On The Way to Immortality and Eternal Life

On The Way to Immortality and Eternal Life

a Series of Radio Talks by

PRESIDENT J. REUBEN CLARK, JR.

of the First Presidency of the Church
of Jesus Christ of Latter-day Saints

With Appendix

DESERET BOOK COMPANY
Salt Lake City, Utah

1953

Copyright 1949 by
Deseret Book Company

Printed by
DESERET NEWS PRESS
In the United States of America

FOREWORD

During the first six months of 1948, President J. Reuben Clark, Jr., delivered the radio talks on the Church Sunday Evening Hour from the Salt Lake Tabernacle. The programs were broadcast over Radio Station KSL, with the music of the Brigham Young University Symphony Orchestra and other University musical groups brought by remote control from Provo, Utah.

The talks were published in the Church Section of the Deseret News, and were also made available in pamphlet form. The public response was so generous, however, that shortly after the series was completed the supply of reprints was exhausted. From then until now numerous requests have been made by those who would like them. Because of the importance of the subject matter and the scholarly manner in which it is set forth, it was felt that a need would be served among missionaries and gospel students through publication of the talks in book form.

President Clark agreed to this, and he has made the work yet more valuable by the inclusion of an appendix of further extensive studies on the apostasy of the Primitive Church.

Those who read the work and note the extensive documentation will gain some small idea of the tremendous labor that went into its production. Already overburdened by his numerous duties incident to responsibilities in the First Presidency, President Clark has done his studying and writing late at night after the day's work at the office. He has brought to this labor those same qualities of industry and scholarship which have distinguished him as an educator, jurist, statesman, and churchman.

As with all other Church radio speakers, he has

received no compensation for this work, and he has declined any royalties of the kind that ordinarily accrue to book writers. The entire work has been prompted by a desire to further the cause of the Lord.

—Church Radio and Mission
Literature Committee

TABLE OF CONTENTS

TALKS

APPENDIX

NOTE

The Radio and Mission Literature Committee having expressed a desire to print in book form my recently delivered radio talks and having assured me of their belief the book would be faith-promoting, I have willingly assented to their wish in the hope their belief might be justified.

In the book I have expanded slightly some of the talks, so partially to overcome the effect of brevity of treatment that was imposed by time limits in the delivery over the air. I have added an appendix containing brief discussions on some further matters touching the Great Apostasy.

The book is not light reading. Perhaps much of it will be tedious, even dull. But the matters treated are not light. They are of the very last importance to our own Church membership and to Christians everywhere.

I am fully conscious of my own scholastic deficiencies for an exhaustive and adequate treatment of the apostasy—the "falling away" predicted by Paul in his Second Epistle to the Thessalonians, and the "damnable heresies" foretold by Peter in his Second General Epistle. But the hope is harbored that this inadequate effort will spur some of our own scholars, who are properly equipped, to go forward with historical studies in which the adequacy of treatment shall fully equal the importance of the subject matter. So will be made clear, even for the man with little faith, the need for the restoration to the earth of the Gospel of Jesus Christ and of the Holy Priesthood after the Order of the Son of God, if man is to be saved and exalted according to God's plan made "in the beginning."

—J.R.C.

January, 1949.

I

ON THE WAY TO IMMORTALITY
AND ETERNAL LIFE

I AM appointed to give on the Church Radio Hour, a series of short talks under the general title, "On the Way to Immortality and Eternal Life." God declared to the Great Lawgiver:

"For behold, this is my work and my glory— to bring to pass the immortality and eternal life of man."[1]

The shortness of each talk will not permit amplifying the theme by discussions. We shall generally state principles and draw conclusions, leaving our listeners to fill in the reasoning.

The annual season set apart for remembering the birth of our Lord has just closed. Properly kept, it brought to us the reflections that come from a knowledge that he, whose birth we remembered, gave us the gift of life in resurrected bodies for the eternities.

During the season, we have pondered, again and again, our own lives of which he is the way and the light. Sobered by this thought, we felt we had somehow drifted afield. We recalled Christ's words to his disciples, "Enter ye in at the strait gate; for strait is the gate, and narrow is the way that leads to life, and few there be that find it; but wide is the gate, and broad the way which leads to death, and many there be that travel therein, until the night cometh, wherein no man can work."[2]

Aware of our own weakness to overcome the infirmities of the flesh, humbled by the sense of our own waywardness, yet enheartened by the spirit of righteousness which lighteneth every soul not too deep in sin, we have with broken hearts and contrite spirits, reached out for help to that final source of all help, our Heavenly Father. And he has blessed us by bringing to our memories that glorious, sovereign formula revealed to us through James,— the formula that opened the door for the ushering in of this, the Last Dispensation of the Fullness of Times:

"If any of you lack wisdom, let him ask of God, that giveth to all men liberally, and upbraideth not; and it shall be given him."[3]

Recollecting this, we were comforted, for this sovereign promise is not to the few, nor to those of high degree only, but to every one of us, high and low, rich and poor, who live on God's footstool it is universal, unrestricted—to you and to me, to our neighbor and to his neighbor, and to our loved ones afar off. God will give liberally to each and all who properly come to him and to the established Church of his Son. Reflecting thus, we had joy in our hearts, for here was great hope.

But we now remembered the further words of James, teaching us how we might make certain to gain the promised wisdom:

"But let him ask in faith, nothing wavering. For he that wavereth is like a wave of the sea driven with the wind and tossed.

"For let not that man think that he shall receive any thing of the Lord."⁴

Wondering, almost doubting, we thought, have we the faith necessary to gain the wisdom we seek? We recalled Paul's discourse to the Hebrews on the power of faith, and the mighty works done through the ages by this all-compelling force, even since the beginning days when "through faith . . . the worlds were framed by the word of God."⁵

We felt we had not the faith that performed the great wonders of which Paul told, yet we recollected that faith is a gift of God, and that Jesus speaking to the multitudes on the mount said, "Ask, and it shall be given you; seek, and ye shall find; knock, and it shall be opened unto you."⁶

Then there was borne in upon us the everlasting truth that the Lord stands always ready to help; that all spiritual aid comes from him; that this we may always have if we go to him in such way that we can receive his blessings. We know he has unnumbered blessings to give to every one of his children, if they but put their lives and their spirits in such tune with his that he may bestow his gifts, and that we may so attune our lives and spirits with his if we keep his commandments.

Then recollection brought us the memory of his great commitment to us:

"I, the Lord, am bound when ye do what I say; but when ye do not what I say, ye have no promise."⁷

So from out this season we gathered anew into our hearts the solemn conviction that in our wanderings, even in our transgressions, we might have help, the help of wisdom to overcome, which is one of God's most precious gifts, if we but sought him in faith for the wisdom to meet our trials and tribulations, and, further, that, as he promised the multitude on the mount, if we asked we should receive and if we knocked, it should be opened unto us.

This sovereign formula brings help and peace now as it did two millenniums ago. The heavens are as open today as they were in the days of Peter, and James, and John, and Paul, and all the rest of those olden Apostles, mighty in the strength of the Holy Ghost. God still answers the prayers of the righteous, still reveals his mind and will to the established Church of his Son.

I give you my testimony that these things are true.

May we all, in humility, seek his wisdom on our way to immortality and eternal life, I humbly pray, in the name of the Son. Amen.

[1]Moses 1:39. [2]3 Nephi 27:33. [3]James 1:5. [4]James 1:6-7. [5]Heb. 11:3. [6]Matt. 7:7; Luke 11:9. [7]D.C. 82:10.

II

EXCEPT YE BECOME AS LITTLE CHILDREN

O N HIS way from Perea to Jerusalem to attend his last Passover, and following the giving of his great parable about the Pharisee and the sinning Publican, the people brought little children to Jesus to be blessed of him. The disciples forbidding this, Jesus rebuked them, saying:

"Suffer little children to come unto me, and forbid them not: for of such is the kingdom of God. Verily I say unto you, Whosoever shall not receive the kingdom of God as a little child shall in no wise enter therein."[1]

To his disciples disputing among themselves as to who should be greatest, Jesus said:

"Except ye be converted, and become as little children, ye shall not enter into the kingdom of heaven. Whosoever therefore shall humble himself as this little child, the same is greatest in the kingdom of heaven."[2]

Yet, in the words of an ancient prophet, many men "are lifted up in the pride of their eyes, and have stumbled, because of the greatness of their stumbling block . . . they put down the power and miracles of God, and preach up unto themselves their own wisdom and their own learning."[3]

Paul declared to the Corinthians the truth about the proud man of the world:

"But the natural man receiveth not the things of the Spirit of God: for they are foolishness unto him: neither can he know them, because they are spiritually discerned."[4] "For what man knoweth the things of a man, save the spirit of man which is in him? even so the things of God knoweth no man, but the Spirit of God,"[5] and "the Spirit of God dwelleth in you."[6]

Men must put pride of their learning and their achievement from their hearts. And why not? For how like a drop in the ocean is the knowledge of the wisest compared with the fullness of the truth of the universe. Men must humbly confess Jesus as the Christ, "for there is none other name under heaven given among men, whereby we must be saved."[7]

To the natural man who scornfully scoffs at this, I again quote Paul, "the foolishness of God is wiser than men,"[8] while "the wisdom of this world is foolishness with God."[9]

Concerning the wisdom of men the Preacher said: "Vanity of vanities . . . all is vanity,"[10] and God, speaking of the mysteries of creation and existence, taunted Job:

"Who is this that darkeneth counsel by words without knowledge? Gird up now thy loins like a man; for I will demand of thee, and answer thou me. Where wast thou when I laid the foundations of the earth? declare, if thou hast understanding. . . . When the morning stars sang together, and all the sons of God shouted for joy? . . . Hast thou commanded the morning since thy days; and caused the dayspring to know his place . . . Have the gates of death been opened unto thee? or hast thou seen the doors of the shadow of death? . . . Canst thou bind the sweet influences of Pleiades, or loose the bands of Orion? Canst thou bring forth Mazzaroth in his season? or canst thou guide Arcturus with his sons? Knowest thou the ordinances of heaven? canst thou set the dominion thereof in the earth?"[11]

Man today may understand, through the wisdom God has bestowed upon his children in these latter days, many things Job did not understand. But not yet can man do the simplest arithmetic of God's creations and compute the relationship even of the earth, the moon, and the sun, to say nothing of the sun and his whole planetary system, and infinitely farther beyond this, the mysteries of the universe,— man still does not understand the laws that govern the Pleiades and Orion, and Mazzaroth and Arcturus, and that keep them in their places in the visible universe, and that hold this universe on its way in orderly procession through the deep reaches of endless space. Narrow indeed are the limits of the finite mind touching infinity.

So on our way to immortality and eternal life we must humbly try to comprehend and live the simple truths of the everlasting Gospel, framed for the weakest and most unlearned amongst us, so simple indeed that "wayfaring men, though fools, shall not err therein."[12] For eternal truth is not foolishness, but infinite wisdom.

Truth found, brings to the humble, contrite

soul a gleam of the glory and majesty and saving power of him who died that we might live, who declared to them who would have made him their king, because he fed them with loaves and fishes: "I am the bread of life: he that cometh to me shall never hunger; and he that believeth on me shall never thirst";[13] who in the Temple, at the Feast of the Tabernacles, said: "I am the light of the world: he that followeth me shall not walk in darkness, but shall have the light of life";[14] and who declared to Martha complaining that he was not with Lazarus before he died: "I am the resurrection, and the life: he that believeth in me, though he were dead, yet shall he live: And whosoever liveth and believeth in me shall never die";[15] and who in the Passover Chamber proclaimed to the Apostles: "I am the way, the truth, and the life: no man cometh unto the Father, but by me."[16]

Men without humility must always hold in remembrance the wisdom of Solomon, son of David: "Pride goeth before destruction, and an haughty spirit before a fall."[17]

May God bless our efforts to know Christ is the way, the truth, and the life, that we may be on our way to immortality and eternal life, I humbly pray, in the name of the Son. Amen.

[1]Luke 18:10 ff.; Mark 10:13 ff. [2]Matt. 18:1-6; Mark 9:33-37; Luke 9:46-48. [3]2 Nephi 26:20. [4]I Cor. 2:14. [5]I Cor. 2:11. [6]I Cor. 3:16. [7]Acts 4:12. [8]I Cor. 1:25. [9]I Cor. 3:19. [10]Eccles. 12:8. [11]Job 38:2-4, 7, 12, 17, 31-33. [12]Isa. 35:8. [13]John 6:35. [14]John 8:12. [15]John 11:25-26. [16]John 14:6. [17]Prov. 16:18.

III

GOD, UNCHANGED, EVERLASTING

L AST week we spoke to the point that to enter the
kingdom of God men must put pride and self-
sufficiency from their hearts, and become as little children. Tonight we shall speak to the point
that the scriptures declare that the Father and the
Son are "the same, yesterday, today, and forever."

Every child of God born on this earth, from the
most benighted savage to the most learned savant un-
touched by infidelity, has in his heart a belief in a
supreme being,—a deity. The concept of deity in
the savage will differ from the concept of the savant,
but basically their concepts will have in common a
belief in the omnipotence, omniscience, and omnipresence of that deity, whether it be one god or a
galaxy. What all men have by a universal, instinctive birthright of earth-existence, we may assume as
truth. Some of us are blessed not only with this
birthright but with a spiritual knowledge[1] which is
more sure than the sense-knowledge of the body.

So in the talks which follow, we shall assume
without doubt or uncertainty that God is and lives;
that he is omnipotent, omniscient, and, through his
Spirit and agencies, omnipresent. Thus all things
are possible with God.[2] He cannot be limited. Moreover, God's ways are not man's ways[3]; indeed, "his

ways (are) past finding out,"[4] since God is infinite, man finite. Sometimes his Spirit enlightens man's understanding, and man may, for a brief space, vision eternity and its creations.[5] These visions come when the Lord has some special purpose to serve or some particular blessing to bestow.

God is our Father. We are his children. He created us; we did not create him.

No greater heresy exists, or one more destructive of Christian faith, than that man makes his own god, who changes with the times and with the cultural and intellectual development possessed by the man creating him.

This heresy lies at the base of all such man-made doctrines as that the God of Abraham, Isaac, and Jacob, and of Moses and of the Israel of the time of Moses and later, is not the God of the Christian world, not the God of today, but that now we have another, a more humane God, one of love and mercy. If this heresy were true, the whole body of scripture we know would be a delusion and a snare and would fall to the ground, false and worthless.

John opens his gospel with this great exposition of eternal truth:

"In the beginning was the Word, and the Word was with God, and the Word was God. The same was in the beginning with God. All things were made by him; and without him was not any thing made that was made. In him was life; and the life was the light of men. . . . And the Word was made flesh, and dwelt among us, (and we beheld his glory, the glory as of the only begotten of the Father,) full of grace and truth."⁶

This declares the Father and the Son, each as God⁷; John tells us that "in the beginning" they were together; that the Son—the Word—created all things that were created; that Father and Son were together before the Son was tabernacled in the flesh⁸; and after the Son was resurrected, he ascended into heaven to the Father⁹—his disciples saw this¹⁰; and Stephen, after Christ's ascension, "being full of the Holy Ghost," declared to his executioners: "Behold, I see the heavens opened, and the Son of man standing on the right hand of God"¹¹; and in mighty vision vouched to modern prophets, the Son has been seen standing on the right hand of God, with holy angels attending and worshipping.¹²

Jesus repeatedly declared his Sonship to those about him¹³ and to the Father himself in the great intercessory prayer in the Garden, saying: "Father, the hour is come; glorify thy Son, that thy Son also may glorify thee."¹⁴

The Father himself formally introduced the Christ as his Son, at the baptism by John,¹⁵ and so announced him to Peter, James, and John at the time of the transfiguration.¹⁶

The Father and the Son were one in all the Son did and in all he taught.¹⁷ There were no differences between them; there could not be, for both were infinitely wise.

Paul declared to the Hebrews: "Jesus Christ the same yesterday, and to day, and for ever," and added warningly, "Be not carried about with divers and strange doctrines."[18]

There is no room in Christian faith for the heresy that man makes his own god, who changes with the times and with the cultural and intellectual development of the man creating him—this at best is anti-Christ; nor is there space in Christian faith for that other heresy that the God of Abraham, Isaac, and Jacob, and of Moses and of Israel of the time of Moses and later, is not the God of the Christian world, not the God of today. These heresies will condemn all who hold them.

The scriptures hold one language, that God the Father and his Only Begotten, Jesus Christ, are the same yesterday, today, and forever, from everlasting to everlasting, unchangeable.[19]

May this necessary testimony come to all on their way to immortality and eternal life, I pray, in the Son's name. Amen.

[1]I Cor. 2:11 ff. [2]Mark 14:36. [3]Jacob 4:6 ff. [4]Rom. 11:33. [5]Moses 1. [6]John 1:1-4, 14. [7]Jude 25. [8]John 17:5. [9]John 16:16, 28. [10]Mark 16:19; Luke 24:50-51; Acts 1:9-11. [11]Acts 7:55-56. [12]D.C. 76:20-21. [13]Matt. 7:21; 12:50; 16:17; 18:19; 26:29. [14]John 17:1. [15]Matt. 3:17; Mark 1:11; Luke 3:22. [16]Matt. 17:5; Mark 9:7; and see 3 Nephi 11, and History of Joseph Smith, P. of G.P. [17]John 5:17; 8:13 ff. [18]Heb. 13:8-9; and see D.C. 20:12, 17; 35:1; 38:1-4; 39:1; 68:6; 76:4; 136:21. [19]D.C. 20:12-17.

IV

PERSONALITY OF GOD, THE FATHER

L AST WEEK we saw that God lived, that he is the same, yesterday, today and forever, unchangeable, from everlasting to everlasting, and that he is not a god changing with the times or with the reason of men.

Jesus, on that last evening he spent with his Apostles before his death, went with them from the Passover Chamber to Mount Olivet, and there petitioned his Father in the great intercessory prayer, saying:

"And this is life eternal, that they might know thee the only true God, and Jesus Christ, whom thou hast sent."[1]

Of what manner of being is God that we may know him and gain eternal life?

Much confusion has grown in the Christian sects on this matter from the days following the Primitive Church that was taught, officered, and directed by Christ's Apostles. While avowedly trying to exclude rationalizing on the subject, nevertheless the post-Primitive Church has sought by human reason and wisdom to describe God and his attributes acceptably to human reason instead of accepting him as he has declared himself to be.

One creed declares "there is one true and living

God, Creator and Lord of heaven and earth, almighty, eternal, immense, incomprehensible, infinite in intelligence, in will, and in all perfection, who, as being one, sole, absolutely simple and immutable spiritual substance, is to be declared as really and essentially distinct from the world, of supreme beatitude in and from himself, and ineffably exalted above all things which exist, or are conceivable, except himself."[2]

Another creed affirms: "There is but one living and true God, everlasting, without body, parts, or passions; of infinite power, wisdom, and goodness; the Maker, and Preserver of all things both visible and invisible. And in unity of this Godhead there be three Persons, of one substance, power, and eternity: the Father, the Son, and the Holy Ghost."[3]

Higher critics, essentially atheistic in their approach, have developed the heresy referred to last week, that man makes his own god, that so-called religious truths are man-made, that such truths vary and change as human reason develops or retrogrades, adding that miracles are mere deceptions, myths, and that Jesus Christ himself is a myth, and then they have added a multitude of other heresies that disturb the thoughtless and entrap the unwary.

But how far afield these go from the simple statements of the scriptures!

The Holy Bible, which every Christian must accept, declares in the plainest of English, that man is in the image of God:

"And God said, Let us make man in our image,

after our likeness. . . . So God created man in his own image, in the image of God created he him; male and female created he them."[4]

The Savior was in the image of the Father. Preaching in the Temple, Jesus declared:

"And he that seeth me seeth him that sent me."[5]

Paul, speaking to the Colossians, declared Christ was "the image of the invisible God"[6] and to the Hebrews he said, speaking of God and the Son, that the Son was "the express image of his person," that is, God's person.[7]

The scriptures are filled with incident and description that declare God possesses the attributes that are also the Christ's, attributes found in the children of God:

He *talked* with Moses "face to face, as a man speaketh unto his friend,"[8] "even apparently, and not in dark speeches."[9]

He had attributes that Christ showed, and that men possess. He himself declared in the Ten Commandments that he was *"jealous"*[10]; and he so spoke at other times.[11] Joshua warned the people that their God was a holy and a *jealous* God.[12] In the ancient days the *anger* of the Lord was declared as hot against Israel,[13] and he visited his *anger* and *wrath* upon the people time and time again, and especially against their wickedness.[14]

But God is also full of *love* and *mercy*. How tenderly he spoke as he passed before Moses: "The Lord, The Lord God, *merciful* and *gracious*, long-suffering, and abundant in *goodness* and *truth*, keeping mercy for thousands, forgiving iniquity and transgression and sin,"[15] and mark Daniel's testimony:

"To the Lord our God belong mercies and forgivenesses, though we have rebelled against him."[16]

Moses declared to Israel in the wilderness:

"Only the Lord had a delight in thy fathers to love them. . . . He doth execute the judgment of the fatherless and widow, and loveth the stranger, in giving him food and raiment."[17]

Jesus declared in his great discourse on the Mount of Olives, already referred to:

"For the Father himself loveth you, because ye have loved me, and have believed that I came out from God"[18]; and John said: "He that loveth not knoweth not God; for God is love."[19]

Another ancient prophet declared:

"But behold, the Lord hath redeemed my soul from hell; I have beheld his glory, and I am encircled about eternally in the arms of his love."[20]

Finally, Jesus discoursing to the timorous Nicodemus, who came to him by nightfall, declared:

"For God so loved the world, that he gave his only begotten Son, that whosoever believeth in him should not perish, but have everlasting life."[21]

If plain English words can ever express a precise meaning, then these words must mean what they say—that man is in the image of God, is God's likeness; that the Only Begotten is in the likeness of the Father, his "express image," and we know man is in the likeness of the Only Begotten for he dwelt amongst us. So God is a person of the same essential form and stature as the Only Begotten and, as his children, he has body, parts, and passions.

Then why mock God with heresies? Why make him a falsifier by teaching he is something else than what he and what his Son have declared him to be? If God be an essence, immense, nebulous, formless, without body, parts, and passions, as the wisdom of men conceive, why did he not so tell us straightforwardly, honestly, explaining:

"Since you cannot conceive or understand me as I am, I am falsifying by telling you that mine Only Begotten and you, my children, are in my image, in my likeness, and I am having my Only Begotten declare the same falsehood."

Why did he not so declare? Why? Because this heresy is error, born of Satan, and he is a God of truth.

God is a person, his Son is in his express image, and man is in his likeness.

This we must know that we may be on our way to immortality and eternal life.

I bear this testimony, in the Son's name. Amen.

[1]John 17:3. [2]The Vatican Council, 1870, Schaff, *Creeds of Christendom*, II, p. 239. [3]The Church of England creed, American Revision, 1801, *op cit.*, III, p. 487-488. [4]Gen. 1:26-27; and see the statement in the Prophet's inspired revision, Moses 3:7. [5]John 12:42 ff. [6]Col. 1:15. [7]Heb. 1:3. [8]Ex. 33:11. [9]Num. 12:8; and see Moses 1:2 ff. [10]Ex. 20:5 [11]Deut. 4:24; 6:15. [12]Josh. 24:19. [13]Judges 2:14. [14]Judges 3:8; II Kings 13:3; Rom. 1:18; 2 Nephi 26:6; D.C. 1:13; 5:8; 19:15; 61:31; 82:6; 97:24; Moses 8:15. [15]Ex. 34:6-7. [16]Dan. 9:9; and see Eph. 4:32. [17]Deut. 10:15, 18; 23:5. [18]John 16:27. [19]I John 4:8. [20]2 Nephi 1:15. [21]John 3:16.

V

THE FATHER AND THE SON

L AST WEEK we spoke of the personality of God, and
read his declaration that he made man in his own
image and likeness, that Jesus was in the likeness of the Father, that he who had seen Jesus had
seen the Father.

We may tonight profitably dwell for a moment
or two on the divinely tender relationship between
Father and Son, a relationship, as told to us by Jesus
himself, that is not conformable to a being on the
one side that is an immense spiritual essence, nebulous, unformed, without body, parts, and passions,
and to a being on the other side with a living, vibrant,
dynamic personality with body, parts, and passions,
with a mission to carry out and in truth fulfilling it.

From the moment when, on the banks of the
Jordan, he directed John to baptize him to fulfill all
righteousness, and the Father in voice from heaven
declared, as the Holy Ghost descended upon the head
of the Son, "This is my beloved Son, in whom I am
well pleased,"[1] until on the cross, expiring, the Son
cried out, "Father, into thy hands I commend my
spirit,"[2] Jesus went forward in an intimate relationship with the Father that was based upon the
fact that the Father, like the Son, was a personal
being. The Son's actions, his teachings, his prayers,
permit no other reasonable explanation.

In his great sermon to the Pharisees in the Treasury to the Temple, Jesus declared:

"I am not alone, but I and the Father that sent me . . . if ye had known me, ye should have known my Father also. . . . I speak to the world those things which I have heard of him . . . as my Father hath taught me, I speak these things . . . for I do always those things that please him."[3]

Later to the Jews in the Temple, he affirmed that he came not of himself, but that God sent him, that he spoke that which he had seen with his Father and concluded with his declaration of Messiahship:

"Before Abraham was, I am."[4]

As the evening in the Passover Chamber drew to a close, he declared to the Apostles:

"I am the way, the truth, and the life: no man cometh unto the Father, but by me . . . he that hath seen me hath seen the Father; and how sayest thou then, Shew us the Father? . . . I go unto my Father."[5]

Later, on the Mount of Olives, he declared:

"I have kept my Father's commandments, and abide in his love. . . . I came forth from the Father, and am come into the world: again, I leave the world, and go to the Father."[6]

And in the great prayer before he went to Gethsemane he declared of the oneness of those who believed, as he had declared many times of the oneness of the Father and himself:

"Neither pray I for these alone, but for them also which shall believe on me through their word; that they all may be one; as thou, Father, art in me, and I in thee, that they also may be one in us . . . that they may be one, even as we are one,'"—one in purpose, one in will, one in faith, one in obedience, one in service, one in righteousness, but different personalities.

In the early morning, standing before Caiaphas, the High Priest, who adjured him to tell:

"Art thou the Christ, the Son of the Blessed?" Jesus said, "I am: and ye shall see the Son of man sitting on the right hand of power, and coming in the clouds of heaven."[8]

In Gethsemane, Jesus, leaving the rest of the Apostles, drew apart with Peter, James, and John, and then asking them to tarry and watch, he "exceeding sorrowful, even unto death,"[9] went on a stone's cast and, falling on his face, prayed in agony while "his sweat was as it were great drops of blood falling down to the ground,"[10] "O my Father, if it be possible, let this cup pass from me: nevertheless not as I will, but as thou wilt."[11] Thrice repeating the prayer, and thrice returning to Peter, James, and John, he found them sleeping each time; "What, could ye not watch with me one hour?" But though they watched not, an angel came from heaven, to strengthen him.[12]

Then, on the cross, when the lees of life were ebbing away, and mortal strength had almost gone, he cried out in the words pre-voiced by the inspired Psalmist a full millennium before, "My God, my God, why hast thou forsaken me?"[13] So questioned the Son of the Father as the darkness of mortal death blinded his eyes.

All these are not the outcries in prayer of a

mighty soul in divine agony to an immense, formless, impersonal, spiritual essence, without body, without parts, without passions. These are the heart out-pourings of a loving Son, weighted with the sins of men, to a divine Father, who knew, who suffered when the Son suffered, who loved his Only Begotten as only God can love; a Father who had mercy; a Father in whose image and likeness the Son was; a Father who could speak and answer back, who could give aid and succor to a Son in distress as he had done time and time again during the Son's mission on earth. The person Son was beseeching the person Father for help, and the Father gave that help to the full, not for the lessening of the mortal agony of the Son, as might seem from the prayer in Geth-semane, such lessening was neither asked for nor given, it was a call for aid to the fulfilling of his mission—the making of the great atonement for Adam's Fall, thus bringing to every one of God's children born on the earth, the power to overcome mortal death and gain the destiny of a resurrection.

May God give to each of us on our way to im-mortality and eternal life the necessary testimony that we are in his image and likeness, I pray, in the Son's name. Amen.

[1]Matt. 3:13-17; Mark 1:9-11; Luke 3:21-22. [2]Luke 23:46. [3]John 8:16, 19, 26, 28-29. [4]John 8:38, 42, 58. [5]John 14:6, 9, 12. [6]John 15:10; 16:28. [7]John 17:20-22. [8]Mark 14:61-62; Matt. 26:64. [9]Matt. 26:38. [10]Luke 22:44. [11]Matt. 26:39. [12]Matt. 26:34-46; Mark 14:32-42; Luke 22:40-46; John 18:1-2. [13]Matt. 27:46-47; Mark 15:34-35.

VI

THE QUESTION EVERY SOUL ASKS

NO MAN is so dead to the spiritual side of life but that some time in a reflective moment he has asked himself: Where did I come from? Why am I here? Where do I go? So questioning he has said to himself: If I knew these things I could shape my life for the best.

Now God has placed in every man's heart a divine spark, which never wholly goes out; it may grow dim, it may become hidden, almost smothered by the ashes of transgression; but the spark still lives and glows and can be fanned into flame by faith, if the heart is touched. This is true of all, save of them who commit the unpardonable sin, and few can do this, for to do so requires greater spiritual knowledge than is vouched to most men.

Behind these questions lies the deeper one — is there a purpose underlying our mortal lives; are we here on earth by chance, nonexistent before our birth, with an aimless existence here, and a void, an endless night of oblivion after death?

Every fibre of being of the normal man cries out against such an existence without purpose. Man in all stages of intellectual development, from the savage in the forest to the most learned and enlightened toiler in the laboratory, has during all history rebelled against such a destiny, and God has supported him in his rebellion by revealing through Holy Writ as much of the great underlying purposes of life as man's finite mind can grasp.

Sometimes men have been so intoxicated by their own learning through the senses—their sensuous knowledge—that they have not only refused to recognize the knowledge of the spirit, but they have scoffed at it and derided that it is.

But doubt and derision do not destroy truth, which lives, finally triumphant.

Where did we come from? had we an antemortal life?

Answering, we turn first to the example, the pattern of the Captain of Salvation,[1] the Prince of the Kings of this Earth,[2] the Only Begotten.[3] Whence was he?

If we had no other words than from John the Beloved, we should not be in doubt on this point. John began his hymn of praise and worshipful homage which opens his gospel:

"In the beginning was the Word, and the Word was with God, and the Word was God."[4]

Thus God the Father and God the Son were together "in the beginning," and this beginning was before even the world was made, because "all things were made by" the Word, and "without him was not any thing made that was made."[5]

In his first epistle John declared: "God sent his only begotten Son into the world,"[6] thus testifying again that the Son was with the Father before he came to earth, and the Word created the world long, long before he entered it. In the great visions which came to him on the Isle of Patmos, John affirmed: "These things saith the Amen, the faithful and true witness, the beginning of the creation of God,'" and Paul told the Colossians that Christ was "the firstborn of every creature."⁸ These sayings bear record that Christ was with the Father from the beginning, the first creation of all.

But the Savior bore his own testimony that he had long association with the Father before he took on mortality.

Attending the Second Passover of his ministry and speaking in the Temple to the Jews, who sought to kill him, Jesus declared:

"The Son can do nothing of himself, but what he seeth the Father do: for what things soever he doeth, these also doeth the Son likewise."⁹

Later, speaking to the Pharisees in the Treasury of the Temple, Jesus said:

"I speak to the world those things which I have heard of him. . . . I do nothing of myself; but as my Father hath taught me, I speak these things."¹⁰

Teaching in the Temple he said to the fearsome believers on him among the chief rulers of the Pharisees:

"For I have not spoken of myself; but the Father which sent me, he gave me a commandment, what I should say, and what I should speak. And I know that his commandment is life everlasting: whatsoever I speak therefore, even as the Father said unto me, so I speak."¹¹ And after this Jesus said: "For all things that I have heard of my Father I have made known unto you."[12]

All this speaks of a long and close relationship with the Father, not for the few years he dwelt in mortality, shackled with the chains of the flesh, but an association in the eternity from before the beginning of the earth.

But again and again Jesus himself declared his antemortal existence with the Father.

Preaching to the multitude whom he had fed and who followed him across the sea, he said:

"What and if ye shall see the Son of man ascend up where he was before?"[13]

To his Apostles with whom, after eating the Passover meal, he had gone to the Mount of Olives, Jesus, predicting his death and resurrection, said:

"A little while, and ye shall not see me: and again, a little while, and ye shall see me, because I go to the Father. . . . I came forth from the Father, and am come into the world: again, I leave the world, and go to the Father. . . . I have overcome the world."[14]

In the great intercessory prayer, the Prayer of the Great High Priest, made just before he crossed the brook Cedron to Gethsemane and its agony, Jesus commenced his prayer:

"Father, the hour is come; glorify thy Son, that thy Son also may glorify thee. . . . I have glorified thee on the earth: I have finished the work which thou gavest me to do. And now, O Father, glorify thou me with thine own self with the glory which I had with thee before the world was."[15]

One cannot but remember here the words which had come to Jesus in the Temple two days before, and just after the Greeks had come to worship him, his crucifixion weighing heavily upon him:

"Now is my soul troubled; and what shall I say? Father, save me from this hour: but for this cause came I unto this hour. Father, glorify thy name. Then came there a voice from heaven, saying, I have both glorified it, and will glorify it again."[16]

Some of the people hearing the voice thought it thundered; others thought an angel spoke.

As then, so now, men understand not the heavenly voices that come unto them. Some hear only the thunders of the air—the natural things of earth; others believe they hear angels, but do not understand the message; a few get the words themselves, the message, and harken, so gaining wisdom and inspiration. This we must all come to on our way to immortality and eternal life.

I leave with you tonight my testimony that Jesus was with the Father from the beginning, that he existed in the eternities before the world was, and that, his mortal mission finished, he returned to the Father. I bear this testimony in the Son's name. Amen.

---

[1]Heb. 2:10. [2]Rev. 1:5. [3]Heb. 11:17. [4]John 1:1. [5]John 1:1-3; I John 1:2; 2:14; Moses 1:32-33; 3:4 ff.; Abraham 4; D.C. 93:7 ff., 21. [6]I John 4:9. [7]Rev. 3:14. [8]Col. 1:15. [9]John 5:19. [10]John 8:26, 28. [11]John 12:49-50. [12]John 15:15. [13]John 6:62. [14]John 16:16, 28, 33. [15]John 17:1, 4-5. [16]John 12:27-28.

VII

MEN LIVED BEFORE THEY WERE MORTAL

L AST WEEK, considering the question whence we came to earth, we saw that Holy Writ plainly taught, and that Jesus himself declared, that he had an antemortal existence with the Father, that he lived with the Father in eternity from the very "beginning," during untold periods before he came to earth to take on a mortal body.

Should anybody question what meaning this has for us, it may be answered that Christ is the archtype of God's creation, he is perfect, even as our Father in Heaven, for he and the Father are one;[1] and he bade us to become perfect even as our Father in heaven is perfect.[2]

If we would be perfect we must share as fully as may be, consistent with his exalted mission and our vastly humbler callings, the experiences of being, of existence, through which he passed. So if he had antemortal existence so must we have had, in order that we might learn of the Father even as he testified, over and over again, that he had learned of Him, and about gospel principles, and the way of life, and so prepare ourselves for mortal existence.

It is fundamental with Christian doctrine that every mortal man has in him a spirit. No honest Christian questions this. One example may be given:

Jesus raised from the dead, the maid, daughter of the ruler of the synagogue, after those about "laughed him to scorn, knowing that she was dead," and Luke records that Jesus "put them all out, and took her by the hand, and called, saying, Maid, arise. And her spirit came again, and she arose straightway."[3]

When Korah and those rebelling with him gathered together unto "the door of the tabernacle of the congregation," Moses and Aaron fell upon their faces and appealed in prayer to the "God of the spirits of all flesh."[4]

Moses addressed the Lord as "the God of the spirits of all flesh," when he asked the Lord to set a man over the congregation, and Joshua was chosen.[5]

Paul said to the Hebrews:

"Furthermore we have had fathers of our flesh which corrected us, and we gave them reverence: shall we not much rather be in subjection unto the Father of spirits, and live?"[6]

Ecclesiastes, the Preacher, said:

"Then shall the dust return to the earth as it was: and the spirit shall return unto God who gave it."[7]

That our spirits were with the Father before our births into mortality is clearly shown by the scriptures.

Jeremiah protested to the Lord he could not speak for he was a child, but the Lord rebuked him:

"Say not, I am a child: for thou shalt go to all that I shall send thee, and whatsoever I command thee thou shalt speak. Be not afraid of their faces: for I am with thee to deliver thee, saith the Lord."

And to show he knew Jeremiah and his abilities, the Lord said:

"Before I formed thee in the belly I knew thee; and before thou camest forth out of the womb I sanctified thee, and I ordained thee a prophet unto the nations."[8]

Paul, speaking to the Ephesians and the Thessalonians, affirmed that the Lord had chosen some "before the foundation of the world," and "from the beginning."[9] This he could not have done, if the chosen ones had not existed from the beginning.

Jesus passing by a man, which was blind from his birth, his disciples asked:

"Master, who did sin, this man, or his parents, that he was born blind?"[10] thus evidencing their teaching from the Master that the spirit of man existed before birth into mortality and that our condition here might be determined by our course before we came.

Furthermore, the Sacred Records make it clear that the Father and Son were not alone in their eternal abode; that they dwelt amongst untold Heavenly Hosts; that a great schism arose amongst these hosts; that part of them rebelled against the Father, led by Lucifer, a Son of the Morning, who sought to make himself above God; that a war ensued; that Lucifer and his followers, a third of the hosts of heaven were cast out and down into the bottomless pit, becoming the devil and his angels. Modern revelation makes all this very clear.[11]

Of these hosts that followed Satan, Jude affirms they kept not their first estate,[12] and Peter declared,

"God spared not the angels that sinned, but cast them down to hell, and delivered them into chains of darkness, to be reserved unto judgment."[13]

The scriptures show that these rebel spirits can not lawfully receive bodies but that they constantly seek to steal them. Over and over again Jesus cast them out from bodies they sought to possess. It was thus with the one possessed in the synagogue at Capernaum, the evil spirits declaring Jesus to be the Holy One and entreating him to leave them alone.[14] So with those evilly possessed who were blind and dumb, and who, Jesus healing, saw and spake[15]; and likewise of the one who was violent and vicious coming to Jesus at Mt. Hermon.[16] But in the two possessed of legions of evil spirits in the country of the Gergesenes or Gadarenes, we find most clearly the reason the evil spirits had for entering mortal bodies. Recognizing the Christ, they asked "art thou come hither to torment us before the time?" Perceiving he was to cast them out, they "besought him that he would not command them to go out into the deep," but to let them enter the bodies of the swine, and he permitting this, the swine rushed down and were drowned in the sea.[17]

Thus the scriptures show us that we lived before we came; that those who were rebels in the antemortal state do not have bodies here; that those who kept their first estate do take on bodies here; that some were chosen before their mortal birth for their work on this earth; that our lives in our antemortal existence have an effect and influence on our lives here; and all Christendom believes that when we go hence our lives in the hereafter will be happy or unhappy depending on how we live here.

There is no place in this great plan, framed in the Council of Heaven[18] for that arch-heresy first preached, if not invented by Tertullian, and still proclaimed by a large part of the sectarian world, that our spirits had no premortal existence, but are propagated, like our mortal bodies, by our mortal parents.[19]

Our spirits were created by our Heavenly Father. We existed before we came to earth.

Thus all who live are on their way to immortality and eternal life, which is the glory of God, if they but live righteously, keeping the commandments of God.

That we may so live I pray in the name of the Son, him who is our advocate with the Father. Amen.

[1]John 17:21 ff. [2]Matt. 5:48; Col. 1:28; James 1:4. [3]Luke 8:53 ff. [4]Num. 16:19-22. [5]Num. 27:15 ff. [6]Heb. 12:9. [7]Eccles. 12:7. [8]Jer. 1:4-8. [9]Eph. 1:4; II Thess. 2:13. [10]John 9:1-2. [11]Isa. 14:12 ff.; Luke 10:18; Rev. 12:3 ff.; 20:2; II Pet. 2:4; Jude 6; D.C. 29:36; 76:25 ff.; Abraham 3:27-28. [12]Jude 6. [13]II Pet. 2:4. [14]Mark 1:21-28; Luke 4:31-37. [15]Matt. 9:32-34; 12:22-23. [16]Matt. 17:14 ff.; Mark 9:14-29; Luke 9:37-43. [17]Matt. 8:28-34; Mark 5:1-20; Luke 8:26-39. [18]Abraham 3. [19]Newman, *A Manual of Church History*, I, p. 262; *The New Schaff-Herzog Encyclopedia of Religious Knowledge*, sub voce *Soul and Spirit*.

VIII

THE ORGANIZATION IN THE PRIMITIVE
CHURCH

I N OUR first talk we quoted the words of our Heavenly Father to Moses: "For behold, this is my work and my glory—to bring to pass the immortality and eternal life of man."[1]

In our talks following the first one, we spoke of the necessity that in spirit men must become as little children if they would but enter the Kingdom of God; that God is not made by man, but that man was made by God; that God is the same yesterday, today and forever; that he is a personal being; that his Son, Jesus Christ, and man are in God's express image and likeness; that Jesus Christ and the spirits of men were with our Heavenly Father before they took on mortal bodies; and as indicated in the revelation of God to Moses, we are here to gain immortality and eternal life in the Kingdom of God.

To help men to come back to him, our Heavenly Father has from the beginning shown the way leading back into his presence, by proclaiming the saving principles of the Gospel to his children,[2] not always in their fullness, but sufficiently so to save men if they harken and obey. Remnants of the Gospel plan have clung in the minds of men from Adam down, part as corrupted memories, part as tradition; some few things God made instinctive in his children.

To assist men in their efforts fully to return to him, our Heavenly Father has provided from time to time, beginning with Adam, organizations of his Priesthood, to bring to men principles they had abandoned and sometimes forgotten, and to reemphasize and where necessary restore, the Priesthood, with its duties and divine powers. These occasions are called dispensations in Holy Writ, and we speak of the dispensations of Adam, Enoch, Noah, Abraham, Moses, the Messiah, and now of the Dispensation of the Fullness of Times. In each pre-Messianic dispensation God gave to the men who established it, special authority and commandments with particular missions.

So to the same end, the Savior during his mission in Palestine, in the Meridian of Time set up an organization, established his Church and provided certain offices therein. He told the disciples who were with him at Caesarea Philippi that he would build up his Church;[3] Paul told the Ephesians that Christ was head of the Church over which the Apostles presided, and that he so loved it that he gave his life for it.[4]

In our Articles of Faith (which are the equivalent of creeds in other religious organizations) we declare:

"We believe in the same organization that existed in the Primitive Church, viz., apostles, prophets, pastors, teachers, evangelists, etc."

Apostles. In the Primitive Church the Savior chose Twelve Apostles,[5] to whom he gave power against unclean spirits, and to heal "all manner of sickness and all manner of disease,"[6] as also a commandment to go to all nations and to baptize in the name of the Father, Son, and Holy Ghost, and to teach "whatsoever I have commanded."[7] Having told Peter at Caesarea Philippi that he would give power and authority to bind on earth and loose in heaven,[8] he later, at Capernaum declared that this power and authority was then vested in all the Twelve, not in Peter alone.[9] On the evening of the day of the resurrection, he confirmed power and authority upon all the Twelve to remit or retain sins.[10] Still later in Galilee, the Lord, declaring "All power is given unto me in heaven and in earth," commissioned and commanded his Apostles: "Go ye therefore, and teach all nations, baptizing them in the name of the Father, and of the Son, and of the Holy Ghost: Teaching them to observe all things whatsoever I have commanded you: and, lo, I am with you alway, even unto the end of the world. Amen"[11]

The Lord, being possessed of all power,[12] gave power and authority to the Apostles; he did not pray the Father to give it, that is, it was a present bestowal of power, not a prayer for power. This fact is most important.

Following the condemnation of Jesus, Judas committed suicide.[13] After the ascension, Peter stood up among the disciples (the Twelve) and told them they should fill the vacancy caused by the death of Judas, which they did by choosing Matthias, Peter declaring that from the beginning of baptism by John till the ascension of the Christ "must one be ordained to be a witness with us of his resurrection."[14]

Paul repeatedly declared himself to be an apostle,[15] and an apostle to the Gentiles.[16] He also affirmed he was so ordained,[17] but there is no record that he was ever a member of the Twelve.

One essential point of the foregoing is that a vacancy in the Council of the Twelve was filled by the Twelve, and that Peter clearly took the lead, presided.[18]

Prophets. Certainly from the time the Lord told Moses, "Aaron thy brother shall be thy prophet,"[19] there have been prophets in Israel and among God's people in all times. Many books (16) of the Bible were written by prophets. Amos declared: "Surely the Lord God will do nothing, but he revealeth his secret unto his servants the prophets."[20] The Savior constantly referred to them in his ministry, as did his Apostles after he went to his Father. They were found in the Primitive Church, the gift of the Lord, as Paul told the Ephesians.[21] They will always be found where the Church of Christ is established.

The seventy. After the Twelve had finished their first formal missionary assignment,[22] Jesus sent out seventy ("other seventy") two and two, "before his face into every city and place, whither he himself would come."[23] He gave the seventy certain rights and powers to represent him, saying: "He that heareth you heareth me; and he that despiseth you despiseth me; and he that despiseth me despiseth him that sent me."[24] The seventy returned, overjoyed, saying: "Lord, even the devils are subject unto us through thy name," and he then gave them further powers.[25]

Elders. While on several occasions, as recorded in the Four Gospels, the word "elders" is used, by or in connection with the work of the Savior,[26] it is clear that the word is there used in the Old Testament sense — as designating men of experience, wisdom, and gravity, and of a resulting authority among the people, originally by appointment thereto[27] rather than as designating a grade of an ordained priesthood order.[28]

But when the Apostles began to carry on the organization which was set up by the Lord, the word "elder" took on a different meaning (though sometimes still evidently used with Old Testament meaning).[29] Writing to Titus in Crete, Paul informs him he was left there to "set in order the things that are wanting, and ordain elders in every city, as I had appointed thee."[30] Peter spoke of himself as an elder.[31] The elders had priesthood authority; they were to anoint the sick with oil and pray over them,[32] and in his first epistle, Peter outlines their duties and directs the young folk to "submit yourselves unto the elder."[33]

Bishops. The word "bishop" seems not to have been used in the Old Testament, though Peter quotes a psalm[34] as using the term.[35]

However, in the Church presided over by the Apostles, the word is used to designate an office with definite duties. Paul speaking to the Church at Ephesus, calls them "overseers, to feed the church of God."[36]

Writing to Timothy, Paul lays down the qualifications of a bishop: he must be blameless, vigilant, sober, given to hospitality, apt to teach, temperate, not quarrelsome, not greedy for filthy lucre, patient, not a brawler nor covetous, must be the husband of one wife — there was no hint of celibacy in the early Church but this positive command against it— ruling his own family, "having his children in subjection with all gravity; (for if a man know not how to rule his own house, how shall he take care of the church of God?)."[37] Instructing Titus as to the Cretians, Paul repeated essentially the same qualifications, adding:

"Holding fast the faithful word as he hath been taught, that he may be able by sound doctrine both to exhort and to convince the gainsayers."[38] This text somewhat confuses "elders" and "bishops."

In the early days following the ascension, the Twelve (yielding to the murmurings that the Greek widows were neglected as against the Hebrew widows) appointed seven men who should attend to the needs of these widows.[39] Scholars assert these were bishops.[40] They were evidently ordained;[41] Paul later abode with one of them, who was then an evangelist.[42] Perceiving here the concern of the Apostles for the welfare of the widows, one recalls the words of James: "Pure religion and undefiled before God and the Father is this, To visit the fatherless and widows in their affliction, and to keep himself unspotted from the world."[43]

The instructions given by Paul show that the bishop was of lesser authority than the apostle, for he, an apostle, directed the bishop. Furthermore, the jurisdiction of the apostle was Church-wide; the bishop was a local officer.

Evangelists. Paul speaking to the Ephesians declared that the "household of God" was "built upon the foundation of the apostles and prophets, Jesus Christ himself being the chief corner stone,"[44] and adding later: "And he gave some, apostles; and some, prophets; and some, evangelists; and some, pastors and teachers."[45] Paul entered into the house of Philip, the evangelist, who had earlier been a bishop.[46] Timothy was directed to do the work of an evangelist.[47] The duties of the evangelist are not clear from the gospels and epistles, but modern revelation has prescribed their duties and called them patriarchs.[48]

Teachers. Teachers were known in Old Testament days. David separated those "who should prophesy with harps, with psalteries and with cymbals," the "small as the great, the teacher as the scholar."[49] The Psalmist referred to them,[50] also Solomon in his Proverbs,[51] and Isaiah warned, "yet shall not thy teachers be removed into a corner any more, but thine eyes shall see thy teachers."[52] Paul said to the Corinthians, "And God hath set some in the church, first apostles, secondarily prophets, thirdly teachers, after that miracles, then gifts of healings, helps, governments, diversities of tongues. Are all apostles? are all prophets? are all teachers? are all workers of miracles? Have all the gifts of healing? do all speak with tongues? do all interpret?"[53] Paul declared to Timothy that he (Paul) was an apostle, an ordained preacher, and a teacher of the Gentiles.[54] There were prophets and teachers at Antioch.[55]

Thus throughout the Old and New Testaments, a record is made of those who were appointed to teach — teachers — and the highest and the lowest in the Church might be so used. But teachers were an essential element in the Primitive Church.

Deacons. The deacons were closely associated with the bishops. Their qualifications as given to Timothy parallel the qualifications of the bishops. A deacon must be grave, not double-tongued, temperate, without greed for money, "holding the mystery of the faith in a pure conscience," all these to be proved before his choice; he must be the husband of one wife (again, no celibacy in the Primitive Church), who must be grave, not slanderous, sober, faithful; he must rule his children and his house well.[56] Paul said they who fill well the office of deacon "well purchase to themselves a good degree, and great boldness in the faith."[57]

Several points should now be kept in mind:

I. After the death of the Savior the Apostles were the possessors of the supreme authority in the Church.

II. They possessed and exercised the right and authority—

1st. To endow others by ordination with the

apostolic powers they possessed, that is, ordain other apostles.[58]

2nd. To endow others with the right to exercise certain apostolic powers, e. g., the choice and ordination of subordinate officers.[59]

3rd. To provide that those ordained should continue to exercise their Priesthood after the life of the one bestowing them.[60]

And of all these matters we must have knowledge on our way to immortality and eternal life.

That this knowledge may come to us, I pray, in the Lord's name. Amen.

---

[1]Moses 1:39.   [2]Moses 5:56-58.   [3]Matt. 16:18.   [4]Eph. 5:23-25. [5]Matt. 10:1-2; Mark 3:14; Luke 6:13.   [6]Matt. 10:1; Mark 3:15. [7]Matt. 28:18-20; Mark 6:7; 16:14 ff.; Luke 9:1 ff.; Acts 1:1-8. [8]Matt. 16:19. [9]Matt. 18:18. [10]John 20:22-23. [11]Matt. 28:18-20. [12]Op. cit. [13]Matt. 27:3-10; Acts 1:16 ff. [14]Acts 1:22, 26; John 15:16; Mark 3:14 ff.; Acts 14:23; 17:31; I Tim. 2:7; Heb. 5:1; 8:3; 9:6; the imposition of hands,—Acts 13:2-3; 6:6; I Tim. 4:14; II Tim. 1:6. [15]Rom. 1:1; I Cor. 1:1; 9:1-2; 15:9; II Cor. 1:1; 12:12; Eph. 1:1; Col. 1:1; I Tim. 1:1; II Tim. 1:1; Tit. 1:1; Gal. 1:1. [16]Rom. 11:13; 15:16; I Tim. 2:7. [17]I Tim. 2:7. [18]Acts 1:15-26. [19]Ex. 7:1. [20]Amos 3:7. [21]Eph. 4:11. [22]Luke 9:1-6; Mark 6:30. [23]Luke 10:1. [24]Luke 10:16. [25]Luke 10:17-20. [26]Matt. 15:2; 16:21; 27:12, 20, 41; 26:59; 28:12; Mark 7:3; 8:31; 14:43; 15:1; Luke 9:22; 22:52. [27]Ex. 3:16; 18:17 ff.; Deut. 1:16-17. [28]D. C. 84:6, 23 ff. [29]Acts 4:8. [30]Tit. 1:5. [31]I Pet. 5:1; D.C. 20:38. [32]James 5:14. [33]I Pet. 5:1 ff. [34]Psa. 109:8. [35]Acts 1:20. [36]Acts 20:28. [37]I Tim. 3:2 ff. [38]Tit. 1:7 ff. [39]Acts 6:1-8. [40]Hastings, *Dictionary of the Bible*, sub voce *Bishop*. [41]Acts 6:6. [42]Acts 21:8. [43]James 1:27. [44]Eph. 2:19-20. [45]Eph. 4:11. [46]Acts 6:5. [47]II Tim. 4:5. [48]D.C. 107:39 ff. [49]I Chron. 25:1, 8. [50]Psa. 119:99. [51]Prov. 5:13. [52]Isa. 30:20; 43:27. [53]I Cor. 12:28-30; Eph. 4:11. [54] I Tim. 2:7; II Tim. 1:11. [55]Acts 13:1. [56]I Tim. 3:8-13. [57]I Tim. 3:13. [58]Acts 1:15 ff. [59]Tit. 1:5. [60]II Tim. 4:5-7.

IX

THE PRIMITIVE CHURCH ORGANIZATION DISAPPEARS

L AST WEEK we saw that, established pursuant to the Lord's declaration that he would build up his Church,[1] the Primitive Church, the Apostolic Church, had as officers therein, apostles, prophets, evangelists, seventies, elders, bishops, teachers, and deacons; that to each of these officers certain powers, authorities, and duties were given; that these officers were ordained to their offices and callings; that the apostles exercised authority over all the other officers; that vacancies were filled in the apostles' council; and that the apostles gave authority to others to install and direct the lower officers.

In his epistle to the Hebrews, Paul explained the difference between the Levitical Priesthood, which was the basis of the temple worship in Jerusalem, with its sacrifices and offerings, and the Melchizedek Priesthood, which Jesus held, "an high priest for ever after the order of Melchisedec."[2]

Paul explained:

"If therefore perfection were by the Levitical priesthood, (for under it the people received the law,) what further need was there that another priest should rise after the order of Melchisedec, and not be called after the order of Aaron?"[3]

He also pointed out that Christ came through Judah "of which tribe Moses spake nothing concerning priesthood," and that this high priest "after the similitude of Melchisedec . . . is made, not after the law of a carnal commandment, but after the power of an endless life," for "the law (Mosaic) made nothing perfect, but the bringing in of a better hope did; by the which we draw nigh unto God. . . . Wherefore he is able also to save them to the uttermost that come unto God by him."[4]

Paul thus declared the Priesthood of Melchizedek as above the Levitical Priesthood, and that Christ exercised the powers and authority of the Melchizedek Priesthood;[5] that perfection did not come by the Levitical Priesthood, which was the law of carnal commandments; that the Levitical Priesthood made nothing perfect; but that, through the Melchizedek Priesthood we draw nigh to God, with the power of endless life. We may become, even as the Lord commanded on the Mount:

"Be ye therefore perfect, even as your Father which is in heaven is perfect."[6]

Unless this were true there was no occasion for the Melchizedek Priesthood, the Levitical Priesthood otherwise sufficing.

The Levitical Priesthood knew nothing of apostles or evangelists, of seventy in the priesthood sense of preparing the way for the Lord, of elders in the priesthood sense of authorized presiding officers in the Church, of bishops presiding over local churches, of teachers clothed with the Priesthood, nor of deacons. These officers exercised powers and authorities, did work, which were not incidents of the Levitical Priesthood. These were offices in Christ's Church which functioned under the Melchizedek Priesthood, Christ, the head of the Church, being, as Paul declared to the Hebrews, the "great high priest, that is passed into the heavens, Jesus the Son of God,"[7] and the "Apostle and High Priest of our profession."[8]

All this makes clear that the prime authority in the Church of Christ, he himself not being resident on earth, is in the Apostle and the High Priest after the order of Melchizedek. There is no word in the canonical scriptures contrary to this, nor any word changing or modifying it. Christ's Church was and is a Church of Melchizedek Priesthood, with the lesser or Levitical Priesthood also existing as an appendage of the Melchizedek or higher Priesthood, but with its duties changed from the Mosaic law days, because the atonement of Christ did away with the animal sacrifices and offerings of the Aaronic Priesthood. Furthermore, the law of Levitical sacrifices was ended — Jesus on the Mount said: "Think not that I am come to destroy the law, or the prophets: I am not come to destroy, but to fulfill"[9] — and Paul's whole epistle to the Hebrews shows that Levitical sacrifice is without further force and effect.[10]

When Christ departed he left the Melchizedek Priesthood, vested in the Apostles, in charge of the Church, his Church.[11] There is no word in canonical scripture authorizing any other Church order for his Church; no word that so says expressly or that by implication sanctions any other order for his Church. Thus, under the Holy Scriptures Christ's Church must be a church in which the Melchizedek Priesthood exists and exercises plenary authority. If a church is set up under any other order it cannot be his, Christ's, Church.

The preparedness of the Church to meet its problems at the beginning of the second Christian century following the passing of John the Beloved, the last of the Apostles to go, has been told thusly by a not unfriendly hand:

"The age of inspiration is over, — that peerless century which began with the birth of Christ, and closed with the death of John — and the course of the ages descends once more to the ordinary level of common time.

"It was with the Church now as with the disciples at Bethany, when the last gleam of the Savior's ascending train had passed from their sight, and they turned their faces, reluctant and sad, to the dark world again. The termination of the age of inspiration was in truth the very complement and consummation of the ascension of the Lord . . .

"That time has now fully come. The last gleam of inspired wisdom and truth vanished from the earth with the beloved apostle's gentle farewell, and we pass at once across the mysterious line which separates the sacred from the secular annals of the world, — the history of the apostolic age from the history of the Christian Church."[12]

Now, what is the situation today in the great churches in the world professing Christ,

— the Eastern Church, the Russian Church, and the Western Church and its dissident offspring? Where are their apostles, their prophets, their seventies, who were in Christ's time the possessors under ordination by Christ of the Melchizedek Priesthood and authority in the Church established by Christ? They do not exist. Dr. Fawkes, Vicar of Ashby St. Ledgers, declares:

"And with the disappearance of the Apostles a new age set in. They left no successors; and Peter was no exception to the rule."[13]

These Churches of today have other offices, — the Pope, the cardinals, originally "deacons" in the parishes of Rome,[14] exarchs, primates, patriarchs, (the last three designating or applied to the bishop of the chief city of the diocese)[15] archbishops, archdeacons, and others; but these were not known to the Church in the time of Christ nor to the Primitive Church that followed. Moreover these offices so known in post-Primitive Churches are not subordinate offices to the offices existing in the Primitive Church, that is, they are not helpers to higher ruling officers, they are the ruling officers themselves, yet in some cases laying claim to apostolic authority.

Insofar as the New Testament record shows, Christ, during his mortal mission, appointed only apostles and seventy, endowing them with the powers and authorities of the Melchizedek Priesthood. There is no record that he appointed any bishop, though, as stated, the Apostles did ordain bishops.

As will appear from our later talks, the doctrine we shall now discuss is without significance to the

Lord's Church established under and pursuant to the principles of the Restored Gospel. Yet because of current reiterations of the doctrine with reaffirmations of its validity, so making it still a matter of acute controversy to the disturbance of some, we can hardly escape, in following the theme of our discussions, a brief examination of the doctrine. I refer to the doctrine of the primacy of the Pope, with certain fundamental assumptions incident thereto. The doctrine has had a long evolutionary history. We undertake the discussion with some hesitancy, and regret that time compels such brevity and conciseness as forbids even an attempt at diplomatic phrasing.

History seems clearly to show this development: When the Apostles passed on, leaving no successors, the bishops of the localities became of increasing importance. Lacking a directing authority at the head, as the Apostles had been, they assumed independent leadership in their localities. Quite naturally they arrogated to themselves the functions of leadership belonging to the Apostles. In course of time they asserted the rightful possession of certain of the apostolic powers. Then came the evolution that finally produced the pope.

The Western Church gradually developed, during the early Christian centuries, the claim that the Apostle Peter was a bishop of Rome. No word has been found in the accepted canon of scriptures that would justify this claim.[16] Scholars of great learning affirm there is no accepted history establishing that Peter was ever bishop of Rome.[17]

Out of this claim the Western Church evolved

the further claims that the bishop of Rome was Peter's successor, that Peter was the rock on which Christ was to build his Church, and therefore head of the Christian Church. (It appears that the first unreserved assertion that Peter was the first bishop of Rome was made in "the famous Chronicle of 354," and that the claim to be Peter's successor was made about A.D. 217-222.)[18]

On this point, Dollinger, a Roman Catholic writer of "unrivaled knowledge" and great ability (excommunicated for his refusal to accept the dogma of the infallibility of the Pope), is quoted as declaring:

"Of all the Fathers who interpret these passages in the Gospels (Matt. 16:18; John 21:17), not a single one applies them to the Roman Bishops . . . not one of them whose commentaries we possess— Origen, Chrysostom, Hilary, Augustine, Cyril, Theodoret, and those whose interpretations are collected in catenas—has dropped the faintest hint that the primacy of Rome is the consequence of the commission and promise to Peter! Not one of them has explained the rock or foundation on which Christ would build His Church of the office given to Peter to be transmitted to his successors, but they understood by it either Christ Himself, or Peter's confession of faith in Christ; often both together. Or else they thought Peter was the foundation equally with all the other Apostles, the Twelve being together the foundation-stones of the Church."[19]

The scriptures prove that Peter was not a bishop; he was an apostle. As an apostle he might perform, if he chose to do so, the functions of a bishop, because the greater apostolic authority embraced the lesser authority of the bishop.

There is no word in the canonical scriptures justifying a claim that the supreme apostolic authority can be possessed or exercised by any lesser authority in the Church than the full apostleship.

There is no record in these scriptures of the conferring upon anyone of a part of the apostolic authority. The only scriptural record showing that the apostles conferred their authority upon any one, was upon Matthias, and this was the full authority for he was made a member of the Twelve.[20]

Now the canonical Acts and Epistles clearly show that in the Primitive Church, bishops were local officers with the function of caring for the needs of the flock,[21] hence of a lesser authority than the apostolic, and further that they were under the direction and jurisdiction of the Apostles who were in general charge of the Church, being so ordained, set apart, and charged by Christ himself.

Furthermore, a basic ecclesiastical principle is that a lesser ecclesiastical officer does not possess the authority and cannot exercise the functions of a higher ecclesiastical officer. This principle seems fully recognized by the Roman Church.

This situation presents the Western Church with this dilemma: Since the Roman Pope (prior to the time of Gregory VII, the title *pope* "continued to be bestowed on bishops in general" in countries of the west, in eastern usage the title "was commonly restricted to the bishops of Rome and Alexandria")[22]

claims as bishop of Rome apostolic authority allegedly derived from Peter[23]—and if not already a bishop,
the Pope must, before coronation, receive "the orders
which are still owing to him inclusive of the priestly
consecration"[24]—there must be found further scripture, further revelation from God, in addition to the
accepted canonical scriptures authorizing a bishop
in perpetuity to act lawfully as an apostle. But, this
scripture not appearing in the accepted canonical
scripture, such scripture could come only as all
other scripture has come, by revelation from God.

Once more, the Primitive Church was built on
revelation of the Divine will. There must be further
revelation to change, to add to, or to take from, the
revelations already given.

So the Roman Church must either produce the
revelation from God authorizing a bishop to exercise
the apostolic calling (and it is understood the Church
does not admit the principle of continuous revelation
from God, nor claim it), or it must surrender the
claim of the alleged divine apostolic authority of
the Pope, for which it has no such authorizing revelation.   And in this relation we may observe that
argument is not revelation, and neither is tradition,
however old, either accepted or ex parte.[25]

These principles and conclusions apply equally
to every Church in Christendom claiming apostolic
authority through and from the Primitive Church.

The doctrine of the infallibility of the Pope
which, though mooted before, was apparently not
formally adopted by the Church until it appeared in
the decrees of the Vatican Council of 1869-1870, a

doctrine which rests on inadequate authority[26] and which the history of the papacy, with its varying pronouncements and recants (see for example, history following Leo I, and of Vigilius and Honorius I) will not support,[27] this doctrine seems inadequate to cover for the Roman Church new and additional revelation from God, and apparently it has not been so affirmed.

We who are on the way to immortality and eternal life, must pray constantly for guidance that we may not be led astray by such fallacies. That God may give to each of us this guidance, I pray in the name of the Son. Amen.

---

[1]Matt. 16:18. [2]Heb. 6:20. [3]Heb. 7:11. [4]Heb. 7:14, 15, 16, 19, 25. [5]Heb. 7:26 ff. [6]Matt. 5:48. [7]Heb. 4:14. [8]Heb. 3:1. [9]Matt. 5:17. [10]See 3 Nephi 9:17; 15:3 ff.; 4 Nephi 1:12. [11]See Matt. 16:18. [12]Burns, *The First Three Christian Centuries*, p. 49; and see Schaff, *History of the Christian Church*, I, p. 853 ff. [13]Fawkes in Hastings, *Encyclopaedia of Religion and Ethics*, sub voce *Papacy*, p. 620-21. [14]Benton, *The Church Cyclopaedia*, sub voce *Cardinal*. [15]Robertson, *History of the Christian Church*, I p. 429-30. [16]See on question of Pope as successor to Peter, and denying the succession, Hastings, *Encyc.*, sub voce *Infallibility*, p. 271. [17]See *The Cambridge Bible*, notes by Carr, Matt. 16:18; Benton, sub voce *Pope*, p. 598; Sehling in *The New Schaff-Herzog Encyclopedia of Religious Knowledge*, sub voce *Pope*; Schmiedel in *Encyclopaedia Biblica*, sub voce *Simon Peter*, col. 4589 ff.—this latter article exhaustively discusses the evidence covering all of Peter's life outside Palestine, and his death; and see, also in this relation, Hastings, *Dictionary of the Bible*, sub voce *Peter*, *IV*, 1-2, p. 777 ff. [18]Schmiedel in *Encyc. Biblica*, sub voce *Simon Peter*, col. 4596. [19]Quoted, Hastings, *Encyc.*, sub voce *Infallibility*, p. 270b-271a. [20]Acts 1:26. [21]Acts 6:1-8; 20:28; I Tim. 3:2 ff.; and see James 1:27. [22]Robertson, II, p. 328. [23]Sehling, *Schaff-Herzog*, sub voce *Pope*. [24]*Op. cit.*, p. 130. [25]See Newman, *A Manual of Church History*, touching the "Old Catholic" movement, II, p. 515. [26]See Luke 22:31-32. [27]Newman, II, p. 509 ff.; Hastings, *Encyc.*, sub voce *Infallibility*, p. 272a; Schaff, *Creeds of Christendom*, I, p. 163 ff.

X

THE POST PRIMITIVE CHURCH
GRAPPLES WITH PAGANISM

L AST WEEK we saw that the organization of the
Primitive Church passed from the earth following the expiration of the first Christian century.
We presented briefly the problem involved of the
claimed primacy of the Pope. We noted that a not
unfriendly historian has said of the end of that first
century:

"The age of inspiration is over . . . and the
course of the ages descends once more to the ordinary
level of common time. . . . The last gleam of inspired
wisdom and truth vanished from the earth with the
beloved apostle's (John) gentle farewell."[1]

But the loss of organization was only the commencement of darkness. Almost a millennium before
the Messianic time, the Lord, speaking through the
great prophet Isaiah, declared:

"And it shall be, as with the people, so with
the priest; . . .

"The land shall be utterly emptied, and utterly
spoiled: for the Lord hath spoken this word.

"The earth mourneth and fadeth away, the
world languisheth and fadeth away, the haughty
people of the earth do languish.

"The earth also is defiled under the inhabitants

thereof; because they have transgressed the laws, changed the ordinance, broken the everlasting covenant.

"Therefore hath the curse devoured the earth, and they that dwell therein are desolate: therefore the inhabitants of the earth are burned, and few men left."[2]

This mighty prophet thus forecast the future.

Differences regarding doctrines and Church administration began during the lives of the Apostles: Paul and Barnabas disputed, seemingly quarreled, and separated,[3] the Apostles and elders disputed over the circumcision of non-Jewish Christians as contended for by the Pharisee converts;[4] Paul censured Peter to the Galatians,[5] and Peter accused Paul of preaching things "hard to be understood" and which the "unlearned and unstable wrest, as they do also the other scriptures, unto their own destruction."[6]

In their epistles the Apostles chastise the Church membership for their transgressions. Paul warned Timothy against "profane and vain babblings, and oppositions of science falsely so called,"[7] and admonished Titus not to give "heed to Jewish fables, and commandments of men, that turn from the truth"[8]; he exhorted the Corinthians not to be idolators and to "flee from idolatry"[9] and warned about heresies;[10] Peter warned against "damnable heresies, even denying the Lord that bought them"[11]; John condemned the Nicolaitanes,[12] and declared there were then many anti-Christs and warned that "many false prophets are gone out into the world."[13]

Paul instructed Timothy that "in the latter

times" there would come "seducing spirits, and doctrines of devils; . . . forbidding to marry"[14]; Jude
tells the Church that the Apostles told them "there
should be mockers in the last time, who should walk
after their own ungodly lusts."[15] Paul declared to
the Thessalonians that the "day of Christ" should
"not come, except there come a falling away first,
and that man of sin be revealed, the son of perdition"[16]; and to the Ephesians he said he knew that
after his departing "shall grievous wolves enter in
among you, not sparing the flock."[17]

These forebodings and warnings and prophecies
of heresies and the "falling away," the apostasy,
took on a speedy fulfillment. The Church writhed in
spiritual agony that came soon to be a death struggle
with paganism. Darkness was falling, and before
long night came down.

The next two hundred years (100 to 301) is
called the martyr age, and many went rejoicing and
singing to martyrs' deaths for the cause of Christ.
Some in excess of zeal courted it, sometimes it seems
almost to the point of suicide. In their last moments,
many saw in glorious vision the heavens opened.

But the "damnable heresies" of which Peter
spoke, arose; the "seducing spirits, and doctrines
of devils" predicted by Paul came and his "grievous
wolves" entered the fold, and the idolatries and "falling away" of which he spoke descended relentlessly
upon the Church, the "man of sin . . . the son of perdition" was revealed.

During the time of the Apostles, Demetrius,
pretending to the Messiahship promised by the Lord

to ancient Israel through Moses at Horeb,[18] set up a sect; so also Simon the Sorcerer, with his female assistant purchased in a brothel. Some claim Simon was the founder of gnosticism, yet some authorities say gnosticism had its roots in Egyptian literature of one or two centuries before Christ,[19] and Simon's disciple, Menander, playing the Messiah, set up another sect.[20]

Christian recruits from paganism, not fully converted to Christ and his Gospel with its simplicity of ordinance and worship and with its lofty idealism of a rigorously righteous life, sought by fair means or foul, to bring into the new religion the sensuous appeals, so hard to give up, of the old.

In the immediate post-Primitive time, gnosticism (under which may be included "all the manifold systems of belief, prevalent in the first two centuries of our era, which combined the Christian teachings with a ... higher knowledge,"[21]) aimed to amalgamate the Grecian and Oriental philosophy with Christianity. The gnostics were in part Christians, widely scattered. In the beginning it was the learning, the culture, the philosophy of the great of the earth, against the truth proclaimed by the humble Nazarene Carpenter and the far humbler fishermen of the Sea of Galilee. This was the same old fight of worldly learning and wisdom against spiritual knowledge.[22] Newman says gnosticism "led the way in the amalgamation of Christian and pagan thought and life that was to transform the religion of Christ and his apostles into the Christianity of the third and following centuries."[23] The gnostics brought about the

development of dogmas in the Church, bred a fondness for mysteries, taken largely from the Greek
and Egyptian mysteries, and secured the "introduction of elaborate and pompous liturgical services,"[24]
which, when blended with parts of the ceremonies
of the Aaronic sacrifices, formed a spectacular service that completely wiped out and displaced the beautiful simplicity of the ordinations of Christ's Apostles and the eating of the sacrament of the Last Supper. Harnack is quoted as saying that gnosticism
acted to "the acute . . . hellenising of Christianity."[25]
Manichaeism which "is Gnosticism, with its Christian elements reduced to a minimum,"[26] was another
heretical movement having its origin in Persia, with
a mystic, and to us fantastic philosophy.[27] It continued and was "among the heresies of the middle
ages."[28] This system also played its part in introducing "pompous ceremonial" into the Church; it
promoted the ascetic spirit, the degradation of marriage, its devotees abstaining from marriage, and
also from animal food. Manichaeism exalted virginity, and developed a sacerdotalism that is said to have
eventually led to the introduction of indulgences.[29]
Another heretical sect may be mentioned that warred
against the true Christian faith—the Ebionites or
Judaizing Christians.[30]

Another sect, the Monarchians (A. D. 250),
drew the heretical distinction, now stressed by higher critics—principally, it seems, of Protestant leanings—between the synoptic gospels and the gospel of
John, and taught the further heretical doctrine that

the Father, Son, and Holy Ghost were one person,[31] which came to be known later as Sabellianism.

The fires of doctrinal corruption were fed by other sects.

The Marcionites taught the heresy which some modern critics—again, it seems, especially those professing some form of Protestantism—have newly discovered,—that Jehovah of the Old Testament was not the God of the New Testament; they also argued that if God were good, he would not have permitted man to sin,[32] a view held also by the gnostics.[33]

On the other side, in an effort to stop the innovations coming into the churches from gnosticism and paganism, other sects arose: The Montanists (originating 135-160) inclined to Judaism and rebelled against the immoralities creeping into the Church; to meet immorality they advocated the exaltation of widowhood and virginity, distinctions as to kinds of sin, exaltation of martyrdom, and affirmed that all sensual pleasures were lustful; they forbade second marriages as equivalent to adultery, advocated long continued fasts, all of which, while repudiated by the Church at the time, were many of them later adopted by the Church[34] and are part of the dogmas now accepted by the post-Primitive Church. Novatianists, organized after the Decian persecutions (251 A.D.) to obstruct the rebaptism of those who had denied the faith to escape persecution,[35] and the Donatists, who organized after the Diocletian persecutions (303 A.D.), both protested against corruptions in the Churches, against receiving back into the Church those who had, to escape persecution, burned or otherwise destroyed the scriptures, which to them was a sin not to be pardoned; they protested against the superstition of worshipping relics,[36] which the Church later took on.

Against the gnostic heresies particularly, and also against the corruption that was overrunning the Church, great churchmen, no longer of the humble, unschooled Petrine character, but learned in the lore of the pagans and of the Church, waged an aggressive, valiant fight. We can but name some of them: Origen (b. 185), the tragic figure of Alexandria, persecuted by his early friend and by fellow Christians, "the most learned man and one of the profoundest thinkers in the ancient church"[37]; Quintus Septimus Florens Tertullianus (b. 150-160), whom we know as Tertullian,[38] of Carthage, who in large measure adopted the philosophy of Montanus, who, a stoic and ascetic, taught doctrines upon which the heresy was later built that called for a marriageless clergy—a principle that the Lord never taught, for this would have disqualified Peter and others of the Apostles, and under the Apostles, the bishops and deacons, upon whom marriage was expressly enjoined.[39] Tertullian also taught, if, indeed he did not invent, the heresy, still preached in the sectarian world, that our spirits had no pre-mortal existence, but were begotten, like our mortal bodies, by our parents,[40] a doctrine contrary to that recognized by the Savior when he healed the man, blind from his birth,[41] and contrary to modern revelation.[42] Then Cyprian (b. 200), a disciple of Tertullian, who destroyed in his own area the position of the presbyters (the elders) and built up the primacy of the bishop, but who repudiated and fought the attempt of Stephen, the bishop at Rome, to become the head of the whole Christian Church.[43]

The Church was in utter confusion. The people had no Moses to lead them through the wilderness of conflicting dogmas, no Moses through whom God might reveal his will. Truly, as Burns says:

"The age of inspiration is over . . . and the course of the ages descends once more to the ordinary level of common time. . . . The last gleam of inspired wisdom and truth vanished from the earth with the beloved apostle's gentle farewell, and we pass at once across the mysterious line which separates the sacred from the secular annals of the world,—the history of the apostolic age from the history of the Christian Church."[44]

May the Lord help us so to live that we may keep open the line of communication between God and his children which was again cleared by the ushering in of the Dispensation of the Fullness of Times, I pray, in the Son's name. Amen.

[1]Burns, *The First Three Christian Centuries*, p. 49. [2]Isa. 24:2-6. [3]Acts 15:39. [4]Acts 15:4 ff. [5]Gal. 2:11 ff. [6]II Pet. 3:16. [7]I Tim. 6:20; 1:20; II Tim. 2:17-18, naming Hymenaeus, Alexander, and Philetus as offenders. [8]Titus 1:14. [9]I Cor. 10:7, 14. [10]I Cor. 11:19; Gal. 5:20. [11]II Pet. 2:1. [12]Rev. 2:6, 15. [13]I John 2:18; 4:1; II John 7. [14]I Tim. 4:1 ff. [15]Jude 18. [16]II Thess. 2:3. [17]Acts 20:28 ff. [18]Deut. 18:18. [19]Scott in Hastings, *Encyclopaedia of Religion and Ethics*, sub voce *Gnosticism*, p. 233a. [20]Burns, p. 237. [21]Scott, *op cit.*, p. 231a. [22]I Cor. 2:11, 14, 16; but see, as to Paul, *Encyclopaedia Biblica*, sub voce *Gnosis*. [23]Newman, *A Manual of Church History*, I, p. 194. [24]*Op cit.* [25]Scott, *op. cit.*, p. 232a. [26]Newman, op. cit. [27]Robertson, *History of the Christian Church*, I, p. 189 ff.; Newman, I, p. 197. [28]Robertson, I, p. 200. [29]Newman, I pp. 196-197. [30]*Id.* p. 174 ff. [31]*Id.* pp. 198-199. [32]*Id.*, pp. 191-192, 261. [33]*Id.*, p. 286, 359. [34]*Id.*, p. 202 ff. [35]*Id.* p. 206 ff. [36]*Id.*, p. 208. [37]*Id.*, p. 281. [38]Burns, p. 149. [39]Matt. 8:14; I Cor.

9:5; I Tim. 3. [40]Newman, I, p. 262. [41]John 9:1-2. [42]See Talk No. 7, *Men Lived Before They Were Mortal.* [43]Newman, I, p. 265 ff.; and see Talk No. 9, *The Primitive Church Organization Disappears.* [44]Burns, p 49.

XI

GREAT ERRONEOUS DOGMAS DEVELOP

I N OUR last talk we spoke of the fight of the early post-Primitive Church against paganism. We noted that various pagan beliefs persist today that were first urged against Christian truths in those earlier days.

Tonight we shall see that the Church continued in tense turmoil out of which came great dogmas untaught in the Primitive Church and contrary to basic principles proclaimed by God through the ages. We shall notice a few only of such dogmas.

There were rivalry, jealousy, and quarreling, and scheming for power and primacy among the early bishops—as for example, among the bishops of Alexandria, Jerusalem, and Caesarea over Origen[1]; as affecting the bishop of Antioch, excommunicated (A.D. 269) "after years of bitter controversy"[2]; as between the bishop of Rome and certain eastern bishops and Cyprian, bishop of Carthage[3] (255 A.D.); as between the two rival bishops in Carthage in a schism that spread all over northern Africa (311 A.D.).[4] There were many other controversies unnecessary to name.[5]

Heresies, schisms, and contests for power and authority left the Church torn and mangled over doctrines. The post-Primitive Church was made up

of many flocks, without a shepherd. Councils—
Diocesan, Provincial, Plenary, Patriarchal, National,
General, of a part or of the whole Church, Ecumenical, or world-wide, were held one after the other
over the centuries in an effort to reach agreement on
points of doctrine and matters of discipline. Agree-
ments reached often involved compromises on matters of principle,[6] to the bringing of errors into the
Church. In A.D. 325, Emperor Constantine, a Christian, solicitous for the peace of his empire which
seemed threatened by bitter controversies in Alexandria, called the first ecumenical (world-wide) conference at Nicaea.

One Arius, a presbyter (elder) in charge of a
district of the Alexandrian Church[7] had formulated
and preached a more or less obscure and indefinite[8]
heretical doctrine—the product seemingly of an
Alexandrian controversy[9]—the net result of which
was to deny the divinity of Jesus, the Christ.[10] The
Council, composed at most of some 318 bishops (one-
sixth of all the bishops of the Empire) with lesser
officers and attendants to the number of perhaps
2,000 began with some twenty bishops in favor of
Arius and his heresy. At the conclusion of the Council they had dwindled to two with Arius, who, with
his writings and the two bishops who finally refused
to sign, were anathematized and also excommunicated. Constantine approved the findings of the
Council and put the sanction of the civil law, the
State, behind the decision and thereupon banished
Arius and the bishops to Illyria.

From this point of time the State—the govern-

ment in all parts of post-Primitive Christendom—
greatly influenced the course and control of the
Church. Political, not spiritual, considerations often
largely ruled, and the State lent its sovereign political power to enforce the Church doctrine favored
by it.

The Church was divided after Nicaea into three
divisions—sees—corresponding to political divisions,
with headquarters at capitals—Rome, Alexandria,
Antioch.[11] The whole Church covering the entire
Christian world was called "the Catholic Church,"[12]
and the declarations of the creed were termed
orthodox. Later, after the division of the Western
and Eastern Churches, the former, the Western
Church, appropriated the word "Catholic," and the
latter, the Eastern Church, the word "Orthodox."[13]

The philosophy of Arianism is pagan. "Arius
tried to interpret the Christian revelation in such a
way as to render it acceptable to men whose whole
conception of God and of life was heathen."[14] Arianism had its birth in the fear of Sabellianism, the
doctrine that the Father, Son, and Holy Ghost are
but one person.

But the Arian heresy did not die with the decree
of excommunication and banishment of Arius and
his friends. Constantine himself, after the Council
had finished its work, was swayed from one side to
the other of the controversy.

After Constantine's death, council after council
was called to try to bring harmony into the Church.
But Arianism persisted through the middle ages; it
revived in England in the eighteenth century, to

the great disturbance of the English Church.[15] The basic element of the heresy is found today in the doctrine that portrays Christ as a great philosopher, as the founder of a profound code of ethics, as the supremely righteous man, but denies to him divine parentage, the Sonship of God. This doctrine now finds principal support among the liberal scholars of the Protestant Churches. It drags Christianity down to the level of paganism. The true God and his plan of redemption for his children are utterly wiped out.

As the centuries went on, other errors crept into the Church; councils of all kinds were called to settle urgent controversies. Some of them approved dogmas that were heresies if tested by the canonical scriptures.

Notwithstanding the great commandment to Adam and Eve to multiply and replenish the earth[16] and the further commandment that "therefore shall a man leave his father and his mother, and shall cleave unto his wife: and they shall be one flesh"[17]; notwithstanding the Savior, speaking to the Pharisees, renewed this commandment of the relationship of husband and wife, adding what "God hath joined together, let not man put asunder"[18]; notwithstanding that Jesus chose men with wives for his Apostles[19]; notwithstanding that the Primitive Church directed that bishops and deacons should have wives[20]; notwithstanding the loftiest, holiest relationship we mortals know among ourselves is that of mother and child, and that the Christ declared that except we become as little children we could not enter the kingdom of heaven[21]; notwithstanding all this and more, and contrary thereto, men began in the early days of the post-Primitive Church to preach that the loftiest type of earthly existence was the unmarried state. This, as we know from modern revelation, would defeat the very purpose of earth-life and destroy the destiny God has provided for his children.[22] The examples of Elijah, Elisha, and John the Baptist[23] were erroneously invoked to support this heresy, as were also Paul and his teachings.[24] And so trailing after pagan teachings, men began to retire from their fellowmen and live as hermits, thus they robbed their fellowmen of whatever influence they might have used for righteousness, so typifying a consuming selfishness for themselves and a complete disregard of the welfare of their brethren. Men abandoned the world instead of seeking to reform it.[25]

The practice existed among heathen nations long ante-dating the Christian era, going back among the Hindoos to the time of Moses.[26] It existed among the American Indians before the time of Columbus.[27]

But the affinity of male and female implanted in the hearts of men by God himself in the beginning, that his purposes might not be thwarted, soon led hermits to take what were termed "spiritual wives" ("uxores spirituales"), with whom they were supposed to live in a purely spiritual, platonic relationship. Sometimes they succeeded; too often they did not.[28]

The idea that an ascetic life was the highest type began to take root in the clergy in the third and fourth centuries of the Christian era, and afterwards celibacy became the ordered standard of the righteous life, first, as an unorganized, individual movement, practiced more or less by recluses, next by real hermits, beginning perhaps with St. Paul and St. Anthony (b. about 250 A.D.) in the east,[29] and brought to the west by Athanasius, disciple of St. Anthony,[30] and ending by the grouping of such men into cloisters,[31] the beginning of monasticism.

The movement was doubtless hastened and intensified by the heathenish sexual abominations that were present in the Church, against which Tertullian inveighed, particularly after he adopted Montanism.[32]

The reaction to this celibate concept was a sort of mass pseudo-asceticism, in which the sexes associated together on terms of greatest physical intimacy, in order to show that the spirit was mightier than the flesh,[33] too frequently with disastrous results.

Many of the clergy adopted celibacy. The Eastern Church was more liberal than the Western in favor of marriage. In the east, both priests and bishops lived in wedlock, and at one time were forbidden under pain of deposition and excommunication to put away their wives, but finally, nearly seven hundred years after Christ (A.D. 692) they required celibacy from bishops, but allowed marriage of presbyters and deacons. In the west, the prohibition against marriage operated against the whole clergy.[34] It seems that by the end of the fourth century "the religious life was identified with asceticism."[35]

Forbidden lawful wedlock many of the clergy followed the example of the hermits (took to themselves "spiritual wives"), with the same natural result. Schaff declares: "This spiritual marriage, which had begun as a bold ascetic venture, ended only too often in the flesh, and prostituted the honor of the church."[36]

These illicit relations on the part of some of the clergy were recognized in the Council of Nicaea (A.D. 325), which, in its third canon, provided: "The great Synod absolutely forbids, and it cannot be permitted to either bishop, priest, or any other cleric, to have in his house a *subintroducta*" (women "secretly brought in")[37] "with the exception of his mother, sister, aunt, or such other persons as are free from all suspicion."[38]

But immorality among the clergy increased in the Church during the middle ages. Councils in Italy, Africa and Rome repeatedly condemned transgressions against celibacy,[39] yet transgression continued.

Forbidden lawful wedlock, concubinage amongst the clergy became all too common, apparently in some areas the rule, sometimes it seems, even among the very highest officers. The Council of Trent (A.D. 1545-1563) formally condemned it. Before this time, however, bishops in some countries derived a considerable revenue from assessing a fine upon priests for the third child born to them. Gregory VII, both before and after he became Pope, did his best to stamp out immorality of the clergy, including concubinage, but the sin went on because the rule for-bidding marriage was against and contrary to the revelations of God. In the fourteenth century the German bishops refused to give up their wives.⁴⁰

Thus the tumult and confusion arising out of the bickerings and disputes in the post-Primitive Church, led to the development of great fundamental dogmas that were not taught by Jesus nor by the Apostles, and that are born of error. We have noted that Arianism—the dogma that robs Christ of his divinity—persists in an only slightly disguised form today; we have noted the creeping into the Church of political influences and considerations, that often overshadowed the spiritual welfare and influence of the Church (in the middle centuries this was reversed and the Church claimed and exercised a sort of political suzerainty over the State, to the great harm of the Church); we have noted the "falling away" predicted by Paul when he said there would come "seducing spirits, and doctrines of devils . . . forbidding to marry,"⁴¹ this condemned doctrine finding its fruition, in part, in the rule of a marriage-less clergy.

We, on our way to immortality and eternal life, must be constantly watchful that we do not take on these heresies. That we may be able to avoid them and to live the righteous life, I pray, in the name of the Son. Amen.

¹Newman, *A Manual of Church History*, I, p. 281; Robertson, *History of the Christian Church*, I, p. 145; Burns, *The First Three Christian Centuries*, p. 141. ²Newman, I, p. 198. ³*Id.*, p. 270. ⁴*Id.*, p. 209. ⁵Hastings, *Encyclopaedia of Religion and Ethics*, sub voce *Infallibility*, p. 272a. ⁶Hastings, *Encyc.*, sub voce *Councils*. ⁷Hefele, *History of the Christian Councils*, p. 242. ⁸Robertson, I,

p. 288. [9]Hefele, p. 249. [10]Schaff, *History of the Christian Church*, III, p. 620; Robertson, I, p. 287; Foakes-Jackson in Hastings, *Encyc.*, sub voce *Arianism*, p. 777a; Newman, I, p. 327; Benton, The *Church Cyclopaedia*, p. 192. [11]Robertson, I, p. 431; Hastings, *Encyc.*, sub voce *Infallibility*, p. 272; Hefele, p. 394; and see Schaff, *Hist.*, III, p. 622 ff.; Newman, I, p. 330. [12]See *Nicene Creed*, Hefele, p. 295. [13]Hastings, *Encyc.*, sub voce *Greek Orthodox Church*. [14]Hastings, *Encyc.*, sub voce *Arianism*, Foakes-Jackson quoting Bethune-Baker, p. 781. [15]Hastings, *Encyc.*, sub voce *Arianism;* sub voce *Coptic Church*, p. 117b ff.; sub voce *Councils*. [16]Gen. 1:28. [17]Gen. 2:24. [18]Matt. 19:5-6; Mark 10:7-9. [19]I Cor. 9:5. [20]I Tim. 3. [21]Matt. 18:3; Mark 9:33-37; Luke 9:46-48. [22]Abraham 3-4. [23]Schaff, *Hist.*, III, pp. 156, 161. [24]See I Cor. 7. [25]Schaff, *Hist.*, III, p. 159. [26]Schaff, *Hist.*, III, p. 149 ff.; Newman, I, p. 316. [27]Hastings, *Encyc.*, sub voce *Celibacy*. [28]Hastings, *Encyc.*, sub voce *Agapetae*, p. 179. [29]Schaff, *Hist.*, III, p. 181. [30]Schaff, *Hist.*, III, p. 201. [31]Schaff, *Hist.*, III, p. 156 ff.; Newman, I, p. 318. [32]Burns, p. 154 ff. [33]*The Ante-Nicene Fathers*, Coxe ed., II, *The Pastor of Hermas*, Sim. IX, ch. XI. [34]Schaff, *Hist.*, III, p. 242 ff. [35]Newman, I, p. 371. [36]Schaff, *Hist.*, III, p. 249. [37]Schaff, *Hist.*, III, p. 249; Hastings, *Encyc.*, sub voce *Agapetae*, p. 179a. [38]Hefele, p. 379; and see Schaff, *Hist.*, III, p. 622 ff., Hastings, *Encyc.*, sub voce *Concubinage*, p. 817b. [39]Schaff, *Hist.*, III, p. 248 ff. [40]Hastings, *Encyc.*, sub voce *Concubinage;* Schaff, *Hist.*, V, Pt. I, p. 14, 36, 39, 42, 44, 807, 821; as to Popes, see Newman, I, p. 495 ff.; and as to Alexander VI, the Borgia family, *id.*, p. 537, and *Rankes's History of the Popes*, I, p. 35. [41]I Tim. 4:1 ff.

XII

JESUS THE CHRIST, THE RESURRECTED
SON OF GOD

NINETEEN and a half centuries ago this morning, as men have counted it, a lone woman, love-driven, moved hurriedly, but carefully, over the rough cobblestones of the streets leading to Golgotha and the newly hewed tomb of Joseph of Arimathaea in the garden, where they had laid the Master. In the deep stillness of the morning air, listening, she might have heard the priests in the Temple court calling to the lookout, peering southward from the topmost pinnacle of the Temple wall: "Is the sky lit up as far as Hebron?" for then the morning sacrifice began. But the lookout would not answer back, for it was still dark.

Reaching the tomb and finding the great sealing stone rolled back and the guard of the high priests gone, Mary Magdalene, for she it was, ran back to Peter and John, telling them the body was gone; she knew not where it was laid. Hastening to the tomb, John outrunning Peter, they found the tomb empty, the burial clothes lying about. They returned, Peter wondering and John 'seeing and believing.'

Mary Magdalene, out of whom he had cast seven devils, stood weeping without the sepulchre. Stooping down and looking in, she saw two angels sitting, one at the head, the other at the feet of where Jesus had lain.

"Why weepest thou?"[1] said they, and she answering, said, "Because they have taken away my Lord, and I know not where they have laid him."

And there stood a man beside her, who asked, "Why weepest thou? whom seekest thou?" Thinking it was the gardener, she answered, "Sir, if thou have borne him hence, tell me where thou hast laid him, and I will take him away."

Then Jesus, for it was he, saith unto her, "Mary," and she, recognizing, overwhelmed with emotion, turned and saith unto him, "Rabboni," Master. As she would have touched him, he, gently, affectionately, forbade her, saying: "Touch me not; for I am not yet ascended to my Father: but go to my brethren, and say unto them, I ascend unto my Father, and your Father; and to my God, and your God."

Returning, she told the disciples all that had happened, but they believed not.

Mary saw, talked with, and would have touched, but that she was withheld, the resurrected Christ.

At sunrise, Mary, the Mother of James, and Salome, and other women came to the tomb with spices to prepare the body for final burial, wondering who would roll back the heavy stone sealing the tomb that they might enter. But the tomb was open. Two men stood before them in shining garments, declaring: 'Ye seek Jesus of Nazareth. Why seek ye the living among the dead? He is not here; he is risen. Go tell his disciples and Peter that he will go before you into Galilee; there shall ye see him as he said unto you.'

As they quickly fled from the sepulchre, with fear and great joy, to tell the disciples, "Jesus met them, saying, All hail. And they came and held him by the feet, and worshipped him. Then said Jesus unto them, Be not afraid: go tell my brethren that they go into Galilee, and there shall they see me."

So telling no man on the way, they, with Mary Magdalene, returned and told all "unto the eleven, and to all the rest. . . . And their words seemed to them as idle tales, and they believed them not."

The Marys and Salome and the other women saw and talked with and touched the risen Christ.

As this first day grew older, Jesus lingered about, seemingly loathe to leave the scenes of his mortal ministry and his beloved disciples, he knowing how much they needed his help, being bereft of his presence.

So as Cleopas and another sadly journeyed to Emmaus, Jesus drew near and went with them. But their "eyes were holden that they should not know him." He asked of what they talked. They told him of Jesus and of their trust "that it had been he which should have redeemed Israel"; they told him of the death, the burial, the empty tomb, of the angels who had been seen by the women. And Jesus, trying to teach them to walk in the strength of the spirit, said to them, "O fools, and slow of heart to believe all that the prophets have spoken." He then explained to them, beginning at Moses, the teachings of the prophets about the Christ. Journeying on towards the village, he made as though he would go on, but they asked him to tarry with them, for the day was far spent. So he went in and sat down with them at meat. He took bread and blessed and brake it, and gave to them; then their eyes were opened; they knew him; and he vanished from their sight.

"They said one to another, Did not our heart burn within us, while he talked with us by the way, and while he opened to us the scriptures?"

They sensed it not, but they had the testimony of the spirit before there came to them the witness of the eyes.

Returning to Jerusalem they found gathered together in a chamber the disciples, who told them, "The Lord is risen indeed, and hath appeared to Simon." They told the disciples of how they themselves had walked and talked and sat at meat with Jesus.

And even as they spoke one with another, Jesus suddenly stood amongst them in the chamber. Terrified and affrighted they "supposed that they had seen a spirit." Asking why they were troubled, why thoughts arose in their hearts, he said:

"Behold my hands and my feet, that it is I myself: handle me, and see; for a spirit hath not flesh and bones, as ye see me have."

While "they yet believed not for joy, and wondered," he asked for food; they gave him a piece of fish and honeycomb, and he ate before them. The Christ, the creator of all things whatsoever that were made, the second member of the Godhead, himself created in the express image of the Father, now returning to sit on the right hand of God, his Father, was a tangible person in human form, that talked and walked and ate, doing what he had seen his Father do. Then he taught them as he taught the two on the way to Emmaus, and they were glad. He saith to them, "Receive ye the Holy Ghost" and the power to remit and retain sins.

These all talked and touched and ate with the risen Lord.

But Thomas was not with them. When told of Jesus' visit he believed not, saying he, too, must see, and adding, unless I "put my finger into the print of the nails, and thrust my hand into his side, I will not believe."

At the end of the week they were all again gathered together in a chamber; the doors were shut. Suddenly Jesus stood amongst them, asking Thomas to touch him, saying, "be not faithless, but believing. And Thomas answered and said unto him, My Lord and my God." Jesus saith unto him:

"Thomas, because thou hast seen me, thou hast believed: blessed are they that have not seen, and yet have believed."

Once more the disciples had talked with the resurrected Christ, and touched his body.

But the disciples yet knew not their calling and their work. Peter said to Thomas, and Nathanael, and the sons of Zebedee, and two others, "I go a fishing," and they said, "We also go with thee." Hieing themselves to the Sea of Tiberias, they went fishing, the work from which he had called them into his service. They fished the night through; they caught nothing. In the early morning, drawing near the shore, they saw standing there a man who, calling to them, asked if they had any meat. They answering no, he called back, "Cast the net on the right side of the ship, and ye shall find," and doing so, they filled their net. This was the sign which, three years before, Jesus had given to Simon Peter, and Andrew and James and John, when he called them to his service, saying:

"Follow me, and I will make you fishers of men."[2]

This memory must have surged into the mind of John, for he said to Peter: "It is the Lord," and Peter, girding his fisher's coat about him, for he was naked and would not so come unto the Lord, cast himself into the sea, and went to the Master. Then, again in mild reproof, this time because they had so soon left his service, going back to the old ways, he, "when they had dined," thrice questioned, "Simon, son of Jonas, lovest thou me?"; thrice Peter answered, "Yea, Lord; thou knowest that I love thee"; and thrice the Christ instructed, "Feed my sheep."

Again they talked, sat at meat, and were instructed by the risen Lord.

Thereafter Jesus was seen of James, of above five hundred brethren at once, and of Paul, "as of one born out of due time."[3]

He shewed himself again to his Apostles, on the mount in Galilee to which he had called them, and while they worshipped him, some yet doubted. Declaring all power was given unto him in heaven and earth, he gave them their charge and commission to teach all nations, baptizing, and instructing in the principles he had taught to them.

Finally, having instructed them to tarry in Jerusalem "until ye be endued with power from on high," he lifted up his hands and blessed them, then "he was taken up; and a cloud received him out of their sight," heaven-bound to sit on the right hand of God.

As the disciples stood gazing after him, two men in white apparel stood by them, saying:

"Ye men of Galilee, why stand ye gazing up into heaven? this same Jesus, which is taken up from you into heaven, shall so come in like manner as ye have seen him go into heaven."

Thus for forty days after the morning Mary had first seen him at the tomb's mouth, Jesus had moved among his disciples. They saw him, heard him, walked with him, talked with him, sat at meat with him, touched him,—they fearing him as a spirit, he said to them, "a spirit hath not flesh and bones, as ye see me have." He was risen indeed, a resurrected being of flesh and bone, a man made in the express image of the Father, a perfect soul, the first fruits of the resurrection, the only Begotten of the Father, the second member of the Godhead.

The Christ came also to this hemisphere, to the other sheep of whom he spoke to the Jews in Jerusalem,[4] and ministered among their multitudes for three glorious days.[5] With these other sheep he talked, he blessed their little children, he fed them, he administered the Sacrament to them, he called

other disciples to whom also he gave divine com-
missions.

Yet while Jesus still moved and ministered in
mortality in Palestine, there came two great occasions when he was called the Christ.

The first came as he and the disciples paused
in their great Galilean Mission for a needed moment-
ary respite from their labors. They were in the coasts
of Caesarea Philippi. As they rested Jesus asked,
"Whom do men say that I the Son of man am?"
They answered, some say John the Baptist, some
Elias, some Jeremias, or one of the prophets. Then
plumbing their own knowledge and testimony, Jesus
asked, "Whom say ye that I am?" And Simon Peter
answered: "Thou art the Christ, the Son of the
living God." Saith the Savior, "Blessed art thou,
Simon Barjona: for flesh and blood hath not revealed
it unto thee, but my Father which is in heaven." So
Peter for an instant glimpsed the full truth.[6]

So also the humble Martha, gently chiding
Jesus: "If thou hadst been here, my brother had not
died." Jesus saith unto her: "Thy brother shall rise
again. Martha saith unto him, I know that he shall
rise again in the resurrection at the last day. Jesus
said unto her, I am the resurrection, and the life: he
that believeth in me, though he were dead, yet shall
he live: and whosoever liveth and believeth in me
shall never die. Believest thou this? She saith unto
him, Yea, Lord: I believe that thou art the Christ,
the Son of God, which should come into the world."[7]

Thus while he yet lived amongst them, there
came to the humblest of them—Peter, the fisherman,

and Martha, the good housewife "cumbered about much serving"[8]—the testimony for which men since have devoutly lived and gloriously died,—that Jesus was the Christ, the Son of God.

At the beginning and ushering-in of this Last Dispensation, the Father and Son appeared in person, in the form in which Jesus returned to the Father, to the boy Joseph in the woods, in the most glorious vision vouched to man in all time.

And thereafter, Joseph and Sidney at Hiram, Ohio, declared a vision:

"And now, after the many testimonies which have been given of him, this is the testimony, last of all, which we give of him: That he lives!

"For we saw him, even on the right hand of God; and we heard the voice bearing record that he is the Only Begotten of the Father—

"That by him, and through him, and of him, the worlds are and were created, and the inhabitants thereof are begotten sons and daughters unto God."[9]

And now may I, of the lowliest of the lowly who seek to serve him, and fully acknowledging my own weaknesses and imperfections, bear in deep humility my own testimony, born of the Spirit, that Jesus is the Christ, the Son of the Living God, the Only Begotten in the flesh, chosen before the foundations of the earth were laid to be the Redeemer of the World, the First Fruits of the Resurrection, through and by whom the spirits and bodies of all men will, in the due time of the Lord, be reunited and resurrected from the grave, "they who have done good in the resurrection of the just, and they who have done evil in the resurrection of the unjust."[10]

May I be preserved in this testimony till I lay down my body in my last sleep, I pray, in the Lord's name. Amen.

---

[1]For texts see Matt. 28; Mark 16; Luke 24; John 20-21; Acts 1. [2]Matt. 4:19. [3]I Cor. 15:6-8. [4]John 10:16. [5]3 Nephi 11-28. [6]Matt. 16:13 ff. [7]John 11:13 ff. [8]Luke 10:40. [9]D.C. 76:22-24. [10]D.C. 76:17.

XIII

OTHER ERRONEOUS DOGMAS APPEAR

WE have seen that, in the centuries following the Primitive Church there developed great dogmas that were contrary to the teachings of the Christ; we noted the Arian doctrine, still persisting, which denies the divinity of Christ; we noted the false doctrine of celibacy introduced into the Church from pagan sources, and some of the transgressions ensuing therefrom; we observed that the mixing of State and Church brought about commotion, uncertainty, and irregularity, and the subjection of the spiritual to the temporal. As Gibbon observes: ". . . the will of the prince was the rule of episcopal faith."[1]

We shall tonight call attention to another dogma which is not in accord with the principles of the Gospel; it concerns the sacrament of bread and wine, instituted by the Savior at the Last Supper.

The sacrament of the Lord's Supper in certain great Christian Churches long since lost the beautiful simplicity of the Upper Room, when, as he and they were gathered round the eating board of the "passover,"[2] for he had said, "I have desired to eat this passover with you before I suffer,"[3] "Jesus took bread, and blessed it, and brake it, and gave it to the disciples, and said, Take, eat; this is my body. And he took the cup, and gave thanks, and gave it to them, saying, Drink ye all of it; for this is my blood of the new testament, which is shed for many for the remission of sins," and "they all drank of it."[4]

In lieu of this simplicity, the post-Primitive Church developed an elaborate ritual carried through with great pomp and ceremony. The Lord gave bread and wine to all the Twelve, and on this continent to all the assembled people.[5] A part of the post-Primitive Church has developed the practice of passing the bread (wafers) to the people, but the drinking of the wine is confined to the celebrant only. Wafers as used by the Roman Church were unknown till the eleventh or twelfth centuries.[6]

The administration of the sacrament has been variously named during Christian centuries. In the Acts of the Apostles it is called "breaking of bread."[7] Paul termed it "cup of blessing," "cup of the Lord," "communion of the blood of Christ," "communion of the body of Christ," "the Lord's supper."[8]

"The sub-apostolic writers call the Sacrament by the names of Oblation (Clement of Rome), Sacrament (Pliny), Eucharist (Ignatius), Sacrifice (Justin Martyr), and Commemoration (Justin Martyr). For the first three centuries these appear to be the only titles by which the Sacrament of the Body and Blood of Christ was known. Commencing with the fourth century, we find Origen using the term Passover, and towards the close of that century we find St. Ambrose using the term Mass in reference to this Sacrament."[9] The term Eucharist became popular from the time of Ignatius on, he being, it is said, the first of the Fathers to use it.[10]

Furthermore, while the sacrament originally "and in itself . . . had nothing whatever to do with the idea of sacrifice, it has in the course of centuries come to convey an exceedingly definite idea of sacrifice."[11]   So in the sacramentary prayers and procedure incident to the celebration of the Lord's Supper there were introduced, as time went on, some of the essential characteristics of the Aaronic animal sacrifice ceremonies: for example, the host is "waved" and "heaved" as were the breasts in a "peace offering" by the individual,[12] as were the parts named in the ceremony of the consecration of priests,[13] as the peace offering for the people,[14] as the sheaf of the first fruits,[15] as the two lambs offered with the first fruits,[16] as the "jealousy" offering,[17] as the offering of the Nazarite "when the days of his separation are fulfilled,"[18] and as the offering of the leper "in the day of his cleansing."[19]

Indeed, in these Churches the whole sacramentary ceremony has taken on as the centuries lengthened, characteristics incident to the Aaronic offering of sacrifice instead of the simple eating of bread and drinking of wine under the Lord's example and command: "this do in remembrance of me."[20]   The concept of sacrifice was finally carried, in the Greek and Roman Churches,[21] to its logical conclusion with the dogma that Christ himself is again sacrificed each time the eucharist is celebrated.   The whole service became that "of a Priest sacrificing a Victim"[22]; the Roman Mass "has engrafted on the Jewish worship, and on the primitive Christian worship the Roman pagan idea of sacrifice."[23] So far was this idea of sacrifice carried, that to make it more realistic, as it would seem, the Roman Church for centuries "actually slew at Easter a living Victim, a lamb, roasted its flesh, had it brought whole to the altar, and offered as a sacrifice." This was done during the Mass; "the flesh of the lamb was distributed to the faithful"; this practice was followed as late as the end of the twelfth century.[24]

A further and critical "falling away" officially appeared when the Fourth Lateran Council (1215) defined the dogma of transubstantiation (the only dogma, it is said, "that had not been defined by one of the first eight Ecumenical Councils"[25]).

Beginnings of this last "falling away" apparently came in the late 700's,[26] when the phrase, *substance of the Lord's body and blood* was used of the sacrament in the writings of Bede and Alcuin. The term *transubstantiation* was apparently not used until the eleventh century, when Peter Damiani (b. 1007) used it in one of his works.[27]

In the controversies of the two centuries following the Fourth Lateran Council, which culminated in the rebellion of Luther and the Reformation, Berengar (Berengarius) preached against a *material* change in the bread and wine. While under pressure he recanted his teachings, yet he later returned to them.[28]

This dogma of transubstantiation, which did not become official until the thirteenth century, is highly mystical and apparently declares that the bread and wine of the sacrament of the Lord's Supper is changed in the sacramental ceremony to the actual flesh and blood of the Savior, who is thus again sacrificed, killed, every time a priest officiates at Mass, following which Christ's flesh and blood are then mysteriously borne to heaven "by the hands of Thy Holy Angel to Thine Altar on high in sight of Thy Divine Majesty," as the prayer is quoted.[29] Under this dogma, those partaking of the sacrament eat the actual flesh and drink the actual blood of Jesus, the Christ, who is, under this dogma, sacrificed thousands of times each day, and day after day, growing into millenniums. Thus the sacrament of the Lord's Supper becomes, in essence, under this dogma, an Aaronic sacrifice, as if of a beast of the field, with elaborate, pompous ceremonies. The divine nature of the atoning sacrifice of the Son of God, the Great High Priest after the order of Melchizedek,[30] for the sins of the world, is swallowed up and lost in an empty meaningless ceremony, because the atonement of Christ did away with the Aaronic sacrifices,[31] in the image of which these Churches administer this holy ordinance.

How different this is from the simple prayers of the Didache as they existed shortly after the last of the Apostles had gone.[32]

The underlying fallacy of the dogma of transubstantiation was treated by Paul as if he foresaw its coming.

Speaking to the Hebrews, he declared these principles in contrasting the sacrifice offered by the high priest under the Mosaic law in the Temple and the sacrifice made by Christ.

"For Christ is not entered into the holy places made with hands, which are the figures of the true; but into heaven itself, now to appear in the presence of God for us: nor yet that he should offer himself often, as the high priest entereth into the holy place every year with blood of others; for then must he often have suffered since the foundation of the world: but now once in the end of the world hath he appeared to put away sin by the sacrifice of himself. And as it is appointed unto men once to die, but after this the judgment: so Christ was once offered to bear the sins of many . . ."[33]

Speaking further of Christ's sacrifice, Paul says:

"By the which we are sanctified through the offering of the body of Jesus Christ once for all . . . But this man, after he had offered one sacrifice for sins for ever, sat down on the right hand of God . . . For by one offering he hath perfected for ever them that are sanctified."[34]

There should be repeated here, Paul's other statement to the Hebrews, where he was exhorting them to go on to perfection. He first referred to those "who were once enlightened, and have tasted of the heavenly gift, and were made partakers of the Holy Ghost, and have tasted the good word of God, and the powers of the world to come," and then declared "it is impossible" for these "if they shall fall away, to renew them again unto repentance; seeing they crucify to themselves the Son of God afresh, and put him to an open shame."[35]

Thus did Paul condemn the principle underlying this dogma of transubstantiation, more than thirteen centuries before it became an official tenet of the Church. Here indeed was a "falling away" against which he had so earnestly and prophetically warned the Thessalonians.[36]

This whole heresy comes from a misinterpretation of the words of the Savior (already quoted) on the night he instituted the sacrament during the Last Supper, where, as to the bread, he said, "Take, eat; this is my body," and as to the wine, he said, "Drink ye all of it; for this is my blood of the new testament, which is shed for many for the remission of sins."[37]

But the super-literal interpretation which these churches have given to these words ignores certain other parallel scriptures. Talking to the woman of Samaria, Jesus declared that if she had known "the gift of God," and had asked him, knowing who he was, for a drink, he would have given her *living water*, that whosoever should drink of it would never thirst, for "the water that I shall give him shall be in him a well of water springing up into everlasting life."[38] Obviously, Jesus was not speaking of earthly water, but of a spiritual fountain of eternal existence. Thus early in his ministry did Jesus begin to speak of eating and drinking in a spiritual sense.

To the multitude that had followed him across the lake to Capernaum, the day after he fed them with the loaves and fishes, he preached his great sermon on the bread of life, in the course of which he repeatedly spoke of *eating* his flesh and drinking his blood.[39] In considering this sermon, in reality one of Christ's greatest declarations as to his own divinity and mission, we must read it remembering that it was addressed to those who believed in the efficacy of the sacrifice of flesh and blood, and in meat-offerings (which were offerings of flour and oil, not flesh) and drink-offerings, in sin offerings and "outer" and "inner" offerings, all, in one way or another, for the atonement for sin and the readjustment of the lives of the offerers to bring them into harmony with God's ways.[40] In their sacrifices they themselves at times ate the flesh of the sacrifice (the paschal lamb), and the priests ate a part of the burnt and other offerings. Nor should it be overlooked that their sin offerings were for sins "through ignorance," or "involuntary sins," not for those that were deliberate or premeditated, those done "presumptuously," for the doers of these latter sins were to be "cut off from among his people," and must await the judgment of God. Jesus thus used concepts with which they were entirely familiar, to teach them the meaning and purpose of his own mission and atonement,—the sacrifice of his own flesh and blood.

The multitude, quoting the Psalms,[41] declared that manna was "bread from heaven." But Jesus denied this, saying:

"My Father giveth you the true bread from heaven. For the bread of God is he which cometh down from heaven, and giveth life unto the world."[42]

This clearly refers to spiritual food, the bread

from heaven, contrasting it with the manna, food for the flesh. To their request that he give them this bread, he replied:

"I am the bread of life: he that cometh to me shall never hunger; and he that believeth on me shall never thirst."[43]

He makes clear here, that *coming* to him, not actually eating of his flesh, satisfies spiritual hunger, and *believing* on him slakes spiritual thirst, thus clarifying his words to the woman of Samaria. He was again speaking of things of the spirit, in terms of eating and drinking.

Continuing his teaching, he said to the multitude:

"He that believeth on me hath everlasting life. I am that bread of life."[44]

Thus *belief* is that bread of life, which gives eternal life.

Declaring that a man eating of the bread which cometh down from heaven should never die, thus paralleling his saying to the woman of Samaria that those drinking the living water he would give would never thirst, he added:

"I am the living bread which came down from heaven: if any man eat of this bread, he shall live for ever: and the bread that I will give is my flesh, which I will give for the life of the world."[45]

Jesus is here obviously speaking in highly figurative language of his atonement, and, in the sacrificial vernacular with which they were familiar, of his sacrifice of his own flesh and blood for the life of the world. He is again using *eating* in a spiritual sense. He is not thinking or speaking of the actual eating of his own mortal flesh.

When he again explained and repeated, "except ye eat the flesh of the Son of man, and drink his blood, ye have no life in you,"[46] he obviously did not mean mortal life, for those to whom he spoke were living beings. He made this clear when he added: "Whoso eateth my flesh, and drinketh my blood, hath eternal life," speaking of the life hereafter.[47]

Continuing, he said:

"For my flesh is meat indeed, and my blood is drink indeed. He that eateth my flesh, and drinketh my blood, dwelleth in me, and I in him. As the living Father hath sent me, and I live by the Father: so he that eateth me, even he shall live by me."[48]

Jesus made clear here that he is speaking of a relationship of himself to the Father as being of the same kind as our relationship to the Son. No one will venture to say that Christ eateth of the actual flesh of the Father in any literal sense, in order to live by the Father, so no one may rightly say one eats of the actual flesh of the Son in order that he shall live by the Son.

He continues:

"This is *that* bread which came down from heaven: not as your fathers did eat manna, and are dead:"—manna, the food of the mortal body, but "he that eateth of this bread shall live for ever," that is, shall have eternal life.[49] The Jews did not understand and murmured, "This is an hard saying; who can hear it?" Knowing "in himself" that they murmured, he asked, "Doth this offend you?" and then, after forecasting his ascension into heaven, he concluded:

"It is the spirit that quickeneth; the flesh profiteth nothing: the words that I speak unto you, they are spirit, and they are life."[50]

Thus Jesus declared to them that the spirit quickeneth, and that the flesh as flesh—the Jews were thinking of his mortal flesh as contrasted with the manna—*"profiteth nothing,"* and then he expressly affirmed that the words he spoke were spirit and they gave life.

That he spoke spiritually and not of his mortal body and blood, and that so speaking spiritually he was speaking of belief in him as giving life, are shown by the words of John the Baptist, when he declared:

"He that believeth on the Son hath everlasting life: and he that believeth not the Son shall not see life; but the wrath of God abideth on him."[51]

In the great intercessory prayer on the last night before the crucifixion, he declared, addressing the Father:

"And this is life eternal, that they might know thee the only true God, and Jesus Christ, whom thou hast sent."[52]

Thus it is knowledge of the Christ, which comprises belief in him, and the keeping of his commandments, that gives eternal life, and not the profanation of pretending to eat of his flesh and drink of his blood, a heresy that did not begin until seven hundred years after Christ's death, and that did not become an official dogma until the thirteenth century.

Before closing these observations, another "falling away" should be noted, namely, the erroneous dogma that partaking of the sacrament brings about a remission of the individual sins committed by the partaker, apparently such a remission as results from baptism. No warrant whatever has been found in the scriptures for such a doctrine. It was not even hinted at by the Savior in the Passover Chamber, the remission of sins Christ spoke of being the atonement for the fall of Adam, thus making truthful Paul's basic dictum: "As in Adam all die, even so in Christ shall all be made alive."[53]

No clear explanation of the origin of this dogma has been found. It may have arisen in this way: St. Cyprian (the Carthagenian bishop martyred Sept. 14, 258, almost two and a half centuries after the crucifixion) taught: "When we drink the Blood of the Lord, and the cup of salvation, we put off the remembrance of the old man and forget our former secular conversation, and our sorrowful and heavy heart, which before was pressed with the anguish of our sins, is now absolved or set at liberty by the joyfulness of the divine indulgence or pardon."[54]

This is a curious quirk of reasoning. The phrase *"remembrance of me,"* the atoning sacrifice of the Passover ordinance, is now twisted to mean *remembrance of our individual sins;* then this remembrance of sin is to bring anguish, and next, seemingly, repentance, which is to be followed by joy, which in turn brings "divine indulgence or pardon." Of

course there is nothing of this in the Savior's commandment.

The simple words of the Passover Chamber were these, as recorded by Matthew:

"Jesus took bread, and blessed it, and brake it, and gave it to the disciples, and said, Take, eat; this is my body. And he took the cup, and gave thanks, and gave it to them, saying, Drink ye all of it; for this is my blood of the new testament, which is shed for many for the remission of sins," and "they all drank of it."[55]

Luke's account reads: "And he took bread, and gave thanks, and brake it, and gave unto them, saying, This is my body which is given for you: *this do in remembrance of me*. Likewise also the cup after supper, saying, This cup is the new testament in my blood, which is shed for you."[56] This clearly shows the thought of *remembering* the Savior, that we may have the *communion* with him of which Paul wrote, and the shedding of his blood for all mankind, a doctrine that is basic to Christianity.

Without attempting to trace out here the steps of the development of the idea of remission of individual sins by partaking of the sacrament, it seems clear that the idea of an actual sacrifice at the sacrament table gained ground, and a concept developed of a two-fold sacrifice, a spiritual sacrifice and a commemorative sacrifice.[57] The concept of a commemorative sacrifice required that something be sacrificed, that the priest must sacrifice something (as pointed out above). There reacted on this concept the developing dogma that in the sacrament the flesh of Christ was eaten and the blood of Christ was drunk. Then came the dogma that at a certain moment Christ came down to the altar with a "mystical and yet most dread Presence,"[58] that he was present even as he was at the Last Supper[59] and was there sacrificed,[60] that "Christ's Body becomes killed by the words of consecration,"[61] and that God was present to receive the sacrifice.[62] The ceremony came to be "an offering of the immaculate Victim for the remission of sins."[63] This all finally developed into the dogma of transubstantiation, with its implementing cult.

Thus under this dogma and cult, the officiating Roman priesthood logically, but erroneously came to claim that Christ was crucified at each celebration of the Mass, (we call attention to Paul's words to the Hebrews regarding re-crucifying the Christ), and a sacrifice having been found, the Aaronic concept of sacrifice came into play which called for a sacrifice for individual transgressions, and so this renewed sacrifice of Christ by the priest is held to atone for the individual sins of him who partakes thereof.

In this connection it is interesting again to note that in the Passover Chamber, the Lord had all of them drink of the wine for the witness to him. If the drinking of the wine is to bring remission of sins to the individual, then on the basis of the Passover Chamber where all drank, every one must drink to get forgiveness. But under the Roman Mass ceremonial, only the officiating priest gets the wine, the faithful laity merely watch him drink it. This does not fulfill the divine command as to drinking the wine.

Having in mind this dogma and its implementing cult as to the purpose and efficacy of the Mass, it is easy to understand why Leo XIII in his Bull against Anglican Orders declared that the grace and power of the "Sacred Order of Priesthood . . . is chiefly the power 'of consecrating and of offering the true body and blood of the Lord.' "[64] Thus officiating at Mass is the chief function of the Roman priests.

And speaking of this power, one is reminded of the pastoral letter of Cardinal Katsschler which is quoted by Newman as pointing out that God has given up his omnipotent power to forgive sin to the "plenipotentiary priest," a power which, he says, earthly kings, archangels, patriarchs, seraphim, cherubim, thrones, and dominions do not possess, nor can even Mary, the Mother of God, the Queen of the Heaven, the bride of the Holy Spirit, the Mistress of the Universe, exercise such power. The devout Cardinal also declares that priests should be honored because while Mary brought the divine Child into the world once only, yet the priest does this not once but hundreds of thousands of times. He adds that it may be questioned "whether the priest whom God has so highly exalted, bound so intimately with himself, really given power over himself, is still a man? Christ, the only begotten Son of God, through whom the heavens and the earth were created, and who administers the universe, is herein subject to the will of the Catholic priest."[65]

On the perverted premises from which the learned Cardinal starts his argument, one might concede his logic. But how inexpressibly impudent and arrogant is this monumental sacrilege! What treason against our Lord and Master! Such claims, if not so tragic, would be deemed ridiculous.

Lowndes affirms that this whole dogma and the cult attaching thereto is neither Scriptural nor Primitive,[66] and such investigation as has been possible to us confirms this conclusion.

Concerning this power to sacrifice, Lowndes makes this learned and searching observation:

"The power of offering sacrifice by a Christian Priest may be said not to lie in any divine command, but in the nature of the office. Christ gave no definite command to His Apostles to offer any particular sacrifice, nor did He even give them any general command to that effect. We look in vain among the powers entrusted to the Apostles for any clear power to offer sacrifice. It may be said, therefore, that if there is any sacrificial power belonging inherently to the successors of the Apostles, it must be contained among the indefinite powers conveyed by the general command to teach and to observe all things whatsoever Christ commanded to His Apostles. The only way to arrive at any degree of certainty in such a matter is to ascertain in what light the Apostles and their immediate successors regarded their ministry, and further to see what traces of sacrificial intent may be found in the very earliest Liturgies or services for the administration of the Holy Eucharist.

"In other words, we now leave the solid domain of fact, and enter upon an investigation of theories."[67]

Lowndes affirmation seems wholly justified.

Lowndes further declares: "It is the greatest misfortune that has ever happened to Christendom, and, therefore, to the whole world, that Christians have not been content to leave the great Sacrament which was intended to be the bond of union and communion between them and their Lord just as Holy Writ leaves it."[68]

The evidence offered by the Romanists, of the rightfulness of innovations is "that if Roman innovations are not right, then the Church of God must long since have perished."[69]

This argument would validate the wickedness of every dispensation from the murder of Abel down, for an idolatrous, apostate religious system, of one sort or another, has always maintained itself on the earth. Lowndes calls the argument "absurd," and so it is.

There is no scripture to prove that remission of individual sins comes to him who partakes of the sacrament, or that such remission is a function of the ordinance; nor is there any reasonable deduction from scriptures nor reasonable interpretation thereof, justifying any such dogma.

Modern revelation gives the truth about the sacrament: In simple ceremony we eat the bread and drink the water in remembrance of the flesh and blood of the Savior, sacrificed in the great atonement, and we thereby covenant always to remember

him and to keep his commandments which he has
given us, that his spirit may always be with us.

May the Lord keep us from this and other
heresies that lead us away from his paths and into
the realms of darkness, I pray in the name of the
Son. Amen.

[1]Gibbon, *The Decline and Fall of the Roman Empire*, Milman
New Edition, III, p. 450. [2]Matt. 26:18; Mark 14:14; Luke
22:13-15. [3]Luke 22:15. [4]Matt. 26:26-28; Mark 14:22-24; Luke
22:19-20; Acts 2:42 ff.; 20:7; I Cor. 10:16 ff.; 11:17 ff. [5]3 Nephi
18:1 ff., 28-33; 20:1 ff.; 26:13; Moroni 4:3. [6]Lowndes *Vindication of Anglican Orders*, p. 370. [7]Acts 2:42, 46. [8]I Cor.
10:16, 21; 11:20. [9]Lowndes, p. 385; see also an elaborate article
Mass, in *The New Schaff-Herzog Encyclopedia of Religious Knowledge*. [10]Lowndes, p. 390. [11]*Op cit.*, p. 386. [12]Lev. 7:30. [13]Lev.
8:27 ff. [14]Lev. 9:21. [15]Lev. 23:11-12. [16]Lev. 23:20. [17]Num. 5:25.
[18]Num. 6:13. [19]Lev. 14:2-12. [20]Luke 22:19. [21]See Schaff, *Creeds
of Christendom*, I p. 922. [22]Lowndes, p. 401. [23]*Op. cit.*, p. 402.
[24]*Op. cit.*, p. 422-423. [25]Hastings, *Encyclopaedia of Religion and
Ethics*, sub voce *Councils*, p. 193. [26]Robertson, *History of the Christian
Church*, III, p. 235. [27]Robertson, IV, p. 216; V, p. 411; and see on
whole subject, Hastings, *Encyc.*, sub voce *Eucharist*. [28]Robertson,
IV, p. 361 ff.; and see VI. p. 439 ff. [29]Meyrick, *The Doctrine of the
Holy Communion*, p. 80 ff.; see for the Tridentine pronouncements
on transubstantiation, Schaff, *Creeds*, Symbola Romana, II, p. 126,
136. [30]Heb. 6:20. [31]3 Nephi 9:17; 15:4-5; 4 Nephi 12; D.C. 74. [32]*The
Ante-Nicene Fathers*, Coxe ed., VII, *The Teaching of the Twelve
Apostles*, IX. [33]Heb. 9:24-28. [34]Heb. 10:10, 12, 14. [35]Heb. 6:1-6. [36]II
Thess. 2:3. [37]See earlier citations (4). [38]John 4:10 ff. [39]John 6:22
ff. [40]Edersheim, *The Temple*, p. 82, 83, 105. [41]Ps. 78:24-25. [42]John
6:32-33. [43]John 6:35. [44]John 6:47-48. [45]John 6:51. [46]John 6:53.
[47]John 6:54. [48]John 6:55-57. [49]John 6:58. [50]John 6:61-63.
[51]John 3:36. [52]John 17:3. [53]I Cor. 15:22. [54]Lowndes, p. 331.
[55]See citations above (4). [56]Luke 22:19-30. [57]Lowndes, p. 390-391.
[58]*Id.*, p. 414. [59]*Id.*, p. 400. [60]*Id.*, p. 403. [61]*Id.*, p. 423. [62]*Id.*,
p. 399. [63]*Id.*, p. 406. [64]*Id.*, p. 150, 300 (Sentence 64). [65]Newman,
A Manual of Church History, II, p. 724, 725. [66]Lowndes, p. 340.
[67]*Id.*, p. 384-385. [68]*Id.*, p. 358. [69]*Id.*, p. 318.

TOPICALLY THE APPENDIX SHOULD BE READ AT
THIS POINT, BEFORE CONSIDERING THE SUBJECT
OF THE RESTORATION OF THE GOSPEL AND
PRIESTHOOD

XIV

THE NEED FOR RESTORATION

IN earlier talks we have pointed out that the organization of the Primitive Church was lost to the post-Primitive Church, which set up a system of its own, some essential features of which developed slowly over the centuries.

We called attention to the fact that even in the Primitive Church there began to be differences of opinion regarding points of doctrine, even among the Apostles themselves, as for example between Peter and Paul. We noted Paul's warnings to Timothy, to the Corinthians, to the Thessalonians, and to the Ephesians,—speaking to them about heresies that were to come in amongst them, that men would walk after their own ungodly lusts, that grievous wolves would enter in amongst them. We called to notice that Peter spoke of "damnable heresies," and that Paul declared the "day of Christ" should not come save there be a "falling away" first.

We then hastily scanned the early history of the Christian Church and noted the introduction therein of principles and practices of paganism. We commented briefly on gnosticism and named a few of the errors that came into the post-Primitive Church from this prolific source of false doctrine. We observed that some of these doctrines still plagued various Christian sects. We also named Manichaeism, the source through which much pagan pomp and ceremony came into the early Church; and Sabellianism, from which arose the heresy that there is but one divine essence and that Father, Son, and Holy Ghost are but different manifestations of that essence; we noted the Ebionites, the Judaizing Christians, the Marcionites, teaching that the God of the Old and of the New Testaments were different deities, a heresy which persists today. We called attention to the Montanists, the Novatianists, and Donatists, who vainly tried to curb certain corruptions creeping into the Church, and to shape doctrines touching baptism and rebaptism.

We considered the doctrine of Arius, which denied the divinity of Christ, and the efforts beginning with the first Council of Nicaea (A.D. 325) to put an end to this heresy, and it was so recognized by the Church. We quoted the estimate that "Arius tried to interpret the Christian revelation in such a way as to render it acceptable to men whose whole conception of God and of life was heathen." We pointed out that this heresy had appeared and reappeared over the centuries, and that its essentials were found in the doctrine that portrays Christ as a great philosopher, as the founder of a profound code of ethics, as the supremely righteous man, but denies to him the divine parentage, the Sonship of God,—a doctrine utterly destructive of the basis of Christian faith.

We traced briefly the rise of celibacy as the standard of the highest life, showed that the concept

came in from paganism, that it led to a corruption
of the clergy, that in the first Council of Nicaea a
canon was drawn aimed to correct the immoralities
that had followed the practice of the dogma. We also
observed that the influence of the doctrine that the
celibate life was the highest type, led at times to a
sort of mass asceticism that was most demoralizing
to the early saints and led to grave excesses.

We also noted the effect on the Church of the
assumption by the State of an over-lordship over the
Church, and we quoted Gibbon that "the will of the
prince was the rule of episcopal faith"; we also commented that at one time the Church claimed, and for
a time, exercised a sort of political suzerainty over
the State, to the great harm of the Church.

We called attention to the peculiar dogma, held
apparently by both the Roman and the Eastern
Church, and known by the name of *transubstantiation*, and we considered the dogma in the light of the
Master's great sermon in which he declared he was
the bread of life.

We call attention to the fact that each of these
dogmas was developed in the Church long before the
days of Luther (1483-1546), Calvin (1509-1564),
and Knox (1505-1572), and the other reformers.
Thus the whole of Christendom was the recipient of
the heresies, the "falling away" declared by Paul.

We have hardly made a beginning on the subject of Paul's "falling away," but we have considered
enough to show that Peter and Paul spoke with the
spirit of prophecy when they declared that there
would come upon the Church before "the day of

Christ," a great apostasy from the true Gospel of
Christ, and to make it apparent that the post-Primitive Church has for centuries been as a flock without
a shepherd, lacking the Melchizedek Priesthood,
which, with its powers and authorities, must be operative upon the earth for the salvation and exaltation of man. In this connection we noted Paul's
epistle to the Hebrews, patiently explaining the difference between the Aaronic Priesthood and its purposes and the Melchizedek Priesthood and its functions and powers.

We have laid the foundation that makes clear
the truth of the declarations of Dr. Burns, when he
spoke of the condition of the world when the beloved
Apostle, John, ended his mission:

"The age of inspiration is over,—that peerless
century which began with the birth of Christ, and
closed with the death of John—and the course of the
ages descends once more to the ordinary level of common time.

"It was with the Church now as with the disciples at Bethany, when the last gleam of the Savior's
ascending train had passed from their sight, and
they turned their faces, reluctant and sad, to the
dark world again. The termination of the age of
inspiration was in truth the very complement and
consummation of the ascension of the Lord. The sun
can then only be said to have fairly set, when his
departing glory has died away from the horizon,
and the chill stars shine out sharp and clear on the
dim and naked sky.

"That time has now fully come. The last gleam

of inspired wisdom and truth vanished from the earth with the beloved apostle's gentle farewell, and we pass at once across the mysterious line which separates the sacred from the secular annals of the world, —the history of the apostolic age from the history of the Christian Church."[1]

How terrible, indeed, the thought that "the age of inspiration is over," that the Lord has retired to the Father and left us alone to work out our own destinies without the inspiration he alone can give.

We recall here the words of Isaiah: "The earth also is defiled under the inhabitants thereof; because they have transgressed the laws, changed the ordinance, broken the everlasting covenant."[2]

But God still lives. He still has infinite love for his children. He still wishes to inspire them, to reveal his mind and will to them. The Only Begotten, our Advocate with the Father, who gave his life for us, still loves us as dearly as ever. He would help us. The Father and Son will both draw near unto us if we thrust them not away from us by our transgressions.

So there was need in these latter days for God to reopen the channel of communication with him, that he might inspire us again, and again reveal his mind and will unto us, his wayward, wandering children.

Blessed are we who, on our way to immortality and eternal life, know that God has not left his children alone, but that his boundless love still encircles us, to guard and to guide us, that through his Kingdom which he has set up on earth his inspira-

tion still abides with us to our salvation and exaltation finally in his presence if we walk in his paths
and keep his commandments, that he still grants us
his revelations, still speaks to us, and that we shall
hear and know, if we shall attune our lives to his
righteousness.

May the Lord bring to each of us the testimony
of the Holy Spirit that this is true, I pray, in the
Son's name. Amen.

---

[1]Burns, *The First Three Christian Centuries*, p. 49. [2]Isa.
24:5.

XV

THE DISPENSATION OF THE FULLNESS
OF TIMES

W E HAVE sketched in prior talks, the apostasy
of the post-Primitive Church. We indicated
that we had need for the restoration of the
true Gospel of Christ, which the Church had lost,
and of the Melchizedek Priesthood, for the full possession of which there seemed to be no claim among
the various great Christian denominations.

A reasonable reading and interpretation of the
scriptures leave no doubt that an apostasy of the
children of God from his way of life, is nothing new
to this earth. Over and over and over again, men
have had revealed to them the Gospel of the Christ,
and as often as revealed they have let Satan into their
hearts, they have become "carnal, sensual, and devilish,"[1] and have forsaken—apostatized from the true
faith.

God in his infinite knowledge knew all this; he
saw the end of all things even from the beginning.
Isaiah declared the word of the Lord saying:

"Remember the former things of old: for I am
God, and there is none else; I am God, and there is
none like me,

"Declaring the end from the beginning, and
from ancient times the things that are not yet done,

saying, My counsel shall stand, and I will do all my pleasure."[2]

Thus God knew men in the beginning, not only en masse, but as individuals. He knew they would 'fall away' from the truth. So he provided that at periods when spiritual darkness became too great, he would restore the light, and again give men the chance to live in his ways and gain their salvation.

But Satan commenced his abominable work in the very beginning, intruded himself into the inner household of Adam, and made Cain the first murderer, shedding the blood of his own brother. From this time men began to stray away. The Lord warned: "My spirit shall not always strive with man."[3] Wickedness so increased that the Lord was 'grieved at his heart.'[4] The dispensation of Adam closed, as the people apostatized from the Gospel truths given to Adam and his children.

But the plan of God, as worked out in the great council of heaven, provided that all of God's children should have opportunity to "prove" themselves "to see if they will do all things whatsoever the Lord their God shall command them," that so keeping his commandments they might "have glory added upon their heads for ever and ever."[5]

So the Gospel plan being lost after Adam, the Lord, to make good his promise and to carry out his plan, again brought the Gospel to the earth through Enoch, who opened his dispensation. Enoch taught the people and pleaded with them to keep the commandments. Some of them did, and Enoch "walked with God: and he was not; for God took him."[6]

Paul declares: "By faith Enoch was translated that he should not see death; and was not found, because God had translated him: for before his translation he had this testimony, that he pleased God."[7] Enoch took with him the righteous of his generation, "and Enoch and all his people walked with God."[8]

But those who followed not Enoch increased in wickedness till, in his mercy, God ordained their destruction. Concerning them he told Enoch, "among all the workmanship of mine hands there has not been so great wickedness as among thy brethren."[9]

So again filled with infinite love and mercy for his children, God again set up his work through Noah, who brought in his dispensation. Noah was directed to preach to the people the Gospel that God had revealed to Enoch, and "Noah called upon the children of men that they should repent; but they hearkened not unto his words."[10] But the earth's peoples who were not of Enoch, so increased in wickedness, they became such a stench in the Lord's nostrils, that he resolved to destroy mankind, and bring a new race through Noah and his posterity. Then came the Flood, and the antediluvians died in their sins, rejecting the truth.

Noah and his family began his dispensation.

But again, as time went on, men 'fell away' from the truth. Apostasy from the Gospel came. Idolatry and heathenish rites and ceremonies were set up, seemingly among all peoples.

Again the Lord made good his promise and plan, and called Abraham from a pagan family[11] to set up a reign of Gospel righteousness. Then came the great promise to Abraham and his seed. Isaac and Jacob and Jacob's twelve sons were born.

Driven by famine, they went to Egypt, where they, too, lapsed into idolatry. The dispensation of Abraham insensibly merged into the dispensation of Moses, the great lawgiver. By a rich outpouring of miraculous power, Moses led the children of Israel from their Egyptian bondage to the Promised Land. Once more God had vindicated his mercy and love in preserving his people.

But even while on their way to the new home, the people lapsed into their idolatry at Sinai in the wilderness. But God forgave them, and they pushed on. By the time the conquest of the new land was complete, they had again turned to strange gods, the gods they worshipped in Egypt.[12] Joshua, the mighty warrior, called them to choose whom they would serve, solemnly declaring "but as for me and my house, we will serve the Lord."[13] Though the people covenanted with Joshua to serve the true God, they soon again fell into transgressions, departed from the true worship, and for the next generations wandered away from the righteous life, were again and again recalled to the true path by the prophets of the Lord, only again and again to wander, the Lord punishing them from time to time for their rebellion. He permitted them to be led into captivity and to become again an enslaved people. He let them divide their kingdom and afflict themselves with fratricidal wars. He suffered them to come under the Roman yoke. He did not stop the corruption of their priesthood, nor the twisting from their ancient

THE DISPENSATION OF THE FULLNESS OF TIMES

purity of the laws and commandments he had given them.

But God's grand plan must be fulfilled. There must come a Redeemer who should atone for the Fall of Adam. The Gospel had before been preached from the beginning, but now the keystone of the gospel arch must be laid, so that the soul of man—the spirit and the body[14]—could come back into the presence of God, the Father, and there dwell eternally. Then came the Messianic dispensation. The Christ was born. He lived. He performed his ministry. He was crucified, lay in the tomb, on the third day was resurrected—the First Fruits of the Resurrection, then ministered for a few days to his disciples, and ascended to Heaven, the angels standing by declaring to the Apostles:

"This same Jesus, which is taken up from you into heaven, shall so come in like manner as ye have seen him go into heaven."[15]

As we have seen in earlier talks, there began, even while the Apostles lived, another "falling away," and it has continued during the generations since then. This was predicted by Peter and Paul. Left without inspiration, as Burns points out,[16] the Church has wandered far afield. It has been torn and mangled from within, and, at times, in the early days, persecuted from without. Spiritual darkness 'covered the face of the earth as the waters cover the mighty deep.'

But God's love and mercy was again to be manifested. Men were not to be left without the knowledge of the essentials of the plan of salvation, nor

without opportunity to enjoy the blessings of a righteous life under the reign of the God-given Gospel
plan.   That knowledge and that plan were to be
restored to the earth, for it had been again lost, as
it had been after Adam, after Enoch, after Abraham,
after Moses. And so it has been.

This restoration was foreseen by Paul, writing
to the Ephesians, when he said (after speaking of
our redemption through Christ and his making
known his will) :

"That in the dispensation of the fullness of
times he might gather together in one all things in
Christ, both which are in heaven, and which are on
earth; even in him."[17]

And Peter, speaking with John in the Temple
after their first miracle, declared:

"Repent ye therefore, and be converted, that
your sins may be blotted out, when the times of re-
freshing shall come from the presence of the Lord;

"And he shall send Jesus Christ, which before
was preached unto you:

"Whom the heaven must receive until the times
of restitution of all things, which God hath spoken by
the mouth of all his holy prophets since the world
began."[18]

From the earliest days of our own Church, we
have known the meaning of the "fullness of times."
It was then declared:

"Now the thing to be known is, what the fullness
of times means, or the extent and authority thereof.
It means this, that the dispensation of the fullness
of times is made up of all the dispensations that ever

have been given since the world began, until this time."[19]

May the Lord cause that to every soul seeking the truth shall come the testimony that we today live in the Dispensation of the Fullness of Times, I pray, in the Son's name. Amen.

---

[1]Moses 5:13; D.C. 20:20; Gen. 6:5. [2]Isa. 46:9-10; see also 41:26. [3]Gen. 6:3. [4]Gen. 6:6. [5]Abraham 3:25-26. [6]Gen. 5:24. [7]Heb. 11:5. [8]Moses 7:69. [9]Moses 7:36. [10]Moses 8:20. [11]Abraham 1. [12]Josh. 24:14. [13]Josh. 24:15. [14]D.C. 88:15. [15]Acts 1:11. [16]Burns, *The First Three Christian Centuries*, p. 49. [17]Eph. 1:10. [18]Acts 3:19-21. [19]*The Millennial Star*, XVI, p. 220.

XVI

THE GOSPEL RESTORATION—
THE FIRST VISION

WE RETURN again to the words of that poet-prophet Isaiah of ancient times, declaring the future and the will of God:

"And it shall be, as with the people, so with the priest....

"The land shall be utterly emptied, and utterly spoiled: for the Lord hath spoken this word.

"The earth mourneth and fadeth away, the world languisheth and fadeth away, the haughty people of the earth do languish.

"The earth also is defiled under the inhabitants thereof; because they have transgressed the laws, changed the ordinance, broken the everlasting covenant.

"Therefore hath the curse devoured the earth, and they that dwell therein are desolate: therefore the inhabitants of the earth are burned, and few men left."[1]

A boy fourteen years of age, Joseph Smith, with the innocence of Samuel ministering before the Lord in the Tabernacle at Shiloh, and with the trust of David, sling-armed, facing Goliath, was seeking truth,—the truth of immortality and eternal life.

A great religious revival among the sects of his

neighborhood, a concourse of seekers for truth, had come together. The ministers were contending one against another. It was "a scene of great confusion and bad feeling ensued," said the boy. Some of his family had joined the Presbyterians; he was inclined to the Methodists. But, said he, "so great were the confusion and strife among the different denominations," so torn in spirit was he with this "war of words," that he could not make up his mind what to do.

Reading one day in Holy Writ, he chanced on the words of James:

"If any of you lack wisdom, let him ask of God, that giveth to all men liberally, and upbraideth not; and it shall be given him."[2]

"Never," says he, "did any . . . scripture come with more power to the heart of man than this did at this time to mine." He pondered, as best his youthful mind allowed, upon his own lack of knowledge and the promise of James. At last, it came certainly to him, he must do as James bid, and ask God.

Now let Joseph tell his own story:

"So, in accordance with this, my determination to ask of God, I retired to the woods to make the attempt. It was on the morning of a beautiful, clear day, early in the spring of eighteen hundred and twenty. It was the first time in my life that I had made such an attempt, for amidst all my anxieties I had never as yet made the attempt to pray vocally.

"After I had retired to the place where I had previously designed to go, having looked around me, and finding myself alone, I kneeled down and began to offer up the desires of my heart to God. I had scarcely done so, when immediately I was seized upon by some power which entirely overcame me, and had such an astonishing influence over me as to bind my tongue so that I could not speak. Thick darkness gathered around me, and it seemed to me for a time as if I were doomed to sudden destruction.

"But, exerting all my powers to call upon God to deliver me out of the power of this enemy which had seized upon me, and at the very moment when I was ready to sink into despair and abandon myself to destruction—not to an imaginary ruin, but to the power of some actual being from the unseen world, who had such marvelous power as I had never before felt in any being—just at this moment of great alarm, I saw a pillar of light exactly over my head, above the brightness of the sun, which descended gradually until it fell upon me.

"It no sooner appeared than I found myself delivered from the enemy which held me bound. When the light rested upon me I saw two Personages, whose brightness and glory defy all description, standing above me in the air. One of them spake unto me, calling me by name, and said, pointing to the other—This is My Beloved Son. Hear Him!

"My object in going to inquire of the Lord was to know which of all the sects was right, that I might know which to join. No sooner, therefore, did I get possession of myself, so as to be able to speak, than I asked the Personages who stood above me in the light, which of all the sects was right—and which I should join.

"I was answered that I must join none of them, for they were all wrong; and the Personage who addressed me said that all their creeds were an abomination in his sight; that those professors were all corrupt; that: 'they draw near to me with their lips, but their hearts are far from me; they teach for doctrines the commandments of men, having a form of godliness, but they deny the power thereof.'

"He again forbade me to join with any of them; and many other things did he say unto me which I cannot write at this time. When I came to myself again, I found myself lying on my back, looking up into heaven. When the light had departed, I had no strength; but soon recovering in some degree, I went home."[8]

So did the Father and Son open the Dispensation of the Fullness of Times, by a personal appearance to the boy Joseph.

From that sacred hour in the grove, Satan never forgot Joseph for a moment until his murderers had finished their work, and never to this day has Satan forgotten Joseph's mission and work. Slander, vilification, falsehood, persecution, plunderings, whippings, mobbings, law courts, jails, were daily piled upon Joseph for a quarter of a century, and then he was massacred by a mob, against the wrath of whom a Governor had solemnly promised to protect him. Joseph died a martyr to the cause of truth, sealing his testimony with his blood, the highest proof mortal can give of his own belief in the cause he espouses.

The holy vision in the grove, ushering in this Last Dispensation of the Fullness of Times, with the Father and Son present in person, marked the opening of the last chapter of the mortality of men. It was one of the greatest hours of all time, surpassed only by the hours that saw the birth, life, death, and resurrection of the Only Begotten, the Son.

God was present, in voice, at the baptism of Jesus, when the Holy Ghost was also manifest,—the only time in recorded scriptures when the Father, Son, and Holy Ghost all manifested themselves at the same time and place to the physical senses of man. The Father manifested himself, but in voice only, at the time of the transfiguration, when Peter, James, and John were on the Mount with Jesus[4]; and again, in voice only, in the Temple on the third day of the week of the atoning sacrifice, when the Father comforted the Son in distress over the approaching crisis.[5] Thereafter, on this hemisphere after the resurrection, when Christ, descending from heaven in resurrected body, visited the Nephites, the Father introduced him by voice only to the assembled multitude.[6]

Each time the Father has introduced the Son, he has declared the Sonship of the Only Begotten. As John the Baptist baptized Jesus while others stood on the river bank, the Father declared to Jesus: "Thou art my beloved Son, in whom I am well pleased."[7] At the transfiguration, the Father said to Peter, James, and John: "This is my beloved Son, in whom I am well pleased; hear ye him."[8] And to the people on this hemisphere, the Father proclaimed: "Behold my Beloved Son, in whom I am well pleased, in whom I have glorified my name—hear ye him.'"

And now, to the boy, praying in the woods on that bright spring morning, the Father, calling the youth by name, pointed to the Son, and said: "This is My Beloved Son. Hear Him!"

Atheists have jeered at the naivete of the boy's story, and at the credulity of them who believe in him. To those who so jeer, it need only be said: Repent and turn to God, lest his judgments come upon you.

Others, professing Christ, have ridiculed the fact that God and the Son should come to a boy. But is this stranger than that the Lord should come to young Samuel in the temple after nightfall, and call Samuel to his service,[10] or that the spirit of the Lord should rest upon the youth David,[11] to the performance of his task?

Others have scoffed at his struggle with the evil power, and at his coming to, lying upon his back upon the ground, at the shaft of light, at the appearances of the heavenly beings, and at his weariness, declaring that all this was but an epileptic fit.

But what will these scoffers say of the experience of Saul, of the light that shone about him, of his falling to the ground, of his blindness, so that he must be led by the hand, of his extreme exhaustion?[12] Will any Christian dare characterize that as an epileptic fit?

And what of Daniel's experience, when his vision came to him, when he was left without strength, fell into a deep sleep on his face which was towards the ground, when the personage spoke to him, and gave him commands, and then afterwards Daniel was strengthened.[13] Was this, too, epilepsy?

Was Jacob's wrestling with the Lord, at the time the Lord gave him the name of Israel, and he saw God face to face,—an epileptic fit?[14]

When at the time of the transfiguration, a great light appeared, and heavenly beings appeared, with whom Jesus talked, while Peter, James, and John slept, and awakened confused, but saw the glory of these beings? Was this, too, a fit?[15]

When Jesus went to the Garden to pray on the night of the betrayal, while Peter, James, and John waited "a stone's cast" away, and falling to the ground on his face, he prayed: "Abba, Father, all things are possible unto thee; take away this cup from me: nevertheless not what I will, but what thou wilt."[16] Was this reality, or some physical impairment?

And what of Stephen, the first martyr of the Primitive Church, who, responsive to the enquiry of the high priest, bore his testimony of the Christ to the Council of the Jews, and they hearing and frenzied by Satan "gnashed on him with their teeth," and he, "being full of the Holy Ghost, looked up steadfastly into heaven, and saw the glory of God, and Jesus standing on the right hand of God, and said, Behold, I see the heavens opened, and the Son of man standing on the right hand of God." Are Christians ready to dismiss this as epilepsy, or as an hallucination? And before they answer yes, let them listen and try to hear the crunching of Stephen's bones as the mob stoned this martyr to death, Saul witnessing; let them try to vision Stephen, with pain-taut, agonized features, as his spirit struggled to be free, but with glorious exaltation in his eyes, crying out as he neared death:

"Lord Jesus, receive my spirit. . . . Lord, lay not this sin to their charge. And when he had said this, he fell asleep."[17]

And what of Pentecost, and the "sound from heaven as of a rushing mighty wind," and the coming "unto them cloven tongues like as of fire, and it sat upon each of them," and of their speaking in tongues, being filled with the Holy Ghost, and then the great multitude, "devout men, out of every nation under heaven," each hearing the Apostles' testimony in his own tongue, saying among themselves, what meaneth this, and some, mocking, declaring: "These men are full of new wine."[18] Was this, too, epilepsy, a mob hallucination? Deny the verity of this, Christians who can, and then try to get on your knees and pray to God, through our mediator, Jesus Christ.

The vision of Joseph, when he saw the Father and the Son, was real, just as all these we have named were real. It was not the vagary or hallucination of a disease-preyed mind. Joseph saw, even as Moses saw,—the one no less certainly than the other.

The Spirit hath borne its witness to me of this, and I so declare, in the name of the Son. Amen.

[1]Isa. 24:2-6. [2]James 1:5. [3]History of Joseph Smith, P. of G.P. [4]Matt. 17:1-13; Mark 9:2-13; Luke 9:28-36. [5]John 12:28. [6]3 Nephi 11:5-7. [7]Matt. 3:13-17; Mark 1:9-11; Luke 3:21-22. [8]Matt.

17:5; Mark 9:7; Luke 9:35. [9]3 Nephi 11:7. [10]I Sam. 3:3 ff. [11]I Sam. 16:13. [12]Acts 9:1-8. [13]Dan. 10. [14]Gen. 32-24 ff. [15]Matt. 17:1-3; Mark 9:2-13; Luke 9:28-36. [16]Matt. 26:36-46; Mark 14:32 ff.; Luke 22:39 ff. [17]Acts 7:54 ff. [18]Acts 2.

XVII

THE BUILDING OF A DISPENSATION

WE TALKED last time of the vision, unequalled
in the recorded history of man, of the boy
Joseph, praying in the woods, when there appeared to him two heavenly beings, glorious beyond
description, the Father and the Son, and the Son,
introduced by the Father, told the boy of his mission.
The simple, straightforward, modest story of the
boy is its own witness of truth.

It will be well to have in mind at this time that
each of the Gospel dispensations that have been upon
the earth began with a direct revelation of God to
man. "Adam hearkened unto the voice of God,"[1]
both before and after the Fall. "Enoch walked with
God,"[2] and 'the Lord stood before his face and talked
with him, even as a man talketh to another, face to
face.'[3]

God spake unto Noah[4] and renewed the command he had given to Adam: "Be fruitful, and
multiply, and replenish the earth,"[5] "and the Lord
ordained Noah after his own order."[6]

The Lord appeared unto Abraham time and
time again.[7] He was called the "Friend of God."[8]

Moses talked with God from the beginning of
his mission till the end,[9] God appeared to him at
Sinai; he talked with Moses "face to face, as a man
speaketh unto his friend."[10]

And the Son of God himself opened the Messianic Dispensation, after the preparation therefor by the Forerunner, John the Baptist.

So the Dispensation of the Fullness of Times was opened just as all other dispensations have been opened, by a divine manifestation of God himself.

Men have asked, without thinking, why did God choose an unschooled rustic to be the tool in his hand to build up the last dispensation? Why did he not take of the wise men of the earth, those trained in the learning of men, widely read in human history and in the sacred annals of God's dealings with his children, men schooled in the ancient tongues that they might read the scriptures in the languages in which they were written, men of strength in logic and philosophy, and science?

We will answer that question by another. Why did God choose the family of a humble Nazarene carpenter in which to rear his Son and against the day he should be sacrificed as the Redeemer of the World? The blood of David must have coursed through the veins of some of the mighty ones of Judah.

Why did not Jesus, beginning his work and choosing those who should follow him, seek out those of great learning, from among the scribes, the Pharisees, the Sadducees, the elders, why did he not choose them that were schooled in the law and in its refinements and perversions,—Jesus knew these since the time he was in the Temple at twelve years and they "were astonished at his understanding and answers."[11] Why instead of that, did he go along the

seashore among the humble fishermen, and finding
Peter and Andrew and James and John, say unto
them: "Follow me, and I will make you fishers of
men," and they, dropping their nets on the sand,
followed him?[12]   Would Gamaliel, the teacher of
Paul, have done as did these fishermen, or would
Paul himself without the miracle that afterwards
came to him, or the timorous Nicodemus, or Joseph
of Arimathea, or any of the haughty Pharisees,
scribes, Sadducees, or elders? And if they had followed, would they, short of a Pauline miracle, have
hearkened and believed—they who disputed every
doctrine he taught, who disbelieved and derided every
miracle he wrought as born of Beelzebub, who, for
his teachings and acts of mercy, sought constantly his
life,—would any of them have so humbled himself
as to gain the testimony and then declare, as did
Peter, unlearned, unschooled, untaught, save by the
spirit of the Master: "Thou art the Christ, the Son
of the living God"?[13]

Men would choose the wise and confound the
weak, but God chooses the weak things of the earth
to confound the mighty.[14] Nor does he put new wine
into old bottles.[15]

Men steeped in the lore of the ages, with prejudices fixed, with convictions set, with thought-
habits formed, with unwillingness to receive the
new or to travel new roads, or to take on new guides,
or to move toward hitherto unknown or forgotten
countries, cannot lead a new cause, cannot yield to
the promptings of the spirit, cannot open their souls
to further revelation.

So the Son of God chose the fishermen on the seashore to march with him, and the Father and the Son chose the humble rustic to lead the way into a new and the last dispensation. They chose a virgin mind that, unpolluted by heresies and sensitive to the promptings of the Spirit, could be taught and led.

Some three years after the great vision in the woods, a heavenly messenger, Moroni, came to Joseph, now almost eighteen years old, and began instructing him in the duties of the great mission that had been given to him. The instructions came gradually, for his mind was finite, while the subject was infinite. So, as time went on, God revealed to the boy prophet the things he should know in order to restore and again build up the Church of Christ on earth. The Book of Mormon was translated and printed, out of which came principles and doctrines long since lost to the world. The Priesthood—Aaronic and Melchizedek—was restored. The Church was organized in counterpart of the Primitive Church. Then began a long series of revelations from God to Joseph, sometimes in rapid succession, sometimes at considerable intervals, all for the guidance and building up of the Church, and for the instruction of the Saints in the principles of the Restored Gospel. These revelations came as they were needed, to build up, encourage, and direct the activities of the Church and its membership.

Some have sought to discredit Joseph and the Church by the charge that Joseph's revelations came only when he was in trouble, and that to get out of the trouble he always had a revelation. It is the implication of this statement, and not the statement itself, upon which the scoffers rely for its pregnancy.

Of course the Lord fed Joseph spiritually as he and the Church had need. When they were enhungered the Lord gave bread; when they were thirsty he gave them drink. How else could he have done?

This growth from the simple to the complex, from the elementary to the abstruse, is the great natural law of the mind. First comes the multiplication table, and then, way out beyond, the formula for the tearing down of the atom. This advance did not follow in days, but came slowly with the marching of the centuries.

The same great law controls in the realm of the spirit.

God, delivering Israel from the Egyptians, did not bring freedom in a day. Israel had to be prepared with great demonstrations of God's power working mighty miracles; Pharaoh had to be softened by one sore affliction after another, and finally by the death of the first-born, before he commanded Moses:

"Rise up, and get you forth from among my people, both ye and the children of Israel; and go, serve the Lord, as ye have said. Also take your flocks and your herds, as ye have said, and be gone; and bless me also."[16]

All the miracles that Moses and Aaron worked, came one by one as the need was, to relieve them of a crisis arising during this gigantic duel between good and evil.

Israel was scarcely on its way till Pharaoh sent his hosts in pursuit. Israel seemed caught; before them lay the sea, behind them pressed a destroying army. Israel was in dire distress. A crisis faced them. God ordered them forward, commanding Moses to lift up his rod and stretch out his hand over the waters,[17] and "the waters were gathered together, the floods stood upright as an heap, and the depths were congealed in the heart of the sea."[18] Israel passed over dry-shod; and Pharaoh's hosts racing after, the sea returned to its wonted place, and they died. Thus another crisis was met as it came. Israel was not told of this in Egypt. The revelation of God's power came at the moment it was needed, and not before.

Great as was Moses' training in the royal courts of Pharaoh, it was not enough for his new duties. So Jethro, the priest of Midian and father-in-law of Moses, having learned of God's dealing with Moses and his people, came to Israel's camp and instructed Moses in the rudiments of government for a people dwelling in tents and on the march. This revelation from a high priest of God[19] did not come while Israel was yet in Egypt, as a matter of fitting them for their trek, but it came at the hour when Moses needed it, lest he should "wear away," as also his people which were with him.[20] And Jethro counselled: "And thou shalt teach them ordinances and laws, and shalt shew them the way wherein they must walk, and the work that they must do,"[21] for as Israel moved forward, knowing only the heathenish laws of the Egyptians, they must be patiently, gradually taught. Being God's people, they must live his laws, they must worship in his way.

So in the third month, Israel came into the wilderness of Sinai and camped before the Mount. Obedient to God's command, Moses went upon the Mount, where he received the Ten Commandments which should rule Israel.[22] These might have been given back in Egypt; they were not. Thus, since Moses was in trouble in his leadership of Israel, God gave him a revelation.

As they wandered in the wilderness, other crises, other troubles came.

Aaron and Miriam spake against Moses because of the Egyptian woman; they challenged his authority. Moses was meekly enduring their censure and taunts; he was again in trouble. But God spoke suddenly to him and gave him a revelation, reproving and punishing the erring brother and sister. A revelation rid Moses of this trouble.[23]

Korah, Dathan, Abiram, with two hundred and fifty of the princes of the assembly, challenged the authority of Moses and Aaron. A rebellion faced the Levites and their priesthood. Moses was in dire straits. God revealed to him what he should do. Korah and his rebels were swallowed up in an opening earth crack.[24] Thus came another revelation of God's power to relieve a crisis.

Then the whole of Israel murmured at the destruction of these conspirators; Moses and Aaron had killed them, the people said. Again Moses stood in critical necessity. God gave him a revelation directing his course.[25]

And so, time after time, while Israel wandered in the wilderness for forty years that she might learn of God's ways and be trained in his laws, because reforming and rebuilding a nation was a mighty undertaking, God revealed his mind and will to Moses as the need for the revelation arose. He gave his general revelations on worship and conduct no faster than Israel could absorb and reasonably live them. When crises came he revealed his mind and will to his servant Moses, showing him what he should do to meet them. God did not anticipate the troubles of Israel, but he gave, as they arose, the solution thereof.

So it has been with God's people since time began, with Abraham, Isaac, and Jacob, and with Joseph sold into Egypt, with Elijah challenging the priests of Baal.

So it was with the Prophet Joseph. As problems came, the Lord revealed the solution. Usually the Lord did not anticipate. It has been thus with each of them who followed Joseph as the head of the Church. God has given and does now give special revelations to his mouthpiece whenever the need therefor arises. His inspiration dwells with his prophets at all times.

I bear witness to the truth of this great principle, in the name of the Son. Amen.

---

[1]Moses 6:1, 53, 55, 68. [2]Gen. 5:22. [3]Moses 7:4. [4]Gen. 6:13. [5]Gen. 9:1. [6]Moses 8:19. [7]Gen. 12:7; 17:1; 18:1. [8]James 2:23; and see II Chron. 20:7; Isa. 41:8. [9]Ex. 3 ff. [10]Ex. 33:11. [11]Luke 2:47. [12]Matt. 4:19. [13]Matt. 16:16. [14]I Cor. 1:27. [15]Matt. 9:17. [16]Ex. 12:31-32. [17]Ex. 14:15 ff. [18]Ex. 15:8. [19]D.C. 84:6. [20]Ex. 18:18. [21]Ex. 18:20. [22]Ex. 19 ff. [23]Num. 12:1 ff. [24]Num. 16:1-32. [25]Num. 16:41.

XVIII

A HEAVENLY BEING BRINGS
GOOD TIDINGS

TWO WEEKS AGO we told the story of the First
Vision of the boy Joseph Smith, as the Father
and Son came to him, praying in the woods for
direction as to which of the many Christian churches
he should join. We read the boy's own story of this
glorious experience and learned that the Son told
him he should join none of these churches, for they
were all wrong, that they drew near to the Lord
with their lips, but that their hearts were far from
him; that they taught for doctrines the commandments of men, having a form of godliness, but denying the power thereof. We met and answered the
charge sometimes made, that this great theophany
was either an hallucination, or a fit, and that it
could not come to an unlettered rustic.

This was the first step in the opening of the
Last Dispensation.

Tonight we are to note the next definite step
forward in the establishment of the Dispensation of
the Fullness of Times.

For a little more than three years after the
visit of the Father and Son, the boy received no
further heavenly manifestation. At first he guile-
lessly told the story of his vision, only to find himself

treated with contempt, derided, scoffed at, reviled, and even persecuted, his contemners saying "there were no such things as visions or revelations in these days; that all such things had ceased with the apostles, and that there would never be any more of them." But the boy stood adamant; "it was," said he, "a fact that I had beheld a vision."

In after years he reflected how much his experiences were like to those of Paul, especially as Paul stood before Agrippa. And as he suffered his trials, he 'was led to say in his heart,' "Why persecute me for telling the truth? I have actually seen a vision; and who am I that I can withstand God, or why does the world think to make me deny what I have actually seen? For I had seen a vision; I knew it, and I knew that God knew it, and I could not deny it, neither dared I do it; at least I knew that by so doing I would offend God, and come under condemnation."

He marvelled that an "obscure boy, of a little over fourteen years of age . . . who was doomed to the necessity of obtaining a scanty maintenance by his daily labor," should stir up the "great ones of the most popular sects" so that they had a "spirit of the most bitter persecution"—a fact that "was often the cause of great sorrow" on his part.

But in September, 1823, over three years after his first vision, meanwhile "all the time suffering," as he says, "severe persecution at the hands of all classes of men, both religious and irreligious, because I continued to affirm that I had seen a vision . . . I betook myself to prayer and supplication to Almighty God for forgiveness of all my sins and follies." (He had earlier in his account assured us that "no one need suppose me guilty of any great or malignant sins. A disposition to commit such was never in my nature.") And now he asked for a manifestation "that I might know of my state and standing before him; for I had full confidence in obtaining a divine manifestation, as I previously had one."

His prayer was answered:

"While I was thus in the act of calling upon God, I discovered a light appearing in my room, which continued to increase until the room was lighter than at noonday, when immediately a personage appeared at my bedside, standing in the air, for his feet did not touch the floor.

"He had on a loose robe of most exquisite whiteness. It was a whiteness beyond anything earthly I had ever seen; nor do I believe that any earthly thing could be made to appear so exceedingly white and brilliant. His hands were naked, and his arms also, a little above the wrist; so, also, were his feet naked, as were his legs, a little above the ankles. His head and neck were also bare. I could discover that he had no other clothing on but this robe, as it was open, so that I could see into his bosom.

"Not only was his robe exceedingly white, but his whole person was glorious beyond description, and his countenance truly like lightning. The room was exceedingly light, but not so very bright as immediately around his person. When I first looked upon him, I was afraid; but the fear soon left me.

"He called me by name, and said unto me that

he was a messenger sent from the presence of God to me, and that his name was Moroni; that God had a work for me to do; and that my name should be had for good and evil among all nations, kindreds, and tongues, or that it should be both good and evil spoken of among all people."

Moroni then told Joseph of a record written upon gold plates (which Moroni had finished and hidden up) of the ancient peoples of this hemisphere and that the book contained, besides a history, "the fulness of the everlasting Gospel . . . as delivered by the Savior to the ancient inhabitants" of America. Moroni described other things that were deposited with the record plates, including the Urim and Thummim, which should be used in translating the record.

Having finished this, Moroni began quoting to Joseph from the Old and New Testament scriptures, with explanations as he went along, at times making changes in some of the texts that had been mistranslated or corrupted in the texts as we have them. He first quoted to the youth a part of the third and also the fourth chapter of Malachi, but with changes in the first, fifth and sixth verses of the fourth chapter. He also quoted the eleventh chapter of Isaiah, and the twenty-second and twenty-third verses of the third chapter of Acts, with some explanation. He quoted the second chapter of Joel, from verse twenty-eight on, saying that "this was not yet fulfilled, but was soon to be. And he further stated that the fulness of the Gentiles was soon to come in."

Joseph continues:

"He quoted many other passages of scripture,

and offered many explanations which cannot be mentioned here."

Moroni told Joseph that in due time he should receive the record plates, and 'the vision was opened to his mind' so that he "could see the place where the plates were deposited."

Joseph continues:

"After this communication, I saw the light in the room begin to gather immediately around the person of him who had been speaking to me, and it continued to do so until the room was again left dark, except just around him; when, instantly I saw, as it were, a conduit open right up into heaven, and he ascended till he entirely disappeared, and the room was left as it had been before this heavenly light had made its appearance.

"I lay musing on the singularity of the scene, and marveling greatly at what had been told to me by this extraordinary messenger; when, in the midst of my meditation, I suddenly discovered that my room was again beginning to get lighted, and in an instant, as it were, the same heavenly messenger was again by my bedside.

"He commenced, and again related the very same things which he had done at his first visit, without the least variation; which having done, he informed me of great judgments which were coming upon the earth, with great desolations by famine, sword, and pestilence; and that these grievous judgments would come on the earth in this generation. Having related these things, he again ascended as he had done before."

As Joseph lay in his bed pondering, Moroni returned a third time, in the manner of his first coming, and repeated to Joseph all he had said in the first visit, with an added caution about efforts that would be made to get the records from him.

On the day following, Moroni again appeared to Joseph and delivered the same message, instructing the lad to tell his father of the incident, which Joseph did. The father told the boy his message "was of God" and that he should obey the messenger. Joseph then visited the place where the records were deposited, uncovered the cemented stone box in which they were stored, opened it, viewed the contents, but Moroni would not permit him to remove them.

Moroni told Joseph to come to the place the year following, and so yearly for four years, which Joseph did, each time receiving further instructions "respecting what the Lord was going to do, and how and in what manner his kingdom was to be conducted in the last days."

Finally the time came for Joseph to receive the plates, and on September 22, 1827, the plates were delivered to him.[1] Joseph, by the power of God, translated a part of these plates, and printed the translation as the Book of Mormon.

With the trials, vicissitudes, hardships, disappointments, stratagems by others to obtain the plates, and persecutions—and there were many—incident to the translation and printing of this translation, we cannot now be concerned. We may say here only that under a copyright issued by R. R. Lansing, Clerk of the Northern District of New

York, and bearing date of June 11, 1829, it was printed and ready for distribution in the spring of 1830. Three special witnesses testified they were shown the plates by a heavenly messenger and eight others witnessed that Joseph had shown them the plates. The Book is almost half as large as the King James translation of the Bible. It is the history of the ancient inhabitants of America and of God's dealings with them. It contains many pieces of great literature.

From its publication it has been the subject of bitter attack, as being fraudulent, it being charged that it was a stolen manuscript, or that it was an uninspired writing of some person other than Joseph. Because the accusations were false, they have all fallen to the ground. The charges urged against Joseph, and considered in our last two previous talks, have been, in principle, vehemently repeated against this great Book, but these charges also vanish as did those against Joseph personally. It was urgently affirmed that the Book was a steal from a manuscript of fiction written by one Spaulding, but that manuscript was found and the examination thereof destroyed that attack. But every now and again some one revives the story and it gains currency for a time, then dies out again. It has also been affirmed that Sidney Rigdon wrote the Book, as well as many of Joseph's revelations. But this is more absurd than the Spaulding story. Sidney Rigdon gave no evidence of even the beginning of an ability to write the Book, and he never made claim thereto, even after he drifted from the Church.

It is but natural that in this inspirationless age, men will throw away all the miraculous in life, notwithstanding the millenniums of manifestations of God's powers that do not square with men's reason or knowledge; and this covers the full history of God's dealings with the men of this earth from the creation, through the flood, through Abraham's experiences, and those of Israel under Moses, and even the parentage, birth, mission, death, and resurrection of the Messiah himself. One need not then be disturbed because the rationalizing of atheistic savants, unlearned in spiritual truths, the greatest of all truths—and how little the best of them know of the full eternity of truth—shall now seek to cast doubt on the facts attending the opening of the Dispensation of the Fullness of Times.

And after all, as to the bringing forth of the Book of Mormon, the account of it as given by the Prophet Joseph is certainly a no greater drain on the credulity of the rationalizing doubter than is the account of the revelation of the Ten Commandments amidst the thunders of Mount Sinai, and the tracing of the commandments on the two tables of stone by the finger of God himself.[2]

But Moroni himself provided the formula, specified the sovereign test, by which the genuineness of the ancient record might be judged and proved. He said:

"And I seal up these records, after I have spoken a few words by way of exhortation unto you.

"Behold, I would exhort you that when ye shall read these things, if it be wisdom in God that ye should read them, that ye would remember how merciful the Lord hath been unto the children of men, from the creation of Adam even down until the time that ye shall receive these things, and ponder it in your hearts.

"And when ye shall receive these things, I would exhort you that ye would ask God, the Eternal Father, in the name of Christ, if these things are not true; and if ye shall ask with a sincere heart, with real intent, having faith in Christ, he will manifest the truth of it unto you, by the power of the Holy Ghost."[3]

Tens of thousands of the Church membership testify that they have prayed as Moroni instructed and have been rewarded as the ancient prophet promised.

There is no explanation to this Book except the one the Prophet himself gave and the eleven witnesses confirmed.

I bear my own testimony to this same truth, in the Son's name. Amen.

---

[1]History of Joseph Smith, P. of G. P. [2]Ex. 31:18; Deut. 9:10 ff.
[3]Moro. 10:2-4.

XIX

THE RESTORATION OF THE PRIESTHOOD

IN an earlier talk of this series, under the title "The Primitive Church Organization Disappears," we cited and quoted from Paul's epistle to the Hebrews, in which he discussed and distinguished the Levitical, or Aaronic Priesthood, and the Melchizedek Priesthood. We noted the care Paul took to make clear the superiority of the Melchizedek Priesthood over the Aaronic, or Levitical Priesthood. Paul explained:

"If therefore perfection were by the Levitical priesthood, (for under it the people received the law,) what further need was there that another priest should rise after the order of Melchisedec, and not be called after the order of Aaron?"[1]

In our talk we noted that Paul further pointed out that Christ came through Judah "of which tribe Moses spake nothing concerning priesthood," and that this high priest, (Christ—"called of God an high priest after the order of Melchisedec")[2] "after the similitude of Melchisedec . . . is made, not after the law of a carnal commandment, but after the power of an endless life," for "the law (Mosaic) made nothing perfect, but the bringing in of a better hope did; by the which we draw nigh unto God. . . . Wherefore he is able also to save them to the uttermost that come unto God by him."[3]

All through his epistle Paul stressed to the Hebrews the importance of the Melchizedek Priesthood in contrast with the Aaronic, or Levitical Priesthood. He exhorted his brethren, "consider the Apostle and High Priest of our profession, Christ Jesus. . . . For this man was counted worthy of more glory than Moses."[4] Again, ". . . we have a great high priest, that is passed into the heavens, Jesus the Son of God."[5] "For every high priest taken from among men is ordained for men in things pertaining to God. . . . And no man taketh this honor unto himself, but he that is called of God, as was Aaron."[6] Speaking of the Priesthood of Melchizedek, Paul said: "Without father, without mother, without descent, having neither beginning of days, nor end of life; but made like unto the Son of God; abideth a priest continually."[7] "But this man, because he continueth ever, hath an unchangeable priesthood."[8] And there are many other passages.

From Adam till now, God has guarded with jealous care the exercise of the rights and functions of his Holy Priesthood.

Abel offered an acceptable offering;[9] Cain did not, and God reproved Cain for his failure.[10]

The ancient patriarchs, Abraham, Isaac, and Jacob, made offerings to the Lord.[11]

Moses, fleeing the wrath of Pharaoh, went to Jethro, the Midian priest (from whom he received the Melchizedek Priesthood).[12] He with Aaron, his mouthpiece, exercised the powers of the priesthood in a great contest with the powers of evil manifested through the Egyptian magicians, to the vindication of the priesthood powers. Before the special Levitical Priesthood endowment to Aaron (at the hands of Moses),[13] Moses offered sacrifice, showing he possessed the right and power,[14] and Jethro, visiting him thereafter, made a burnt offering to God.[15] Israel, seducing Aaron to make a golden calf, offered sacrifices thereto. Under the instructions of the Almighty, Moses came down from the Mount, broke up the calf, ground it to powder, "strawed it upon the water," and compelled the Israelites to drink it.[16]

After the Levitical, or Aaronic Priesthood, was set up, Aaron and Miriam sought to challenge the authority of Moses under the higher priesthood—the Melchizedek—but God vindicated Moses.[17]

After the observance of the Levitical ritual was established, Nadab and Abihu died for offering "strange fire."[18] The incidents of God's Priesthood must not be trifled with.

When God sets up his Priesthood, and ordains and consecrates his priests, others not so commissioned may not pretend to priesthood powers. It was thus with Korah, Dathan, and Abiram, claiming equal authority with Aaron, and against these rebels God poured out speedy punishment for their sacrilege;[19] likewise, afterwards, when God manifested his choice of the Levites, by the blossoming of Aaron's rod, and its bearing of almonds.[20]

God, on occasion, vindicates his Priesthood, even before the multitude—as time and again with Moses and Aaron before Pharaoh, and with Elijah tempting and challenging the prophets of Baal, when God displayed his power in great clearness before all Israel.[21]

And so through the whole history of God's dealing with Israel, and with the Primitive Church.

The Priesthood of God is the authority delegated to man, by God, to act for and in his name in the matters and to the extent which he stipulates when he bestows the endowment.

Whenever God places the true Priesthood on the earth, there is always present a false priesthood, pretending the powers of the true Priesthood. It was so with Cain, with the magicians of Pharaoh, with the prophets of Baal, and with countless others, and these counterfeits are sometimes so well formed as to deceive many. Paul cautioned: "Satan himself is transformed into an angel of light."[22] The false priesthood always survives and operates after the true Priesthood has been lost through the transgressions of men.

No Christian will question that the Christ bestowed the Priesthood upon his Apostles, nor that they afterwards bestowed it upon others, as we showed in our talk on "The Organization in the Primitive Church."[23]

In the early part of the second year of his ministry, Jesus chose and "ordained twelve, that they should be with him, and that he might send them forth to preach."[24] Peter affirmed, at the choosing and ordination of Matthias: "Beginning from the baptism of John, unto that same day that he was taken up from us, must one be ordained to be a witness with us of his resurrection,"[25] thus showing that a special spiritual virtue came from ordination, because ordination would not make an eye witness of the resurrection of those who did not physically see the Christ risen.

Jesus sent out the Twelve, with "power and authority over all devils, and to cure diseases . . . and to heal the sick," clearly the power and authority of the Priesthood;[26] and the Twelve "went out, and preached that men should repent. And they cast out many devils, and anointed with oil many that were sick, and healed them."[27] Speaking to Peter at Caesarea Philippi, early in the third year of his ministry, Christ said:

"I will give unto thee the keys of the kingdom of heaven: and whatsoever thou shalt bind on earth shall be bound in heaven: and whatsoever thou shalt loose on earth shall be loosed in heaven."[28]

Later he fulfilled this promise by bestowing these powers, not upon Peter alone, but upon all his disciples, saying:

"Whatsoever ye shall bind on earth shall be bound in heaven: and whatsoever ye shall loose on earth shall be loosed in heaven."[29]

In the evening of the day of his resurrection, he said to the Twelve:

"Peace be unto you: as my Father hath sent me, even so send I you."[30]

He then gave them the great commission to remit and retain sins,[31] and breathing upon them, he said, "Receive ye the Holy Ghost."[32] He added the commission to preach the Gospel, to baptize, declared the blessing of the believer, and the punishment of the unbeliever, and added the blessings that should follow the believer.[33]

As to the Holy Ghost, it should be noted that Jesus had earlier said the "Comforter, which is the Holy Ghost"[34] would not come unless he went away, "but if I depart, I will send him to you."[35] And on the day of his ascension he told the Twelve "that they should not depart from Jerusalem, but wait for the promise of the Father, which, saith he, ye have heard of me. For John truly baptized with water, but ye shall be baptized with the Holy Ghost not many days hence . . . ye shall receive power after that the Holy Ghost is come upon you."[36] The Holy Ghost came at Pentecost with a sound from heaven "as of a rushing mighty wind . . . and there appeared unto them cloven tongues like as of fire, and it sat upon each of them. And they were all filled with the Holy Ghost."[37]

The conferring of these powers and authorities was not precatory,—that is, prayers to the Father that he would bestow these powers, authorities, and blessings, but an actual present endowment of the Priesthood and of its powers and authorities.

But by the middle of the third century, this Priesthood had been wholly lost, as we have already seen. The earliest ordinal (form of ordination) known, accredited to the Canons of Hippolytus (A.D. 236) makes no pretense at an actual bestowal or endowment of power and authority, it merely offers prayers that God will give certain powers and authority. Furthermore, this ordinal does not meet the requirements for the bestowal of the Priesthood, now laid down by some of the great modern churches claiming the possession of the Priesthood. All other early ordinals in the time following Hippolytus are equally defective.

With one of these great churches at least, the principle is adopted (and it is obviously sound) that one cannot pass a Priesthood power which one does not possess. Therefore, since these ordinals did not bestow the Priesthood in those early days, according to their own present standards and requirements, and since the candidates for whom the prayers of the ordinals were offered, received nothing as nothing passed to them, they in turn passed nothing on, and thus, as already pointed out, the Melchizedek Priesthood, before called the Holy Priesthood after the Order of the Son of God,[38] with its appendage, the Aaronic Priesthood, had disappeared from the earth by the middle of the third century.[39]

Having thus been lost, it must be restored, if it is to be on the earth. And restored it was, by the hands of heavenly beings, in ceremonies that actually, and in express terms, bestowed it, not prayed for it, upon the heads of those ordained.

The Priesthood was restored by two ordinations, first, the Aaronic, and later, the Melchizedek.

The restoration of the Aaronic Priesthood was on this wise, as recorded by the Prophet Joseph Smith:

"We still continued the work of translation, when, in the ensuing month (May, 1829), we (Joseph Smith and Oliver Cowdery) on a certain day went into the woods to pray and inquire of the Lord respecting baptism for the remission of sins, that we found mentioned in the translation of the plates. While we were thus employed, praying and calling upon the Lord, a messenger from heaven descended in a cloud of light, and having laid his hands upon us, he ordained us, saying:

" 'Upon you my fellow servants, in the name of Messiah, I confer the Priesthood of Aaron, which holds the keys of the ministering of angels, and of the Gospel of repentance, and of baptism by immersion for the remission of sins; and this shall never be taken again from the earth, until the sons of Levi do offer again an offering unto the Lord in righteousness.'

"He said this Aaronic Priesthood had not the power of laying on hands for the gift of the Holy Ghost, but that this should be conferred on us hereafter; and he commanded us to go and be baptized, and gave us directions that I should baptize Oliver Cowdery, and afterwards that he should baptize me. Accordingly we went and were baptized. I baptized him first, and afterwards he baptized me, after which I laid my hands upon his head and ordained him to the Aaronic Priesthood, and afterwards he laid his hands on me and ordained me to the same Priesthood—for so we were commanded.

"The messenger who visited us on this occasion, and conferred this Priesthood upon us, said that his name was John, the same that is called John the Baptist in the New Testament, and that he acted under the direction of Peter, James and John, who held the keys of the Priesthood of Melchizedek, which Priesthood he said would in due time be conferred on us, and that I should be called the first Elder of the Church, and he (Oliver Cowdery) the second. It was on the 15th day of May, 1829, that we were ordained under the hand of this messenger, and baptized."[40]

Thus was the Aaronic Priesthood restored to the earth, and has been bestowed and rebestowed, transmitted, from one to another, from its restoration till now by an equivalent ordination, an actual bestowal, upon the heads of all those receiving the ordination.

The Melchizedek Priesthood was restored in June, 1829. Peter, James, and John appeared to Joseph Smith and Oliver Cowdery and conferred upon them, ordained them to, the higher, or Melchizedek Priesthood, by a ceremony equivalent to that by which the Aaronic Priesthood was restored, and this higher Priesthood likewise has been bestowed and rebestowed, transmitted, from one to another, from its restoration till now by an equivalent ordination upon the heads of all those receiving the ordination.

By modern revelation we know that the resurrected Christ, on the shore of Galilee in the early morning, when, as they sat at meat, Jesus thrice instructed Peter, "Feed my sheep," said to John:

"And I will make thee to minister for him (Peter) and for thy brother James; and unto you three I will give this power and the keys of this ministry until I come."[41]

The restoration of this Priesthood, and various keys, have been described by the Prophet Joseph in these words:

"The voice of Peter, James, and John in the

wilderness between Harmony, Susquehanna County, and Colesville, Broome County, on the Susquehanna River, declaring themselves as possessing the keys of the kingdom, and of the dispensation of the fullness of times!

"And again, the voice of God in the chamber of old Father Whitmer, in Fayette, Seneca County, and at sundry times, and in divers places through all the travels and tribulations of this Church of Jesus Christ of Latter-day Saints! And the voice of Michael, the archangel; the voice of Gabriel, and of Raphael, and of divers angels, from Michael or Adam down to the present time, all declaring their dispensation, their rights, their keys, their honors, their majesty and glory, and the power of their priesthood; giving line upon line, precept upon precept; here a little, and there a little; giving us consolation by holding forth that which is to come, confirming our hope!"[42]

In August, 1830, the Prophet Joseph received a revelation from the Lord in which he recounted the men with whom he would "drink of the fruit of the vine with you on the earth," including, "and also with Peter, and James, and John, whom I have sent unto you, by whom I have ordained you and confirmed you to be apostles, and especial witnesses of my name, and bear the keys of your ministry and of the same things which I revealed unto them."[43]

Thus the Holy Priesthood of God has been again restored to the earth in this, the Dispensation of the Fullness of Times, with its keys, powers, and authorities, as it has been in every other dispensation from the beginning,[44] and this Priesthood has continued, since its restoration, and is now, in the Church of Jesus Christ of Latter-day Saints, which is thus fully authorized "to preach the Gospel and administer in the ordinances thereof."

To this I bear witness, in the name of him whose Priesthood is with us. Amen.

[1]Heb. 7:11. [2]Heb. 5:10; 6:20. [3]Heb. 7:14-16, 19, 25. [4]Heb. 3:1, 3. [5]Heb. 4:14. [6]Heb. 5:1, 4. [7]Heb. 7:3. [8]Heb. 7:24. [9]Heb. 11:4. [10]Gen. 4:2 ff. [11]Gen. 22; 26:25; 31:54. [12]D.C. 84:6, 17 ff. [13]Lev. 8. [14]Ex. 17:15. [15]Ex. 18:12. [16]Ex. 32:20. [17]Num. 12:1 ff. [18]Num. 3:1-4. [19]Num. 16:1 ff. [20]Num. 17:8. [21]I Kings 18:15 ff. [22]II Cor. 11:14. [23]Talk No. 8. [24]Mark 3:14. [25]Acts 1:22. [26]Luke 9:1-2. [27]Mark 6:12-13. [28]Matt. 16:14-19. [29]Matt. 18:18. [30]John 20:21. [31]John 20:22-23. [32]John 20:22. [33]Matt. 28:18-20; Mark 16:15 ff. [34]John 14: 26. [35]John 15:26; 16:7. [36]Acts 1:4-5, 8. [37]Acts 2:1-4. [38]D.C. 107:2-3. [39]See Lowndes, *Vindication of Anglican Orders.* [40]Documentary History of the Church, I, p. 39-41. [41]D.C. 7:7. [42]D.C. 128:20-21. [43]D.C. 27:12. [44]Parry, *Teachings of Joseph Smith,* p. 122.

XX

SALVATION UNIVERSAL

IN the greatest sermon ever preached on the resurrection, Paul declared this elemental truth:

"For since by man came death, by man came also the resurrection of the dead. For as in Adam all die, even so in Christ shall all be made alive."[1]

This is the glorious message that comes from out the ministry of Christ,—by the Fall of Adam, all die, but by the Atonement of Christ, all shall again live, —every man, woman, and child born to this earth shall in due time rise from the grave to everlasting life.

Israel over the centuries had lost this truth, that all men should rise in a resurrection, though the Gospel, of which the atonement is a basic part, had been preached to Abraham[2]; and the Savior, speaking to the Jews as he was in Jerusalem for the second Passover of his ministry, said:

"Do not think that I will accuse you to the Father: there is one that accuseth you, even Moses, in whom ye trust. For had ye believed Moses, ye would have believed me: for he wrote of me. But if ye believe not his writings, how shall ye believe my words?"[3]

And before that, it had been taught to Adam himself, for the record reads, after reciting his offerings of sacrifice of the firstlings of his flocks:

"And after many days an angel of the Lord appeared unto Adam, saying: Why dost thou offer sacrifices unto the Lord? And Adam said unto him: I know not, save the Lord commanded me.

"And then the angel spake, saying: This thing is a similitude of the sacrifice of the Only Begotten of the Father, which is full of grace and truth.

"Wherefore, thou shalt do all that thou doest in the name of the Son, and thou shalt repent and call upon God in the name of the Son forevermore.

"And in that day the Holy Ghost fell upon Adam, which beareth record of the Father and the Son, saying: I am the Only Begotten of the Father from the beginning, henceforth and forever, that as thou hast fallen thou mayest be redeemed, and all mankind, even as many as will.

"And in that day Adam blessed God and was filled, and began to prophesy concerning all the families of the earth, saying: Blessed be the name of God, for because of my transgression my eyes are opened, and in this life I shall have joy, and again in the flesh I shall see God.

"And Eve, his wife, heard all these things and was glad, saying: Were it not for our transgression we never should have had seed, and never should have known good and evil, and the joy of our redemption, and the eternal life which God giveth unto all the obedient.

"And Adam and Eve blessed the name of God, and they made all things known unto their sons and their daughters."[4]

So from the time of the Fall, men knew of the

atoning sacrifice that would be offered by the Only Begotten, that it would bring to all mankind a redemption from the mortal death brought into the world by Adam.

The day of the transgression of Adam brought his separation from the Father, with whom, before that day, he had walked and talked,—this separation was a spiritual death.[5] But Adam's transgression also brought mortality and the death of the body. Thus all men must die, and, as Adam left them when he passed on, they must sleep forever.

But that was not God's plan set up at the beginning. That plan provided that his children should come to earth, take on mortal bodies, and, if they lived his laws and kept his commandments, they should "have glory added upon their heads for ever and ever," in the life hereafter.[6]

So there must be a rising from the dead in order that the mortal body and the spirit might be reunited to form the soul,[7] even as God had planned.

To bring this about, Christ was born, ministered, died, and was resurrected, and being resurrected, his body and spirit were again reunited, for he declared to his disciples, in the evening of the day of his resurrection, that he was not a spirit, but a being of "flesh and bones."[8]

This redemption from death, this resurrection of the mortal body, is to come to all men who have ever lived, from the beginning till the end, to those who heard the truth while living and to those who have died without the truth. Resurrection from the

dead is humanity-wide, none, even the most de-
praved, lose this blessing.

In his great discourse to the Jews in Jerusalem
as he attended the second Passover of his ministry,
Jesus declared, speaking of his relationship to the
Father:

"The dead shall hear the voice of the Son of
God. . . . Marvel not at this: for the hour is coming,
in the which all that are in the graves shall hear his
voice, and shall come forth; they that have done
good, unto the resurrection of life; and they that
have done evil, unto the resurrection of damnation."[9]

Thus as to the dead, all shall rise, but only they
who do good shall be exalted.

As to the living, Christ commanded his Apostles: "Go ye into all the world, and preach the gospel to every creature. He that believeth and is baptized shall be saved; but he that believeth not shall
be damned."[10] The mandate was to "teach all nations."[11] And John on Patmos declared he saw "another angel fly in the midst of heaven, having the
everlasting gospel to preach unto them that dwell on
the earth, and to every nation, and kindred, and
tongue, and people."[12]

No living man, no woman, no child of whatever
race, creed, or nation, is to be deprived of the right
to hear the Gospel of Christ and to live the commandments of God. And Jesus said in that same sermon
to the Jews at the Passover:

"Verily, verily, I say unto you, The hour is coming, and now is, when the dead shall hear the voice
of the Son of God: and they that hear shall live."[13]

Peter had difficulty with the principle that all men had a right to the Gospel and its salvation, to this resurrection from the dead, the reuniting of the spirit with the resurrected body. The beneficiary of centuries of teaching that Israel was the chosen people of God, he could not understand that the Gospel with its blessings should go to the Gentiles. But the Lord gave him the vision of the vessel, "as it had been a great sheet knit at the four corners, and let down to the earth," filled with "all manner of four footed beasts of the earth, and wild beasts, and creeping things, and fowls of the air. And there came a voice to him, Rise, Peter; kill and eat. But Peter said, Not so, Lord; for I have never eaten any thing that is common or unclean. And the voice spake unto him again the second time, What God hath cleansed, that call not thou common. This was done thrice: and the vessel was received up again into heaven."

And while Peter yet doubted the meaning of the vision, messengers came to him to bring him to Cornelius. But Peter, though the vision was still fresh in his mind, still hesitated, and a voice said, "Get thee down, and go with them, doubting nothing: for I have sent them."

When he had come to Cornelius and asked why the messengers sought him, Cornelius told of the vision that had come to him, giving Peter's name, the place where he lodged, and that Peter would come to speak to those whom Cornelius had gathered together. Hearing these things, "Peter opened his mouth, and said, Of a truth I perceive that God is no respecter of persons: But in every nation he that feareth him, and worketh righteousness, is accepted with him,"[14] and Peter might have added, whether he be living or dead.

And so it is. "Adam fell that men might be; and men are, that they might have joy,"[15] the joy of living righteously, that into the soul may come the peace that Christ gave to his Apostles in the Upper Chamber:

"Peace I leave with you, my peace I give unto you: not as the world giveth, give I unto you. Let not your heart be troubled, neither let it be afraid."[16]

And with our righteous lives, lived obediently all our days to the principles and ordinances of the Gospel, so bringing us his peace, we shall ourselves redeem ourselves from the spiritual death which came to us through Adam from the day of his transgression, and thus find our way back to the presence of God to be with him through the eternities to come.

How merciful are the words of Jesus to those who have slipped by the way, who have not lived the righteous life, who have sinned.

Over and over again he spoke of himself as the tender, watchful shepherd and of us as his flock.

To the disciples disputing about who should be greatest in heaven, he taught the lesson of the greatness of little children, and declared:

"For the Son of man is come to save that which was lost. How think ye? if a man have an hundred sheep, and one of them be gone astray, doth he not leave the ninety and nine, and goeth into the mountains, and seeketh that which is gone astray?

And if so be that he find it, verily I say unto you, he rejoiceth more of that sheep, than of the ninety and nine which went not astray."[17]

How infinite his love and mercy for the wayward ones, how far he reaches for them, how he seeks for them in the wilderness of transgression.

Speaking to the Jews in Jerusalem at another time, Jesus said:

"Verily, verily, I say unto you, I am the door of the sheep . . . I am the door: by me if any man enter in, he shall be saved, and shall go in and out, and find pasture. . . . I am the good shepherd: the good shepherd giveth his life for the sheep . . . I am the good shepherd, and know my sheep, and am known of mine. As the Father knoweth me, even so know I the Father: and I lay down my life for the sheep."[18]

He laid down his life for his sheep, not for one only, nor for the few, but for every member of the flock, black and white.

Unto the woman of Canaan, whom, seeking mercy for her stricken daughter, the disciples would have driven away, Jesus said: "I am not sent but unto the lost sheep of the house of Israel." Yet she came worshipping, craving the healing of her daughter. Jesus said to her, "It is not meet to take the children's bread, and to cast it to dogs." Then came from the Canaanite, one not of the chosen seed, the one reply made to him in all his recorded ministry that successfully challenged one of his own sayings: "Truth, Lord: yet the dogs eat of the crumbs which fall from their masters' table." Deeply touched, Jesus answered: "O woman, great is thy faith: be it unto thee even as thou wilt. And her daughter was made whole from that very hour."[19]

How blind was Peter that after this lesson he must needs have a thrice-repeated vision to convince him that God is no respecter of persons, that his love and mercy are for all, even for those whom the chosen seed despised. But even before this, Peter had been taught the lesson by the incident of Jesus at the well with the woman of Samaria. The converted Samaritans, hearing him, testified:

"We have heard him ourselves, and know that this is indeed the Christ, the Savior of the world."[20]

Yet this acceptance of the Samaritans, the race hated by Judah, left Peter untaught. Peter, as well as Paul, 'kicked against the pricks,'—Peter against the principle of the universal salvation of men, — men of all creeds, races, and colors.

But while every mortal shall be raised from the dead through the atonement of Christ, we shall not all rise equal in all things, any more than we are all equal, spiritually and intellectually in mortality. Jesus said, as we have quoted: men are to come forth "they that have done good, unto the resurrection of life; and they that have done evil, unto the resurrection of damnation."[21] Paul, speaking to the Corinthians to the same principle declared that in the resurrection there were celestial bodies with their glory, and terrestrial bodies with their glory, and compared the difference among these glories by comparing them to the sun, the moon, and the stars.[22] Modern revelation has broadened our knowledge on this matter, and we now know that, according to their deeds, men will rise to celestial glory, to terrestrial glory, or to telestial glory, or to a resurrection without glory, depending upon the kind of lives they lived while on the earth. Blessed are they who rise to a celestial glory for they shall live with the Father. Sad will be they who rise to no glory, for they shall not live with the Father.[23]

Paul, speaking to the Corinthians and paraphrasing Isaiah[24] declared: "But as it is written, Eye hath not seen, nor ear heard, neither have entered into the heart of man, the things which God hath prepared for them that love him."[25]

May God help each of us so to live that we may be resurrected with celestial bodies, heirs to immortality and eternal life with the Father, I pray, in Jesus' name. Amen.

---

[1]I Cor. 15:21-22. [2]Gal. 3:8. [3]John 5:45-47. [4]Moses 5:6-12. [5]D.C. 29:4-45. [6]Abraham 3:26. [7]D.C. 88:15. [8]Luke 24:39. [9]John 5:25, 28-29. [10]Mark 16:15-16. [11]Matt. 28:19. [12]Rev. 14:6. [13]John 5:25. [14]Acts 10:9-35. [15]2 Nephi 2:25. [16]John 14:27. [17]Matt. 18:1-13. [18]John 10:7, 9, 11, 14-15. [19]Matt. 15:21-28. [20]John 4:42. [21]John 5:29. [22]I Cor. 15:36 ff. [23]D. C. 76 and 88. [24]Isa. 64:4. [25]I Cor. 2:9.

XXI

THE ORGANIZATION OF THE CHURCH UNDER THE RESTORED GOSPEL AND PRIESTHOOD

IN OUR talks already given we considered the organization in the Primitive Church; we noted that this organization disappeared in the very early history of the Church, the last of the Apostles who served being John the Beloved.[1]

We found also that the Priesthood possessed in the Primitive Church had disappeared as early as the middle of the third century, and probably many decades before.[2]

We learned that in fulfillment of the prophecies of Peter, "damnable heresies" (these are Peter's words)[3] crept into the Church, and that in fulfillment of the prophecies of Paul there was a "falling away" from the principles and doctrines taught by Christ and his Apostles.[4]

We have called attention to the history of God's dealings with his children, showing that over the generations from Adam down, there have been periods of apostasy which, time and again, have required that God restore to the earth his gospel plan and his Priesthood in order that men might work out for themselves the salvation and exaltation which God has designed that his children might obtain.[5]

We related further the opening of another gospel dispensation in our time, this one the anciently predicted Dispensation of the Fullness of Times, which was ushered in by the glorious vision, unequalled in the prior recorded history of the human race, in which the Father and Son appeared to the humble, prayerful boy Joseph Smith.⁶

We also told the story of the later appearance to the boy of the angel Moroni, who instructed him in his great mission and, after a time of preparation, entrusted to him the plates of gold on which was recorded the history of the ancient inhabitants of America; we explained that this record was translated through the power of God and is now printed as the Book of Mormon.⁷

We also gave the account of the restoration of the Lesser, the Aaronic Priesthood, and the High Priesthood, the Melchizedek Priesthood, which includes the Aaronic Priesthood, and "is after the holiest order of God."⁸

We shall now consider some details that will indicate the completeness of the preparation which the Lord made for the organization of his Church in this dispensation.

The spiritual training of Joseph began with the First Vision. It was intensified by the visits and teachings of Moroni, and amplified by the principles and doctrines set out in the Book of Mormon as its translation progressed. During this full period of translation the Lord gave revelations to Joseph that bore upon the work he was doing and was thereafter to do. Some of these were recorded, but others were not, a fact which later brought from Joseph a lament.[9]

The earliest revelations recorded, following those given by Moroni, were given, one in July, 1828,[10] and the other in the same summer[11]—Joseph was then 22 years old. These revelations deal with the unfaithful care that Joseph had theretofore bestowed upon the records under translation and upon certain parts of that translation. Joseph was censured by the Lord for his carelessness, was sternly admonished as to his relationship to the work of the Lord, and warned as to the guile and wiles of designing men. No greater or better evidence can be offered or given of Joseph's own convictions of the character of his mission and of its divine origin, nor evidence of his own personal moral and spiritual courage, than the publication of these two revelations in which he, himself, comes under condemnation. No man perpetrating a fraud would hazard such a step that could so easily lead to the failure of the evil end a fraud would aim at. And speaking of fraud — and Joseph has been so spoken of — what had Joseph to gain by the perpetrating of a fraud? We shall return to this question again.

As time moved on during 1828, 1829, and 1830, other revelations came, all preparatory to the formal establishment of the work — the setting up of the Church, christened by the Christ himself as the Church of Jesus Christ of Latter-day Saints.

In February of 1829, a revelation came regarding the relationship of Joseph's father to the work and what he might do.[12]

In March of the same year (1829), a revelation came regarding Martin Harris and others who were to become witnesses to the verity of the Book of Mormon; also regarding Joseph's gift of translation —his first gift; referring to this as "the beginning of the rising up and the coming forth of my church out of the wilderness"; noting Joseph had not yet been ordained and referring to baptism; pointing out that "a desolating scourge" should come upon the earth, if they rejected the truth; intimating to Joseph the character of his death, saying, "behold I grant unto you eternal life, even if you should be slain . . . and there are many that lie in wait to destroy thee from off the face of the earth"; and admonishing Martin Harris against his waywardness.[13]

In April of 1829, the Lord gave a revelation to Joseph Smith and Oliver Cowdery, who had just begun to act as Joseph's scribe in the translation of the Book of Mormon, urging them to diligence in their work; promising them spiritual blessings from doing good—they should be made rich, "behold, he that hath eternal life is rich"; declaring that if they were faithful to the end they should be saved in the kingdom of God, "for there is no gift greater than the gift of salvation." In this revelation, the Lord told Joseph of matters about Oliver, theretofore known only to God and Oliver, to the strengthening of Oliver's faith and testimony.[14]

In the same month (April, 1829), the Lord revealed an answer to an enquiry of Joseph and Oliver regarding the work of John the Beloved, and declared

to them that at the morning breakfast on the shores
of the Sea of Galilee, he had said to John, desiring to
tarry till Christ should come, that he might bring
souls to Christ:

"And I will make thee to minister for him
(Peter) and for thy brother James; and unto you
three I will give this power and the keys of this ministry until I come."[15]

Thus the Lord was preparing the minds of
Joseph and Oliver for the restoration of the Priesthood.

Two other revelations (April, 1829) dealt with
Oliver's desire to do translating work, and explained
why he could not do so. Oliver had thought that all
he need do was to ask, but the Lord told him he must
work for his blessing.[16]

In May, 1829, as we have already learned, the
Lord restored the Aaronic Priesthood at the hands
of John the Baptist (May 15, 1829), and then in
June, 1829, the Melchizedek Priesthood at the hands
of Peter, James and John, of whose visitation and
ordination they had received an intimation in April[17]
and of which John the Baptist advised them at the
time he ordained them to the Aaronic Priesthood.[18]

The establishment of the Church was drawing
near. Revelations continued to come. Joseph and
Oliver began carefully to teach others, at the same
time sensing the incompleteness of their own knowledge. The translation of the Book of Mormon continued to go forward, and the knowledge of the
brethren grew proportionately, for the book contained "the fulness of the everlasting Gospel . . . as

delivered by the Savior to the ancient inhabitants"
of America.[19]

Special revelations were given for the Prophet's
brother, Hyrum,[20] for Joseph Knight, Sen.,[21] for
David Whitmer,[22] for John Whitmer,[23] for Peter
Whitmer, Jun.,[24] all for their spiritual encourage-
ment and building up, for they were of great assistance to the Prophet in his work of translating, and
bringing forth of the Book of Mormon. Oliver
Cowdery, David Whitmer, and Martin Harris were
promised a view of the plates.[25]

Shortly after this, following earnest prayer by
each of them in a spot in the woods to which they
had retired, a heavenly messenger displayed the
golden plates to each of them, in a glorious vision
that brought rejoicing and a never-dying conviction
of the verity of the plates to each of them.[26] These
three men—Oliver Cowdery, David Whitmer, and
Martin Harris—signed a formal document affirming
the facts of this great vision. This document is
called the Testimony of the Three Witnesses.

Soon thereafter, Joseph himself displayed the
plates to eight other men, and these likewise signed
a formal document affirming that they had seen the
plates, had hefted them, had seen the writing thereon, and knew Joseph had the plates. This document
is known as the Testimony of the Eight Witnesses.

But there were three other great revelations
that came before the establishment of the Church.

The first of these was given in June, 1829. It
declared the world was ripening in iniquity and men
must be stirred to repentance. The Lord, Jesus

Christ, gave a message to Oliver Cowdery and David Whitmer, telling them they were called to the same calling as Apostle Paul. He spoke of the atonement of Christ and of the joy of bringing one soul to repentance; he promised the Holy Ghost and indicated its service; he affirmed that through the Lord's name only could men be saved; he referred to the work of the Twelve in preaching, and in ordaining priests and teachers, and said men must repent and be baptized, including children "arrived at the years of accountability"; he declared that by their hands he would "work a marvelous work among the children of men." The revelation closes with these words:

"Behold, I, Jesus Christ, your Lord and your God, and your Redeemer, by the power of my Spirit have spoken it. Amen."[27]

The Brethren now had the Book of Mormon; Joseph had translated it and Oliver had acted as his scribe for a great part of it. They had discussed the Gospel principles therein taught. The Book of Mormon contained not only Gospel principles long lost to the world, but also specific instructions concerning baptism, giving the form of ordination, and the prayers for the administration of the sacrament. At times, Joseph and Oliver had gone to the Lord for answers to questions. They had gone far in their searchings, for this revelation (Sec. 18) discusses matters in terms that connote a knowledge background of great breadth. The Lord was preparing for the final step in his program of establishing his Church.

The next revelation was given for Martin Harris, some nine months later (March, 1830). Declaring his own omnipotence and Godhood, the Lord defines eternal punishment and endless punishment as God's punishment; commands Martin Harris to repent, and points out the position of the unrepentant sinner. The Lord tells of his own suffering—in the Garden and on the cross—and again calls for repentance. In their preaching they are to preach only repentance, and states that this is the last commandment he will give on this matter. He commands Martin Harris to give of his property to pay the cost of printing the Book of Mormon. The revelation concluded with urgent commands, admonitions, and pleadings to Martin Harris.[28]

The third of these revelations came in April, 1830,[29] it would seem just before the 6th of the month, on which date the Church was organized. (The text of this section as now printed in the Doctrine and Covenants appears to include two other shorter revelations received at different times.) This whole revelation relates to Church order and government, and was the capstone both to the doctrines and ordinance procedures given in the Book of Mormon and in the revelations and instructions theretofore received from the Lord.

This revelation opens by declaring the time of the organizing of the Church, and naming Joseph and Oliver as apostles, Joseph to be the first elder and Oliver the second.[30] The next section notes transgressions by Joseph and the Lord's forgiveness therefor, and declares that God is the same yesterday, today, and forever.[31] The next following verses[32] treat of the rewards and punishments of the righteous and unrighteous. Next is the section dealing with the character of God, the creation, the action of men, the atoning sacrifice of the Only Begotten, the universality of salvation, the necessity for repentance, the possibility of men transgressing, therefore the Church must pray always, and the relationship of these scriptures to the writings of John.[33] The verses following[34] name certain Priesthood offices,— apostles, elders, priests, teachers, and deacons, and give the duties thereof and the identifying papers they must carry. These verses lay down the rule that no person is to be ordained to any office in this Church where there is a regularly organized branch of the same, without the vote of the Church. Next considered[35] was the duty of the members after they are received by baptism. The order and manner of baptism were then given, together with the words to be used in the ordinance, which had already been given in the Book of Mormon.[36] The Church was to meet often and partake of the sacrament, and the words of the prayer on the bread and on the wine were given in the words already familiar to them from the Book of Mormon.[37] Instructions followed as to the discipline of the Church, the handling of the records of expelled members, and of members removing from one place to another, with other pertinent and necessary instructions to implement the rules and principles of the Gospel of Christ and his Priesthood.

Thus the needed instructions in doctrine had been given, the necessary Priesthood had been restored, the offices essential to the organization of the Church had been named, all in order that the Church of Jesus Christ of Latter-day Saints should be established in this, the last dispensation, the Dispensation of the Fullness of Times.

Accordingly, on Tuesday, April 6, 1830, at the home of Peter Whitmer, Sr., in Fayette township, New York, the Church was organized by six men,— Joseph Smith, Jr., Oliver Cowdery, Hyrum Smith, Peter Whitmer, Jr., Samuel H. Smith, and David Whitmer.

Joseph and Oliver were possessed of the Melchizedek Priesthood (possibly others[38]), and also, as we have seen, they held the apostleship.[39]

The Documentary History of the Church contains the following brief account of the organization:

"Whilst the Book of Mormon was in the hands of the printer, we still continued to bear testimony and give information, as far as we had opportunity; and also made known to our brethren that we had received a commandment to organize the Church; and accordingly we met together for that purpose, at the house of Mr. Peter Whitmer, Sen., (being six in number,) on Tuesday, the sixth day of April, A. D., one thousand eight hundred and thirty. Having opened the meeting by solemn prayer to our Heavenly Father, we proceeded, according to previous commandment, to call on our brethren to know whether they accepted us as their teachers in the things of the Kingdom of God, and whether they were satisfied that we should proceed and be organized as a Church according to said commandment which we had received. To these several propositions they consented by a unanimous vote. I then laid my hands upon Oliver Cowdery, and ordained him an Elder of the 'Church of Jesus Christ of Latter-day Saints'; after which, he ordained me also to the office of an Elder of said Church. We then took bread, blessed it, and brake it with them; also wine, blessed it, and drank it with them. We then laid our hands on each individual member of the Church present, that they might receive the gift of the Holy Ghost, and be confirmed members of the Church of Christ. The Holy Ghost was poured out upon us to a very great degree—some prophesied, whilst we all praised the Lord, and rejoiced exceedingly. Whilst yet together, I received the following commandment:" (Here was given the revelation appearing as D. C. 21; Joseph was to be called "a seer, a translator, a prophet, an apostle of Jesus Christ.") "We now proceeded to call out and ordain some others of the brethren to different offices of the Priesthood, according as the Spirit manifested unto us: and after a happy time spent in witnessing and feeling for ourselves the powers and blessings of the Holy Ghost, through the grace of God bestowed upon us, we dismissed with the pleasing knowledge that we were now individually members of, and acknowledged of God, 'The Church of Jesus Christ,' organized in accordance with commandments and revelations given by Him to ourselves in these last days, as well as according to the order of the Church as recorded in the New Testament."[40]

The name of the Church as organized, "The

Church of Jesus Christ," was later (April 26, 1838) changed by revelation to "The Church of Jesus Christ of Latter-day Saints."[41]

The Dispensation had been opened by the great vision to Joseph in the grove, ten years before. Joseph was then between 14 and 15 years of age; he was now between 24 and 25 as the Church was organized.

Pursuant to the revelations, the Church was established with the same organization provided for in the Primitive Church,—apostles, prophets, elders, priests, teachers, and deacons; other offices and priesthood grades were added in the ensuing months until the modern Church functioned, fully officered as was the Primitive Church.

The Church of the Christ was again restored to the earth, with his Gospel and his Priesthood.

Beginning with a revelation in the very meeting of organization, a stream of other revelations followed, the Lord leading and directing modern Israel under Joseph, even as he had led ancient Israel under Moses,—leading Joseph no less certainly than he led Moses.

Thus was fulfilled Daniel's interpretation of the dream of Nebuchadnezzar:

"Thou sawest till that a stone was cut out without hands, which smote the image upon his feet that were of iron and clay, and brake them to pieces.

"Then was the iron, the clay, the brass, the silver, and the gold, broken to pieces together, and became like the chaff of the summer threshingfloors; and the wind carried them away, that no place was found for them: and the stone that smote the image became a great mountain, and filled the whole earth."[42]

To the truth of all this I bear witness, in the name of the Son. Amen.

[1]See Talks 8 and 9. [2]Talk 19. [3]II Pet. 2:1. [4]Talks 10, 11, and 13. [5]Talk 15. [6]Talk 16. [7]Talk 18. [8]D.C. 84:18; Talk 19. [9]Documentary History of the Church, II, p. 198-199. [10]D.C. 3. [11]D.C. 10. [12]D.C. 4. [13]D.C. 5. [14]D.C. 6. [15]D.C. 7:7. [16]D.C. 8-9. [17]D.C. 7:8. [18]D. H. C., I, p. 39; D.C. 7, 13. [19]Moroni's statement, History of Joseph Smith. P. of G. P., v. 34. [20]D.C. 11. [21]D.C. 12. [22]D.C. 14. [23]D.C. 15. [24]D.C. 16. [25]D.C. 17. [26]D. H. C., I, p. 52 ff. [27]D.C. 18. [28]D.C. 19. [29]D.C. 20. [30]D.C. 20:1-4. [31]Id., v. 5-12. [32]Id., v. 13-16. [33]Id., v. 17-36. [34]Id., v. 38-67. [35]Id., v. 68-84. [36]3 Nephi 11:25. [37]Moro. 4-5. [38]See D.C. 18:9. [39]D.C. 20:2-3. [40]D. H. C., I, p. 74-79. [41]D.C. 115:3-4. See D. H. C., I, Ch. 8; Roberts, Comprehensive History of the Church, I, Ch. 16, n. 13. [42]Dan. 2:34-35.

XXII

KEYS AND POWERS OF THE PRIESTHOOD

IN OUR talk on the restoration of the "Holy Priest-hood, after the Order of the Son of God,"[1] we briefly defined Priesthood as the authority dele-gated to man by God, to act for and in his name, in the matters and to the extent which he stipulates when he bestows the endowment, God being the source of all power and all authority whatsoever.

We noted that at Caesarea Philippi, after Peter's great testimony that Jesus was the Christ, Christ promised to Peter (then an apostle and so bearing the Priesthood) :[2]

"And I will give unto thee the keys of the king-dom of heaven: and whatsoever thou shalt bind on earth shall be bound in heaven: and whatsoever thou shalt loose on earth shall be loosed in heaven."[3]

We also noted that, a little later, Christ fulfilled the promise and bestowed this power, these keys for binding and loosing, upon all the Twelve, not upon Peter alone, by declaring:

"Whatsoever ye shall bind on earth shall be bound in heaven: and whatsoever ye shall loose on earth shall be loosed in heaven."[4]

It is clear from this incident that the mere pos-session of the Priesthood does not carry with it the right to exercise all the powers and authorities em-

braced by it, but only those which are specifically
authorized by the Lord, either directly or by delega-
tion by one who holds the specific authority from the
Lord.

It will be recalled that when John the Baptist
conferred the Aaronic Priesthood upon Joseph and
Oliver, he said:

"Upon you my fellow servants, in the name of
Messiah I confer the Priesthood of Aaron, which
holds the keys of the ministering of angels, and of
the gospel of repentance, and of baptism by immersion for the remission of sins."[5]

The Priesthood of Aaron did not carry the
powers or keys for confirmation into the Church, the
bestowal of the Holy Ghost, nor the power to bind
and loose, nor to retain or remit sins, as the ancient
Apostles possessed, these keys and powers came later
to Joseph.

In the revelation given to Joseph, in connection
with the organization of the Church,[6] the Lord pointed out that the Aaronic Priesthood had three grades,
or orders: deacons, teachers, and priests, and defined
the right, duties, obligation, and service of each
grade. We speak of these functions as callings, and
so they are, but they involve also the bestowal of
keys, as John the Baptist said,—"*keys* of the ministering of angels," that is, this Priesthood had the
authority and right to receive visitations from
angels, as for example, the visit of the angel Gabriel
to the priest Zacharias, ministering in the Temple
at Jerusalem.[7] John the Baptist further said, in
conferring the Aaronic Priesthood on Joseph and

Oliver, that this Priesthood held the *keys* "of the gospel of repentance, and of baptism by immersion for the remission of sins," that is, holders of the Aaronic Priesthood may preach repentance, and teach the people and may baptize, being duly authorized thereto.

That revelation[8] and others make it clear that deacons can not perform the duties nor do the work of the teacher; that the teacher can perform his own duties, meet his calling, use his keys, and can also act as deacon, but the teacher can not perform the duties of a priest, and that the priest has still other duties, possesses further powers, and can in addition exercise all the rights and powers of the lesser offices of teacher and deacon.

The elder (and an apostle is an elder) possesses the higher, or Melchizedek Priesthood, which embraces the Aaronic Priesthood; he may exercise all the callings of the Aaronic Priesthood, but has in addition other callings.

This principle that the holder of a higher office of the Priesthood possesses the powers and authorities of all offices of a lesser grade than the one he holds, but may normally exercise none of those powers and functions of higher offices than his own, is fundamental to the Restored Gospel and the administration thereunder of the Church of Jesus Christ of Latter-day Saints and of the Priesthood through and by which the Church operates. No bearer of the Priesthood has any right to perform any Priesthood function until either he has been ordained to the office which carries with it the authority to perform the function, or until he has been duly authorized, by special ordination or otherwise, to perform it.

This principle has been operative since the days of Adam, when Cain failed to offer an acceptable sacrifice.[9] It operated when Nadab and Abihu offered "strange fire"—they lacked the authority to make the offering they made;[10] it operated against the claim of the conspirators Korah, Dathan, and Abiram, claiming to function as priests as did Aaron, for which they did not possess the right;[11] and so when Uzza steadied the ark when the oxen stumbled, the right to care for the ark resting in the Kohathites,[12]—this latter incident has become the classic illustration of one seeking to function without authority, invading the rights of others; and so with the rights and authority of the High Priest to enter the Holy of Holies and perform the rites to be celebrated therein,—the High Priest alone held the keys for that service.

So in carrying on the discipline and government of the Church, and in administering the rituals and ordinances thereof, the Lord has established a control that there may be order in the Church— the Lord has said his house is a house of order.[13] Those controls make it necessary to have special authority for the exercise of the Priesthood functions and powers which are involved in these matters of discipline, government, and administration. Not every bearer of the Priesthood, no matter what grade he holds, can perform these special services, rituals, and ordinances; he must be authorized to perform them by one holding the right to authorize, and this right of performance under authorization is called a *key*.

As already stated, Christ said to Peter, "And I will give unto thee the keys of the kingdom of heaven: and whatsoever thou shalt bind on earth shall be bound in heaven: and whatsoever thou shalt loose on earth shall be loosed in heaven."[14] We have already noted that though the Apostles had been ordained and therefore held the Priesthood, they had not this binding and loosing power, until Christ gave them the keys, which he later did, bestowing these powers upon all the Twelve.[15]

Later in the Upper Chamber on the evening of the day of the resurrection, he bestowed upon his Apostles other *keys* which theretofore they had not possessed:

"Whose soever sins ye remit, they are remitted unto them; and whose soever sins ye retain, they are retained."[16]

The command to preach and baptize given to the Twelve on the mount, prior to Christ's ascension, was not a bestowal of special powers as of that time, for the Apostles had been preaching and baptizing from the beginning of their ministry with Jesus;[17] it was a direction as to their service. In our day the Lord has revealed that he bestowed upon Peter, James, and John "the keys of this ministry until I come."[18]

John the Revelator, being "in the Spirit on the Lord's day," heard a voice that declared, "I am Alpha and Omega, the first and the last. . . . I am he that liveth, and was dead; and, behold, I am alive for evermore, Amen; and have the keys of hell and of death."[19]

This being the Dispensation of the Fullness of Times, and "made up of all the dispensations that ever have been given since the world began, until this time,"[20] it was necessary that all powers and authorities and functions, ever heretofore existing on the earth since the beginning, as well as all those additional and necessary for the full salvation and exaltation of man, must be restored to the earth or newly bestowed thereon. As Paul said:

"That in the dispensation of the fullness of times he might gather together in one all things in Christ, both which are in heaven, and which are on earth."[21]

So even before the Church was organized the keys incident to the Gospel in the last dispensation began to be restored.

Moroni came to Joseph with the "keys of the record of the stick of Ephraim."[22]

John the Baptist came and bestowed the keys of the Aaronic Priesthood.[23]

Shortly after the organization of the Church (August, 1830), the Prophet Joseph was told of the keys held by Elias[24] and Elijah,[25] and Peter, James, and John, the Lord declaring, as to these latter:

". . . By whom I have ordained you and confirmed you to be apostles, and especial witnesses of my name, and bear the keys of your ministry and of the same things which I revealed unto them; unto whom I have committed the keys of my kingdom, and a dispensation of the gospel for the last times; and for the fulness of times, in the which I will gather together in one all things, both which are in heaven, and which are on earth."[26]

In a later revelation the Lord declared:

"Which power you hold, in connection with all those who have received a dispensation at any time from the beginning of the creation; for verily I say unto you, the keys of the dispensation, which ye have received, have come down from the fathers, and last of all, being sent down from heaven unto you."[27] And again, "And the keys which I have given unto him, and also to youward, (the Apostles) shall not be taken from him till I come."[28]

A like bestowal was made upon Joseph of "the keys of the mysteries of the kingdom," never to be taken from him "while he liveth, inasmuch as he obeyeth mine ordinances."[29]

At another time the Lord spoke of "the keys of this kingdom and ministry"[30] which he had bestowed upon Joseph and also "the keys of the church."[31] The Lord also said, in a revelation directed to Frederick G. Williams, as a Counselor to the Prophet:

"Unto whom (the Prophet) I have given the keys of the kingdom, which belong always unto the Presidency of the High Priesthood."[32]

And speaking of the Twelve, the Lord said:

"Which Twelve hold the keys to open up the authority of my kingdom upon the four corners of the earth, and after that to send my word to every creature."[33]

In this same revelation,[34] the Lord, after naming general ward and stake offices, said:

"The above offices I have given unto you, and the keys thereof, for helps and for governments, for the work of the ministry and the perfecting of my saints."[35]

Speaking in connection with the matter of baptism for the dead, of the keys promised to Peter at Caesarea Philippi[36] and later bestowed upon all the Twelve,[37] that is, the power to bind or loose, the Prophet said:

"For him to whom these keys are given there is no difficulty in obtaining a knowledge of facts in relation to the salvation of the children of men, both as well for the dead as for the living."[38]

Sometimes special keys are bestowed upon particular individuals for especial reasons, as for example the exceptional power and authority conferred upon Hyrum Smith, the Patriarch,[39] and some keys are held by only one person on the earth at a time.[40]

Two great visions were given to Joseph Smith and Oliver Cowdery in the Kirtland Temple on April 3, 1836, in the first, 'the veil being taken from their minds and the eyes of their understanding being opened,' they beheld the Lord standing in majesty on the breastwork of the pulpit, declaring he was Jehovah.

"After this vision closed, the heavens were again opened unto us; and Moses appeared before us, and committed unto us the keys of the gathering of Israel from the four parts of the earth, and the leading of the ten tribes from the land of the north.

After this, Elias appeared, and committed the dispensation of the gospel of Abraham, saying that in us and our seed all generations after us should be blessed. After this vision had closed, another great and glorious vision burst upon us; for Elijah the prophet, who was taken to heaven without tasting death, stood before us, and said: Behold, the time has fully come, which was spoken of by the mouth of Malachi—testifying that he (Elijah) should be sent, before the great and dreadful day of the Lord come—To turn the hearts of the fathers to the children, and the children to the fathers, lest the whole earth be smitten with a curse—Therefore, the keys of this dispensation are committed into your hands; and by this ye may know that the great and dreadful day of the Lord is near, even at the doors."[41]

The Prophet, recounting other heavenly manifestations, declared:

"And again, the voice of God in the chamber of old Father Whitmer, in Fayette, Seneca County, and at sundry times, and in divers places through all the travels and tribulations of this Church of Jesus Christ of Latter-day Saints! And the voice of Michael, the archangel; the voice of Gabriel, and of Raphael, and of divers angels, from Michael or Adam down to the present time, all declaring their dispensation, their rights, their keys, their honors, their majesty and glory, and the power of their priesthood; giving line upon line, precept upon precept; here a little, and there a little; giving us consolation by holding forth that which is to come, confirming our hope!"[42]

Thus has there come to earth and been bestowed upon God's servants, those whom he chose to lead his Kingdom in this the Last Dispensation, the Dispensation of the Fullness of Times, the great keys of authority that set in motion the Gospel principles by and through which all men may be saved and exalted, if they will. And all these keys have been duly transmitted and are now held by the leadership of the Church.

May we who may profit by their use, gain testimony that they are and that they operate to the blessing of each of us on our way to immortality and eternal life, I humbly pray, in the Lord's name. Amen.

---

[1]D.C. 107:3. [2]Mark 3:14 ff. [3]Matt. 16:14-19. [4]Matt. 18:18. [5]D.C. 13. [6]D.C. 20. [7]Luke 1:11 ff. [8]D.C. 20. [9]Gen. 4:5. [10]Num. 3:4. [11]Num. 16. [12]I Chron. 13:9-10; Num. 1:51; 3:31, 38. [13]D.C. 132:8. [14]Matt. 16:19. [15]Matt. 18:18. [16]John 20:23. [17]John 3:22, 26; 4:1-2. [18]D.C. 7:7. [19]Rev. 1:10-11, 18; and see I Cor. 15:55 ff. [20]The Millennial Star, XVI, p. 220. [21]Eph. 1:10. [22]D.C. 27:5. [23]D.C. 13. [24]D.C. 27:6. [25]D.C. 27:9. [26]D.C. 27:12-13; and see 97:14. [27]D.C. 112:31-32. [28]D.C. 112:15; and see 90:3. [29]D.C. 64:5; see also 28:7; 35:18. [30]D.C. 115:19; see also 65:2. [31]D.C. 42:69. [32]D.C. 81:2. [33]D.C. 124: 128. See as to keys connected with the baptism for the dead, D.C. 124:33. [34]D.C. 124. [35]D.C. 124:143. [36]Matt. 16:18-19. [37]Matt. 18:18. [38]D.C. 128:11. [39]D.C. 124:91-92, 97. [40]D.C. 132:7. [41]D.C. 110:11-16. [42]D.C. 128:21.

XXIII

SALVATION FOR THE DEAD

IN an earlier talk[1] we learned that through the atonement of Christ all men may live again in a life everlasting, with body and spirit reunited. This blessing Jesus purchased for us with his own life. But we also saw that our place, or station and position, in the hereafter must be bought by ourselves by and through our good works.[2] Ancient and modern revelations make clear that because we are not all equally righteous, are not equally zealous in good works, some of us will rise to a celestial glory—the highest glory; others, to a terrestrial glory, the next highest; still others, to the telestial glory, the lowest glory of all; while some will rise to an existence without glory.[3] Out of the upper chamber and from the Last Supper, comes the word of Christ: "In my Father's house are many mansions: if it were not so, I would have told you. I go to prepare a place for you."[4]

We noted that these good works and this righteousness of ours are measured by the fullness with which we keep the commandments of the Lord, obeying the laws, principles, and ordinances of the Gospel; and men's obedience thereto is determined partly by their own willingness to obey, and partly by the knowledge they have of truth.

We may say in passing, that these Gospel laws, principles, and ordinances are not born of the caprice of Deity, but are founded upon, indeed are the expressions of, great fundamental truths that govern and control the growth of the spirits of men; and that, therefore, where these principles are unheeded there is no resultant growth, and where there is no spiritual growth there is no glory.

When these laws, principles, and ordinances are unknown, they will be observed only as a matter of accident.

An ancient prophet has said:

"Where there is no law given there is no punishment; and where there is no punishment there is no condemnation."[5]

Thus men will not be punished for not keeping a spiritual law of which they had no knowledge. But by the same token they, not observing the law, cannot receive the blessing of spiritual growth which observance thereof brings.

As we noted in our talk on the Dispensation of the Fullness of Times,[6] there were periods following each dispensation opening, when man became "carnal, sensual, and devilish,"[7] so that the Lord at one time declared "My spirit shall not always strive with man," since "every imagination of the thoughts of men's hearts was only evil continually."[8]

In these long periods of spiritual darkness which closed each dispensation and was at once the need and the cause for a new dispensation—another revealing of the Gospel laws, principles, and commandments—untold millions lived and died without any knowledge of the great spiritual truths. Thus they were without opportunity to keep them, and without the opportunity for growth which comes to those who know of them. That the Divine teachings were not on the earth when they lived was no fault of theirs. (I pass for now the question of why these spirits came to the earth in apostate eras instead of in a gospel dispensation.)

What is to become, in the hereafter, of these myriads, dying without opportunity to live the Gospel and obey its principles, laws and ordinances? What is their place, their station? Are they to live on in eternity, reunited in body and spirit because of the atonement of Christ, but without any glory, left in that realm of action where their chance obedience, or disobedience, as might have been their lot, placed them?

Clearly such a fate would not accord with our human estimate of right and justice, of equity and humanity. The Scriptures leave us without doubt, indeed with a knowledge beyond dispute, that such a fate is not in accord with God's justice, mercy, and love. He has planned far otherwise.

But how shall the dead, who have not heard the Gospel, have opportunity to hear, know, and obey?

In this relation we can never forget the words of Jesus to Martha as she spoke to him in gentle reproof that he was not with them when Lazarus died, else he had not died; that Jesus replying that Lazarus would rise again, Martha responded she knew he would rise again in the resurrection at the last day; and then the great declaration of Jesus to her, and to all who have ever lived on earth, a declaration of one of the great ultimate truths:

"I am the resurrection, and the life: he that believeth in me, though he were dead, yet shall he live: and whosoever liveth and believeth in me shall never die."[9]

Answering the Jews who, angered by his healing on the Sabbath of the man at the pool of Bethesda, sought to kill him, Jesus said:

"Verily, verily, I say unto you, He that heareth my word, and believeth on him that sent me, hath everlasting life, and shall not come into condemnation; but is passed from death unto life.

"Verily, verily, I say unto you, The hour is coming, and now is, when the dead shall hear the voice of the Son of God: and they that hear shall live. . . .

"Marvel not at this: for the hour is coming, in the which all that are in the graves shall hear his voice,

"And shall come forth; they that have done good, unto the resurrection of life; and they that have done evil, unto the resurrection of damnation."[10]

Jesus evidently taught his Apostles the Gospel plan on this subject, for it was later directly touched upon by two of them.

Peter in his first epistle explains:

"For Christ also hath once suffered for sins the just for the unjust, that he might bring us to God, being put to death in the flesh, but quickened by the Spirit:

"By which also he went and preached unto the spirits in prison;

"Which sometime were disobedient, when once the long suffering of God waited in the days of Noah, while the ark was a preparing, wherein few, that is, eight souls were saved by water."[11]

It was concerning these people of the days of Noah, to whom Christ now went to preach, that the Lord had said:

"My spirit shall not always strive with man . . .

"And God saw that the wickedness of man was great in the earth, and that every imagination of the thoughts of his heart was only evil continually.

". . . And it grieved him at his heart."[12]

Peter went still further in his teachings and told us in what position the spirits in prison were left by this preaching. After telling of the wickedness in which the people walked, Peter said:

"Who shall give account to him that is ready to judge the quick and the dead.

"For for this cause was the gospel preached also to them that are dead, that they might be judged according to men in the flesh, but live according to God in the spirit."[13]

Peter referred again to this matter when he was speaking to Cornelius and the many that were with him as Peter met them,—for after first pointing out that the resurrected Christ appeared "unto witnesses chosen before of God, even to us, who did eat and drink with him after he rose from the dead," Peter added:

"And he commanded us to preach unto the people, and to testify that it is he which was ordained of God to be the Judge of quick and dead."[14]

Thus Peter taught that Christ is to judge all men, both the quick and the dead; that to fit them for this judgment all are to have the Gospel preached to them; that Christ himself set the example by going and preaching to the imprisoned spirits of the disobedient of Noah's day; that these spirits so taught were to be judged according to men in the flesh, but to live according to God in the spirit.

Thus the dead are to have opportunity to secure blessings that come from living the Gospel.

We should recall here that Jesus, in Jerusalem attending his First Passover after the beginning of his ministry, was visited by the cautious, yet believing Nicodemus, who came to Jesus after nightfall, and that to him Jesus preached his first great recorded sermon,—a sermon about baptism and the Holy Ghost. After a few opening words, Jesus declared:

"Verily, verily, I say unto thee, Except a man be born of water and of the Spirit, he cannot enter into the kingdom of God."[15]

Before this, Jesus had come to the Jordan where John was baptizing, asking baptism of John, and, John demurring, Jesus said to him: "Suffer it to be so now: for thus it becometh us to fulfill all righteousness."[16] Thus baptism is of such prime need and value, that even the Son of God, the Only Begotten, must be baptized to fulfill all righteousness.

We may refer to another instance. The resurrected Christ, giving his final instructions just before his ascension into heaven to sit on the right hand of the Father, commanded the Apostles, saying to them, "All power is given unto me in heaven and in earth,"[17] "go ye into all the world, and preach the gospel to every creature,"[18] "teaching all nations,"[19] "he that believeth and is baptized shall be saved; but he that believeth not shall be damned."[20]

Thus if words can make anything clear it is certain that belief and baptism are necessary for salvation. Then what shall be done for the untold millions who have died without belief and baptism? Paul understood the matter, for speaking to the Corinthians in an oft quoted passage, he said:

"Else what shall they do which are baptized for the dead, if the dead rise not at all? why are they then baptized for the dead?"[21]

This is a plain recognition of the principle that all men must be baptized to be saved, and that baptism for those who are dead is to be done vicariously. The doctrine of vicarious service is instinct in the whole law of Moses, and is basic to Christian faith, because Christ vicariously suffered and died for all in an atonement for the fall of Adam.

In an article on baptism (early Christian) Dr. Kirsopp Lake (Professor of Ecclesiastical History in Harvard University) writes as follows:

"It would also seem from I Cor. 15:29 that St. Paul recognized the practice of vicarious baptism for the dead. It is impossible that 'Else what shall they do who are baptized for the dead? If the dead are not raised at all, why then are they baptized for them?' can refer to anything except vicarious baptism."[22]

But the principle was lost early in the history of the post-Primitive Church. There was still some vestige of it in the middle of the second century after Christ, when the Pastor of Hermas[23] spoke of the matter but seemingly taught that not only was the Gospel preached to the spirits of the dead by the spirits of those who had the Gospel in the flesh, but that the spirits of the righteous baptized in the spirit world the spirits of the unrighteous, the Pastor saying: "Accordingly they descended with them into the water, and again ascended."

But obviously Paul was not speaking of such an ordinance as this taking place in the spirit world. He spoke of mortals being baptized vicariously for those who were dead.

The teachings of the Pastor drew the approval of Clement of Alexandria (writing at about the same time), but with still further corruption of the principle.[24]

Tertullian (virtually a contemporary of both the Pastor and Clement of Alexandria) in his argument against Marcion (who contended the God of the Old Testament was not the God of the New Testament),[25] dismissed Paul's statement about baptism for the dead by saying: "Now, never mind that practice, (whatever it may have been). The Februarian lustrations will perhaps answer him (quite as well), by praying for the dead."[26]

A special propitiatory rite or ceremony (amburbium) was held on each February 2. "It was the interest of the State to see that its concord with the gods remained unbroken. This purpose was secured in particular by the periodical observance of lustrations, which served both to purify their object from all contracted stains and to ensure a renewal of divine protection against the danger of further contamination. The lustration was accomplished by symbolic acts of cleansing with water or fire, or by a procession conducting the sacrificial victim round the area which required purification."[27]

Dr. Lake doubts that Tertullian "was acquainted with any contemporary Christian custom of baptism for the dead."[28] If this be true then by Tertullian's time the principle had been lost. But Tertullian's words would suggest that by the end of the second century they were offering prayers for the dead in lieu of baptism for the dead, a great corruption of the vicarious baptism for the dead of which Paul wrote, a corruption which still maintains in certain great churches.

But in this the Dispensation of the Fullness of Times, this great principle has been again revealed; the ordinance of baptism for the dead has been reestablished; temples have been built, dedicated to the Most High, in which this sacred ordinance is performed.

The members of the Church are hunting out the names of their ancestors, and, learning the names, they are baptized for these ancestors, that the dead may hear the Gospel, believe, if they are so blessed, and so "be judged according to men in the flesh, but live according to God in the spirit."[29] Hundreds of thousands of those who have gone to the other side have been blessed by the performance of this vicarious ordinance in their behalf.

Thus the keys bestowed upon the Prophet Joseph Smith in the Kirtland Temple by Elijah the ancient prophet, have opened the door of salvation to the numberless dead,—"the hearts of the fathers have been turned to the children, and the hearts of the children to the fathers," so escaping the threatened curse that otherwise would have afflicted the earth.

So the plan is perfected in this dispensation of the restoration of all things, for the tender of salvation to every being born to this earth, in whatever place and at whatever time he lived. This plan makes certain that no soul shall be without salvation, except by his own choice.

May the Lord speed the carrying out of this glorious plan by which all may be saved and given opportunity for exaltation in the kingdom of God, I pray, in the name of him who died for us all. Amen.

---

[1]Talk No. 20. [2]John 5:29. [3]I Cor. 15:36 ff.; D.C. 76 and 88. [4]John 14:2. [5]2 Nephi 9:25 ff. [6]Talk No. 15. [7]Moses 5:13. [8]Gen. 6:3, 5. [9]John 11:21-26. [10]John 5:24-25, 28-29. [11]I Pet. 3:18-20. [12]Gen. 6:3, 5-6. [13]I Pet. 4:5-6. [14]Acts 10:41-42; II Tim. 4:1; Rom. 14:9. [15]John 3:5. [16]Matt. 3:15. [17]Matt. 28:18. [18]Mark 16:15. [19]Matt. 28:19. [20]Mark 16:16. [21]I Cor. 15:29. [22]Hastings, *Encyclopaedia of Religion and Ethics*, sub voce *Baptism*, p. 382a. [23]*The Ante-Nicene Fathers*, Coxe ed., The Pastor of Hermas, III, S. IX, Ch. XV-XVI. [24]*Op cit.*, Stromata, II, Ch. IX; for Pastor of Hermas, see II, p. 49; Clement, p. 357. [25]Newman, *A Manual of Church History*, I, p. 191 ff. [26]Tertullian against Marcion, *The Ante-Nicene Fathers*, III, p. 449. [27]A. C. Pearson in Hastings, *Encyc.*, sub voce *Propitiation (Roman)* p. 399. [28]Hastings, *Encyc.*, sub voce *Baptism*, p. 387a. [29]I Pet. 4:6.

XXIV

THE LORD STILL SPEAKS
TO HIS CHILDREN

WE quoted in our talk on the visit of Moroni to Joseph[1] that Joseph's first vision of the Father and the Son was scoffed at by many people, who said "there were no such things as visions or revelations in these days; that all such things had ceased with the apostles, and that there would never be any more of them."[2] This continues to be the doctrine of the great churches of the sectarian world,—Catholic and Protestant.

It is not put quite so plainly and bluntly as this in their creeds, but it is the principle lying behind their provisions.

We shall not have time tonight for a consideration of the actual texts of their creeds, but we may draw therefrom some important conclusions.

The Western Church—the Catholic Church—laid down its dogmas on this question at the Council of Trent (Session of April 8, 1546) and reaffirmed them in the Vatican Council of 1870 where the doctrine of the infallibility of the Pope was announced and formally adopted. The creed of the Church seems clearly to come to this: The written words of the canons of the Old and New Testament and the unwritten traditions of the Church are to be received as the full revelation of God to man; the written word must be received in all its parts as containing the Gospel of Christ and anyone not so receiving it is anathema. In matters of faith and morals the Pope is infallible in determining and declaring the true doctrine thereon, and any person contesting this infallibility is anathema.[3]

In other words, there is no further revelation of Gospel truths pertaining to faith and morals either necessary or acceptable; thus continuous revelation from God is in effect denied. In the provisions defining infallibility no claim is found that the Pope may or does receive further revelations from God on the matters concerning which he issues his pronouncements, but only that his decisions on matters of faith and morals are infallible. He is an interpreter, not a revelator.

The Eastern Church—the Orthodox Catholic Church—apparently follows the Western Church in the essential parts of doctrine on this point, and defines tradition thusly:

"By the name holy tradition is meant the doctrine of the faith, the law of God, the sacraments, and the ritual as handed down by the true believers and worshipers of God by word and example from one to another, and from generation to generation."

St. Basil is quoted as citing as matters of tradition,—the making of the sign of the cross, invocation in the ceremony of the eucharist, the 'blessing of the water of baptism,' the oil of unction, the anointing with oil, the rule of trine immersion. St. Basil then asks. 'What is the written word for these,' "from what Scripture are they taken?   Are they not all from this unpublished and private teaching, which our Fathers kept under a reserve inaccessible to curiosity and profane disquisition. . . ."[4]

Thus admittedly for these named matters of tradition there is no authority therefor in the recorded words of Christ and the Apostles. It seems clear that the great Eastern and Western Churches hold virtually the same views and they adhere to the same dogmas in the matter of the non-continuance of further revelation from God.

The Old Catholic Union Church has the same dogma, but guards the matters of tradition.[5]

The Church of England holds that the "Holy Scripture containeth all things necessary to salvation: so that whatsoever is not read therein, nor may be proved thereby, is not to be required of any man, that it should be believed as an article of the Faith, or be thought requisite or necessary to salvation."[6]

The Reformed Episcopal Church has virtually the same provision,[7] as also the Belgic Confession (the Reformed Church),[8] the Free-Will Baptist,[9] and the New Hampshire Baptist Churches,[10] as also the Methodist.[11]

It is not necessary at this time to comment upon the creeds of other churches. All of those considered make clear two doctrines: That the canon of scriptures is full (though they differ among themselves as to which books are canonical and which are not), and that nothing which is not found in the canon of scripture, is required of any man either to believe or practice for his salvation.

At this point we might note the provisions of our own creed (our Articles of Faith) in respect of these matters. These read:

"We believe the Bible to be the word of God as far as it is translated correctly; we also believe the Book of Mormon to be the word of God.

"We believe all that God has revealed, all that He does now reveal, and we believe that He will yet reveal many great and important things pertaining to the Kingdom of God."

We may offer here a few observations on the canon of scriptures to which the sectarian Christian world ties its faith.

In the first place, the scriptures which the sectarian world regard as containing the full revelation of God's will to man, are not the full scriptures. There are lost books. Dr. James E. Talmage in his doctrinal classic, "The Articles of Faith," lists a number of them in his notes at the end of his Lecture XIII, "The Holy Bible."

If man is to be fully taught, then the truths of these books must be placed before God's children, either by a recovery of the books themselves or by direct revelation of the truths contained in them.

We may note again that not only are some books lost, but even as to those which we have, not all sects accept the same books. The Protestant churches seem generally to use the King James Bible, the same Bible that is used by our Church. The Catholic Church, however, has added to their Bible several books not found in the King James Bible.[12]

These collections of accepted sacred writings

are called the Canon of Scripture. Our purpose and our time do not call for, nor permit us to discuss the formation of our Bible,—the Canon of Scripture. What books should make up the Old Testament Canon was discussed back in the days of ancient Israel. Some writings were included, some rejected; some were declared canonical, others apocryphal. As Sanday said:

"It is true that no book either of the New Testament or of the Old 'was born with the predicate "canonical." ' " But, he adds further, "we are prepared to maintain that all the books both of OT and NT, though no doubt with very considerable differences of degree, were born with the qualities which caused them to be labelled 'canonical'; in other words, with the marks that are summed up under the name of Inspiration."[13]

The final Canon of the New Testament was also fixed after long discussions and disputes, with inclusions and exclusions, until an acceptable canon was at last found.

Concerning these inclusions and exclusions in the Old Testament, Dr. Ryle is quoted as saying:

"They reflect the subtlety of academic discussion more than the anxiety of a perplexed conscience."[14]

It would seem that any claim that the building of the Canon of Scripture is the result of God's revelation or inspiration to men, is a matter of grave question in the minds of many critics, and theologians also, and one writer logically says:

"Thus we have the rather remarkable result that inspiration in the sense of a supernatural guar-

antee for their truth and authority is claimed for
a series of writings, while no claim is, or can be,
made for a supernatural determination of the precise writings which are to be included in the series.
. . . So long as inspiration cannot be claimed for the
process by which canonicity is determined, canonicity cannot be held to fix the bounds of inspiration."[16]

Thus, on the thesis that God has made his final
revelation to man, we note that some books containing such revelations are lost, that others are accepted
by some only, and rejected by others. So, if we are
to consider the sacred scriptures given down to the
forming of the canons as the final revelation from
God to man, there must be further revelation from
God to someone declaring what books contain the
revelations he has already given. This situation
poses a dilemma that can only be solved by admitting
the necessity for and seeking further revelation.

Then there is, in this matter of further revelation, this added dilemma involving eternal justice,—
how is it that God during the pre-Messianic Dispensations should believe it both necessary and in
accordance with his infinite love and mercy, to reveal
his mind and will and at times to manifest himself to
his children wandering in a wilderness of spiritual
darkness and sin, and yet following the Meridian of
Time, and the offering of the great Atoning Sacrifice, the Lord should shut off these revelations, and
make of the Heavens a barren sanctuary, offering
neither spiritual food nor drink to the hungry pilgrims treading the road of a transgressing mortality.

The divine word has always spoken of help to God's children as individuals, as well as *en masse.*

Jesus so spoke to the multitudes after John's questioning disciples had left to return to John;[16] so also his final words to his disciples before his ascension.[17] David sang in poetic line that the Lord "leadeth me in the paths of righteousness for his name's sake."[18] Amos declared, "Surely the Lord God will do nothing, but he revealeth his secret unto his servants the prophets;"[19] and Daniel declared the same principle to Nebuchadnezzar.[20] Paul so spoke of the Lord's help, to the Galatians,[21] to the Corinthians,[22] to the Ephesians,[23] and to the Hebrews,[24] while Peter spoke of the revelations that might come to the saints.[25]

Looked at calmly and without previous prejudice or conviction, is it not really a monstrous thought that, while all through the ages from Adam down to the time of the Primitive Church (the Church of Christ and his Apostles) God continuously spoke to his children; to Noah, for the guidance of himself and family and of the people; to Abraham, as he left the parental roof and also in Egypt and Palestine; to Moses, as he led the children of Israel; to Joshua in his work of conquest; to Samuel, to Elijah, to Elisha, to David, to Solomon, and to the Apostles in their labors, at times in daily ministrations, counselling and advising all of them, giving them laws, principles, and ordinances by which they should guide their lives, likewise revealing his mind and will to them from time to time in their great trials, tribulations, persecutions, sorrows, in their path-determining crises, and in their personal problems, and yet, that with all this help to his children in past ages, and indeed since the closing of the ministry of John the Beloved, that now the Lord has closed the heavens; that God no longer speaks to us, his children, though averring for us, over and over again, his infinite love and mercy; that he leaves us to make our way as best we may with no current counsel or advice or commandment from him; that he watches us unmoved as we wander in densest darkness, stumbling in wickedness, plunging forward to destruction? I say again, is not this a monstrous thought? And it will not do to answer that we have the Gospel of Christ and the ancients did not, for Paul tells us the Gospel was preached to Abraham,[26] and Jesus told the Jews at the Second Passover that Moses 'wrote of him,'[27] and we know from modern scriptures that the Gospel was preached from the beginning.

An earthly father would not so treat his children, to say nothing of the holy mother love that reaches down even into the depths of hell to claim her own. How infinitely less would our Heavenly Father, with his boundless, eternal love and mercy, see his children plunge to destruction without stretching forth his hand to stay or guide them, without whispering to them his will, without revealing through his ordained servant the way that would lead them back to him out of the morass of iniquity through which they struggle.

But the reason for this monstrous concept is not far to seek. Leaders, knowing in their hearts that they do not possess the Priesthood of God, and, therefore, that they have not the right to receive revelations from God for the guidance of his children, have found convenient escape from their dilemma in the doctrine that the canon of revelation is full and that God no longer speaks to his children. How great the responsibility of those who so teach!

But we of our Church know God does still speak to his children in their joys and in their distress; that he leads them, occasion requiring, in their personal affairs, in their daily trials. He makes known his will and wisdom to the righteous in divers ways— by the visitation of heavenly beings, by his own voice, by dreams and visions (as he has promised), by the whisperings of the still, small voice (as to Elijah on the mount), by the sweet influence of his Spirit, and by the promptings of the Holy Ghost.

He promised all this to us, through the Prophet James, who declared:

"If any of you lack wisdom, let him ask of God, that giveth to all men liberally, and upbraideth not; and it shall be given him"—this promise is to every one of God's children—any man—not to the select few only, not to the chosen people alone, not to a favored nation, but to each and every one of us born on the earth.

James continues:

"But let him ask in faith, nothing wavering. For he that wavereth is like a wave of the sea driven with the wind and tossed.

"For let not that man think that he shall receive any thing of the Lord.

"A double minded man is unstable in all his ways."[28]

From the ancient days, from Adam down through all dispensations till this the Last Dispensation of the Fullness of Times, the Lord has revealed his mind and will to his prophets and the leaders of the dispensations. He has come to them in personal appearance, as to Adam in the Garden, to Enoch,[29] to Abraham,[30] to Jacob, [31] to Moses,[32] to Daniel,[33] to the Brother of Jared.[34] He has also spoken by audible voice to his servants, as to Adam after the Fall, to Noah,[35] to Abraham, to Moses, to Samuel,[36] to Elijah on the Mount,[37] to Saul of Tarsus,[38] to Jesus at the time of his baptism,[39] to Peter, James, and John at the time of the transfiguration,[40] to Jesus in the Temple,[41] to the Nephites on the American continent.[42]

To the major and minor prophets of olden times, the Lord gave his messages, spoke his will.

Jeremiah declared:

"The word of the Lord came unto me saying" (Jeremiah 1:4), and Enos said: "The voice of the Lord came into my mind again, saying."[43]

This dispensation has proceeded from the very first as have the others: An opening theophany to Joseph, a visitation of the Father and Son in person in the First Vision, so opening the dispensation; and this was followed in due course by the visitation of an angel, Moroni. Then a great series of revelations in which, speaking through Joseph, the Lord declared, as he declared through David in the Psalms, through Isaiah, Jeremiah, and all the rest, speaking in variant phrase in his own proper person: "Behold,

I am God;"[44] "I am Alpha and Omega;"[45] "I am the Great I am;"[46] "even Jesus Christ your Redeemer;"[47] "Behold I say unto you;"[48] 'Listen to my words or voice;"[49] "Hearken unto the voice of the Lord,"[50] or unto "my word,"[51] or "unto me;"[52] "Behold, thus saith the Lord;"[53] "Behold, blessed, saith the Lord;"[54] 'Hearken, O ye elders or people of my Church;'[55] "Behold, and hearken;"[56] "Hearken, and lo, a voice;"[57] "Hearken, and listen to the voice of the Lord;"[58] "Hear, O ye heavens, and give ear, O earth;"[59] "Verily I say unto you;"[60] "Verily, thus saith the Lord;"[61] or "Verily this is the word of the Lord;"[62] "It is my will;"[63] "I, the Lord your God, am not displeased;"[64] "I am the Lord thy God."[65]

The account of the great vision in the Kirtland Temple is opened by the sublime announcement, "The veil was taken from our minds, and the eyes of our understanding were opened."[66]

Thus God has spoken, is speaking, and will continue to speak, so long as we keep open the line of communication with him. God is a God of continuous revelation. He stands always ready to speak to us in a way we shall understand, if we keep his laws and commandments. He has spoken and is speaking to his Church, through his chosen and ordained servant, his Prophet, Seer, and Revelator, who, through the continuous revelation God gives to him, will direct the Lord's work and the Lord's people, if they will but listen to him.

I bear testimony to all this in the name of him who died that we might live, Jesus Christ. Amen.

[1]Talk 18. [2]History of Joseph Smith, P. of G. P., v. 21. [3]Schaff, *Creeds of Christendom*, II, p. 80 ff., 240 ff., 253, 270-271. [4]*Id.*, p. 448-455. [5]*Id.*, p. 548. [6]The Thirty-Nine Articles of Religion of the Church of England, —English Edition 1571, American Revision 1801, Schaff, *Creeds*, III, p.489-492. [7]Schaff, *Creeds*, III, p. 815-816. [8]*Id.*, p. 384-389. [9]*Id.*, p. 749. [10]*Id.*, p. 742. [11]*Id.*, p. 808. [12]See Douay's Bible; also Fourth Session, Council of Trent, April 8, 1546, Schaff, *Creeds*, II, p. 79 ff.; for the canon of the Eastern Church see p. 451. [13]Hastings, *Encyclopaedia of Religion and Ethics*, sub voce *Bible*, p. 577a. [14]A *New Standard Bible Dictionary*, sub voce *Old Testament, Canon of* p. 637. [15]Dr. Alexander Stewart, St. Mary's College, University of St. Andrews, in Hastings, *Dictionary of the Bible*, sub voce *Bible*, p. 297a. See on the whole subject of the Canon of Scripture, Hastings, *Encyc.*, sub voce *Bible; The New Schaff-Herzog Encyclopedia of Religious Knowledge*, sub voce *Canon of Scripture; Stand. Bible Dict.*, sub voce *Old Testament, Canon of*, and *New Testament, Canon of;* Hastings, *Dict.*, sub voce *Bible;* (see same article for an understandable discussion of inspiration and revelation from the sectarian standpoint); and sub voce *Canon.* [16]Matt. 11:28-30. [17]Matt. 28:20. [18]Psa. 23:1-4. [19]Amos 3:7. [20]Dan. 2:28. [21]Gal. 2:2. [22]I Cor. 14:6-26; II Cor. 12:1 ff. [23]Eph. 1:17. [24]Heb. 1:1 ff. [25]I Pet. 1:13. [26]Gal. 3:8. [27]John 5:46. [28]James 1:5-8. [29]Gen. 5:22; Moses 7:4. [30]Gen. 12:7; 17:1; 18:1. [31]Gen. 28:12 ff.; 32:30. [32]Ex. 33: 11. [33]Dan. 10. [34]Ether 3. [35]Gen. 6:13; 9:1. [36]I Sam. 3. [37]I Kings 19:11 ff. [38]Acts 9:3-8; 22:6-11; 26:12-18. [39]Matt. 3:13-17; Mark 1:9-11; Luke 3:15-22. [40]Matt. 17:1-13; Mark 9:2-13; Luke 9:28-36. [41]John 12:28. [42]3 Nephi 9 ff. [43]Enos 10. [44]D.C. 6, 11, 12, 14. [45]D.C. 19, 35, 38, 75. [46]D.C. 29, 38. [47]D.C. 34. [48]D.C. 5, 8, 9, 10, 17, 22, 23, 26, 28, 30, 32, 33, 36, 42, 53, 96. [49]D.C. 1, 15, 16, 27, 29. [50]D.C. 25. [51]D.C. 49. [52]D.C. 51, 69, 78. [53]D.C. 44, 52, 55, 60, 64, 66, 71, 99. [54]D.C. 59. [55]D.C. 41, 42, 43, 45, 46, 50, 56, 57, 58, 62, 63, 67. [56]D.C. 70. [57]D.C. 65. [58]D.C. 72. [59]D.C. 76. [60]D.C. 7, 79, 81, 82, 94, 97, 98, 101, 103, 104, 105. [61]D.C. 80, 83, 86, 87, 88, 90, 91, 92, 93, 95, 100, 108, 112, 113, 114, 115, 117, 118, 119, 120, 124, 132. [62]D.C. 84. [63]D.C. 106. [64]D.C. 111. [65]D.C. 132. [66]D.C. 110.

XXV

OUR SCRIPTURES

WE shall say a few words tonight about the sources to which we Latter-day Saints look for our knowledge of the Gospel as restored to the earth in these last days.

Since the Gospel has been preached in all ages from Adam on down[1]—Paul declared it was preached to Abraham,[2] and Jesus declared that Moses "wrote of me"[3]—we of the Church draw without limit from all the records we have of God's dealings with men as recorded by his holy prophets, for as Amos said:

"Surely the Lord God will do nothing, but he revealeth his secret unto his servants the prophets."[4]

In modern days he has affirmed that whatsoever his servants, duly authorized thereto, shall declare "when moved upon by the Holy Ghost shall be scripture, shall be the will of the Lord, shall be the mind of the Lord, shall be the word of the Lord, shall be the voice of the Lord, and the power of God unto salvation."[5]

The Articles of Faith (thirteen in number) of the Church of Jesus Christ of Latter-day Saints, the equivalent of the ordinary church creed, were drawn up by the Prophet Joseph Smith in early March, 1842. The eighth Article reads:

"We believe the Bible to be the word of God as

far as it is translated correctly; we also believe the Book of Mormon to be the word of God."

As to the Bible, the Prophet Joseph on another occasion (October 15, 1843) said:

"I believe the Bible as it read when it came from the pen of the original writers. Ignorant translators, careless transcribers, or designing and corrupt priests have committed many errors."[6]

We should keep in mind this appraisal of the Prophet as we proceed in our discussion tonight.

Furthermore, in what follows tonight, we should also keep foremost in our minds that the Christian sectarian world declares as a fundamental belief that the full revelation of God to man is contained in the Bible, and that God no longer gives revelations to his children.

Now, scholars do not deny that the original texts of the Bible have been corrupted, though they do not agree in all cases on the portions that are corrupted, nor in which of the variant texts is the corruption found, nor on the probable original text. But we are not concerned with these details tonight. We are interested only in the fact that there are corruptions and in how they came about.

Among the causes for corruption in the original texts, as listed by the distinguished scholars, Burgon and Miller of the Church of England, we may mention these: "inadvertency of the scribes," and later attempts to rectify them, but, as the authors observe: "A systematic and perpetual mutilation of the inspired Text must needs be the result of design, not

of accident.'" These authors then list as accidental
causes for corruption:

"Pure accident;"

Errors resulting from the omission or addition
of identical or nearly identical letters in close prox-
imity to one another;

Errors arising from the use of uncial "character, without accents, punctuation, or indeed any
division of the text;"[8]

Errors from "itacism," that is, misspelled words
and misplaced words, and from "liturgical influence," that is, "accommodating an ordinary copy,
whether of the Gospels or of the Epistles, to the requirements of the Church."[9]

Other causes of text corruption, listed as "chiefly intentional," are:

The "harmonistic influence," which resulted
from an effort to bring the narrative of the four
Gospels into harmony;

"Assimilation," or the improper transfer of the
expressions of one Evangelist to the writings of
another;

"Attraction," or "the proneness of words standing side by side in a sentence to be attracted into a
likeness of ending,—whether in respect of grammati-
cal form or of sound; whereby sometimes the sense
is made to suffer grievously,—sometimes entirely to
disappear;"[10]

"Omission" of words and clauses, "the largest
of all classes of corrupt variations from the genuine
Text," the authors stating that "omissions are much
in favour with a particular school of critics," and

citing as an illustration the discarding, as spurious, by some critics of the last twelve verses of St. Mark's Gospel, on what the authors regard as wholly insufficient evidence.[11]

The authors add as other intentional causes of text corruption—transposition, substitution, and addition, stating, "All the Corruption in the Sacred Text may be classed under four heads, viz. Omission, Transposition, Substitution, and Addition,"[12] the authors further adding as to certain kinds of changes: "they were inserted by men who entirely failed to realize the wrongness of what they did,— the mischievous consequences which might possibly ensue from their well-meant endeavours to improve the work of the HOLY GHOST."[13]

To the foregoing "chiefly intentional" causes of corruptions of the sacred text, the authors name:

"Glosses" (usually in the form of additions or substitutions), that is, "those explanatory words or clauses which have surreptitiously insinuated themselves into the text, and of which no more reasonable account can be rendered than that they were probably in the first instance proposed by some ancient Critic in the way of useful comment, or necessary explanation, or lawful expansion, or reasonable limitation of the actual utterance of the SPIRIT."[14]

There was also the corruption of heretics. The authors say, "In the age which immediately succeeded the Apostolic there were heretical teachers not a few, who finding their tenets refuted by the plain Word of GOD bent themselves against the written Word with all their power. From seeking to evacuate (sic) its teaching, it was but a single step to seeking to falsify its testimony."[15] Speaking of heretical doctrines concerning Christ's divine personality, and the attack by the heretics on the texts dealing therewith "with restless ingenuity," the author declares: "I do not say that Heretics were the only offenders here. I am inclined to suspect that the orthodox were as much to blame as the impugners of the Truth."[16]

Finally, the authors name corruption from "orthodox" sources, and make these preliminary observations to their own detailed study thereof:

"Another cause why, in very early times, the Text of the Gospels underwent serious depravation, was mistaken solicitude on the part of the ancient orthodox for the purity of the Catholic faith. These persons, like certain of the moderns, Beza for example, evidently did not think it at all wrong to tamper with the inspired Text. If any expression seemed to them to have a dangerous tendency, they altered it, or transplanted it, or removed it bodily from the sacred page. About the uncritical nature of what they did, they entertained no suspicion: about the immorality of the proceeding, they evidently did not trouble themselves at all. On the contrary, the piety of the motive seems to have been held to constitute a sufficient excuse for any amount of licence."[17]

In an earlier part of their discussion, the authors state:

"Indeed, the Ancient Liturgy of the Church has frequently exercised a corrupting influence on the text of Scripture."[18]

Having in mind the effect of all this textual tampering and corruptions upon the understanding and teachings of uninspired men, it is little wonder that the Lord in the First Vision repeated to Joseph what he had said in Palestine to the Pharisees who were complaining that the disciples violated "the tradition of the elders:"

"Well hath Esaias prophesied of you hypocrites, as it is written, This people honoreth me with their lips, but their heart is far from me.

"Howbeit in vain do they worship me, teaching for doctrines the commandments of men. . . .

"And he said unto them, Full well ye reject the commandment of God, that ye may keep your own tradition."[19]

This would seem a fitting and sufficient commentary on the traditions of some modern churches.

In another place the author affirms:

"I can but reflect on the utterly insecure basis on which the Revisers and the school which they follow would remodel the inspired Text."[20]

A consideration of the whole problem suggests that the virus of modern criticism is found in part, possibly principally, in the fact that these altered texts, including those the heretics and the Church tampered with, are treated by these higher critics, not as texts that have been deliberately corrupted, but as texts of variant readings having equal value and authority as original texts. The approach of the higher critics seems clearly to be to search out and use the corruptions in order to destroy the Bible as an inspired volume that sets out the dealings of

God with his children and his commandments to them, instead of attempting to find the corruptions and then eliminating them so as to establish the original text, as nearly as may be, and thereupon to learn its teachings.

It is a challenging fact that the unschooled Joseph Smith, in 1843, appraised the defects of the Bible on the very same points as these modern scholars, that is, that the original texts were corrupted by "ignorant translators, careless transcribers, or designing and corrupt priests." This was not a mere fortunate, haphazard appraisal; it was not based on worldly learning, for he did not possess it; it came only through inspiration.

The Bible accepted and used by this Church of ours is the King James translation.

Having in mind these corruptions, and particularly those deliberately made to make God's words conform to man-made dogmas, surely no one would be so careless as to say there is no more need for revelation from God, that the Bible as it is contains all. It did contain God's words as it came from the original inspired writers; but only part of God's words are there now. Further revelation must come to supply the omissions and to correct the corruptions. That revelation did come and is coming, and as God's work moves on more will come as needed.

Accordingly, alongside the Bible we place the Book of Mormon, which contains an account of God's dealings with and teachings to branches of the house of Israel, who came to this hemisphere in ancient times, of whom the American Indians are a residuary remnant. We have heretofore spoken of the coming forth of the Book of Mormon through the instrumentality of Moroni and Joseph Smith.

At about the time of the issuance of the Articles of Faith (March 1842), the Prophet Joseph published a translation of an Egyptian papyrus—The Book of Abraham—containing a partial history of Abraham and an account of the creation of the earth and the purpose thereof.

The Prophet worked upon an inspired revision of the Bible, correcting and supplementing the text of the King James translation with additional material. But he was martyred before this work was completed. The opening chapters of this revision (under the title, "Book of Moses") and the Book of Abraham, plus a retranslation of the twenty-fourth chapter of Matthew (beginning with the last verse of chapter twenty-three) are printed by the Church as the Pearl of Great Price.

From before the organization of the Church (April 6, 1830) until his martyrdom, the Prophet Joseph received from the Lord revelations containing principles and doctrines of the Gospel of Jesus Christ; as well as commandments, exhortations, directions, and sometimes reproofs—all dealing with the Restored Gospel and the organization of the Church, with its functioning and administration under the Holy Priesthood of God, and all having to do with the work, powers, and duties of the Church and its officers and members in this the Dispensation of the Fullness of Times. These revelations and others received by the Prophet's successors, are printed as the Doctrine and Covenants.

These four books—the Bible, the Book of Mormon, the Pearl of Great Price, and the Doctrine and Covenants—are of equal authority in the Church and have been so used in our talks. These scriptures declare the divine will of God, reveal his dealings with his peoples, and proclaim the Restored Gospel of Jesus Christ.

A further thought should be added: Higher critics are exhausting their learning and acute ingenuity in evilly casting doubt upon the traditionally ascribed authorship of the books of the Bible, as if such ascribed authorship being disproved, the books themselves would fall as spurious and worthless. Their attack seems often based upon such finespun and technical comparisons, innuendoes, and interdependent "ifs," and relate usually to matters of such secondary or little importance as would not be listened to in the practical affairs of men. In the profession of the law their attacks would be called pettifogging.

I am not really concerned, and no man of faith should be, about the exact authorship of the books of the Bible. More than one Prophet may well have written parts of books now collected under one heading. I do not know. There may have been "ghost writers" in those days, as now. The Lord gave Aaron to Moses in an equivalent capacity, and spoke to Israel through Moses by the mouth of Aaron. He may have done the same in other cases. If so, what of it? Shakespeare's literature is neither lost nor dimmed because Bacon may have written it.

Textual corruptions and discrepancies are magnified by the critics, essential spiritual truths are minimized, so destroying, by design or otherwise, confidence in the messages carried by the texts. The critics treasure the husks and throw away the wheat.

But in spite of all this criticism, usually atheistic in its concept, and notwithstanding the corruptions themselves, the Good Old Book stands as a record of God's dealings with and commandments and promises to his children, in their days of righteousness and in their generations of sin. It still, though corrupted, points out the way of righteousness to the man of faith seeking to serve God. It contains some of God's counsel to his children. It has been so treated and esteemed in these talks, along with the other sacred modern scriptures which have been named.

How blessed are we to know that out of our sacred scriptures we may learn the full plan of life and salvation; to know that our salvation and exaltation hereafter depend solely upon our own efforts and lives, under divine guidance and help; to know that we are in no sense dependent upon the goodness someone else has built up in heaven—save only the atonement of the Lord Jesus Christ; and to know that we are the full beneficiaries of our own work for ourselves, and that among these works are the unselfish deeds we bestow upon others.

May the Lord give to all of us strength always

to live as his scriptures teach, I pray, in the Lord's
name. Amen.

[1]Moses 5:58-59. [2]Gal. 3:8. [3]John 5:46. [4]Amos 3:7. [5]D.C.
68:4. [6]Documentary History of the Church, VI, p. 57. [7]Burgon
and Miller, *Causes of Corruption in the Traditional Text*, pp. 21, 23.
[8]*Id.*, p. 42. [9]*Id.*, p. 69. [10]*Id.*, p. 123. [11]*Id.*, pp. 128-129. [12]*Id.*, p.
164. [13]*Id.*, p. 158. [14]*Id.*, p. 172. [15]*Id.*, p. 192. [16]*Id.*, p. 197. [17]*Id.*,
p. 211; and see also Paton in *A New Standard Bible Dictionary*,
sub voce *Old Testament Text*. [18]Burgon and Miller, p. 81. [19]Mark
7:5-7, 9; Matt. 15:7-9. [20]Burgon and Miller, p. 81.

XXVI

THE PROPHET JOSEPH SMITH

TONIGHT we are come to the last talk of our series. Another series will follow by Elder William E. Berrett, who will speak about "What Shall Men Believe." I commend to your attentive listening the talks of Brother Berrett. He is a man of ripened scholarship and genuine faith. You will gain from him enlightenment, spiritual strength, and upbuilding.

I thank all who have helped in these broadcasts, —The Brigham Young University Symphony Orchestra and the University's choral groups, as well as those who directed them; and Brothers Harold H. Bennett and Frank W. Asper who are furnishing the music for us tonight; also Elder Gordon B. Hinckley of the Church Radio Committee, for his valued kindness and suggestions, and President Richard L. Evans, our talented, excellent, and veteran announcer; then our skilled technicians, Howard Smith and David Sears; likewise the able radio staffs at the Brigham Young University and at KSL, who have so helpfully cooperated; and last but not least my most competent secretary, Sister Rowena Miller, whose industry, great care, and devotion to her tasks, have been of inestimable help to me in this work.

I thank you friends of the air for the time you have given us. I have tried not to waste it. I know the principles we have treated are among those by which we may guide our footsteps along the way to immortality and eternal life.

In the closing words tonight I shall speak of one of the greatest souls of all time,—the modern Prophet, Joseph Smith, who under God's authority and direction, opened this, the Last Dispensation, the Dispensation of the Fullness of Times, and organized for the last time on this earth the Church of the Savior of the world.

To those who will not accord to Joseph this place it may be said that truth is truth, no matter what the unbeliever may say. Puny, designing men may impose ignorance and error upon the children of men for a time, even for generations, but they never finally prevail. Joseph's truths proclaimed through God's inspiration, will finally triumph, because light always dispels darkness.

Joseph's life and work fitted the life pattern of the leaders of each of the other prior dispensations:

Each of these leaders, save Adam, was born into a world-setting of spiritual darkness; the people were wandering in ignorance and sin, ridden with priestcraft and apostate from the eternal truths of mortal life and everlasting existence.

In each dispensation when preparations therefor were completed, revelations came from God to the man of destiny, chosen from before the foundation of the world to open a dispensation, these revelations re-discovering to men the truths of the Gospel of Christ and the purpose and end of existence.

Having received the revelations, each of these chosen men proclaimed the Gospel truths under divine approval and direction. Always a few of the earth accepted the message; the mass rejected it.

Following his proclamation of truth, there came first to each of these men, sneers, scoffs, and derision of the many for him and for the few following him. Afterwards came persecution, huntings, drivings, burnings, plunderings, rapings, even martyrdom of some of the few by the many, even of the Christ himself in his dispensation.

Then, always in the past dispensations, the few waxed stronger for a time, then tolerance came for them, then good will, then a gradual "falling away" by the followers themselves, then absorption of them by the many; then another lapsing of the earth into apostasy, paganism, idolatry, with ignorance and sin once more taking over the ruling of the people.

So with Adam and Noah and Abraham and Moses, and even with the Primitive Church set up by the Christ himself.

But this is not the destiny declared by God for this Last Dispensation.

For our good earth has its life term, too, and under God's plan mortal man must run his course thereon before time dies and eternity comes. Man, instinct from the Fall with evil, having become "carnal, sensual, and devilish,"[1] "every imagination of the thoughts of his heart was only evil continually,"[2]

must have a final chance to save himself and his
ancestry even from the beginning. Till now every
such chance has been lost. So as the days of earth-
life are running out, and the spirits to be tabernacled
in mortality on this earth are nearing the last, a final
dispensation of the Gospel must come that should
gather all that has gone before into one, that all
men from the beginning of time, dead and living, may
have a chance to come to a knowledge of the truth.*

God has so decreed.

So Joseph, like Abraham* and all the rest of the
great and mighty ones in God's work, was called to
his work for which he was fore-ordained in the Grand
Council in Heaven.*

Like Samuel of old, Joseph was called early to
his work. He was but fourteen when he beheld the
greatest recorded vision of all time—the visit of the
Father and Son.

Just as John the Baptist, who baptized the
Christ, afterwards declaring him to be the Lamb of
God, yet later, persecuted and imprisoned, sent his
disciples questioning, "Art thou he that should come?
or look we for another,"* so Joseph, after the First
Vision, the spirits of youth running high and the
memory of the vision dwindling in brilliance, went
again to the Lord for renewed assurance. Moroni
came in answer.

Just as Moses, that he might lead a great host,
was under a divine plan taught and trained for his
task in the royal court of Pharaoh, so Joseph, not
merely with a host to lead, but with a host to build
and then to lead, and a Church to establish, was

taught and trained thereto in Gospel truths through the translation of the Book of Mormon and the revelations of the Lord which poured in upon him.

Just as Moses, so taught and trained in the beginning, must be helped in his growing task by the constant revelation of God's mind and will, so Joseph, the Church organized, had need for further light and direction, and God gave it to him, by revelation after revelation, without stint, as the needs of the days came.

Unlike Noah, Abraham, and Moses, who came to their tasks in the strength of physical and mental maturity, Joseph came to his work as a boy, untaught, unlearned, inexperienced, unknown.

The First Vision came to him at 14 (Spring 1820); almost four years later (Sept. 21, 1823) at 17, the Angel Moroni first came to him; following a spiritual preparation and instruction of another four years, Moroni entrusted to him (Sept. 22, 1827) the plates Moroni had prepared and hidden away against this day,—Joseph was almost 22; then more preparation, more training, with trial after trial and harsh persecution, and the translation was completed and the Book of Mormon published in 1830,—Joseph was not yet 25. Now by divine authority and direction, Joseph organized the Church, April 6, 1830.

Then began a wandering of modern Israel, with a slow multiplication of their numbers, that was to last, in Joseph's era, not for forty years, as with ancient Israel, but a scanty 17 years till the Saints found final refuge and comparative peace in the Rocky Mountains.

They had gone from New York to Pennsylvania; then to Ohio; then to Missouri; then to Illinois, all under the leadership of the Prophet,—14 years of great trials, abject poverty, testing persecutions. Joseph's steps were dogged with cruel hardships, groundless prosecutions; with false and blasted friendships of men trusted to the life; with the apostasy of some upon whom he leaned most,—14 years of plunderings, mobbings, burnings, drivings, rapings, for him and his people, in all which he fully shared. Finally came his martyrdom at the hands of a mob against the wrath and murderous plans of which the Governor of Illinois had promised to protect him. He so sealed his testimony with his blood at 38, younger it seems likely than when his great predecessors, the leaders of other dispensations, came to the beginning of their work.

Yet, during all these years, he was close to the Lord, even as Moses of old; he had days on end of great spiritual joy and exaltation, when the Lord spoke to him as a friend, when he received as needed, for himself and his people, the revelations of the Lord God Almighty. He had days of dire distress and tribulation,—but never one day of doubt.

No more relentless war of slander and abuse has ever been waged against any man affirming and manifesting spiritual leadership than has been fought against Joseph.

Pseudo-friends have damned with faint praise and with half-told truths.

Every act and word and deed of his has been probed to the very bottom of its underpinnings to find some equivocal act, some casual word, some careless deed upon which to hang suspicion, innuendo, derision, falsehood, all to destroy him.

Every rumor, however slender, every suspicion, however unfounded, every charge, however false, that could be dug up from the mire of evil, has been built up, magnified, and strewn to the four winds to bring upon him dishonor and ignominy.

Even more,—falsehoods, palpably so on the actual facts, have been told; false situations have been invented; court records have been invented and used as the basis of whole books of vilification and misrepresentation.

Born and serving in a modern world, with modern communications and a press wholly free to print his words, his incomings and outgoings, his expressed and assumed attitudes and views, his weaknesses (and he was human), and with a deliberate hiding or denying, or both, of his virtues, he has run the gauntlet of a publicity that no other leader of a dispensation ever had to meet, nor any leader of a reformation.

Hell has no weapon so foul that it has not been used and re-used against him.

To the scriptures he gave us, by translation and revelation, has been applied every test that evil ingenuity could invent. These scriptures have been the beneficiaries of attacks as vigorous, as evilly purposed, as intendedly destructive, as any that have been aimed at the Bible itself. Both scriptures have been the victims of the most intense warfare by atheists, open and covert, ever levied at any books in the history of the world. Yet both have stood all tests, both have repelled every attack. That Joseph's scriptures should be the subject of the same onslaughts that have been aimed against the Bible, is a testimony that Satan recognizes that the two scriptures—the Bible and the Prophet's translations and revelations— stand on the same footing as comprising the commandments of the Lord to men.

But during all this time of slander, libel, and defamation, Joseph held the loyalty of his people,— some forsook and even betrayed him, but the bulk of them cherished him to the last as their Prophet, Seer, and Revelator, the Presiding High Priest of Christ's Church on earth, the holy man chosen by God to open the Dispensation of the Fullness of Times.

We would ask those who would belittle Joseph or make sport of his work and his teachings to give heed to these facts:

A veritable spiritual magnet, he drew to himself, while yet a young man, mature men of experience, and of far greater learning than he possessed. His own family early believed in him, though the family is sometimes the last to recognize spiritual superiority in one of their own. (The brothers and sisters of Jesus seem not to have accepted him till after the crucifixion.)[1]

As his work grew older, other men, great in their own right, gave Joseph full allegiance and complete respect, obedience, and honor,—Brigham Young, Heber C. Kimball, Willard Richards, Daniel H. Wells, Jedediah Grant, Wilford Woodruff, John

Taylor, Lorenzo Snow, the Pratts, and many, many others.

He was a man of unsurpassed qualities of lea-dership. Out of the seeming disaster of Zion's Camp and amongst those who had followed him in military order to fight, if necessary, for the repossession of their Jackson County lands and who, plague scourg-ed, dribbled back to their homes singly or in dis-organized small groups, he rose to call forth from his people even greater trust and devotion, for, while some criticized, the people generally and the greater ones of the Camp, still held him to be the Presiding High Priest of the Church, the Prophet, Seer, and Revelator of the Lord towards his people. Few men in history have survived such a seeming disaster.

Great was his faith, as on that day of miracles in the swamps along the lowlands of the Mississippi, when exhausted, for 'virtue had gone out of him' as he healed the many sick, he gave to Brother Wood-ruff the kerchief which he blessed, and Brother Wood-ruff, smoothing with it the fevered brows of the af-flicted, healed them even as they in olden days were healed to whom were brought the kerchiefs and aprons from the body of Paul.[8]

His faith knew only the bounds that God placed upon it, for God gives to no man a faith that might defeat his infinite wisdom and purposes, or alter the course he has charted.

We would ask those who scoff and belittle, to consider that while he was being fitted to organize and while organizing and building up the Church; while he was leading his people, driven from place to place with dire, sometimes murderous persecutions; while he planned and directed the building of city after city, and the erection of great public buildings, the people themselves being always in great poverty and none poorer than himself,—he produced a scripture (by translation and revelation) that is almost three-quarters the size of the Old and New Testaments combined; that the Book of Mormon alone has a vocabulary of 5500 different words (Joseph was an unschooled, unlettered young man of 24 when this book was finished);— that this scripture contains many passages of the very highest literary excellence; that there is not one salacious story or erotic incident in all the scripture he produced,—more than can be said of the Bible; that the Book of Mormon is almost four times as large as the Books of Moses; that the bulk of Joseph's work, the Book of Mormon, was done in perhaps not to exceed 6 to 8 months; that all this scripture was produced over a period of some 17 years (1827-1844) and the bulk of it within 12 years (1827-1839); that this scripture is filled with references and allusions to the Bible,—the Book of Mormon to the Bible books existing prior to the captivity of Israel, though the Book of Ether, written by those who had no knowledge of the books of the Bible, even the Books of Moses, contains no Bible references.

I would ask those who scoff to consider that notwithstanding their jibes and jeers, their derision and defamation, their evil designs and falsehoods, a million people honor and revere Joseph; this people have

a spiritual knowledge that he was a Prophet of the
living God; that he founded under the Lord's direction the Church of Jesus Christ of Latter-day Saints;
that heavenly beings sent by the Almighty, bestowed
upon him the Holy Priesthood of God.

I would ask the scoffers to observe that in all the
trials and tribulations with which he and his people
were hounded, day in and day out, he drove forward
the missionary work of the Church—he, himself,
repeatedly going into the field—and that even in the
darkest hours the Church membership grew by leaps
and bounds and that loyalty to Joseph was basic to
the lives of the Saints.

I would bring to the attention of his defamers
that even while away from his people, unjustly imprisoned in a vile dungeon, he still was their leader,
they still placed their faith and hope in him, they
obeyed his direction, not as weaklings ridden by
priestcraft, but as normal men and women, among
whom were such spiritual and mental giants as I
have already named,—Brigham Young and a host
of others.

I would ask his enemies to take note of his claim
to statesmanship by looking at his plan for doing
away with slavery, his visions as to the northwest,
his concept of principles of government, as set out
in his writings and also in the truly marvelous organization of the Church itself; his appraisal of the
Constitution and of our government set up under
it; his views on matters of basic economics as contained in the plan of the United Order, and care of
the poor; his grasp of problems of administration

and the principles underlying them; his scientific concepts in astronomy and in the constitution of matter.

I would cite to his deriders the great dramas he wrote,—about Nephi, Alma, Helaman, the Brother of Jared, Mormon, Moroni, and a host of others.

For all of this we of the Church claim divine inspiration; and for all of which those hostile unbelievers who deny him revelation from God, must either grant his authorship and creative genius, thereby proclaiming his greatness, or they must produce others who are the real authors, and there are no others. The work was his, done under the inspiration of the Almighty. Joseph's defamers must take one horn of this dilemma or the other, because, one hundred years of unparalleled achievement of the Church he organized and of the people who reverence him as a Prophet, Seer, and Revelator of Almighty God, may not be blinked or waived aside.

And now at the end of my talks, I bear in all humility my own testimony that Joseph Smith was the instrument in God's hands of setting up in this Dispensation of the Fullness of Times and for the last time on this earth, the Church of Jesus Christ of Latter-day Saints; that through Joseph the Gospel of Jesus Christ and the Holy Priesthood after the order of the Son of God° were restored to the earth and are still among Christ's people in his Church; that Joseph was and is a Prophet, Seer, and Revelator of the Most High; that the Restored Gospel of Jesus Christ will save and exalt all those who believe and live its principles; and that 'there is no other way under heaven whereby men may be saved and exalted' than that laid out by the restored teachings of Christ, as revealed and restored through the Prophet, Joseph Smith. I bear this testimony and bring this witness, in the name of the Redeemer of the World, Jesus Christ, and I call upon all who hear or read it to hearken to its import! Amen.

---

[1]Moses 5:13. [2]Gen. 6:5. [3]Parry, *Joseph Smith's Teachings*, p. 127. [4]Abraham 3:23. [5]Parry, p. 132. [6]Luke 7:19. [7]Matt. 12:46-50; Mark 3:31-35; Luke 8:19-21; also John 7:2-9; and the Epistles of James and Jude. [8]Acts. 19:11-12. [9]Parry, p. 112.

APPENDIX

STILL OTHER GREAT ERRONEOUS DOGMAS IN PAUL'S "FALLING AWAY"

Perhaps it would be well to begin the consideration of other great "fallings away" by the Church after the ascension of Christ, by quoting a passage from an article by the Catholic author, Herbert Thurston, B.A., S.J., in Hastings, "Encyclopaedia of Religion and Ethics," XI, *sub voce* "Saints and Martyrs":

"The almost ineradicable tendency among the rude and uneducated to cling to their primitive customs led beyond doubt to a certain amount of compromise in matters which were not judged to be distinctively pagan. It was the advice of St. Gregory Thaumaturgus, of St. Augustine, and of St. Gregory the Great that an attempt should be made to Christianize their popular observances, if not absolutely evil in themselves, rather than to extirpate them. If a particular day had been kept as a holiday, let it be transformed into a Christian festival; if there had been resort to a particular site for superstitious purposes, let some worthier object of pilgrimage be substituted; if certain practices connected with funerals, weddings, or other ceremonial occasions had established themselves firmly in the hearts of the people, let them be given a Christian coloring or significance."

The Jesuit Father admits, "certainly there was much danger of grave abuses resulting from such condescensions." The Father suggests the work of conversion might have been hindered by any other course. Yet the facts show that once entered upon, this road led finally to a complete apostasy. This will become clear as we proceed.

It should be remembered that a good part of these "fallings away" had fully matured long before the Reformation, and that some of them, indeed led to that religious revolution.

A

THE FALSE DOGMA THAT FORGIVENESS OF SIN MAY BE PURCHASED WITH GOLD

We have heretofore dealt with the false doctrine of transubstantiation, and the theory that the administration of the sacrament of the Lord's Supper was, at each celebration of the eucharist, actually a renewed sacrifice of the Savior's life, under ceremonies that aped, in some matters, the Aaronic sacrifices of lambs, rams, and bullocks. We pointed out the true doctrine of the sacrament as revealed by modern revelation.

We shall now speak of the false dogma which sanctions the buying of forgiveness for sin by the payment of gold.

Jesus, visiting Jerusalem for the second Passover of his mission, went to the pool of Bethesda, and found there a man sick of an infirmity for thirty-eight years. Jesus enquired of the man whether he would be healed. The man replied he had no one to put him into the water when it was troubled. The tradition was that he who first touched the water after it was troubled by the angel would be healed of his sickness. "Jesus saith unto him, Rise, take up thy bed, and walk. And immediately the man was made whole, and took up his bed, and walked. . . Afterward Jesus findeth him in the temple, and said unto him,

Behold, thou art made whole: sin no more, lest a worse thing come unto thee."[1]

To the woman caught in the very act of adultery and taken to him for judgment as he was in the temple during the Feast of Tabernacles, Jesus said, declaring he would not condemn her to death, "Go, and sin no more."[2]

Thus, the doctrine of Jesus was go and sin no more, lest a worse thing come upon thee. Modern revelation declares that upon the head of the repentant sinner whose sins are forgiven shall his former sins return if he sins again.[3]

Nullifying this doctrine, another "falling away" from the pure Gospel of Christ crept into the Church in the early centuries.

The Christ speaking to the ten Apostles in the Upper Room on the evening of his resurrection day,[4] and Peter speaking to the multitudes on the day of Pentecost,[5] announced repentance and baptism for the remission of sins. Very early the Church, recognizing that the convert was by baptism remitted of sins committed before baptism, faced the problem of the forgiveness of sins, whether by rebaptism or otherwise, committed after baptism. Controversies arising thereon that shook the Western Church (Cyprian-Stephen controversy, last half of the third century) as to rebaptism,[6] the Council of Constantinople (A.D. 381) declared, in an effort to settle the question, "we acknowledge one baptism for the remission of sins."[7]

To bring about the forgiveness of post-baptism sins, the dogma was developed that there must be acts of self-abasement or self-punishment called penance, which was described as a "laborious kind of baptism."[8] Men must pay for their sins, — not repent and forsake them.

At first there was a public penance before the Church, but this went out of use during the seventh and eighth centuries, except for gross offenses. This was replaced by private auricular confession before a priest, and private penance, which was first recognized in the West by Leo the Great (440-461).

Thus it took between 400 and 500 years for this false doctrine to secure recognition.

The priest fixed the penance and gave absolution, to obtain which the penitent should have a contrite heart, should confess, and satisfy by good works,[9] such as works of reparation, fasting, giving alms, prayers, psalms, mortification, and the making of pilgrimages to holy places, to all of which actions was attached an atoning efficacy for the sin committed.[10] Some recommended the voluntary whipping of one's self, but this was condemned by Clement VI.[11]

Every sin had its penance assigned, covering days, weeks, months, or years. The system provided for alms as a basis for compensation for the penances, the alms varying with the wealth and charity of the penitent, so finally there came to be a "redemption" of penances.[12]   One writer says that piety involved in the "pious exercises" of penance was measured by the quantity of good works rather than by the character of the sinner.[13]

Gibbon has the following to say regarding these

practices of the Church, his comments embracing not only the early history of the practices but the later developments: "A literal accomplishment of penance was indeed impracticable: the guilt of adultery was multiplied by daily repetition; that of homicide might involve the massacre of a whole people; each act was separately numbered; and, in those times of anarchy and vice, a modest sinner might easily incur a debt of three hundred years. His insolvency was relieved by a commutation, or *indulgence*: a year of penance was appreciated at twenty-six *solidi* of silver, about four pounds sterling, for the rich; at three solidi or nine shillings, for the indigent: and these alms were soon appropriated to the use of the church, which derived, from the redemption of sins, an inexhaustible source of opulence and dominion. A debt of three hundred years, or twelve hundred pounds, was enough to impoverish a plentiful fortune; the scarcity of gold and silver was supplied by the alienation of land; and the princely donations of Pepin and Charlemagne are expressly given for the *remedy* of their soul. It is a maxim of the civil law, that whosoever cannot pay with his purse, must pay with his body; and the practice of flaggellation was adopted by the monks, a cheap, though painful equivalent. By a fantastic arithmetic, a year of penance was taxed at three thousand lashes; and such was the skill and patience of a famous hermit, St. Dominic of the iron Cuirass, that in six days he could discharge an entire century, by a whipping of three hundred thousand stripes. His example was followed by many penitents of both

sexes; and, as a vicarious sacrifice was accepted, a
sturdy disciplinarian might expiate on his own back
the sins of his benefactors. These compensations of
the purse and the person introduced, in the eleventh
century, a more honorable mode of satisfaction. The
merit of military service against the Saracens of Africa and Spain had been allowed by the predecessors
of Urban the Second. In the council of Clermont, that
pope proclaimed a *plenary indulgence* to those who
should enlist under the banner of the cross; the
absolution of *all* their sins, and a full receipt for *all*
that might be due of canonical penance. The cold
philosophy of modern times is incapable of feeling
the impression that was made on a sinful and fanatic
world. At the voice of their pastor, the robber, the
incendiary, the homicide, arose by thousands to redeem their souls, by repeating on the infidels the
same deeds which they had exercised against their
Christian brethren; and the terms of atonement were
eagerly embraced by offenders of every rank and
denomination. None was pure; none was exempt
from the guilt and penalty of sin; and those who were
the least amenable to the justice of God and the
church were the best entitled to the temporal and
eternal recompense of their pious courage. If they
fell, the spirit of the Latin clergy did not hesitate to
adorn their tomb with the crown of martyrdom; and
should they survive, they could expect without impa-
tience the delay and increase of their heavenly reward. They offered their blood to the Son of God,
who had laid down his life for their salvation: they
took up the cross, and entered with confidence into

the way of the Lord. His providence would watch over their safety; perhaps his visible and miraculous power would smooth the difficulties of their holy enterprise. The cloud and pillar of Jehovah had marched before the Israelites into the promised land. Might not the Christians more reasonably hope that the rivers would open for their passage; that the walls of their strongest cities would fall at the sound of their trumpets; and that the sun would be arrested in his mid career, to allow them time for the destruction of the infidels?"[14]

But a vicious extension of the doctrine of penances appeared about 700 A.D.; it showed its head first in Britain. The northern and western pagan barbarians had a custom of making money payments to compensate for their crimes instead of suffering punishment therefore.[15] This pagan custom was first taken over and applied to penances by Archbishop Theodore of Canterbury, England (d. A. D. 690), whence it rapidly spread over the Western Church.[16] The step was made easily. Instead of the physical amends, — fasting, prayers, pilgrimages, or other temporal punishments — which the sinner made for his transgressions, he could now make a payment of money. Under the original Church theory, it was affirmed that while God and he only forgives the eternal punishment for sin, yet the Church has temporal punishments for sin (both on earth and in purgatory) under its control, and it can sell relief therefrom for gold.

This was the official Church view of money payments. "But the people in general understood them, and persisted in understanding them, as promises of eternal forgiveness, while they overlooked any conditions of repentance or charity which had been annexed to them."[17]

To Simon the Sorcerer offering gold for the power of conferring the Holy Ghost, Peter gave vigorous rebuke: "Thy money perish with thee, because thou hast thought that the gift of God may be purchased with money. Thou hast neither part nor lot in this matter: for thy heart is not right in the sight of God."[18] Can sound distinction be drawn between selling the power of the priesthood to forgive sin and selling the power of the priesthood to bestow the Holy Ghost with its gifts? If Peter were here he would condemn each equally, not being deceived by hair-splitting distinctions.

This "falling away" dogma was based on another erroneous concept, namely, that the Saints and the righteous generally — usually the Savior was also included — had built up in heaven a great credit "treasury," one might say bank of extra good, and that the Roman Church priesthood had the power to draw on this treasury of good to meet the bad debits of the sinners.[19] This doctrine was first 'made much of' by Clement VI in his bull promulgating the jubilee of 1350.[20]

Later the principle was extended to the dead, under the influence of the schoolmen, Alexander of Hales and Aquinas being the leading proponents of the doctrine, which was first included in a public document by Sixtus IV in 1477, and was applied by Innocent VIII in 1490.[21]

This erroneous dogma did not appear until nearly a millennium and a half after the crucifixion. Such was its slow growth.

The means that were developed for carrying out this dogma was a granting of what are called indulgences (indulgentia), which is defined "in the legal language of Rome" as "a term for amnesty or remission of punishment."[22]   This in effect means buying forgiveness for sins commited or, on the other hand, buying permission to commit sin.   It has been also said that indulgences came into the post-Primitive Church through the sacerdotalism of Manichaeism.[23]

In the course of time, there came to be two kinds of indulgences, plenary indulgences, and partial indulgences, — "a plenary indulgence is one which covers all penance required of the penitent; a partial indulgence covers a part of the penance, and is counted by days, months, or years."[24]

Indulgences were given not only to cover particular sins, but Gregory VII (1073-1085) promised absolution of all sins for those who would take up arms against Henry IV; and Victor III (1086-1087) made a like promise for those who would wage a religious war against the Saracens of Africa.[25]

Urban II (1095) offered a plenary indulgence, seemingly the first ever granted, to cover sins past and future of all who engaged in a crusade to free the Holy Land, — this being the crusade preached by Peter the Hermit.[26]   This action was made legal by a decree of the Council of Clermont (1095), which said: "Whoever, out of pure devotion and not for

the purpose of gaining honor or money, shall go to
Jerusalem to liberate the Church of God, may count
that journey in lieu of all penance."[27] This had in
effect the astounding meaning that such a person
was forgiven for whatsoever sin he had committed
or might commit.

Robertson, after commenting upon the understanding of the people as to the efficacy of indulgences
— that the people "persisted in understanding them,
as promises of eternal forgiveness, while they overlooked any conditions of repentance or charity which
had been annexed to them" — observes, "And the
license which marked the lives of the crusaders, and
of the Latins who settled in the Holy Land, is an
unquestionable proof of the sense in which the papal
offers were interpreted."[28]

As to the temporal advantages coming to the
crusaders, and the effect of granting them, Dr.
Workman says: "The *cruce signati* were freed from
arrest for debt, and from usury; they were guar-
anteed justice; the Pope was the guardian of their
wives, families, etc. In consequence the crusaders
were a mixed company, debtors and criminals
abounding."[29]

Out of this situation came the wild, riotous living of the crusaders, their savage excesses towards
their enemies, and the carnage and butchery against
the people of Jerusalem after the walls were finally stormed (following a vain attempt by the clergy
to repeat the miracle of Joshua at Jericho). When the
city came into the hands of the Christians, "so terrible, it is said, was the carnage which followed that

the horses of the crusaders who rode up to the mosque of Omar were knee-deep in the stream of blood. Infants were seized by their feet and dashed against the walls or whirled over the battlements, while the Jews were all burnt alive in their synagogue. In the midst of these horrors Godfrey entered the church of the Sepulchre, clothed in a robe of pure white, but barefooted as well as bareheaded, and knelt at the tomb to offer his thanksgiving for the divine goodness which had suffered them to realize the yearning of their hearts. In the profound enthusiasm and devotion of the moment his followers beheld the dead take part in the solemn ritual, and heard the voice of Adhemar (bishop and papal legate) rejoicing in the prayers and resolutions of penitence offered by the prostrate warriors of the cross. Among the living, too, there were those who called forth the deepest gratitude; and the vast throng fell at the feet of the hermit Peter, who thus saw the consummation of the enterprise which was mainly his work, and of whom after the completion of his task we hear no more. On the next day the horrors of that which had preceded it were deliberately repeated on a larger scale. Tancred had given a guarantee of safety to 300 captives. In spite of his indignant protest these were all brought out and killed; and a massacre followed in which the bodies of men, women, and children were hacked and hewn until their fragments lay tossed together in heaps. The work of slaughter ended, the streets of the city were washed by Saracen prisoners."[30]

One can but recall the Messianic lamentation:

"O Jerusalem, Jerusalem, thou that killest the prophets, and stonest them which are sent unto thee,
how often would I have gathered thy children together, even as a hen gathereth her chickens under
her wings, and ye would not! Behold, your house
is left unto you desolate. For I say unto you, Ye
shall not see me henceforth, till ye shall say, Blessed
is he that cometh in the name of the Lord."[31]

Boniface VIII (1294-1303) in 1299, declared a
jubilee on the 1300th year and granted therewith a
plenary indulgence (the second one granted) of extraordinary fullness (with certain residential re-
strictions and certain exceptions) to all who should
with due penance and devotion visit the tombs of
Peter and Paul. He directed the repetition of this
every hundredth year. It is said that as many as
200,000 strangers were in the city of Rome at one
time on this Jubilee. At Christmas time, the indulgence was extended to the following Easter.
Enormous contributions were received. Robertson
says that as time went on plenary indulgences were
"extended to religious wars in Europe, or to wars
undertaken by the popes against Christian sov-
ereigns with whom they had quarrelled."[32]

Honorius III (1216-1227) curtailed granting of
indulgences by inferior persons, but enlarged his own
exercise of the powers, increased the commutation of
penances and obligations for money, held that he
might dispense "with everything except the law of
nature and the articles of the faith," and granted
indulgences not only for past offenses but, by papal

authority, for "future or intended violations of the law."[33]

Boniface IX (1389-1404), first pronouncing a jubilee for 1390 (under a miscalculation)[34] which netted large returns on an indulgence excusing persons from attending the jubilee,[35] later declared a second jubilee for the turn of the century, and gave indulgences to all who would visit Rome in person, but any one might, in lieu of going to Rome, visit a local Church and pay into the papal treasury the sum it would have cost him to make a trip to Rome.[36] Boniface IX revoked indulgences illegally granted and then resold them.[37] "Although it is said that much of the money paid for this indulgence (the jubilee of 1390) was embezzled by the collectors, it brought in a large addition to the profits of the jubilee — which, while a portion of them was bestowed on the repairs of the Roman churches, were mostly retained for the pope's own use."[38]

Alexander VI (1492-1503) sold indulgences for the jubilee of 1500, that might be bestowed on souls in purgatory, "by the way of suffrage." Indulgences had been previously granted on this account by Sixtus IV in 1477, and by Innocent VIII in 1490.[39]

Julius II in 1506 sold indulgences to raise money to rebuild St. Peters in Rome. This plan was repeated by Leo X (1513-1521) for the same purpose, — a house erected for the worship of a sinless, perfect Lord God Almighty, built with the gold that came from licensed sin.[40] Pope Leo's act "became the immediate occasion of Luther's defiance of Rome."[41]

Schaff notes that Jesus began his public ministry by cleansing the Temple of the money changers and the dealers in sacrificial animals. "Make not my Father's house an house of merchandise."[42]

As would be expected, great abuses came into the Church from the granting of indulgences.[43]

The banking house of Fuggers was involved in collecting and transmitting the papal portion of indulgences, sometimes charging 5%. This house also secured from ecclesiastical officers the grant of indulgences to individuals, apparently for a price or commission.[44]

Schaff says: "The difficult and complicated doctrine of indulgences is peculiar to the Roman Church. It was unknown to the Greek and Latin fathers. It was developed by the medieval schoolmen, and sanctioned by the Council of Trent (Dec. 4, 1563), yet without a definition and with an express warning against abuses and evil gains."[45]

The Council of Trent (1563, Pius IV) passed a "decree concerning indulgences," which first affirms that the power to grant indulgences was delivered unto the Church by Christ, and declared that "the sacred holy Synod teaches and enjoins that the use of Indulgences, for the Christian people most salutary, and approved of by the authority of sacred Councils, is to be retained in the Church; and it condemns with anathema those who either assert that they are useless, or who deny that there is in the Church the power of granting them. In granting them, however, it desires that, in accordance with the ancient and approved custom in the Church, moderation be observed; lest, by excessive facility, ecclesiastical discipline be enervated. And being desirous that the abuses which have crept therein, and by occasion of which this honorable name of Indulgences is blasphemed by heretics, be amended and corrected, it ordains generally by this decree, that all evil gains for the obtaining thereof,—whence a most prolific cause of abuses amongst the Christian people has been derived, — be wholly abolished."[46]

Thus this declaration specifically concedes that the doctrine has been "a most prolific cause of abuses amongst the Christian people."

In this connection it should be noted, as declared by Schaff, that "the principal source and the highest standard of the doctrine and discipline of the Roman Church are the Canons and Decrees of the Council of Trent."[47]

In the earlier centuries, indulgences were "precatory," that is, they were prayers that the penances would be effective in their operation upon temporal punishments, but later the indulgences became "declaratory," that is, the sin was wiped out. Aquinas declared that the absolution is from guilt as well as from punishment.[48]

Schaff, writing in 1885, affirms: "The popes still exercise from time to time the right of granting plenary indulgences, though with greater caution than their mediaeval predecessors."[49]

Dr. Boudinhon, writing about indulgences in 1928 under the heading "Practical Remarks," observes: "The chief indulgences are, as formerly, the Crusade (still kept up in Spain in a special form); the Jubilee, which occurs every quarter-century, and is imitated more or less frequently by solemn indulgences called 'in form of Jubilee'; indulgences attached to the most popular devotions, as the Rosary or the Stations of the Cross; those of famous sanctuaries, as Rome, Jerusalem, Compostella, Assisi's Portiuncula, etc.; 'apostolic' indulgences, attached by the pope (or the priest authorized by him) to holy objects blessed by him."[50]

Thus another great "falling away" was developed over the centuries, but not finally ripening into a recognized dogma until a thousand years after the Christ. There is no justification for this dogma in holy writ. The decree of the Council of Trent refers to none, but relies upon synods and councils for the authority therefor.

All this is not the way of the Christ. As we have noted, he drove from the Temple with whips the money changers and those who trafficked for profit with the doves and lambs for the sacrifice, saying: "It is written, My house shall be called the house of prayer; but ye have made it a den of thieves."[51]

Under the Mosaic law, those who sinned deliberately, or with premeditation, "presumptuously," were to be "cut off from among his people," to await the judgment of God.[52] The adulteress taken before Jesus in the Temple was, under this law, to suffer death, if condemned. Jesus refused to pass this condemnation, and instead declared the new law of repentance, — "Go, and sin no more."

Paul, speaking to the Hebrews on his theme "let us go on unto perfection," declares: "For it is impossible for those who were once enlightened, and have tasted of the heavenly gift, and were made partakers of the Holy Ghost, and have tasted the good word of God, and the powers of the world to come, if they shall fall away, to renew them again unto repentance; seeing they crucify to themselves the Son of God afresh, and put him to an open shame."[53]

Again, exhorting the Hebrews to "provoke" one another "unto love and to good works," Paul declared: "For if we sin wilfully after that we have received the knowledge of the truth, there remaineth no more sacrifice for sins, but a certain fearful looking for of judgment and fiery indignation, which shall devour the adversaries."[54]

To this woman sinning in adultery, Jesus *did not* say: "Go thy way, thou art forgiven, sin again, then bring me a loaf and a fish and I will forgive again; and then, so doing, you may sin and sin again till your life runs out." Oh no! He said to this wayward soul: "Go, and sin no more," and to the man of Bethesda pool, he said, "sin no more, lest a worse thing come unto thee." God's mercy and forgiveness for the sinner is infinite; but he never traffics in sin nor sells license therefor.

Modern revelation gives us the law of this dispensation, — repent and sin no more, and upon the head of the repentant and forgiven sinner, shall his former sins return if he sins again.[55] This same principle was announced by Ezekiel.[56]

May God help us to live the law of the Last Dispensation, and not be misled by that grievously evil doctrine of Satan, that forgiveness for repeated sinning may be bought with gold.

[1]John 5:1-15. [2]John 8:1 ff. [3]D.C. 82:7; see Ezek. 3:17 ff. [4]Luke 24:47. [5]Acts 2:37-38. [6]Robertson, *History of the Christian Church*, I p. 172 ff. [7]Schaff, *History of the Christian Church*, III, pp. 667, 669. [8]Schaff, *Hist.*, IV p. 383. [9]*Id.;* see also Robertson, V, p. 427. [10]Schaff, *Hist.*, IV, p. 382 ff.; VI, p. 147 ff.; Robertson, V, p. 425 ff. [11]Robertson, VII, p. 165-166. [12]Schaff, *Hist.*, VI, p. 147; Hastings, *Encyclopaedia of Religion and Ethics*, sub voce, *Indulgences*, p. 252b. [13]Schaff, *Hist.*, IV, p. 383. [14]Gibbon, *The Decline and Fall of the Roman Empire*, IV, pp. 183-184. [15]Schaff, *Hist.*, VI p. 147. [16]Schaff, *Hist.*, VI, p. 147; IV, p. 384. [17]Robertson, V, p. 426; VI, p. 449. [18]Acts 8:9 ff. [19]Robertson, VI, p. 446-7; Schaff, *Hist.*, IV, p. 384. [20]Hastings, *Encyc.*, sub voce *Indulgences*, p. 254a; Robertson, VII, p. 483. [21]Robertson, VIII, p. 376; Hastings, *Encyc.*, sub voce *Indulgences*, p. 254a; see also Lowndes, *Vindication of Anglican Orders*, p. 347 ff. [22]Schaff, *Hist.*, VI, p. 147. [23]Newman, *A Manual of Church History*, I, p. 197. [24]Hastings, *Encyc.*, sub voce *Indulgences*, p. 254b. [25]Robertson, V, p. 425; IV, p. 380. [26]Robertson, IV, p. 387. [27]Hastings, *Encyc.*, sub voce, *Indulgences*, p. 253a. [28]Robertson, V. p. 426. [29]Hastings, *Encyc.*, sub voce *Crusades*, p. 346b. [30]*Encyclopedia Britannica*, 9th (American) Edition, sub voce *Crusades*, p. 627a; see also Gibbon, IV, p. 215. [31]Matt. 23:37-39; Luke 13:34-35. [32]Robertson, VI, p. 327, 447; Hastings, *Encyc.*, sub voce *Indulgences*, p. 253a; Schaff, *Hist.*, VI, p. 148. [33]Robertson, VI, p. 448-9; and see Cardinal Newman's letter to Pusey, quoted, Hastings, *Encyc.*, sub voce *Infallibility*, p. 270a. [34]Robertson, VII, p. 228. [35]*Op. cit.* p. 227. [36]*Op. cit.*, p. 483. [37]*Op. cit.*, p. 226. [38]*Op cit.*, p. 227. [39]Robertson, VIII, p. 376. [40]*Op cit.*, p. 375-376; Schaff, *Hist.*, VI, p 146 ff. [41]Robertson, VIII, p. 375-376. [42]Schaff, *Hist.*, VI, p. 146; John 2:16. [43]Robertson, VI, p. 449; Newman, I, p. 520; Schaff, *Hist.*, V, pt. II, p. 756, VI, p. 148 ff. [44]Schaff, *Hist.*, V, pt. II, p. 761. [45]Schaff, *Hist.*, VI, p. 146. [46]Schaff, *Creeds of Christendom*, II, p. 205. [47]Schaff, *Creeds*, I, p. 91. [48]Robertson, VI, p. 451; see for summary, Schaff, *Hist.*, IV, p. 381 ff. [49]Schaff, *Hist.*, IV, p. 384, n. 2. [50]Hastings, *Encyc.*, sub voce *Indulgences*, p. 255a. [51]Matt. 21:13. [52]Num. 15:30, 31; Edersheim, *The Temple*, p. 101. [53]Heb. 6:4-6. [54]Heb. 10:24-27. [55]D.C.82:7. [56]Ezek. 3:17 ff.

B

MARTYRS AND SAINTS

It would appear wise before proceeding with the next succeeding topics — B to E inclusive — to consider what the scriptures — ancient and modern — say regarding idolatry, for this is the sin which lies behind each of the matters to be discussed and so is applicable to each of them.

On Sinai, God traced with his finger:[1]

"Thou shalt have no other gods before me.

"Thou shalt not make unto thee any graven image, or any likeness of any thing that is in heaven above, or that is in the earth beneath, or that is in the water under the earth:

"Thou shalt not bow down thyself to them, nor serve them: for I the Lord thy God am a jealous God, visiting the iniquity of the fathers upon the children unto the third and fourth generation of them that hate me;

"And shewing mercy unto thousands of them that love me, and keep my commandments."[2]

Even while Moses yet communed with God on the Mount, and the finger of the Almighty was writing the divine code that was to govern God's people from then till now, Israel, seduced by the Egyptian paganism that still lingered in their minds, gathered their gold earrings, and, tickling Aaron's ears with

flattering words of hinted leadership, besought him
to make a golden calf that they might worship. And
he, little, if any, loathe, yielded to their entreaties,
made the molten calf, proclaiming, "These be thy
gods, O Israel, which brought thee up out of the land
of Egypt. . . . Tomorrow is a feast to the Lord."
Then Israel came with burnt offerings and peace
offerings and "sat down to eat and to drink, and
rose up to play."[3]

The Lord told Moses on the Mount what was
carrying on in the camp, condemned the people for
their idolatrous worship and stiff-neckedness, declared their destruction, and promised to make of
Moses a great nation. And Moses, the humble man,
but mighty, pleaded for the people, and the Lord
relented. Moses, descending from the Mount with
Joshua, cast down and broke the tables of the commandments, burnt and ground to powder the golden
calf, casting the powder on the water, making the
people drink it. Then Levi, hearkening to the call
for those who were on the Lord's side, smote Israel
by Moses' command in punishment for their idolatry.[4]

From these days till the Christ came, Israel
lapsed time after time into idolatry, and God time
after time chastised them. While yet in the wilderness
the Lord exhorted Israel to covenant with him, re-
minding them of the peoples they had seen. "And
ye have seen their abominations, and their idols,
wood and stone, silver and gold, which were among
them."[5]

The tragedy of Solomon's transgression is thus told:

"For it came to pass, when Solomon was old, that his wives turned away his heart after other gods: and his heart was not perfect with the Lord his God, as was the heart of David his father.

"For Solomon went after Ashtoreth the goddess of the Zidonians, and after Milcom the abomination of the Ammonites.

"And Solomon did evil in the sight of the Lord, and went not fully after the Lord, as did David his father.

"Then did Solomon build an high place for Chemosh, the abomination of Moab, in the hill that is before Jerusalem, and for Molech, the abomination of the children of Ammon.

"And likewise did he for all his strange wives, which burnt incense and sacrificed unto their gods.

"And the Lord was angry with Solomon, because his heart was turned from the Lord God of Israel, which had appeared unto him twice.

"And had commanded him concerning this thing, that he should not go after other gods: but he kept not that which the Lord commanded.

"Wherefore the Lord said unto Solomon, Forasmuch as this is done of thee, and thou hast not kept my covenant and my statutes, which I have commanded thee, I will surely rend the kingdom from thee, and will give it to thy servant.

"Notwithstanding in thy days I will not do it for David thy Father's sake: but I will rend it out of the hand of thy son.

"Howbeit I will not rend away all the kingdom; but will give one tribe to thy son for David my servant's sake, and for Jerusalem's sake which I have chosen."[6]

And Jeroboam, king of the Ten Tribes, built two golden calves, placing one at Bethel and the other in Dan. And the people sacrificed unto these calves. And Rehoboam, king of Judah, followed the same course. And the vengeance of God descended upon them.[7]

Later, in the days of the kingdoms, Asa, king of Judah and son of Abijam, "took away the sodomites out of the land, and removed all the idols that his fathers had made."[8]

Ahab and Jezebel sinned grievously, —

"But there was none like unto Ahab, which did sell himself to work wickedness in the sight of the Lord, whom Jezebel his wife stirred up.

"And he did very abominably in following idols, according to all things as did the Amorites, whom the Lord cast out before the children of Israel."[9]

For his wickedness, and that of Jezebel, the Lord had Elijah declare the great punishment that was to befall them. Out of this came one of the most dramatic incidents in all sacred history, — the contest between Elijah and the priests of Baal, and Elijah's triumph.[10]

Manasseh 'seduced the people to do more evil than did the nations whom the Lord destroyed before the children of Israel' ... "and hath made Judah also to sin with his idols";[11] he even "set a carved image, the idol which he had made, in the house of

God,"[12] which, after grievous punishment, he moved.[13]

Amon, following his father, ". . . walked in all the way that his father walked in, and served the idols that his father served, and worshipped them: And he forsook the Lord God of his fathers, and walked not in the way of the Lord."[14]

Idolatry still flourishing, Josiah, in the twelfth year of his reign, ". . . began to purge Judah and Jerusalem from the high places, and the groves, and the carved images, and the molten images.

"And they brake down the altars of Baalim in his presence; and the images, that were on high above them, he cut down; and the groves, and the carved images, and the molten images, he brake in pieces, and made dust of them, and strowed it upon the graves of them that had sacrificed unto them.

"And he burnt the bones of the priests upon their altars, and cleansed Judah and Jerusalem. . . .

"And he did that which was right in the sight of the Lord, and walked in the ways of David his father, and declined neither to the right hand, nor to the left."[15]

The Psalmist bemoaned those who "shed innocent blood, even the blood of their sons and of their daughters, whom they sacrificed unto the idols of Canaan: and the land was polluted with blood."[16] and "their idols are silver and gold, the work of men's hands."[17] Again he declared:

"The idols of the heathen are silver and gold, the work of men's hands.

"They have mouths, but they speak not; eyes have they, but they see not;

"They have ears, but they hear not; neither is there any breath in their mouths.

"They that make them are like unto them: so is every one that trusteth in them."[18]

Isaiah, condemning the house of Jacob, rich in the treasures of the earth, declared:

"Their land also is full of idols; they worship the work of their own hands, that which their own fingers have made:

"And the mean man boweth down, and the great man humbleth himself: therefore forgive them not."[19]

Jeremiah, foretelling the destruction of Babylon, proclaimed:

"A drought is upon her waters; and they shall be dried up: for it is the land of graven images, and they are mad upon their idols."[20]

Ezekiel, setting his face "toward the mountains of Israel," prophesied as the Lord commanded:

" . . . I will cast down your slain men before your idols.

"And I will lay the dead carcases of the children of Israel before their idols. . . .

"In all your dwellingplaces the cities shall be laid waste, and the high places shall be desolate; that your altars may be laid waste and made desolate, and your idols may be broken and cease, and your images may be cut down, and your works may be abolished. . . .

"And they that escape of you shall remember

me among the nations whither they shall be carried captives, because I am broken with their whorish heart, which hath departed from me, and with their eyes, which go a whoring after their idols: and they shall lothe themselves for the evils which they have committed in all their abominations."[21]

Hosea proclaimed:

" . . . of their silver and their gold have they made them idols, that they may be cut off. . . .

"And now they sin more and more, and have made them molten images of their silver, and idols according to their own understanding, all of it the work of the craftsmen: they say of them, Let the men that sacrifice kiss the calves.

"Therefore they shall be as the morning cloud, and as the early dew that passeth away, as the chaff that is driven with the whirlwind out of the floor, and as the smoke out of the chimney.

"Yet I am the Lord thy God from the land of Egypt, and thou shalt have no god but me: for there is no savior beside me."[22]

Micah, speaking the will of the Lord regarding Samaria, declared:

"And all the graven images thereof shall be beaten to pieces, and all the hires thereof shall be burned with the fire, and all the idols thereof will I lay desolate: for she gathered it of the hire of an harlot, and they shall return to the hire of an harlot."[23]

The Old Testament prophets never ceased to condemn Israel, in unrestrained vehemence, for her worship of idols.

At the great council of the Apostles and elders held in Jerusalem, concerning the status of gentile converts, at which Peter, Paul, and Barnabas spoke, and James also, they declared that:

" . . . we trouble not them, which from among the Gentiles are turned to God:

"But that we write unto them, that they abstain from pollutions of idols, and from fornication."[24]

Paul's "spirit was stirred in him" at Athens, "when he saw the city wholly given to idolatry."[25]

Repeatedly the Apostles — Paul perhaps more frequently than the others — spoke "touching things offered unto idols."[26] James, at the great council already referred to, commanded: "That ye abstain from meats offered to idols."[27] Paul spoke on the matter to the Corinthians, and added, ". . . that an idol is nothing in the world, and that there is none other God but one. For though there be that are called gods, whether in heaven or in earth, (as there be gods many, and lords many,) but to us there is but one God, the Father, of whom are all things, and we in him; and one Lord Jesus Christ, by whom are all things, and we by him."[28]

He affirmed also:

"But I say, that the things which the Gentiles sacrifice, they sacrifice to devils, and not to God."[29]

The concluding words of John in his first epistle were:

"Little children, keep yourselves from idols."[30]

John on Patmos, beholding the great visions

given in Revelation, and seeing the angels of destruction killing a third part of the men, declared:

"And the rest of the men which were not killed by these plagues yet repented not of the works of their hands, that they should not worship devils, and idols of gold, and silver, and brass, and stone, and of wood: which neither can see, nor hear, nor walk."[31]

On this hemisphere, the Lamanites fell into idolatry;[32] in their days of more ripened iniquity they offered up human sacrifices, even of women and children, to their idols.[33] Idolatry afflicted the Nephites also;[34] and the Zoramites;[35] the Jaredites were not free from it;[36] and even the great Alma was at one time a victim to this curse.[37]

Yet the teachings of the American prophets strongly condemned idolatry. Jacob said:

"Yea, wo unto those that worship idols, for the devil of all devils delighteth in them."[38]

Whenever the American prophets spoke of idolatry it was in terms of strongest condemnation. It was always wickedness in the eyes of the Lord.

In the Lord's preface to the Doctrine and Covenants, he says:

"For they have strayed from mine ordinances, and have broken mine everlasting covenant;

"They seek not the Lord to establish his righteousness, but every man walketh in his own way, and after the image of his own God, whose image is in the likeness of the world, and whose substance is that of an idol, which waxeth old and shall perish in Babylon, even Babylon the great, which shall fall."[39]

The elders watching over the Churches were commanded:

"And let them labor with their own hands that there be no idolatry nor wickedness practised."[40]

Scriptures cited in support of the use of images in worship

But as we shall see, the worship of idols over the centuries crept into the post-Primitive Church. Those who seek to justify the use of images in worship — we will pass for the moment the question as to whether the images are actually worshipped — cite for their justification the following passages:

Exodus 25:17-22: where the Lord gives instructions as to placing two cherubim on the mercy seat, one on each end, the mercy seat to act as a covering for the ark of the covenant. But in this account there is no suggestion whatever of worshipping these cherubim, and the Lord concurrently with ordering the making of the cherubim forbade the worship of idols, with no hint, suggestion, or intimation that the cherubim should be worshipped.

Ezekiel 41:1, 15, 18, 19: where Ezekiel provides for the use of cherubim in decorating posts and pillars in his visioned temple.

Hebrews 9:1-5: where Paul gives some description of the ark of the covenant, the mercy seat, and the cherubim thereon.[41]

But no one of these references does more than tell of the existence of these cherubim, and, it may be repeated, there is not even a suggestion that they were, or were ever intended to be worshipped as images or idols. To repeat: — From the commandments at Sinai, down through all the generations of Israel's history, there is no variant to God's commandment that images should not be worshipped, that idolatry was born of Satan, and that man should worship God only.

Adoration of saints

The scriptures cited for the adoration of saints are equally beside the point.

As justifying a prayer to the Virgin and to saints for their intercession with God, I Chronicles 29:18 is cited, where David cries out: "O Lord God of Abraham, Isaac, and of Israel, our fathers . . ." This is said to show that David prayed " 'as now the Orthodox Church calls upon Christ our true God, by the prayers of His most pure Mother and all His saints.' "[42] Surely no reasonable interpretation of David's words could make of them a prayer by him that Abraham, Isaac, and Israel would intercede with God for him. The plain import of the prayer is that David was praying to the same God to which Abraham, Isaac, and Israel prayed, even as he said.

As justifying the appeal for the mediatory prayers of the saints in heaven, Revelation 8:3 ff. is invoked.[43] This tells of the angel who stood by the altar offering incense which ascended up before God, preceding the pouring out of calamities by the seven angels. While the saints are here said to be offering prayers to God, there is no suggestion that they are so praying at the request of some mortal.

To justify the dogma of "beneficent apparitions" of saints, Matthew 27:52 ff. is cited.[44] This scripture tells of the resurrection of many saints, after the resurrection of Christ, and that they appeared unto many. But these were resurrected beings; they came forth as all shall come forth, resurrected, in the due time of the Lord. They were not apparitions, but bodies of flesh and bone, even as Christ. They were not moving about because of the prayers of mortals, nor in answer to such prayers.[45]

As supporting the dogma "that the saints after their departure work miracles through certain earthly means," two scriptures are cited: II Kings 13:21 and Acts 19:12.[46] The II Kings passage refers to the dead man, who being buried, was let down and touched the bones of Elisha, "and stood up on his feet." There is nothing to show that this was done with the purpose of securing the restoration to life, nor that the prayers of any mortal were involved. It was a manifestation of God's power for a purpose not disclosed. It is not recorded as a procedure on principle, that should operate whenever invoked. The reference to Acts is to the healing power of Paul's handkerchiefs and aprons. But this miracle took place as between living persons; not between a living person and a dead saint or his clothing.[47]

Another scripture cited is Revelation 6:9,[48] where John, speaking of the opening of the seals by the Lamb, says, "And when he had opened the fifth seal, I saw under the altar the souls of them that were slain for the word of God, and for the testimony which they held." Those under the altar were *souls*, not the inanimate bodies of dead men, or the finger, or arm, or head thereof, which relics were, in later centuries, placed under the altars of churches. Moreover, these souls in Revelation were crying 'for the judging and avenging of their blood on them that dwelt on the earth,' and they were counseled patience yet for a little season. There is in this passage no indicated intercession by "souls" upon behalf of earthly persons praying to them for aid, and these souls extending such aid. On the contrary, the "souls" are here asking for vengeance upon those living in mortality.

Still another passage cited is Acts 5:15,[49] which recounts that people brought forth their sick into the streets, that, Peter passing and his shadow falling upon them, seemingly they might be healed. But this has no apparent relationship to the situation of mortals imploring aid to meet the problems of this life, from saints in heaven standing before the throne of God.

Intercession of martyrs and saints

The Western and Eastern Churches seem to hold an essentially common dogma as to martyrs and saints. The Roman catechism, answering the question as to whether the Church on earth has communion with the Church in heaven, says:

"The prayer of faith and love. The faithful who belong to the Church militant upon earth, in offering their prayers to God, call at the same time to their aid the saints who belong to the Church in heaven; and these, standing on the highest steps of approach to God, by their prayers and intercessions purify, strengthen, and offer before God the prayers of the faithful living upon earth, and by the will of God work graciously and beneficently upon them, either by invisible virtue, or by distinct apparitions, and in divers other ways."

The catechism further declares that this rule of the Church is grounded upon " 'a holy tradition, the principle of which is to be seen also in holy Scripture.' "[50] (In our talk, No. 24, we noted that tradition in the Church is not based upon scripture.)

The question of the service of the saints in heaven and their adoration, was considered at the Council of Trent and the Council's action was summarized by Pope Pius IV, as quoted by Hastings:

"In like manner I hold that the saints reigning with God are to be venerated and invoked, and that they offer prayers to God for us, and that their relics are to be venerated."[51]

At the Twenty-fifth Session, December 4, 1563, the Council of Trent defined with punctillious care the official attitude of the Church towards saints and relics. It enjoined bishops and other teachers:

" . . . that, agreeably to the usage of the Catholic and Apostolic Church, received from the primitive times of the Christian religion, and agreeably to the consent of the holy Fathers, and to the decrees of sacred Councils, they especially instruct the faithful diligently concerning the intercession and invocation of saints . . . teaching them, that the saints, who reign together with Christ, offer up their own prayers to God for men; that it is good and useful

suppliantly to invoke them, and to have recourse to
their prayers, aid, (and) help for obtaining benefits
from God, through his Son, Jesus Christ our Lord,
who is our alone Redeemer and Savior; but that
they think impiously who deny that the saints, who
enjoy eternal happiness in heaven, are to be in-
vocated; or who assert either that they do not pray
for men; or that the invocation of them to pray for
each of us even in particular is idolatry; or that it
is repugnant to the Word of God, and is opposed to
the honor of the one mediator of God and men, Christ
Jesus; or that it is foolish to supplicate, vocally or
mentally, those who reign in heaven.

"Also, that the holy bodies of holy martyrs, and
of others now living with Christ, — which bodies
were the living members of Christ, and the temple
of the Holy Ghost, and which are by him to be raised
unto eternal life, and to be glorified, — are to be
venerated by the faithful; through which (bodies)
many benefits are bestowed by God on men; so that
they who affirm that veneration and honor are not
due to the relics of saints; or that these, and other
sacred monuments, are uselessly honored by the
faithful; and that the places dedicated to the memories of the saints are in vain visited with the view
of obtaining their aid, are wholly to be condemned,
as the Church has already long since condemned, and
now also condemns them.

"Moreover, that the images of Christ, of the
Virgin Mother of God, and of the other saints, are
to be had and retained particularly in temples, and
that due honor and veneration are to be given them;

not that any divinity, or virtue, is believed to be in them, on account of which they are to be worshipped; or that any thing is to be asked of them; or that trust is to be reposed in images, as was of old done by the Gentiles, who placed their hope in idols; but because the honor which is shown them is referred to the prototypes which those images represent; in such wise that by the images which we kiss, and before which we uncover the head, and prostrate ourselves, we adore Christ, and we venerate the saints, whose similitude they bear: as, by the decrees of Councils, and especially of the second Synod of Nicaea, has been defined against the opponents of images."

The remainder of this Tridentine canon places paintings and other representations on the same basis as relics and images; refers to miracles "which God has performed by means of the saints," and affirms that any one who entertains "sentiments contrary to these decrees: let him be anathema"; directs the bishops to correct abuses to guard against subversive images, that the people are to be taught the true attitude towards images, superstitions are to be removed, there is to be nothing disorderly or indecorous, the placing of images is to be under the direction of the bishop, new miracles or relics are not to be recognized except upon procedure specified.[52]

The foregoing set out the *official* view of the Roman Church on saints, martyrs, relics, and images. But the whole history of the worship of martyrs and saints, their relics, and the images thereof, show that the common worshipper regarded all these in a far different light from that shown in the official view. And here it may be noted that the adoration, which among the common people became worship, had reached such proportions that the Church of England in its Thirty-Nine Articles, formally declared:

"The Romish Doctrine concerning Purgatory, Pardons, Worshipping and Adoration, as well of Images as of Relics, and also Invocation of Saints, is a fond thing, vainly invented, and grounded upon no warranty of Scripture, but rather repugnant to the Word of God."[53]

But the official view, as expressed in the Tridentine canons, above quoted, came after more than twelve full centuries of customs, practice, and doctrinal discussions and controversies. The earlier practices do not square with the official dogma, nor do present-day practices and concepts, as any one knows who has seen the overflowing emotion of the humble worshippers moaning in an ecstasy, an almost transporting delirium, of joy as they have caressed images of the Virgin and of the saints. The worshipping of martyrs and saints, their relics and images is so real among the great mass of those using them, that the philosophic explanation completely fails to meet the situation.

So it will be well to look at the conditions, early and later, out of which the official view sprang and from which has come the present practice and beliefs of the humble worshipper in all lands.

Development of adoration amounting to idolatry

A "falling away" into adorations and idolatry began to show its head in the post-Primitive Church in the early Christian centuries.

The religions with which Christianity came first into competition and then into a conflict of extermination, were in a large, if not total measure, idolatrous. It would be interesting and valuable, if time and space permitted, to examine the teachings of the various pagan sects, to learn the source of the idolatrous practices that came finally into the post-Primitive Church. But this examination cannot now be made. However, for the benefit of anyone interested, a reference may be made to a series of articles dealing with images and idols of the various world religions to be found in Hastings' Encyclopaedia of Religion and Ethics, sub voce Images and Idols.[54]

However, we might note here that Dr. Moore (of the Andover Theological Seminary) affirms that the earliest religions were aniconic (that is, against image worship), while the later ones were iconic (that is, for image worship). He says:

"Archæological evidence, however, confirms the fact that the iconic age was everywhere preceded by one in which the objects of worship were aniconic."

He explains:

"Thus Varro affirms that for more than 170 years from the founding of the city the Romans had no image of a god in human or animal form; Numa is said to have forbidden such representations; the

Persians had no temples or idols before Artaxerxes I; in Greece also temples and images of the gods were unknown in ancient times; the earliest temples of the Egyptians were without idols. Arab tradition, which is supported by philological evidence, declares that idols like that of Hobal at Mecca were of foreign origin."[55]

To the Latter-day Saints this precedence of the aniconic (non-idol) worship over the iconic (idol) worship can be easily understood, having in mind that Adam's posterity for generations were schooled in the worship of the true God, but that the passage of time took men farther and farther away from the truth.

It is not feasible here to trace in detail as between the worship of martyrs, saints, relics, and images, which corruption came first, nor how closely one followed the other. Indeed, apparently one merged imperceptibly into the other. Moreover, the exact development is not important for us here, nor the precise time thereof.

Robertson has traced out some of the inducing conditions that, over the early centuries, led to the seeping into and adoption by the Church of pagan rituals and practices.[56] We may briefly summarize his discussion of the corrupting influences and conditions of those early centuries, as follows:

He notes the adoption of increased splendor in churches, of gorgeous vestments of the officiating clergy, and of many new ceremonies. He cites St. Jerome (A.D. 340-420) as complaining "of the magnificence which was lavished on churches — their marble walls and pillars, their gilded ceilings, their jewelled altars — which he contrasts with the neglect of all care in the choice of fit persons for the ministry."[57]

The conversion of Constantine brought many pagans into the Church who were quite ignorant of Christian principles, who were still clinging to their heathen notions, and who were spiritually crippled from depravation of heathen morality. The churchmen zealously and blindly sought to win these pagans by elaborate ceremonies and splendid edifices that would rival the paganism they had outwardly repudiated but still inwardly believed, in the hope that the pagans would become true believers. The result could have been easily anticipated, because perfectly natural. True, the new converts, on the one hand, took on some of the Christian belief, but, in equal truth, the Christians, on the other hand, were infected with the doctrines and practices of heathendom. Pagan usages were brought into the Church, — as the burning of lamps and candles in the day, the burning of incense, lustrations (a method of purification) which earlier Christians had ridiculed in the pagans. One Christian writer (the Manich-aean Faustus) is quoted as assailing the Church in this wise:

"The sacrifices of the heathen ye have turned into feasts of charity; their idols into martyrs, whom ye honor with the like religious offices unto theirs; the ghosts of the dead ye appease with wine and delicates; the festival days of the nations ye celebrate together with them (as the kalends and the solstices) ; and of their kind of life ye have verily changed nothing."[58]

The concept of the heathen that external performance of duties was sufficient became the feeling of the Christians, and bounty to the Church covered the guilt of sin. St. Augustine is cited as saying that ordinary Christians pretending to any real seriousness in their worship were mocked by their fellow Christians as much as were the heathen converts to Christianity mocked by their former heathen associates.

The same persons went to Christian Churches to witness the elaborate church ceremonies and then to the pagan theatres and even temples to witness and participate in the heathen ceremonies.

Sermons became rhetorical displays, were received with cheers and the clapping of hands and shouts of "Orthodox" or "Thirteenth Apostle." When the more showy parts of the Church service were over, the people left, not even waiting for the eucharist. Doctrinal controversies, at times very bitter, added to the confusion. The new rituals brought in from the heathen worship, were adopted and regulated by the Church.

Another fostering practice for the adoption of heathenism was found in the use of heathen temples as churches.

Commenting upon this whole resulting situation, Gibbon says: "The sublime and simple theology of the primitive Christians was gradually corrupted; and the MONARCHY of heaven, already clouded by metaphysical subtleties, was degraded by the intro-

duction of a popular mythology, which tended to restore the reign of Polytheism."[59]

As already stated, the growth of this "veneration," which in fact, among the mass of the people
soon became the virtual worship of martyrs, saints,
relics, and images, was gradual. "It is admitted
without dispute that the veneration of saints had
its starting point in the veneration of the martyrs
who suffered death for the Christian faith."[60]

However, the source of the respect in which
martyrs were held almost from the earliest Christian
days, is indicated by certain New Testament scriptures, in which the Lord indicated the persecutions
they would suffer for his sake and the blessings resulting from enduring them.[61] In his charge to the
Twelve, Jesus said: "And he that taketh not his
cross, and followeth after me, is not worthy of me.
He that findeth his life shall lose it: and he that
loseth his life for my sake shall find it."[62]

This was repeated to the disciples and the
people, following the great confession of Peter at
Caesarea Philippi: " . . . Whosoever will come after
me, let him deny himself, and take up his cross, and
follow me. For whosoever will save his life shall
lose it; but whosoever shall lose his life for my sake
and the gospel's, the same shall save it. For what
shall it profit a man, if he shall gain the whole
world, and lose his own soul? Or what shall a man
give in exchange for his soul?"[63]

Authorities also cite to the same point the words
of John: "And I saw the woman drunken with the
blood of the saints, and with the blood of the mar-

tyrs . . .";[64] and, "I saw under the altar the souls
of them that were slain for the word of God, and for
the testimony which they held. . . . And white robes
were given unto every one of them";[65] and further,
"And I saw thrones, and they sat upon them, and
judgment was given unto them: and I saw the souls
of them that were beheaded for the witness of Jesus,
and for the word of God, and which had not worshipped the beast, neither his image, neither had received
his mark upon their foreheads, or in their hands;
and they lived and reigned with Christ a thousand
years."[66]

The respect and honor thus indicated for
him who suffered for Jesus' sake and the spread of
the Gospel were, in the early centuries, prostituted
into unholy and paganish idolatries, so constituting
one of the principal elements in the "falling away,"
the apostasy, predicted by Paul.

Beginning of martyr veneration

It seems that if a date for the beginning of
martyr "veneration" is to be named, it might be the
martyrdom of Polycarp, a little over a century and
a half after the beginning of the Christian era
(about 155). Polycarp's death was highly dramatic,
with some alleged miraculous elements, as related
in a letter "composed in the name of his church."
He was, under his condemning sentence, to be burned
at the stake, so runs the tradition, but the flames
swept around him instead of touching him, while
his body took on the color of bronze, and a perfume
like frankincense filled the air. The tradition con-

tinues,—as the flames seemed to refuse to burn Polycarp, his executioner stabbed him, whereupon blood
gushed out in quantities sufficient to quench the
fire; the heathens and Jews then burnt the body;
afterward the brethren gathered up what bones they
could secure and buried them.[67] The honor shown
to Polycarp's life, memory, and remains, indicated
to the people an 'extraordinary piety which seemed
to reveal the presence of the Spirit in exceptional
fulness,' a feeling that was enhanced by his martyrdom.

The Jews accusing the people of Smyrna of
worshipping the martyrs instead of the Christ, the
people answered they "did not worship (them) as
they did Christ the son of God, but regarded them
with fond affection as witnesses and imitators of the
Lord."[68]

It may be appropriately noted here that the
Scriptures contain no word, suggestion, or even
intimation that the Primitive Church had even the
vaguest notion of "venerating" its first martyr
Stephen. His "veneration" came centuries later,
after the martyr-worship had become thoroughly
established.

Further development of the cult

From this beginning with Polycarp, if it was
the beginning, the "veneration" of martyrs, saints,
relics, and images steadily increased, and easily developed into actual worship.

The recurring day of martyrdom began to be
held in remembrance, — the Greeks and Romans held

in annual commemoration the natal day of their illustrious dead. It was easy for pagans to shift their day of remembrance from the birth date of their heroes to the death date of the saints.

The early Christian fathers — Tertullian, Origen, Clement of Alexandria, and Cyprian — spoke of the martyrs in the most glowing terms. "Already in the Pastor of Hermas the martyrs are represented as wearing crowns; Hippolytus, Dionysius of Alexandria, and Tertullian describe them as fellow-judges with Christ, seated beside Him on thrones." Martyrdom began to be recognized as a "privilege and a trust. . . . Frequently the idea is made prominent that it is Christ Himself who is present and who suffers in the person of the martyr."[69] Persecution brought exceptional recognition. Martyrdom brought complete remission of sins, and entry of the soul immediately into the joys of paradise. The honor and "veneration" often extended to the family of the martyr.

The Apostolic Constitutions so-called (probably composed in the first half of the second century) contain the following: "If any Christian, on account of the name of Christ, and love and faith towards God, be condemned by the ungodly to the games, to the beasts, or to the mines, do not ye overlook him . . . for he that is condemned for the name of the Lord God is an holy martyr, a brother of the Lord, the son of the Highest, a receptacle of the Holy Spirit, by whom every one of the faithful has received the illumination of the glory of the holy Gospel, by being vouchsafed the incorruptible crown, and the testimony of Christ's sufferings, and the fellowship of His blood, to be made conformable to the death of Christ for the adoption of children."[70]

The martyr was even considered "as already possessing the dignity of the priesthood without ordination,"[71] a concept that utterly loses sight of the nature and significance of the priesthood and the manner of its bestowal.

The Jesuit Father, Thurston, (B.A., S.J.) in his article in Hastings, asserts that notwithstanding the facts above set out, "we have no satisfactory evidence of any general practice of cultus before the middle of the 3rd century. The origins of this cultus are no doubt to be found in the funeral rites which the Christians, in accordance with the customs of the pagan society in which they lived, paid to their honored dead. Even in the case of those who had suffered capital punishment, Roman practice usually conceded to the relatives of the deceased the free disposal of their remains. For the most part, therefore, the martyrs, like their fellow-believers, were buried with such observances as everyday usage prescribed, so far at any rate as these rites involved no direct recognition of polytheism or pagan superstition. *For the sacrifices to the gods was substituted the Eucharistic oblation; the banquets offered to the dead at the tomb were replaced by the Christian love-feast, and the same intervals between the celebrations were observed—3rd day, 9th day, 30th day (which in later centuries became the 'month's mind'), and anniversary. It was no doubt from these elements that the cultus of the Christian martyr took its point of departure."*[72] (Italics ours.)

Thus pagan rites incident to burial were transplanted into the Christian service. The usual pagan burial ceremonies thus became incidents of Christian worship that seemingly had no connection with burials — a further step in Paul's "falling away."

Where possible the Eucharist was celebrated at the grave side, not only for members of the bereaved family, but for the whole Christian community, though in the pre-Constantine era the tomb was not treated as an altar, though it was so treated not long thereafter. The banquets were emphasized by the Christians as "love feasts," which later, because of abuses, were largely suppressed. However, the celebration of the liturgy, bringing as it did the Christian communities together, soon took on a different significance at martyrs' graves than at others. These martyr rites increased as time went on. By the end of the 4th century orators preached panegyrics about the martyrs before great assemblies. The Jesuit Father, Thurston, says: "It is true that, as St. Augustine and others expressly pointed out, the sacrifice was offered to God, and in no sense to the saint himself, but it was none the less a supreme recognition of the martyr's dignity and formed the germ from which the whole calendar of saints' days ultimately developed."[73]

Thus this "falling away" further progressed. As Gibbon says: "The sublime and simple theology of the primitive Christians was gradually corrupted."[74]

Schaff notes the following on "The Worship of Saints":

"The Worship of Saints, handed down from the Nicene age, was a Christian substitute for heathen idolatry and hero-worship, and well suited to the taste and antecedents of the barbarian races, but was equally popular among the cultivated Greeks. The scholastics made a distinction between three grades of worship: 1) adoration . . . which belongs to God alone; 2) veneration . . . which is due to the saints as those whom God himself has honored, and who reign with him in heaven; 3) special veneration . . . which is due to the Virgin Mary as the mother of the Savior and the queen of all saints. But the people did not always mind this distinction, and the priests rather encouraged the excesses of saint-worship. Prayers were freely addressed to the saints, though not as the givers of the blessings desired, but as intercessors and advocates. . . . The question, how the saints and the Virgin Mary can hear so many thousands of prayers addressed to them simultaneously in so many different places, without being clothed with the divine attributes of omniscience and omnipresence, did not disturb the faith of the people. The scholastic divines usually tried to solve it by the assumption that the saints read those prayers in the omniscient mind of God. Then why not address God directly?"[75]

By this period (4th century) the invocation of saints was firmly established. "Prayers and appeals to the dead, as many inscriptions on pagan tombstones prove, were by no means unfamiliar to the heathen of Greece and Rome."[76] This practice of tomb prayers was adopted by the Christians. This custom was intensified by the Christians as to those who laid down their lives for the Master. But before this, during the time of Hippolytus and Origen, "we find unmistakable traces of a belief in the power of the holy dead to intercede for those on earth."[77] The memorials in the catacombs offer evidence that protection by the martyrs was sought. "Hence it seems probable," says the Jesuit Father, Thurston, "that the prevalent atmosphere of paganism exercised some vague influence upon Christian feeling, especially in the case of the ruder populace. The strongly marked desire to be buried near the martyrs is no doubt to be attributed to a similar hope of protection."[78]

Father Thurston considers this "a matter not so much of logic as of a deep and primitive instinct"; that burial near martyrs was in itself "a tacit request for their intercession"; and that by the end of the 4th century "the practice of praying to the martyrs was already firmly established."[79]

Father Thurston further observes: " . . . one of the causes which contributed most powerfully to the rapid extension of the veneration of martyrs was the multiplication of shrines and saints' days, due to the Oriental practice of translating and dividing relics,"[80] — that is the transporting from one place to another of the bodies of martyrs which often were cut up and one part sent to one place and another to another place, as *relics*.

As Father Thurston's observation indicates, the "veneration" of saints and of martyrs developed side by side.

Dr. Bonwetsch notes that the conversion of Constantine brought an unprecedented authority to prophets and apostles and to local officers, who "began to receive the veneration of the entire Church. ... Through the veneration of saints," he continues, "heathenism made its way into the Church which had supplanted it. Pagan worship of the dead became Christian martyrolatry, and the birthday feasts of the martyrs were but modifications of the banquets signalizing the pagan *parentalia*. ... Aphrodite became the source of legends connected with the names of Pelagia, Maria, Marina, Margaret, Anthusa, and Eugenia, and during the last years of an expiring paganism marked by the wide-spread worship of female divinities greater emphasis came to be laid on the worship of the 'Mother of God.' With the gods came also the heroes; the hymn to the martyr was but a substitute for the hymn to the hero, the translation of one was the deification of the other, and the pagan statue was replaced by the Christian relic, in the adoration of which such enlightened spirits as Gregory of Nyssa engaged. The host of saints, increased by the accession of a new category, that of ascetics ... as intercessors between man and God. ... The veneration of the saints was formally sanctioned by the second Nicene Council (787) which distinguished, however, between the *proskynesis* or *douleia*, the reverence due to the saints and the absolute worship, *latreia*, to be rendered to God alone. In the West, though the Caroline Books (q.v.) pronounced for the veneration of the saints, Charlemagne was no friend of the cult in its extreme

form. . . . In the case of a Bernard or Francis of
Assisi veneration was paid to a saintly character
even in his lifetime. It was the voice of the people
that at first bestowed the title of holiness; Ulrich
of Augsburg was the first to receive the papal canonization. Scholasticism supplied the dogmatic basis
for the worship of saints by describing them as
friends of God and intercessors before his throne.
The distinction between *douleia* and *latreia* was preserved and the saints were divided into six cate-
gories, patriarchs and prophets, apostles, martyrs,
confessors, virgins, and holy women. Indeed the
close of the Middle Ages was marked by the appearance of many new saints, the worship of Anna, the
mother of Mary, becoming at that time the basis of a
separate cult in Germany."[81]

The Jesuit Father, Thurston, has traced in some
detail the development of the lists of saints, — the
Calendar of Saints. It seemingly began with a recognition of martyrs only; it was then enlarged to
include "confessors" — "one who has borne testimony to his belief at some cost to himself — e.g., by
imprisonment or exile," but "one who has not been
put to the test of grievous bodily torment," these
constituting "a second category of saints," the building of which was facilitated by the practice of "according a special commemoration in the liturgy to
deceased bishops and of keeping locally a formal
record of their anniversaries."[82]

Father Thurston further notes that Cyril of
Jerusalem (c. 349), indicated the classes "of those no
longer living for whom prayer is made in the

liturgy," the first being patriarchs, prophets, apostles, martyrs, and the second " 'holy fathers and bishops who have fallen asleep before.' " He also notes "the famous *Chronography* of Philocalus (A.D. 354)," which contains two documents; one is a record of "the anniversaries of the bishops of Rome with their names and places of interment," the other giving a like record of the "Roman martyrs." These two documents (though seemingly after the 4th century) were later amplified and consolidated into one, in which "we may recognize the first rude outlines of the elaborate *calendaria* and *martyrologia* which came to play so prominent a part in the hagiographical developments of the Middle Ages."[83] This amalgamated list, which seemingly largely destroyed any distinction between martyrs and confessors, was later (apparently in the 6th century) augmented by famous ascetics. However, the term saint (sanctus), in its later technical sense, was not applied to the martyrs, confessors, and ascetics, until the 7th century.[84]

Father Thurston notes, as does Dr. Bonwetsch (supra) that (at first) the people declared this character of saintship upon a martyr or confessor; indeed, Father Thurston speaks of this as "a genuine claim to saintship," and also of the commemorative assemblies of the people for worship at the tomb, where laudatory orations were delivered and the liturgy celebrated. When possible, altars and churches were erected over the tomb. He further observes that as time went on, "when the martyrologies were no longer local and had enlarged their scope, it must be

admitted that many names were added to the roll of
saints without adequate investigation and upon quite
insufficient data." These have been characterized as
"literary canonizations." Father Thurston adds: "An
old-world story familiar to modern readers as that of
Faust was at one time attached to the name of a
mythical St. Cyprian of Antioch; the gruesome
tale of OEdipus seems responsible for the evolution of a St. Albanus and other imaginary personages; while the well-known legend of Buddha re-
appears in Christian hagiography under the guise
of the *Acta* of Saints Barlaam and Joasaph." He
adds further: "On the other hand, there are a number of instances in which a perfectly legitimate
cultus, contemporaneous with the saint's death,
has afterwards become surcharged with all sorts
of legendary excrescences, often preposterous in
themselves, and quite inconsistent with the facts
of history," and he lists the *Acta* of St. Thomas, "or
in those of his fellow-apostles," or of Thecla (reputed
convert of Paul), St. Procopius, the *Lives* of St.
George; and in secular history he mentions the
fables that clustered around Alexander the Great
and Charlemagne. He observes that when the
"existence and the holiness of the person venerated" is even without doubt, "it is not always possible
to explain how the cultus first arose. Often enough
its chief developments were associated with the dis-
covery of relics of doubtful authenticity, or with the
occurrence of cures believed to be miraculous." First
calling attention to the unlikelihood of any credible
record of investigation of the circumstances of mar-

tyrdom, Father Thurston observes: "As a result, legend and historical fact have in many cases become hopelessly confused."[85]

Ado and Usuard (imitators of Bede who 'originated a new type of *martyrologium*') prepared new lists, and "mainly from the work of the last-named the present quasi-official Roman martyrology, which is read in choir as part of the liturgical office, was compiled by Cardinal Baronius at the end of the 16th century."[86]

Out of these lists came the hosts of saints that supplied the demand for the various patron saints of countries, communities, and individuals.

Commenting upon the charged conscious adoption by Christians of pagan rites, ceremonies, and practices, Father Thurston says: "The reproach has constantly been made against the veneration of saints, as it was practised in the Christian Church from the 4th cent. onwards, that it differed little either in its essence or in its manifestations from the pagan worship of gods and heroes." And we quote again the Father's statement that: "The almost ineradicable tendency among the rude and uneducated to cling to their primitive customs led beyond doubt to a certain amount of compromise in matters which were not judged to be distinctively pagan. It was the advice of St. Gregory Thaumaturgus, of St. Augustine, and of St. Gregory the Great that an attempt should be made to Christianize their popular observances, if not absolutely evil in themselves, rather than to extirpate them. If a particular day had been kept as a holiday, let it be transformed into a Christian festival; if there had been resort to a particular site for superstitious purposes, let some worthier object of pilgrimage be substituted; if certain practices connected with funerals, weddings, or other ceremonial occasions had established themselves firmly in the hearts of the people, let them be given a Christian colouring or significance."[87]

Thus is admitted by this scholarly Jesuit the essential fact of the paganizing of Christianity in the post-Primitive Church, of the present existence in the Church to-day of these paganized cults and dogmas, — an admission that the jurists term an admission against interest, and therefore of the highest probative value.

All these paganisms constitute a departure from Gibbon's "sublime and simple theology of the primitive Christians,"[88] and this departure constitutes a "falling away"[89] predicted by Paul, the "damnable heresies"[90] spoken of by Peter, and the idolatry from which Paul exhorted the Corinthians to flee,[91] which added together with other things hereafter to be discussed, make the apostasy which latter-day revelation declares took place in the world following the disappearance of the Primitive Church and its organization.

To Israel, wandering in the wilderness, the Lord declared: "Thou shalt fear the Lord thy God, and serve him, and shalt swear by his name. Ye shall not go after other gods, of the gods of the people which are round about you,"[92] and Jesus, tempted of the Devil, repeated that law as still operative: "Thou

shalt worship the Lord thy God, and him only shalt
thou serve."[93]

To the multitude on the Mount, the Master
said: "No man can serve two masters: for either he
will hate the one, and love the other; or else he will
hold to the one, and despise the other. Ye cannot
serve God and mammon."[94] Later he repeated this to
his disciples, "and the Pharisees also, who were
covetous, heard all these things: and they derided
him."[95]

The whole scriptures hold one language only
as to the worship of idols and images, and anything
other than God himself, and no scriptures can be
found that can be fairly interpreted otherwise. The
commandment at Sinai has stood during all the
centuries and still stands:

"Thou shalt have no other gods before me.

"Thou shalt not make unto thee any graven
image, or any likeness of any thing that is in heaven
above, or that is in the earth beneath, or that is in
the water under the earth:

"Thou shalt not bow down thyself to them, nor
serve them: for I the Lord thy God am a jealous God,
visiting the iniquity of the fathers upon the children
unto the third and fourth generation of them that
hate me;

"And shewing mercy unto thousands of them
that love me, and keep my commandments."[96]

God has always condemned idolatry, always declared that idol worship was for the "devil of all
devils," always commanded that none should be
worshipped but himself.

This is God's law today, and no amount of sophistry, no amount of scriptureless "tradition," no amount of pageantry, of pomp, and of ceremony, can vary a hairsbreadth this divine law or add thereto or take therefrom one jot or tittle.

---

[1]Ex. 31:18. [2]Ex. 20:3-6. [3]Ex. 32:1 ff. [4]Ex. 32:9 ff.; see Acts 7:41. [5]Deut. 29:17. [6]I Kings 11:4-13. [7]I Kings 11-14. [8]I Kings 15:12; 14:21 ff.; II Chron. 14:1 ff. [9]I Kings 21:25-26. [10]I Kings 18:17 ff. [11]II Kings 21:9, 11. [12]II Chron. 33:7. [13]II Chron. 33:11-15. [14]II Kings 21:21-22. [15]II Chron. 34:3-5, 2. [16]Ps. 106:38. [17]Ps. 115:4. [18]Ps. 135:15-18. [19]Is. 2:8-9. [20]Jer. 50:38. [21]Ezek. 6:4-6, 9; and see for a recapitulation of God's dealings with Israel and their transgressions and idolatry, Ezek. 20. [22]Hos. 8:4; 13:2-4. [23]Mic. 1:7; see also Hab. 2:18; Zech. 10:2; 13:2. [24]Acts 15:19-20; 21:25. [25]Acts 17:16; and see Rom. 2:22. [26]I Cor. 8:1. [27]Acts 15:29. [28]I Cor. 8:4-7; and see 10:18 ff.; 28; 12:2; II Cor. 6:14 ff.; I Thess. 1:9. [29]I Cor. 10:20: [30]I John 5:21. [31]Rev. 9:20; and see as to those who worship the beast and its image, Rev. 14 and 15; and as to the woman upon whose forehead was written, "Mystery, Babylon the Great, the Mother of Harlots and Abominations of the Earth," Rev. 17; and as to the Great and Abominable Church, the Church of the Devil, 1 Ne. 13:4 ff; 14:3, 10 ff.; 22:13 ff.; 2 Ne. 6:12; 10:16; 23:19; 4 Ne. 29. [32]Enos 20; Mos. 9:12; Al. 17:15. [33]Morm. 4:14, 21. [34]Mos. 11:6-7; Al. 1:32; 50:21. [35]Al 31:1. [36]Eth. 7:23. [37]Mos. 27:8. [38]2 Ne. 9:37; see He. 6:31. [39]D.C. 1:15-16. [40]D.C. 52:39. [41]See Schaff, History of the Christian Church, IV, p. 460. [42]Hastings, Encyclopaedia of Religion and Ethics, sub voce Saints and Martyrs (Christian), p. 51b. [43]Id. [44]Id. [45]For the explanation of the Eastern Church of this passage, see The Longer Catechism, No. 266, Schaff, Creeds of Christendom, II, p. 486. [46]Hastings, Encyc., op. cit., p. 51b. [47]For Eastern Church view on meaning of these passages, see Schaff, Creeds, II, p. 486-487. [48]Hastings, op. cit., p. 53a. [49]Acts 5:15. [50]Hastings, op. cit., p. 51. [51]Id. [52]Schaff, Creeds, II, p. 199 ff. [53]Schaff, Creeds, III, p. 501, Article XXII; for a summary discussion of the meaning of this Article, as interpreted by the high and low branches of the Church of England, see Hastings, op. cit., p. 52. [54]See also a summary discussion in Encyclopaedia Biblica, sub voce Idolatry and Primitive Religion. [55]Encyclopaedia Biblica, op. cit., II, col. 2155. [56]Robertson, History of the Christian Church, II, p. 43 ff. [57]Op cit., p. 43. [58]Op. cit., p. 44-45. [59]Gibbon, The Decline and Fall of the Roman Empire, Milman Edition, II, p. 314-15. [60]Hastings, op. cit., p. 52b. [61]Matt. 10:16 ff.; Luke 21:12 ff.; John 15:18 ff. [62]Matt. 10:38-39. [63]Mark 8:34-37; Matt. 16:24 ff.; Luke 9:23 ff. [64]Rev. 17:6. [65]Rev. 6:9, 11. [66]Rev. 20:4. [67]Robertson, I, p. 42-44. [68]The New Schaff-Herzog Encyclopedia of Religious Knowledge, sub voce Saints, Veneration of, p. 175. [69]Hastings, op. cit., p. 53a. [70]Constitutions of the Holy Apostles, Book V, Sec. I, The Ante-Nicene Fathers, VII, p. 437. [71]Hastings, op. cit., p. 53b. [72]Op. cit., p. 53b-54a. [73]Op. cit., p. 54b. [74]Gibbon, supra. [75]Schaff, Hist., IV, p. 442-45. [76]Hastings, op. cit., p. 54b. [77]Id. [78]Id., [79]Op cit., p. 54b-55a. [80]Op. cit., p. 55a.

[81]*Schaff-Herzog, op. cit.* [82]Hastings, *op. cit.*, p. 55b. [83]*Op. cit.*, p. 55b-56a. [84]*Op cit.*, p. 56a-56b. [85]*Op. cit.*, p. 56b-57a. [86]*Op. cit.*, p. 57a. [87]*Op. cit.*, p. 58a-b. [88]Gibbon, *supra.* [89]II Thess. 2:3. [90]II Pet. 2:1. [91]I Cor. 10:7, 14. [92]Deut. 6:13-14. [93]Matt. 4:10; Luke 4:8. [94]Matt. 6:24. [95]Luke 16:14. [96]Ex. 20:3-6.

C

RELICS

It seems that a very few basic elements underlie the adoption by the Christians of pagan practices, rites, and ceremonies.

First, there was the almost fanatical desire of the Christians to convert the pagans, and to this end they became willing to yield their principles and doctrines to meet the pagan principle of hero worship. If the pagan, half believing, could be brought into a verbal seeming full fellowship by letting him worship martyrs and saints instead of heroes, — why not?

Then there was, next, the ever-widening influence of this great influx of half-converted pagans upon the existing body of real Christians, — an influence multiplied and fructified by business, social, cultural, and inter-family relations. One is inclined to yield to friends and kinfolk for the sake of peace and harmony and of affectionate association.[1]

The pagans continued to exercise direct influence until the decree of death pronounced by Theodoric the Goth against those who practiced pagan rites, and thereafter 'paganism ceased to appear in the light of history.'[2] But in rural areas the influence continued until long, long after, pagan ceremonies finally finding regular place in Christian services.[3]

For the authority for this innovation of adoration in the Christian worship of the bodies or parts of bodies of saints, one scriptural passage is cited.⁴ It is taken from Daniel's account of his vision of the four beasts, where he says, regarding the four great beasts, which he was told were four kings: "But the saints of the most High shall take the Kingdom, and possess the kingdom for ever, even for ever and ever."⁵ Surely this is a very slender thread upon which to hang so heavy a burden as the worship of men instead of the worship of God, and our Lord Jesus Christ, and the Holy Ghost.⁶

But perhaps as one of the potent causes for the adoption of this non-gospel practice we may note the human infirmity that enables one more easily to yield honor, obedience, and even reverence to an object cognizant to the physical senses, particularly when the material object was a presumed relic of some noteworthy person, than it is to yield such honor, obedience, and reverence to an abstraction or to a being which to most men must be conceived in the mind, without the aid of the physical senses; and so came first the adoration of the man as he lived, then his body, then his grave, then articles connected with his life, then his image, — a statue, a painting. Gibbon affirms that within 150 years from the death of Peter and Paul "the Vatican and the Ostian road were distinguished by the tombs, or rather by the trophies, of those spiritual heroes."⁷

In the age which followed the conversion of Constantine (which he affirmed was the result of the appearance in the noon-day sky of a bright cross,

witnessed by himself and his whole army, around
the cross being traced the words, "In hoc signa
vinces")[8] "the emperors, the consuls, and the gener-
als of armies, devoutly visited the sepulchres of a
tentmaker and a fisherman; and their venerable
bones were deposited under the altars of Christ, on
which the bishops of the royal city continually offered
the unbloody sacrifice."[9]

As the cultus developed, the bodies of martyrs
were dug up, cut into fragments, and transferred
to other places, each fragment — a finger, or an
arm, or a head, or other part — being "supposed to
possess a supernatural virtue, and were deposited
under the altars of churches."[10]

"In his (Julian) time every altar had its
relics."[11]   Indeed, it appears that this was required;[12] and it would seem to be still a requisite that each
altar, at least in cathedrals, must have a relic, such
as a finger, or other fragment of a saint, within or
under it, the placing thus of a relic being a solemn
part of the ceremony of consecration of the
Church.[13]

The digging up and dismembering of the bodies
of saints had become so prevalent by the first half of
the 4th century (356), that St. Antony, after giving away his fewer than half dozen belongings,
charged his disciples that on his death they bury him
in a place unknown to any but themselves, "lest his
remains should be embalmed and kept above
ground."[14]

Because of the numerous fake relics that appeared, Theodosius enacted (in 386) a law forbid-

ding the buying or selling of the bodies of martyrs, or the moving of them from one place to another.[15]

The pagan Eunapius, in vitriolic terms, condemned " 'the new worship' " of the saints, whom he characterized as " 'the meanest and most contemptible slaves.' " He added: " 'The heads, salted and pickled, of those infamous malefactors, who for the multitude of their crimes have suffered a just and ignominious death; their bodies, still marked by the impression of the lash, and the scars of those tortures which were inflicted by the sentence of the magistrate; such' (continues Eunapius) 'are the gods which the earth produces in our days; such are the martyrs, the supreme arbitrators of our prayers and petitions to the Deity, whose tombs are now consecrated as the objects of the veneration of the people.' "[16]

While one can but pity the spiritual blindness which inspired these words about those who died for their testimony and service of the Christ, the comments are of interest as showing in what way the cultus was understood.

Great miracles were claimed as the result of visiting the burial places of the martyrs.[17]

By the middle of the sixth century, churches were dedicated to saints and angels, and whereas originally there was but one altar in the Church, it now became common for altars to be erected to saints.[18]

But the worship of martyrs soon brought along the worship of the Apostles and the early patriarchs. Their burial places were located (frequently through

alleged visions and other manifestations) and their
bodies—sometimes buried centuries before—were
dug up and moved to some other place. The bodies
(so claimed) of Andrew, Luke, and Timothy were
so moved to Constantinople. Likewise the ashes of
Samuel (so claimed), the prophet-judge of Israel,
were brought to the same city with all the pomp and
ceremony of a travelling sovereign. The burial
place of Stephen, the first martyr, was assertedly
revealed by a dream to a presbyter, which to remove
all doubts in the presbyter's mind, was repeated on
three successive Saturdays. According to the account, it was Gamaliel who appeared to the presbyter
in this dream. The presbyter was told that there
were four graves side by side,—Gamaliel's, his son's,
a friend's, and Stephen's. The four graves were
opened, the fourth, Stephen's, was opened last. When
Stephen's remains were "shown to the light, the
earth trembled, and an odor, such as that of paradise, was smelt, which instantly cured the various
diseases of seventy-three of the assistants." Steph-
en's relics were transported to a church on Mount
Zion; "and the minute particles of those relics, a drop
of blood, or the scrapings of a bone, were acknowledged, in almost every province of the Roman world,
to possess a divine and miraculous virtue."[19]

The bishop of Hippo, who felt that Hippo had
been less favorably treated than other places, recorded some seventy miracles, including three resur-
rections from the dead, wrought in two years by the
relics he had, but he wanted more.[20]

But the law of Theodosius (386) above noted,

neither cured, nor even curbed, the credulity of the people nor the cupidity of fakirs. Relics multiplied in unbelievable numbers and of impossible articles.

In England, at Walsingham, Erasmus (1466-1536) was shown the Virgin's congealed milk, and the middle joint of one of Peter's fingers. At Canterbury, Erasmus and Colet were shown relics of Thomas á Becket, including the "rags with which the archbishop had blown his nose, Colet held them only a moment in his fingers and let them drop in disgust."[21]

In Germany the friars purveyed all sorts of merchandise "from the bones of Balaam's ass to the straw of the manger and feathers from St. Michael's wings."[22]

In Vienna they displayed a piece of Noah's ark, drops of the sweat of Jesus in the garden of Gethsemane as well as some of the incense brought to the Christ child by wise men from the East.[23]

The Archbishop of Mainz, Albrecht, collected no fewer than 8133 sacred fragments and 42 entire bodies of saints. This mass of materials included the body of Christ, his own body which lay in the tomb, a statue of the Virgin with a full bottle of her milk hanging from her neck, several of the pots that had been used at Cana and a portion of the wine Jesus made at the marriage feast, some of the actual manna which the Israelites had collected in the wilderness, and some earth from a field in Damascus from which God made Adam.[24]

Frederick the Wise of Saxony, on a pilgrimage to Jerusalem, brought back some 5005 sacred relics, including "a thorn from the crown of thorns, a tunic belonging to John the Evangelist, milk from the Virgin's breast, a piece of Mt. Calvary, a piece of the table on which the Last Supper was eaten, fragments of the stones on which Christ stood when he wept over Jerusalem and as he was about to ascend to heaven, the entire body of one of the Bethlehem Innocents, one of the fingers of St. Anna, 'the most blessed of grandmothers'—*beatissimae aviae,*—pieces of the rods of Aaron and Moses, a piece of Mary's girdle and some of the straw from the Bethlehem manger."[25]

Schaff glosses Calvin's tract on Relics as follows:

"What was at first a foolish curiosity for preserving relics has degenerated into abominable idolatry. The great majority of the relics are spurious. It could be shown by comparison that every apostle has more than four bodies and every saint two or three. The arm of St. Anthony, which was worshipped in Geneva, when brought out from the case, turned out to be a part of a stag. The body of Christ could not be obtained, but the monks of Charroux pretend to have, besides teeth and hair, the prepuce or pellicle cut off in his circumcision. But it is shown also in the Lateran church at Rome. The blood of Christ which Nicodemus is said to have received in a handkerchief or a bowl, is exhibited in Rochelle, in Mantua, in Rome, and many other places. The manger in which he laid at his birth, his cradle, together with the shirt which his mother made, the pillar on which he leaned when disputing in the Temple, the water-pots in which he turned water into wine, the nails, and pieces of the cross, are shown in Rome, Ravenna, Pisa, Cluny, Angers, and elsewhere.

"The table of the last Supper is at Rome, in the church of St. John in the Lateran; some of the bread at St. Salvador in Spain; the knife with which the Paschal Lamb was cut up, is at Treves. What semblance of possibility is there that that table was found seven or eight hundred years after? Besides, tables were in those days different in shape from ours, for people used to recline at meals. Fragments of the cross found by St. Helena are scattered over many churches in Italy, France, Spain, etc., and would form a good shipload, which it would take three hundred men to carry instead of one. But they say that this wood never grows less! Some affirm that their fragments were carried by angels, others that they dropped down from heaven. Those of Poitiers say that their piece was stolen by a maid-servant of Helena and carried off to France. There is still a greater controversy as to the three nails of the cross: one of them was fixed in the crown of Constantine, the other two were fitted to his horse's bridle, according to Theodoret, or one was kept by Helena herself, according to Ambrose. But now there are two nails at Rome, one at Siena, one at Milan, one at Carpentras, one at Venice, one at Cologne, one at Treves, two at Paris, one at Bourges, etc. All the claims are equally good, for the nails are all spurious. There is also more than one soldier's spear, crown of thorns, purple robe, the seamless coat, and Veronica's napkin (which at least six cities boast of having). A piece of broiled fish, which Peter offered to the risen Savior on the seashore, must have been wondrously well salted if it has kept for these fifteen centuries! But, jesting apart, is it supposable that the apostles made relics of what they had actually prepared for dinner?

"Calvin exposes with equal effect the absurdities and impieties of the wonder-working pictures of Christ; the relics of the hair and milk of the Virgin Mary, preserved in so many places, her combs, her wardrobe and baggage, and her house carried by angels across the sea to Loreto; the shoes of St. Joseph; the slippers of St. James; the head of John the Baptist, of which Rhodes, Malta, Lucca, Nevers, Amiens, Besancon, and Noyon claim to have portions; and his fingers, one of which is shown at Besancon, another at Toulouse, another at Lyons, another at Bourges, another at Florence. At Avignon they have the sword with which John was beheaded, at Aix-la-Chapelle the linen cloth placed under him by the kindness of the executioner, in Rome his girdle and the altar at which he said prayers in the desert. It is strange, adds Calvin, that they do not also make him perform mass.

"The tract concludes with this remark: 'So completely are the relics mixed up and huddled together, that it is impossible to have the bones of any martyr without running the risk of worshipping the bones of some thief or robber, or, it may be, the bones of a dog, or a horse, or an ass, or—Let every one, therefore, guard against this risk. Henceforth no man will be able to excuse himself by pretending ignorance.' "[26]

A very celebrated case of the sale of relics was in this wise. In the Imperial chapel at Constantinople was lodged the affirmed crown of thorns that had been placed on the head of the Savior at the time of his crucifixion. Romanian barons borrowed 13,-134 pieces of gold on the security of this crown. The debt being unpaid and the security (the crown) about to be forfeited, a rich Venetian offered to pay the creditors provided the crown, if unredeemed within a certain time, should become the absolute property of Venice. Baldwin, unwilling to let the relic go to Venice, negotiated with the King of France, to whom he delivered the crown, receiving back "a free gift" of ten thousand marks of silver, with which apparently the debt was paid. Frederic having granted the crown a free and honorable passage, the court of France went out devoutly to meet it. Reaching Paris, it was borne "in triumph through Paris by the king himself, barefoot, and in his shirt." Urged by the success of this sale, Baldwin disposed of "the remaining furniture of his chapel; a large and authentic portion of the true cross; the baby-linen of the Son of God, the lance, the sponge, and the chain of his Passion; the rod of Moses, and part of the skull of St. John the Baptist." It was claimed an "inveterate ulcer" was cured by being pricked with a thorn from this crown.[27]

It is unnecessary to follow the matter further. Speaking with all deference, yet with truth, one can only characterize all this as superstition for which there can be found in the Scriptures no sufficient or reasonable justification. The facts, moreover, clearly show the imposition which has been practiced— consciously, it must be—upon the credulity of the people.

May our people guard against any such "falling away" as this. The worship of "relics" must not become part of our system. Historical sites or places noted in our history are not to be worshipped or clothed with sanctity. It is interesting to visit them. On such occasions we may be moved emotionally or spiritually, but this comes, not from the place, but from our inner selves stirred thereto by the thoughts and spiritual reflections our visit has engendered.

---

[1]See Robertson, *History of the Christian Church*, II, p. 44. [2]*Op. cit.*, p. 248; and see Gibbon, *The Decline and Fall of the Roman Empire*, Milman's New Edition, II, p. 295 ff., 309 ff. [3]See Gibbon, supra. [4]See Robertson, III, p. 135 ff. [5]Dan. 7:18-19; *The New Schaff-Herzog Encyclopedia of Religious Knowledge*, sub voce *Saints, Veneration of*, p. 175. [6]See Gibbon, III, p. 467; *Schaff-Herzog, op. cit.*, p. 176a. [7]Gibbon, II, p. 311. [8]*Encyclopaedia Britannica*, 9th (American) Edition, sub voce *Constantine*, p. 300-301. [9]Gibbon, supra. [10]Robertson, II, p. 60. [11]Schaff-Herzog, *op. cit.*, p. 176a. [12]Gibbon, II, p. 311-2; Hastings, *Encyclopaedia of Religion and Ethics*, sub voce *Relics*, p. 657a, Second Council of Nicaea. [13]Hastings, *op. cit.*, p. 657a. [14]Robertson, II, p. 6, 61. [15]*Op. cit.*, p. 62. [16]Gibbon, II, p. 310-311. [17]Robertson, II, p. 62; Gibbon, II, p. 313. [18]Robertson, II, p. 355. [19]Gibbon, II, p. 311-313. [20]*Id.* [21]Schaff, *History of the Christian Church*, V, pt. II, p. 741. [22]*Op. cit.*, p. 742. [23]*Id.* [24]*Id.* [25]*Op. cit.*, p. 742-743. [26]Schaff, *Hist.*, VII, p. 607-609. [27]Gibbon, IV, p. 305 ff.

D

IMAGES

Commenting upon the matters which materially affected the decline and fall of the Roman Empire (and he lists "the propagation of Christianity, the constitution of the Catholic church, the ruin of Paganism, and the sects that arose from the mysterious controversies concerning the Trinity and incarnation"), Gibbon says: "At the head of this class we may justly rank the worship of images, so fiercely disputed in the eighth and ninth centuries; since a question of popular superstition produced the revolt of Italy, the temporal power of the popes, and the restoration of the Roman empire in the West. The primitive Christians were possessed with an unconquerable repugnance to the use and abuse of images. . . . The Mosaic law had severely proscribed all representations of the Deity. . . . The wit of the Christian apologists was pointed against the foolish idolaters, who bowed before the workmanship of their own hands . . . the first notice of the use of pictures is in the censure of the council of Illiberis, three hundred years after the Christian æra. . . . The first introduction of a symbolic worship was in the veneration of the cross and of relics. The saints and martyrs, whose intercession was implored, were seated on the right hand of God; but the gracious and often supernatural favors, which, in the popular belief, were showered round their tomb, conveyed an unquestionable sanction of the devout pilgrims, who visited, and touched, and kissed these lifeless remains, the memorials of their merits and sufferings. But a memorial more interesting than the skull or the sandals of a departed worthy is the faithful copy of his person and features, delineated by the arts of painting or sculpture . . . the images of the Roman emperors were adored with civil, and almost religious honors; a reverence less ostentatious, but more sincere, was applied to the statues of sages and patriots; and these profane virtues, these splendid sins, disappeared in the presence of the holy men, who had died for their celestial and everlasting country. At first the experiment was made with caution and scruple; and the venerable pictures were discreetly allowed to instruct the ignorant, to awaken the cold, and to gratify the prejudices of the heathen proselytes. By a slow though inevitable progression, the honors of the original were transferred to the copy: the devout Christian prayed before the image of a saint; and the Pagan rites of genuflection, luminaries, and incense, again stole into the Catholic church. The scruples of reason, or piety, were silenced by the strong evidence of visions and miracles; and the pictures which speak, and move, and bleed, must be endowed with a divine energy, and may be considered as the proper objects of religious adoration. The most audacious pencil might tremble in the rash attempt of defining, by forms and colors, the infinite Spirit, the eternal

Father, who pervades and sustains the universe. But the superstitious mind was more easily reconciled to paint and to worship the angels, and above all, the Son of God, under the human shape, which on earth they have condescended to assume. . . . The use, and even the worship, of images was firmly established before the end of the sixth century."[1]

Schaff affirms that: "A superstitious fancy even invented stories of wonder-working pictures, and ascribed to them motion, speech, and action."[2]

Those who worshipped images assert that such worship "like many other unwritten things, was matter of apostolical tradition, and had been taught to the church by the Holy Ghost; that it would be as reasonable to ask for scriptural proof in favor of reverencing the cross or the gospels."[3]

This is another instance where there is a tacit admission that there is no scripture for a particular dogma and cult of the Church, and no revelation, only tradition, and a tradition that did not take its full form and secure its complete recognition until centuries after the Primitive Church had lapsed and until the people had forgotten the early doctrines of the Church which abhorred images. It is a curious phenomenon that in this and other matters, the *tradition* that survived was the pagan tradition which corrupted the doctrines of the Gospel of Christ, and not a tradition that kept alive the true Gospel and ordinances. So works Satan, then, now, and while mortality lasts.

The patriarch of Constantinople, Germanus, declining the overtures of Leo the Isaurian to forsake image worship, "argued that images were meant to represent, not the Trinity, but the incarnation; that, since the Savior's appearance in human form, the Old Testament prohibitions were no longer applicable."[4]

To the foregoing thought, John of Damascus added this further idea, that we "must not be in bondage to the mere letter of Scripture," and reiterated the tradition concept by affirming, as stated by Robertson, that "images stand on the same ground with these doctrines, which have been gathered by the fathers from the Scriptures. Holy Scripture countenances images by the directions for the making of the cherubim, and also by our Lord's words as to the tribute-money. As that which bears Caesar's image is Caesar's, and is to be rendered to him; so, too, that which bears Christ's image is to be rendered to Christ, forasmuch as it is Christ's. That images are material, is no good reason for refusing to reverence them; for the holy places are material, the ink and the parchment of the Gospels are material, the eucharistic table, its vessels and its ornaments,— nay, the very body and blood of the Savior,—are material. . . . Images, he continues, are for the unlearned what books are for those who can read; they are to the sight what speech is to the ears."[5]

These observations are the purest sophistry. Regarding the coin, Christ said: "Render therefore unto Caesar the things which are Caesar's; and unto God the things that are God's."[6] Jesus was not talking of worship, but was parrying an entrapping thrust as to the legality of paying taxes. Further-

more, John of Damascus seeks to justify one heresy
by assuming the legality of others. There is no scriptural authority for worship of "Holy places." The
sanctity of the gospels attaches to the truths they
teach, not to the ink and parchment upon which the
gospels are written; and there is no word in the
Scriptures attaching a sanctity to the eucharistic
table.

Still later, in the iconoclastic conflict (A. D.
808), Theodore, appearing before Leo V, declared
that: "The Old Testament prohibitions of images ...
are abolished by the incarnation: if the law of Moses
were to be regarded, how is it that we worship the
cross, which the law speaks of as accursed?"[7]

Here again one heresy is invoked to justify
another. There is no scripture justifying the worship of the cross.

As quoted above, Gibbon declares: "The first
introduction of a symbolic worship was in the veneration of the cross and of relics."[8] But as early as A.
D. 394, Epiphanius, bishop of Constantia in Cyprus,
travelling in the Holy Land, "tore a curtain, which
he found hanging before the sanctuary of a church,
with a figure either of the Savior or of a saint painted
on it—declaring such representations to be contrary
to Scripture";[9] and Augustine (A. D. 354-430) "reluctantly confesses that in his time many were
'adorers of pictures.'" Statues had not yet appeared,[10] but the worship of images had become
"firmly established before the end of the sixth
century."[11]

The worship of saints and of images seems to

have gone forward hand in hand. Schaff says: "With the worship of saints is closely connected a subordinate worship of their images and relics. The latter is the legitimate application of the former."[12]

As to the status or value of image worship, the Second Council of Nicaea (A. D. 787) reached a general conclusion, that "reverence for images would warrant not only unchastity, but breach of oaths."[13] The unchastity clause arose out of a consideration of the following story: An aged monk on the Mount of Olives was greatly tempted by an uncleanly demon that finally proposed to the monk that he would cease his temptations if the monk would cease worshipping a picture of the Virgin and the infant Savior which hung in his cell. The old man asked for time to consider, meanwhile consulting an abbot of renowned sanctity, who reproved him for listening to the devil and told him: "Rather than abstain from adoring Christ and his Mother in their holy images, it would be better for you . . . to enter every brothel, and visit every prostitute in the city," of Jerusalem.[14]

Count Goblet D'Alviella, in his interesting discussion of "Images and Idols (General and Primitive)", observes: "No religion can rival Christianity in the multiplicity of its images. In some large churches, such as the French cathedrals of Paris, Chartres, Reims, and Amiens, there are as many as two, three, or four thousand statues; and in the cathedrals of Chartres, Bourges, and Le Mans, three, four, or five thousand figures on stained-glass. Although quite a number of these are merely figures of unimportant personages, nevertheless we have here what has been called a whole Bible for the use of the unlettered."[15]

The pagan notion of idols—and Christians imbibed freely, even to inebriation, of this notion—may be gathered from D'Alviella's statement that in the time of Pericles, "Stilpo was banished from Athens for having maintained that Phidias's statue of Pallas Athene was not the goddess herself."[16]

The Caroline Books (ascribed to Charlemagne and which were probably in fact largely the work of Alcuin)[17] contains this estimate of "veneration" or "adoration" bestowed upon paintings, and images: "Christ and his saints desire no such worship as that in question; and, although the more learned may be able to practise it without idolatry, by directing their veneration to that which the images signify, the unlearned, who have no skill in subtle distinctions, will be drawn to worship that which they see, without thought of any object beyond it. . . . The only proper use of images is by way of ornament, or as historical memorials. . . . The right use of them for remembrance is strongly distinguished from the plea that it is impossible to remember God without them; those persons (it is said) must have very faulty memories who need to be reminded by an image—who are unable to raise their minds above the material creation except by the help of a material and created object."[18]

But in some of the outlying areas of the Eastern Church there was a strong sentiment against image worship. Leo the Isaurian, from the mountains of

Isauria, came to the throne in the East "with a hatred of images."[19]   He began a war on image worship (A. D. 726) that was not to end until the final triumph of image worship in A. D. 842. Schaff divides this century of conflict: "1) The war upon images and the abolition of image-worship by the Council of Constantinople, A.D. 726-754" (the latter is the year of the Council) ; "2) The reaction in favor of image-worship, and its solemn sanction by the second Council of Nicæa, A. D. 754-787" (the latter date being the date of the Council); "3) The renewed conflict of the two parties and the final triumph of image-worship, A. D. 842."[20]

As Robertson tells us, statues had not yet appeared in the time of Augustine (A. D. 354-430),[21] but there were paintings of Christ, the Virgin, and saints.   Eusebius of Caesarea strongly protested against such representation, contending "that the glory of the Savior cannot be represented, and that the true image of the saints is a saintly life."[22] Gibbon says, as noted above, the first notice of the use of pictures was in their condemnation by "the council of Illiberis, three hundred years after the Christian æra."[23]

We may note two of the most famous pictures that were the objects of worship, one ancient, the other modern.

There are several stories of the impressions of picture likenesses upon cloth by heavenly beings. One of the most famous was that one which said that the Savior himself impressed his image upon a piece of linen which he sent to the king of Edessa.

A later king that came into possession of the image apostatized, and the linen, it was affirmed, was built into a wall to preserve it, but was later discovered through a vision. This linen, together with a picture of the Virgin, "not made with hands," was asserted to have saved Edessa from an attack of the Persians. "Cloths of a like miraculous origin (as was supposed) were preserved in other places; and many images were believed to perform cures and other miracles, to exude sweat or odoriferous balsam, to bleed, to weep, or to speak."[24] However, these images did not save Edessa when a later assault was launched.

This Edessan image has a curious history. After the first alleged preservation of the city as noted above, the image was later carried off by the Mussulmans who conquered Edessa. Other cities in Syria, Palestine, and Egypt which it had been believed were fortified against conquest by the presence of images of the Christ, the Virgin, and saints, were also conquered by the same enemies. The Edessan image was ransomed (after three hundred years) by the court at Constantinople by the payment of "twelve thousand pounds of silver, the redemption of two hundred Mussulmans, and a perpetual truce for the territory of Edessa."[25] "The possession of it (the image) is now contested between Genoa and the church of St. Sylvester on the Quirinal at Rome."[26]

This image was evidently not used or considered merely as a material means of fixing the mind on Deity; it was obviously an image that was supposed to have miraculous powers as *of itself*, as were the images in the other cities mentioned. They were regarded by Christians even as the Greeks regarded the Pallas Athene by Phidias,—as the actual personages themselves.

In America we have the well-known Mexican story of the picture image of the Virgin of Guadalupe, which briefly told, runs thus: A humble Indian, who a few years before had been baptized and christened Juan Diego, was journeying from his home to a neighboring church to hear mass and receive instruction. While crossing the side of a barren mount, he heard sweet music, and looking in the direction from whence it came, he saw an arc of glorious coloring. The rocks about glowed as precious stones. As he drew nearer, he saw a lady of beautiful countenance and form standing in the radiance, who spoke kindly to him, called him her son, told him she was the Virgin Mary, directed that a church be built upon the spot where she stood, and charged him to hasten to the bishop and deliver the message. The bishop did not believe and Juan returned to the spot where he had seen the vision. The Virgin reappeared and told him to return the next day to the bishop and repeat the story. The bishop, more interested, asked him to get a sign from the lady. He ordered two persons to follow Juan, which they did, but reaching the scene of the vision, Juan disappeared from their sight, and the two returned to the bishop, accusing Juan of witchcraft.

However, not knowing of this miracle, Juan

journeyed on; the Virgin again appeared, telling him to return on the morrow and she would provide the sign. His uncle being ill, he did not return on the next day; but on the day following he went along the same route to get a priest for his uncle, but took a different path, fearing reproof from the Virgin. The Virgin intercepted him, however, at a small fountain, she appearing in a dazzling brilliance. She did not reprove him, but told him to go to the top of the hill where there was a miraculous garden of roses, which Juan was to pick. He did as told and returned to the Virgin, who took the roses in her hand, then gave them back to Juan, who placed them in his mantle, and went on to the bishop to deliver the roses. Coming to the bishop, Juan unfolded his mantle to show the roses, and saw, to his astonishment, instead of the roses in the mantle, an image of the Virgin herself, in colors, impressed upon the mantle. This was in early December, 1531. A shrine was erected on the spot and the mantle transferred thereto the following year. The alleged miracle aroused almost a delirium of joy and religious enthusiasm throughout Indian Mexico.

However, it was a century before any Pope would even hear the story of the apparition. In 1667, Pope Clement IX conceded a plenary jubilee in its recognition. By a papal bull of May 25, 1754, (223 years after the proclaimed miracle) the apparition was recognized. The Virgin of Guadalupe then became the Patroness and Protectress of New Spain (Mexico). Many miracles are attributed to this picture, including the bringing to life of a dead person.

The story of the first miracle said to have been performed by the image is told as follows: "While the picture was being transported with great solemnity to the first temple erected in its honor, a number of Indians danced in front of the procession. One of these accidently discharged an arrow which lodged in the jugular vein of another and caused instant death. The yet warm body was carried to the image, the Virgin reached out and removed the arrow, and the dead man returned to life and health."[27] A pestilence visited Mexico City in 1736; the Virgin is credited with causing the plague to disappear.

Another ancient incident may be noted of the same general kind, though this one involves a statue: Over the "Brazen Gate" leading to the imperial palace in Constantinople was a noted statue of the Savior, known as "the Surety." Leo the Isaurian (in beginning his great war on images that was to last, with alternate fortune, for a period of one hundred twenty years)[28] ordered this statue, around which clung marvellous legends and to which attached great veneration, to be removed. A man was sent to remove it. Crowds of women assembled and entreated him to leave it alone. He mounted a ladder and struck an axe into the face of the image. The women dragged down the ladder and tore the man to pieces. A mob formed which was dispersed by troops, with bloodshed.[29]

Thus "the Surety" was likewise more than a

material object to assist in concentrating the mind
on Deity. It was an object of worship that was believed to possess divine powers and that, being
prayed to, might answer prayers.

One more of modern times: There is in Mexico
an image of the Virgin known as "Our Lady of the
Remedies" (Nuestra Senora de los Remedios). It
is claimed the image was brought from Spain by the
Conquistadores, and is said to be to the Mexican
Spaniards what the Virgin of Guadalupe is to the
Mexican Indians. It is thus described in Terry's
Guide Book on Mexico: "The Virgen de Los
Remedios, patroness of the Spaniards in Mexico . . .
is an ugly wooden doll, about 12 inches high, holding
in its arms an infant Jesus; both evidently carved
with a dull penknife. Two holes represent the eyes
and another the mouth; . . . the work bespeaks the
rude, Indian craftsman."[30] (A personal view, at the
distance of a short arm's length, verifies the essential accuracy of this description.)

The account of the image runs thus: a few days
before La Noche Triste, its owner removed it for
safe keeping from Tenochtitlan (Aztec Mexico City)
and placed it beneath a maguey plant. Twenty
years later an Indian cacique found it, and placing
it on an altar in his hut, worshipped it as the Aztec
goddess of water. "The alleged miraculous appearance of the Virgin of Guadalupe opened the eyes of
the clergy to the intrinsic value of such apparitions,
and no sooner was this wooden image found than it
began to do supernatural things." The image fled
from the cacique's home and returned to the maguey.

The cacique brought it back to his hut, put it in a strong box, and slept on top of the box, but the image again fled to the maguey. He told the occurrences to the clergy, who 'perceiving a miracle had been performed,' built a place for the image to repose. "The doll was dressed in satins and pearls, a quantity of false hair was fastened on her head, and a rich crown added. A fine gilded altar was arranged, enclosed by a silver railing, and a huge silver maguey —emblematic of her home for 20 years—was made a feature of the shrine. Despite the fact that the Mexicans derisively called her a gachupina (a vituperative epithet signifying a Spanish woman) her popularity grew apace. Indians came from all parts of the country to worship her, and her shrine was made the object of a fanatical devotion. . . . Marvellous powers of healing, warding off epidemics and of rain-making were soon credited to the Virgin, and she was officially declared the special patroness of the Spaniards in the City of Mexico. When a drought or epidemic threatened the capital the figurine was carried in great state at the head of an impressive procession to Mexico City, where it was solemnly received by the Viceroy, the City Council, the Archbishop and the rest of the clergy. Sometimes the Viceroy headed the holy procession as it wound into the city; in such cases a noble of the highest rank drove the chariot in which the image reposed. The principal convents were visited in succession, and as the Virgin was carried through the cloistered precincts, the nuns ranged themselves on their knees in humble adoration: it was then conducted to the Cathedral where high mass was sung and other ceremonies performed. When rain was desired it came in copious showers immediately after her arrival. Her special protection was earnestly solicited when the royal tribute was sent to Spain, to ensure its safe arrival. Gifts of immense value were deposited at her shrine and a treasurer was appointed to take care of her jewels and her rich wardrobe. (This treasury is now full of rubbish and is not worth looking at.) . . . At the outbreak of the War for Independence (1810) the Spaniards chose the image as their protectress, in opposition to the Virgin of Guadalupe, who guided the Mex. troops to victory. In Sept., 1810, the Spaniards solemnly elevated the Virgen de los Remedios to the position of General of the Royal Army. During the war very uncomplimentary insinuations, relative to the virtue of the two Virgins, were interchanged by the opposing forces. When the Mexicans defeated the Spaniards at the battle of Las Cruces (Oct. 30, 1810), a Mexican general stripped the Spanish patroness of her general's uniform, tore her sash, reproached her for being a gachupina, signed her passport, and ordered her deported to Spain. Upon the promise of the Spaniards that she would not be permitted to influence politics, she was permitted to remain."[31]

This image is still an object of "veneration," worship, and not as a material instrumentality to assist in concentrating the mind of the worshipper on his prayer to the true Virgin, but as an actual object which itself can bestow blessings and on occasion work miracles. A room in the Church in which the image is placed, contains all sorts of articles, such as crutches and like things, attesting the miracles for which the image is given credit.

Thus has a great Church returned to an idolatrous worship against which the Lord has spoken from the beginning, and the thunders of Sinai proclaimed:

"Thou shalt not make unto thee any graven image, or any likeness of any thing that is in heaven above, or that is in the earth beneath, or that is in the water under the earth: thou shalt not bow down thyself to them, nor serve them: for I the Lord thy God am a jealous God, visiting the iniquity of the fathers upon the children unto the third and fourth generation of them that hate me; and shewing mercy unto thousands of them that love me, and keep my commandments."[32]

If this shall happen to those who ignorantly worship, what shall be the punishment of him who, knowing the offense, leads the ignorant so to worship.

Sinai speaks today even as in the days of Moses and transgressing Israel.

May we who know the truth guard against any such "falling away" as this.

---

[1]Gibbon, *The Decline and Fall of the Roman Empire*, Milman's New Edition, III, pp. 444-45.   [2]Schaff, *History of the Christian Church*, IV, p. 451.   [3]Robertson, *History of the Christian Church*, III, p. 291.   [4]*Op. cit.*, p. 45.   [5]*Op. cit.*, pp. 48-49; 135.   [6]Matt. 22:21.   [7]Robertson, III, p. 293.   [8]Gibbon, supra; Robertson, II, p. 50-51.   [9]Robertson, II, p. 49.   [10]*Op. cit.*, p. 50.   [11]Gibbon, III, p. 445.   [12]Schaff, *Hist.*, IV, p. 448.   [13]Robertson, III, p. 137.   [14]Gibbon, III, p. 467; Robertson, III, p. 136.   [15]Hastings, *Encyclopaedia of Religion and Ethics*, sub voce *Images and Idols*, p. 111b.   [16]*Op. cit.*, p. 116a.   [17]Robertson, III, p. 143.   [18]*Op. cit.*, p. 146; see also Schaff, *Hist.*, IV, p. 465 ff.   [19]Gibbon, III, p. 449.   [20]Schaff, *Hist.*, IV, pp. 454-455.   [21]Robertson, II, p. 50.   [22]*Op. cit.*, p. 49.   [23]Gibbon, III, p. 444.

[24]Robertson, III, pp. 39-40; see Gibbon, III, p. 446. [25]Gibbon, III, pp. 447-448. [26]Robertson, III, p. 43, n.b. [27]*Terry's Guide to Mexico*, 1928 ed., p. 394 ff. [28]Gibbon, III, p. 449; or 60 years, Schaff, *Hist.*, IV, p. 454 ff. [29]Robertson, III, pp. 45-46; Gibbon, III, p. 450. [30]Terry, p. 191. [31]*Op. cit.*, pp. 191-192. [32]Ex. 20:4-6.

E

PATRONS, ETC.

Another feature in the "veneration" of saints should be noted. It came in by way of "patrons, shrines, pilgrimages, gilds, etc.," a system developing thereform that "reacted in a thousand ways upon art, literature, trade, and social economics generally." Concerning this, the Jesuit Father, Thurston, says: "Despite many abuses and blunders, even the most rigid censor will find it difficult to maintain that the influence thus exercised was entirely evil," —a tacit admission by the learned Father that there is evil in the system, perhaps that it is almost wholly evil.

The practice developed of praying to certain saints for particular blessings. Individuals adopted particular saints as their own special protectors, or intercessors, or as the source of blessings to the individuals. Special groups followed a like course. For example,—St. Barbara was believed to insure her "clients" that they would receive the sacraments before death. Hence she was appealed to in thunderstorms; so those engaged in more dangerous occupations appealed to her, such as miners, tilers, masons, and gunsmiths. St. Clare (Clara) was the patron saint of people with sore eyes, also glassworkers and laundresses.[1]

Erasmus is cited as saying that "every saint has his distinct office allotted to him. . . . One is appealed to for the toothache, a second to grant easy delivery in childbirth, a third to lend aid on long journeys, a fourth to protect a farmer's live stock. People prayed to St. Christopher every morning to be kept from death during the day, to St. Roche to be kept from contagion and to St. George and St. Barbara to be kept from falling into the hands of enemies. He (Erasmus) suggested that these fabulous saints were more prayed to than Peter and Paul and perhaps than Christ himself."[2]

Speaking of the period A. D. 590-1049, Schaff says: "The number of saints and their festivals multiplied very rapidly. Each nation, country, province or city chose its patron saint, as Peter and Paul in Rome, St. Ambrose in Milan, St. Martin, St. Denys (Dionysius) and St. Germain in France, St. George in England, St. Patrick in Ireland, St. Boniface in Germany, and especially the Virgin Mary, who has innumerable localities and churches under her care and protection."[3]

"In praying to the saints, as formerly to the heathen deities, it was usual for their votaries to promise that, if they would grant the petitions addressed to them, their altars should be richly adorned, and candles should be burnt in their honor; but to threaten that otherwise the altars should be stripped and the lights extinguished. Sometimes, it is said that threats of this kind were the means of obtaining miraculous aid; although, if no such effect followed, the worshippers were generally afraid to

execute them. When petitions had been put up in
vain to one saint, they were transferred to another.
In cases of difficulty, the advice of the saints was
asked, sometimes by prayer, to which an answer was
vouchsafed in visions; sometimes by laying a letter
on the grave or altar which contained the relics of
the saint, with a paper for the expected answer,
which, if the saint were propitious, was given in
writing, while otherwise the paper was left blank."[4]

As showing the manner in which the images of
saints may be appealed to in our own day and the
procedure thereof, a credible witness states that
within months he visited a Catholic cathedral and
saw a humble but rather brazen and insistent communicant, who was not too honest, stand before an
image and with a five centavo piece clasped tightly
between the thumb and forefinger of each hand
which she held up before the image, invoke, almost
threatingly, the aid of the image. She vehemently
declared she was offering the saint five pesos in each
hand. The saint seemed not to respond. She appeared threatening; but still no response. One is reminded of Elijah's admonition to the priests of Baal
who were vainly importuning their gods: "Cry
aloud: for he is a god; either he is talking, or he is
pursuing, or he is in a journey, or peradventure he
sleepeth, and must be awaked."[5]

It is unnecessary to comment upon the unscriptural, unjustifiable character of all this sort of
worship, where the saints, not God, through his
Son, are importuned for aid. It is sufficient to recall that great commandment to Israel and to all

since living: "Thou shalt have no other gods before me"⁶; and to remember that to Satan offering in exchange for the worshipping of him "all the kingdoms of the world, and the glory of them,"⁷ Jesus, the Son of God, said: "Get thee behind me, Satan: for it is written, Thou shalt worship the Lord thy God, and him only shalt thou serve."⁸

[1]Hastings, *Encyclopaedia of Religion and Ethics*, sub voce *Saints and Martyrs (Christian)*, p. 57b. [2]Schaff; *History of the Christian Church*, V, pt. II, p. 741. [3]Schaff, Hist., IV, p. 442; see same page for statement on development of canonization. [4]Robertson, *History of the Christian Church*, II, p. 356. [5]I Kings 18:27. [6]Ex. 20:3. [7]Matt. 4:8. [8]Luke 4:8.

F

MARIOLOGY AND MARIOLATRY

We will note still another "falling away," one of Peter's "damnable heresies," in some respects the greatest of all,—Mariology and Mariolatry.

Mariology is defined as, "The whole body of religious belief and dogma relative to the Virgin Mary"; while *Mariolatry* is said to be, "The worship of Mary, the mother of Christ: an opprobrious term used by some Protestants of the veneration of the Virgin by Roman Catholics."[1]

An underlying concept of the "veneration" bestowed by the Romans on the Virgin Mary is bound up with the dogma of the "immaculate conception," which does not relate to the conception of Jesus, but to the conception of Mary, herself, that is, by this dogma, Mary also was miraculously conceived. Behind the development and framing of the dogma of the "immaculate conception," or perhaps better, growing out of it, or a part of it, lies another dogma that racked the Church for a long time, that is the dogma, officially proclaimed in 1854, which declares that Mary, the mother of Jesus, is "absolutely free from all implication in the fall of Adam and its consequences."[2] This meant she was free from the "original sin," a subject upon which we shall not enter because unnecessary for our present purposes.

Pope Pius IX, who fled from Rome in fear of his life, was, while in temporary exile "a most devout worshipper of Mary." Under date of February 2, 1849, while still in exile, he issued an encyclical letter (a letter addressed by the pope to all the bishops) in which he asked the opinion of the bishops as to the feeling in the Catholic world that the Apostolic See should, by some solemn judgment, define the immaculate conception, and by such means secure great blessings to the Church. He expressed his own feelings thus: " 'You know full well, venerable brethren, that the whole ground of our confidence is placed in the most holy Virgin,' since 'God has vested in her the plenitude of all good, so that henceforth, if there be in us any hope, if there be any grace, *if there be any salvation (si quid spei in nobis est, si quid gratiae, si quid salutis), we must receive it solely from her,* according to the will of him who would have us possess all through Mary.' "[3] (Italics ours.)

One might at this point recall the words of the Savior in the great intercessory prayer: "And this is life eternal, that they might know thee the only true God, and Jesus Christ, whom thou hast sent."[4]

More than six hundred bishops answered the letter; four only dissented; fifty-two thought the time inopportune; the rest went along with the Pope. One of those not sympathetic with the suggestion of the Pope (Archbishop of Paris, Sibour) declared that the immaculate conception "could be proved neither from the Scriptures nor from tradition, and to which reason and science raised insolvable, or at least inextricable, difficulties."[5]

Following the letter, a preliminary special commission of cardinals and theologians, and a consistory of consultation worked over the matter.

The Commission, in 1853, reported (it is said) "that no evidence from Scripture was needed for a dogmatic declaration, but that tradition alone sufficed, and that even this need not be shown in an unbroken line up to the time of the apostles."[6]

Whereupon, Pope Pius IX, on the day of the Feast of the Conception, December 8, 1854, in the Church of St. Peter, before two hundred cardinals, bishops, and other dignitaries, invited to be present, but not to discuss the matter, proclaimed, after the Mass and the singing of *Veni Creator Spiritus*, "with a tremulous voice the concluding formula of the bull *'Ineffabilis Deus:'* "[7]

"In honor of the holy and undivided Trinity, for the glory of the Virgin Mother of God, for the exaltation of the Catholic faith and the Catholic religion, by the authority of our Lord Jesus Christ, of the blessed apostles Peter and Paul, and of our own office, we declare, pronounce, and define the doctrine which holds that the most blessed Virgin Mary was, in the first instant of her conception, by the singular grace and privilege of Almighty God, with regard to the merits of Christ Jesus the Savior of the human race, preserved free from every stain of original sin, has been revealed by God, and therefore is to be firmly and constantly believed by all the faithful."[8]

While seemingly no ecumenical council has approved this dogma, yet since, under the decree of the Vatican Council of 1870, the pope is infallible (to contest which infallibility is anathema), this bull becomes an infallible dogma which may not be questioned.

The dogma of the immaculate conception may, it seems, be laid at the doors of the schoolmen of the middle ages, who, it would appear, are responsible for not a few of the "falling aways" of the Church. Reading of their arguments and contentions, their wild speculations and metaphysical dissertations on the mysteries, one feels that they, in truth, were in the condition of which Festus falsely accused Paul: 'much learning hath made them mad."[9]

Schaff says that "the first traces of the Romish Mariolatry and Mariology are found in the apocryphal Gospels of Gnostic and Ebionitic origin."[10]

Schaff also traces the development of the final dogma through three stages: (1) The idea of the perpetual virginity of Mary which had found some currency in the ante-Nicene age, though he notes that such scholars as the great Tertullian held the view that Mary had children by Joseph after Christ was born. (2) The freedom of Mary from actual sin, which was first clearly taught by Pelagius and Augustine in the fifth century, though Augustine, while exempting her from wilful sin, specifically held her to be involved in the fall of Adam with all its consequences. (3) The final step exempts Mary from original sin, the effects of Adam's fall. Seemingly this first appeared as a "pious opinion" in connection with the festival of the Conception of Mary, introduced in France in 1139, gradually spreading therefrom into England and other countries.

Bernard of Clairvaux (1115-1162), the "honey-flowing doctor," who brought about the second crusade, seemingly condemned the festival and rejected the idea of the immaculate conception as contrary to tradition, as belittling Christ, the only sinless being. He asked: "Whence they discovered such a hidden fact? On the same ground they might appoint festivals for the conception of the parents, grandparents, and great-grandparents of Mary, and so on without end."[11] The legend of the immaculate conception of Mary in her legendary mother Anna, is given in Hastings' *Encyclopaedia of Religion and Ethics*, sub voce *Immaculate Conception*. The legend was taken from certain apocryphal books which Pope Gelasius (A.D. 492-496) condemned as heretical.[12]

The dogma of the perpetual virginity of Mary, developed the other dogma that as Mary conceived *sine viro* so she gave birth *clauso utero*.[13]

In time came also the doctrine (a "pious opinion") of the Assumption, that is, that Mary's body was taken to heaven, and apparently there joined with her spirit.[14]

Legends concerning the Virgin's death grew. Robertson says: "At the time of the council of Ephesus (A. D. 431), she was supposed to have spent her last years with St. John in that city, and to have been interred in the church where the council met. But afterwards it came to be believed that she had been buried in the valley of Jehoshaphat, and

thence had been caught up to heaven. From this
tale, which originated in a conjecture of Epiphanius
that she never died, and was afterwards supported
by sermons falsely ascribed to Jerome and Augustine, the festival of the Assumption took its rise."[15]

Dr. Bernard summarizes the legend thus: that
"first the soul, and after that the dead body, of the
Virgin were assumed to heaven." He quotes Cardinal
Newman as saying: "It was becoming that she
should be taken up into heaven and not lie in the
grave until Christ's Second Coming, who had passed
a life of sanctity and of miracle such as hers."[16]

We may here, as well as elsewhere, note the
legend (apparently first current in the days of
Aquinas and Scotus) that the house in which the Holy
Family had lived in Nazareth was "said to have been
carried by angels, first into Dalmatia, and then into the neighborhood of Loreto, where, after having
thrice changed its place, it finally settled, to draw to
it the devotion and the offerings of innumerable pilgrims."[17]

Her position with reference to her relationship
to the Christ and her position in heaven, were a
matter of more or less gradual development. At first
she was recognized merely as the mother of Jesus,
which naturally developed into the mother of God.
Apparently the next step was to consider her as
sitting just below the Son who sits on a throne. Then
she was represented as a crowned mother sitting on
a level with her Son. Later still she sat on a throne
above the Son. Lastly, she is pictured as interceding
with the Son, angry and about to destroy the world,

in order to save the world from the Son's vengeance. This was the representation of the growth of Mariolatry in art.[18]

A dogma also emerged concerning the santification of Mary: was she "conceived without sin," or was she sanctified in the third hour after conception, or at some other time?[19]   The Pope's bull decided this by declaring it was "in the first instant of her conception."[20]

Dr. Cooper, writing in Hastings, sub voce *Mary*, in an exhaustive summary on the general subject, states, as the result of examining the writings of the leading writers of the first three centuries (Aristides, Ignatius, Justin Martyr, Irenaeus, Origen, and Tertullian) that during these centuries there are few references to her, and those that are found, while speaking of her as the Virgin Mother of the Lord and so worthy of being honored, "give no suggestion of aught that could be called a cult."[21]   This was the condition 300 years after Christ.

During the period of the four great councils (A. D. 325-451)—the conciliar period—there was a beginning of a cult of "adoration" or worship of the Virgin, allegedly it is said to counteract the sensuality coming in from paganism.   Dr. Cooper comments: "In entire consistency with this teaching of the great Fathers, we find that the worship of the Church in the conciliar period shows hardly a trace of any cult of the Virgin.   There are indications that she was *prayed for*."   They were not at this time praying *to her*.   "Cardinal Newman admitted that no prayer to the blessed Virgin is to be found in the voluminous works of St. Augustine."[22]   However, to meet the sensuality present in the Church, her virginity was emphasized, which fitted in with the concept behind the growing monasticism.

This takes us to nearly A.D. 500, with still no cult as to the Virgin Mary. This stupendous "falling away," as it came to be, was but slowly gaining headway.

But during the medieval period (for this purpose from the triumph of Odoacer over the Western Empire, A.D. 476, to the Council of Trent, A.D. 1563) the discussion of the schoolmen greatly furthered the cult.   John of Damascus declared that Mary was the sovereign Lady to whom all creation was made subject by the Son. Bede narrates a vision of St. Wilfred in which he was told he was healed by the Lord through the prayers of his disciples and the intercession of His Blessed Mother Mary of perpetual virginity.

In the great liturgies of the Churches interpolations were made to express the idea that the Son might be approached through the prayers of his spotless Mother. One liturgy had the phrases, in connection with prayers for the holy dead, "especially the most holy, stainless, blessed, our Lady, Mother of God and ever-Virgin"; another used the words "especially the most holy, undefiled, excellently laudable, glorious Lady, the Mother of God, and Ever-Virgin Mary." Mary was also addressed: "Known refuge of the sinful and the low, make known to me thy mercy, O thou pure one, and set me free from the hands of demons."[23]

Gradually it seems the prayer changed in form from a petition for Mary's intercession with the Son, to a petition for Mary's personal help. Seemingly, it was to support this latter concept that the idea of the Assumption of Mary's body to heaven (referred to above) came into being.

The lengths to which the worship of Mary had gone, even before the time of Aquinas and Scotus, is shown by the verbal extravagances of Peter Damiani (b. 1007)[24] whose panegyric regarding the Virgin is glossed by Robertson thus: "Damiani speaks of her as 'deified,' as 'exalted to the throne of God the Father, and placed in the seat of the very Trinity.' 'To thee,' he says, 'is given all power in heaven and in earth; nothing is impossible to thee, to whom it is possible even to raise again the desperate to the hope of bliss. For thou approachest the golden altar of man's reconciliation, not only asking but commanding; as a mistress, not as a handmaid.' "[25]

It was during this period that the schoolmen began to dispute among themselves concerning the immaculate conception. Against the dogma was Thomas Aquinas (d. 1274) and the Dominicans, whose position agreed with such other schoolmen as Anselm (d. 1109), Peter the Lombard (d. 1161), Alexander of Hales (d. 1245), St. Bonaventura (d. 1274), Albertus Magnus (d. 1280). For the dogma was Duns Scotus (d. 1308), and the Franciscans, joined later, as time went on, by the Jesuits.[26]

Irenaeus (d. 202) made a parallel between Eve and Mary, that bore fruit. He called Eve the mother of disobedience, and Mary the mother of obedience.[27]

The controversy continued on during the next two and a half centuries. "Visions, marvelous fictions, weeping pictures of Mary, and letters from heaven were called in to help the argument for or against. . . ."[28]

It might be noted in passing that the Second Council of Nicaea (787) declared that "he who adored the image adored the original."[29]

In the middle of the fifth century Nestorius (d. 451), a Syrian monk, made patriarch of Constantinople in 428, preached that the Savior had two distinct natures, human and divine, that Mary was the mother of the human nature and could not therefore be called the Mother of God (*Theotokos*). This doctrine aroused great opposition. It is said to have been the turning point in the development of the devotion to Mary.[30] Her name was introduced into the prayers of churches, more churches were dedicated to her. Some welcomed the emphasized adoration as a substitute for the pagan female deities.[31]

The doctrine of Mary's perpetual virginity gained ground.[32]

In the fifth century, the perpetual virginity of Mary was denied by writers and officers; a group of female fanatics in Arabia were noted as heretics, because making offerings to Mary. "Anything like worship of angels was as yet supposed to be expressly forbidden by Scripture."[33]

The controversy between the Dominicans and the Franciscans over the dogma became at times very bitter. The Dominicans attempted to perpetrate a fraudulent series of revelations allegedly received by a youth. The fraud was detected and those responsible were tried and burnt.[34] On the other hand various miracles were alleged in the interest of the dogma. One of them was that as "Scotus was on his way to maintain the honour of the blessed Virgin in the schools, an image of her, which he passed, was accustomed every day to bend its head in token of favour."[35]

Some of the popes became involved. Pope Gelasius condemned the apocryphal legend of the bodily assumption of Mary into heaven;[36] Pope Sixtus IV, in earlier life having written against the immaculate conception, issued two bulls in favor of the doctrine;[37] the Feast of the Visitation was withdrawn from the Calendar by Pius V (1566-1572) and reintroduced by Sixtus V (1585-1590); [37a] Pope Siricius (c. 392) confirmed a sentence against Bonosus for following Helvidius in the doctrine that Joseph and Mary had children after Jesus was born.[38]

"The German hymnody of the middle ages, like the Latin, overflows with hagiolatry (the adoration or invocation of saints) and Mariolatry. Mary is even clothed with divine attributes, and virtually put in the place of Christ, or of the Holy Spirit, as the fountain of all grace."[39]

From the time of Gregory VII (Hildebrand, 1073-1085) increased honors were paid to Mary. She was called "Queen of Heaven," and as such she was approached by those "who might fear to approach the Savior immediately," though men such as St. Bernard remonstrated against the dogma of the immaculate conception.[40] She was declared "to be the

rock on which Christ was to build his church, because she alone remained firm in faith during the
interval between his death and his resurrection."[41]
"From the lowly recipient of grace, she became a
source and giver of grace."[42]

The Carmelite order asserted "that the blessed
Virgin every Saturday released from purgatory all
those who had died in the scapulary of the order
during the preceding week," and cited in support of
their assertion two forged bulls, one of John XXII,
the other of Alexander V, though they later were
able 'to extort confirmations of the privilege' from
Pope Clement VII in 1550 and Paul V in 1613.[43]

One incident reported by Schaff, will indicate
the belief and concept of the people in the matter of
the relationship between the Son and his mother.
The Flagellant movement in 1349, during the plague
of the Black Death, broke out again in 1399. According to an account by the "notary of Pistoja,"
the renewed movement began with a vision seen by
a peasant. The account runs as follows:

"After a midday meal, the peasant saw Christ
as a young man. Christ asked him for bread. The
peasant told him there was none left, but Christ
bade him look, and behold! he saw three loaves.
Christ then bade him go and throw the loaves into
a spring a short distance off. The peasant went,
and was about to obey, when a woman, clad in white
and bathed in tears, appeared, telling him to go back
to the young man and say that his mother had forbidden it. He went, and Christ repeated his command, but at the woman's mandate the peasant again

returned to Christ. Finally he threw in one of the loaves, when the woman, who was Mary, informed him that her Son was exceedingly angry at the sinfulness of the world and had determined to punish it, even to destruction. Each loaf signified one-third of mankind and the destruction of one-third was fixed, and if the peasant should cast in the other two loaves, all mankind would perish. The man cast himself on his knees before the weeping Virgin, who then assured him that she had prayed her Son to withhold judgment, and that it would be withheld, provided he and others went in processions, flagellating themselves and crying 'mercy' and 'peace,' and relating the vision he had seen."

Miracles were alleged to accompany the Flagellants in their marches. One is recorded as follows:

"Among the miracles was the bleeding of a crucifix, which some of the accounts, as, for example, von Nieheim's, explain by their pouring blood into a hole in the crucifix and then soaking the wood in oil and placing it in the sun to sweat. According to this keen observer, the bands traversed almost the whole of the peninsula. Fifteen thousand, accompanied by the bishop of Modena, marched to Bologna, where the population put on white. Not only were the people and clergy of Rome carried away by their demonstrations, but also members of the sacred college and all classes put on sackcloth and white. The pope went so far as to bestow upon them his blessing and showed them the handkerchief of St. Veronica."⁴⁴

Schaff affirms: "Mariolatry preceded the Romish Mariology. Each successive step in the excessive veneration . . . of the Virgin, and each festival memorializing a certain event in her life, was followed by a progress in the doctrine concerning Mary and her relation to Christ and the believer. The theory only justified and explained a practice already existing."[45]

A recital of these festivals will serve to emphasize the extent to which this worship of Mary has gone.

Dr. Zöckler names the various festivals or feasts held in honor of Mary as follows:[46]

Annunciation,—probably observed as early as the fourth century. This seems to have been in the earlier days a feast to the Lord.

Purification of Mary,—or Presentation of Christ in the Temple, occurs forty days after Christmas,—February 2. Some writers say it was instituted to take the place of Roman pagan lustrations of February. This seems to have been first a feast to the Lord's presentation in the Temple, but was changed to honor Mary.

Feast of the Nativity,—unknown in early centuries until about A.D. 650, celebrated September 8th.

Assumption of Mary,—commemorating the legend that as the Apostles watched at Mary's deathbed, the Son and his angels appeared, received her soul, turned it over to the archangel Michael; and as they were about to carry her body to the grave, the Son again appeared and took the body in a cloud to paradise, where it was reunited with the soul.

This feast previously fixed for January 18th, was about A.D. 600 fixed for August 15th.

Presentation,—celebrating the presentation of Mary in the temple, at the age of three, in compliance with a legendary vow of her parents. Apparently established in the twelfth century.

Visitation,—found only in the Western Church, commemorates Mary's visit to Elizabeth. First recognized 1247 by Synod of Mans; Franciscans adopting it in 1263, it was extended by Pope Urban VI to all Christendom in 1389.

Espousal of Mary with Joseph,—Since the fourteenth century celebrated on February 23rd; extended to all Christendom by Pope Benedict XIII in 1725.

The Seven Dolors,—celebrated on the Friday before Palm Sunday. Begins with prophecy of Simeon and flight into Egypt, or the parting between Jesus and his mother at the commencement of his Passion, ending in each case with the crucifixion. Feast seems to have originated in the thirteenth century in the Servite order.

Joys of Mary,—a seeming reciprocal of the Seven Dolors; commemorates the "joyful mysteries" of the rosary.

St. Mary of the Snows,—a local Roman feast, celebrated August 5th. According to the legend, a man and wife were directed to build a church on the spot where a miraculous fall of snow occurred in mid-summer.

Other festivals "such as the *Expectation of Mary* (Dec. 18), *the Holy Name of Mary* (Sunday after her Nativity), *Our Lady of Mt. Carmel* or *of the Scapular* (July 16), *Our Lady of Ransom* (Sept. 24), the *Patronage of Our Lady* (third Sunday in November), are of minor importance."

Other feasts said to have had a profound influence in promoting the devotion to Mary are the Dominican instituted *Feast of the Rosary* (first Sunday in October) and the Jesuit instituted *May Devotions*, which runs through the whole month of May.

Feast of the *Immaculate Conception,*—has assumed great importance since the Reformation. Seemingly it has developed from the feast of the Conception of St. Anne, the legendary mother of Mary, which latter feast celebrated the legendary delivery of Anne from the curse of sterility that had been hers.[47] It appears that originally the feast of the *Immaculate Conception* was first the feast of her *Sanctification*, then of her *Conception*, fixed for December 8th.

Protestants seem a unit in saying there is neither Scripture nor tradition justifying the Mariolatry of the Roman Church. Dr. Cooper shows that not only is the Scripture lacking, but, as already pointed out above, there was no doctrine for and many expressions contrary to the concept during the first three Christian centuries, and very little during the conciliar period.[48]

Since the idea of the perpetual virginity of Mary is perhaps basic to the whole dogma and cult involved in Mariolatry, we may make one quotation dealing with this matter from the opposite point of view, which, on the scriptural texts, seems to us the true view. Dr. Zöckler treats the subject as follows:

"The question of her maternal relationship to Jesus on the one hand and to the 'brethren of the Lord' on the other is a less difficult one. The designation of Jesus as her 'first-born son' (Luke ii. 7) and the statement as to her relations with Joseph (Matt. i. 25, cf. i. 13) seem to point to the conclusion that the persons called in the Gospels and in Acts i. 14 the brethren of the Lord were the younger sons of Joseph and Mary. For various reasons the theory of Jerome that they were cousins, and that of Epiphanius that they were children of Joseph by a former marriage, are untenable. The unprejudiced reader of the New Testament can not avoid the view represented in antiquity by Helvidius and stamped as heresy after Jerome and Ambrose, that they were the children of Joseph and Mary, while Jesus was the son of Mary in a miraculous manner, by the Holy Ghost. The latter assertion rests upon distinct passages of Scripture (Matt. i. 18-25; Luke i. 26-38, ii. 7-14), whereas the rationalist and Ebionite view that he also was the son of Joseph and Mary finds no support either in the Gospels or elsewhere in the New Testament."[49]

Schaff, in his *The Creeds of Christendom*, lists the texts cited by the proponents of the immaculate conception dogma and implementing cult regarding the sinlessness of Mary, stating that they "are, with one exception, all taken from the Old Testament, and based either on false renderings of the Latin Bible, or on fanciful allegorical interpretation." He then

lists Genesis 3:15 ("it shall bruise thy head, and thou
shalt bruise his heel," which Paul applied to the
"God of Peace,"[50] and comments upon the Vulgate
translation) ; Songs of Solomon 4:7; and 4:12 ("A
garden inclosed is my sister, my spouse; a spring
shut up, a fountain sealed") ; and Ezekiel 44:1-3,
which, dealing with the closed gate on the east of the
Temple, says: "Then said the Lord unto me; This
gate shall be shut, it shall not be opened, and no
man shall enter in by it; because the Lord, the God
of Israel, hath entered in by it, therefore it shall be
shut.   It is for the prince; the prince, he shall sit
in it to eat bread before the Lord; he shall enter by
the way of the porch of that gate, and shall go out
by the way of the same." These passages are cited
as a type of the concept of closed womb of the Virgin
(noted above) by which Christ entered the world,
"and who added to the miracle of a conception *sine
viro* the miracle of a birth *clauso utero*." Another
passage cited is from an apocryphal book (cited as
Sap. 1:4), and Luke 1:28, the greeting from the
angel to Mary, "Hail, thou that art highly favored,
the Lord is with thee: blessed art thou among
women" (an alternative reading being, "Hail thou
that art graciously accepted," or "much graced," or
as Douay renders it, "Hail, full of grace, the Lord is
with thee: blessed art thou among women").

Schaff comments upon all this as a "frivolous allegorical trifling with the Word of God" to support
the perpetual virginity of Mary and her freedom
from sin.

Saying it is almost useless to cite single passages to controvert this dogma, he lists on the point: Rom. 3:10, 23; 5:12, 18; I Cor. 15:22; II Cor. 5:14-15; Gal. 3:22; Eph. 2:3; I Tim. 4:10; Psalms 51:5. Schaff affirms that the contra-doctrine "runs through the whole Bible, and underlies the entire scheme of redemption," and a little later says, "Great is the glory of Mary—the mother of Jesus, the ideal of womanhood, the type of purity, obedience, meekness, and humility—but greater, infinitely greater is the glory of Christ—the perfect God-man—'the glory of the only-begotten of the Father, full of grace . . . and of truth.' "[51]

One more fancy may be added to the fancies we have noted above, and this the one that Duns Scotus alleged as one of the reasons for keeping Mary free "from all taint of original sin from the very beginning," and that is that "the vacancy, left by the fallen angels in heaven, could be best filled by Mary."[52]

We have not attempted in this short and inadequate summary of the dogma and cult involved in Mariolatry as finally developed, to follow out the erroneous implications and manifold contradictions of the Holy Scriptures as understood by the great Protestant world, and also by the Catholic Churches not subscribing to the dogma and cult. It is not necessary. Any dogma that would destroy or belittle the stature of Christ is a sacrilege, and the Mariolatry of the Roman Church does that.

We have seen that reasonably interpreted there is no scripture, and it is alleged by scholars there is no tradition, supporting the finally developed dogma and cult described by the scholars as Mariology and Mariolatry, and the scholars so asserting are not alone the Protestant scholars, but a great portion of the Catholic scholars as well, speaking over the centuries of a millennium and a half, until they were finally silenced in word (we hope the conscience is still left free) by a Papal Bull that is buttressed by the decree of a Council that the Pope's word is infallible, with the penalty that "if any one—which may God avert—presume to contradict this our definition: let him be anathema,"—seemingly the most terrible curse known to the Roman Church.

We have seen:

That in the minds of the people, at any rate, Mary's body was assumed into heaven to unite with her soul, though without any recognition of the law of the resurrection to which all, even Christ himself, are subject;

That in heaven, she has (as the people appear to believe) assumed a place alongside the Trinity;

That she, according to some, has place even above the Son;

That she is the one from whom comes to us grace;

That she and the Son are in constant warfare, she interceding for humanity, and the Son seeking to destroy it,—she bestowing upon us the blessings;

That she is the rock upon which God's church was to be built;

That she has taken the place of the fallen angels.

For all of this, the record of history shows that the Jesuits—the order of the Society of Jesus ("what's in a name")—must assume the major responsibility.[53]

We observe that Pope Pius IX himself declared that:

"The whole ground of our confidence is placed in the most holy Virgin.

"God has vested in her the plenitude of all good, so that henceforth,

"If there be in us any hope,

"If there be any grace,

"If there be any salvation,

"We must receive it solely from her,

"According to the will of him who would have us possess all through Mary."[54]

Well has it been said, "We may almost call Romanism the Church of the Virgin Mary."[55]

This robs Christ of his place as Redeemer of the World. It makes his crucifixion a mockery. It destroys the very foundation of all Christian faith.

It thus becomes the greatest "falling away" since Paul uttered his prophecy and warning to the Thessalonians; it becomes the most 'damnable heresy' prophesied by Peter.

Surely we may say in truth, it is the greatest sacrilege that a Christian Church has ever perpetrated and the greatest blasphemy that a Christian Church has yet uttered. It could come from one source only,—from him who vainly tempted the Christ himself, as they met in the wilderness and on the pinnacle of the Temple.

---

[1]*New Standard Dictionary.* [2]*The New Schaff-Herzog Encyclopedia of Religious Knowledge,* sub voce *Immaculate Conception,* p. 455a. [3]Schaff, *The Creeds of Christendom,* I, p. 108-109. [4]John 17:3.

[5]Schaff, *Creeds*, p. 109. [6]Schaff-Herzog, *op cit.*, p. 455b. [7]Schaff, *Creeds*, I, p. 109. [8]Schaff-Herzog, *op cit.*, p. 455b-456a. [9]Acts 26:24. [10]Schaff, *Creeds*, I, p. 117. [11]*Op. cit.*, p. 119-121, 126; Robertson, *History of the Christian Church*, V, p. 418; Schaff, *History of the Christian Church*, V, pt. 2, p. 744; *Schaff-Herzog, op. cit.*, p. 457. [12]Hastings, *Encyclopaedia of Religion and Ethics*, sub voce *Mary*, p. 476a; see also *Schaff-Herzog*, sub voce *Mary*, p. 221a for other interesting details. [13]Schaff, *Creeds*, I, p. 114. [14]*Op. cit.*, p. 112; Hastings, *op. cit.*, p. 479a; Robertson, III, p. 242-43. [15]Robertson, III, p. 242-243. [16]Hastings, *Encyc.* sub voce *Assumption*, p. 152-153. [17]Robertson, VII, p. 458. [18]Schaff, *Creeds*, I, p. 118. [19]*Op. cit.*, p. 124. [20]*Supra.* [21]Hastings, sub voce, *Mary*, p. 475. [22]*Op. cit*, p. 477a. [23]*Op. cit.*, p. 478. [24]Robertson, IV, p. 216. [25]*Op. cit.*, p. 187-188. [26]Schaff, *Creeds*, I, p. 122-124. [27]*Op. cit.*, p. 117; *Schaff-Herzog*, sub voce *Mary*, p. 220b. [28]Schaff, *Creeds*, I, p. 124. [29]*Schaff-Herzog, op. cit.*, p. 221. [30]*Id.* [31]*Robertson*, II, p. 357-358; see also Hastings, *op. cit.*, p. 478; *Schaff-Herzog, op. cit.*, p. 221a. [32]Robertson, III, p. 5. [33]Robertson, II, p. 62-63, 67-68, 157. [34]Schaff, *Creeds*, I, p. 124; Robertson, VIII, p. 378. [35]Robertson, VII, p. 489; see also for reported miracles, V, p. 338. [36]Hastings, *op. cit.*, p. 479a. [37]Robertson, VIII, p. 377. [37a]Hastings *op. cit.*, p. 479a. [38]*Schaff-Herzog, op. cit.*, p. 220a. [39]Schaff, *Hist.*, VI, p. 500. [40]Robertson, V, p. 416 ff. [41]Robertson, VI, p. 457. [42]*Schaff-Herzog*, sub voce *Mary*, p. 221b. [43]Robertson, VIII, p. 371; *Schaff-Herzog, op. cit.*, p. 222a. [44]Schaff, *Hist.*, V, pt. 2, p. 509-511. [45]Schaff, *Creeds*, I, p. 118. [46]*Schaff-Herzog*, sub voce *Mary*, p. 222-223; sub voce *Assumption*, p. 321a; Hastings, *op. cit.*, p. 479-80; Robertson, III, p. 242, VII, p. 485-487; V, p. 416-17; VI, p. 455 ff. [47]*Schaff-Herzog*, sub voce *Immaculate Conception*, p. 456b. [48]Hastings, *Encyc.*, sub voce *Mary*, pp. 474 ff.; *Schaff-Herzog*, sub voce *Immaculate Conception*, p. 456a; sub voce *Mary*, p. 220ff.; Schaff, *Creeds*, I, p. 113. [49]*Schaff-Herzog*, sub voce *Mary*, p. 220. [50]Schaff, *Creeds*, I, p. 113 ff. [51]*Op cit.*, p. 113-116. [52]*Schaff-Herzog*, sub voce *Immaculate Conception*, p. 456b. [53]Schaff, *Creeds*, I, p. 125; *Schaff-Herzog*, sub voce *Mary*, p. 223. [54]Pope Pius IX, Encyclical letter to the bishops, Schaff, *Creeds*, p. 109. [55]Schaff, *Creeds*, I, p. 111.

G

THE "FALLING AWAY" FROM AND LOSS OF THE HOLY MELCHIZEDEK PRIESTHOOD AFTER THE ORDER OF THE SON OF GOD

Cardinal Manning, an Anglican archdeacon who was converted to Catholicism, pronounced this far-reaching dictum:

"To appeal to history is treason."[1]

Perhaps his faith admitted of no other declaration, for Lowndes quotes Pope Pius IX (1846-1878) as declaring:

"Alone, notwithstanding my unworthiness, I am the successor of the Apostles, the Vicar of Jesus Christ; alone, I have the mission to govern and direct Peter's bark; I am the way, the truth, and the life."[2]

(It was Christ, in the Passover Chamber, who declared: "I am the way, the truth, and the life: no man cometh unto the Father, but by me.")[3]

Upon this premise of Pope Pius IX, it would necessarily follow, as Leo X (1513-1521) had long before proclaimed:

"It is clear as the noonday sun that the Popes, my predecessors, have never erred in their canons or constitutions."[4]

It would seem that the dictum, "To appeal to history is treason," is necessary to protect this papal claim to infallibility, else would be discovered such

things as that in 1616, Pope Paul V declared in a
"Feria V." (which is a decree by the Pope and the
Inquisition combined and which is infallible and
irrevocable) :

"That the earth moves daily is absurd, philo-
sophically false, and theologically considered at least
erroneous in faith."[5] This decree of Paul V was confirmed by Pope Urban VIII (1623-1644). Other
decrees have similarly proved erroneous.[6]

It may be well to quote here the Decree of the
Vatican Council of 1870 (the Council called and directed by Pope Pius IX) which, after centuries of
dispute and indecision, lays down the dogma of the
infallibility of the Pope.

". . . the Roman Pontiff, when he speaks *ex
cathedra*, that is, when in discharge of the office of
pastor and doctor of all Christians, by virtue of his
supreme Apostolic authority, he defines a doctrine
regarding faith or morals to be held by the universal
Church, by the divine assistance promised to him
in blessed Peter, is possessed of that infallibility
with which the divine Redeemer willed that his
Church should be endowed for defining doctrine regarding faith or morals; and that therefore such
definitions of the Roman Pontiff are irreformable of
themselves, and not from the consent of the Church.

"But if any one—which may God avert—presume to contradict this our definition: let him be
anathema."[7]

We might here give again the words of Paul to
the Thessalonians:

"Now we beseech you, brethren, by the coming

of our Lord Jesus Christ, and by our gathering together unto him, that ye be not soon shaken in mind, or be troubled, neither by spirit, nor by word, nor by letter as from us, as that the day of Christ is at hand. Let no man deceive you by any means: for that day shall not come, except there come a falling away first, and that man of sin be revealed, the son of perdition; who opposeth and exalteth himself above all that is called God, or that is worshipped; so that he as God sitteth in the temple of God, shewing himself that he is God."[8]

We wish to note that, at the expense of space, we have frequently re-quoted (in the remainder of the book) texts already used, instead of paraphrasing them, because they were basic to the discussion in hand and we wished to have in mind the actual words, so tending to lessen the possibility of misunderstanding. We have earnestly sought so to develop the whole subject that the conclusions of the final sections of the book might appear clear and definitive. To this end we have felt it wise to repeat, again and again, certain principles and conclusions that must be ever in mind in disposing of heretical errors and in making self-apparent the "falling away" of which Paul told the Thessalonians and of which Peter spoke as "damnable heresies."

[1]Lowndes, *Vindication of Anglican Orders*, p. 19. [2]*Op. cit.*, p. 11. [3]John 14:6. [4]Lowndes, p. 204. [5]*Op. cit.*, p. 141-2. [6]See exhaustive and historical discussion of "infallibility" in Schaff, *The Creeds of Christendom*, I, p. 163 ff.; and see on heretical popes, p. 176 ff. [7]*Op. cit.*, II, p. 270-271, Chapter 4, "First Dogmatic Constitution on the Church of Christ. Published in the Fourth Session of the holy Oecumenical Council of the Vatican. Pius Bishop, servant of the servants of God, with the approval of the sacred Council, for an everlasting remembrance," July 18, 1870. [8]II Thess. 2:1-4.

a. Sectarian Views on the Christian Priesthood

Apparently the past must not be looked into by the Roman communicants lest dogmas, past or present, are shown to be erroneous. Nevertheless, as we are not subscribers to, nor bound by this dogma of "treason," we shall, in the following pages, make some examination of the past, to our partial enlightenment at least.

But first, and before undertaking a short survey of New Testament scriptures bearing on the Priesthood, its powers and bestowal, we shall note certain matters concerning the dogmas and rituals of the Anglican and Roman Churches, the two great organizations of the West that have elaborate priesthood systems and rituals. It must be admitted that there is, in each system, so much of abstruse metaphysics, so much of unreal and unscriptural symbolism, so much of mystery, that one unschooled in all of it can not be sure he understands accurately either the dogmas or the rituals. But we shall make an honest effort to set out some of the basic matters as they appear to us:

1. It seems clear that both these great Churches look for the justification of their dogmas and rituals pertaining to the priesthood, to the happenings, the teachings, and the instructions that were given by the Lord at Caesarea Philippi, at Capernaum, at the Last Supper, at the meal in the closed room in the evening of the day of the resurrection, at the meeting on the seashore of Jesus and Peter with the rest who had gone fishing, at the meeting on the Mount

between Jesus and the Apostles with the five hundred, at the meeting of the Lord with the Apostles in Jerusalem just before the ascension—the events occurring in the order named according to the *English Harmony of the Gospels* of Robinson, a scholar of recognized authority. All other occurrences, incidents, and instructions prior to the Last Supper, and pertaining to the powers and bestowal of the Priesthood (except the incidents at Caesarea Philippi and at Capernaum), are almost wholly disregarded by these Churches.

This ignores the fact that the Savior bestowed the Priesthood upon his Apostles months before the incident at Caesarea Philippi, indeed it would seem early in his ministry.

2. It would further seem that, as to dogma and ritual, the basic difference between the Anglican and Roman systems has to do with the sacrament, the Romans declaring and the Anglicans denying the dogma of transubstantiation.[1]   Because, seemingly, of this dogma, the Romans affirm that the "Sacred Order of Priesthood, or its grace and power, which *is chiefly the power 'of consecrating and of offering the true body and blood of the Lord'* (Council of Trent, Sess. XXIII., de Sacr. Ord., Can. 1) in that sacrifice which is no 'nude commemoration of the sacrifice offered on the Cross' (Ibid., Sess. XXII., de Sacrif. Missæ, Can. 3)."[2] (Italics ours.)

That the Romans should so consider their Mass, seems a logical necessity from their dogma that Christ is actually and in fact again crucified and offered as a sacrifice every time a priest says Mass.

Lowndes, commenting upon the fact that the Romans assert the first Mass was celebrated in Jerusalem, says: "Roman writers with unscrupulous cleverness beg the whole question by unblushingly asserting that the Apostles celebrated Mass," and adds, "Since the term 'Mass' was not used to designate this Sacrament until near the close of the fourth century, and since the ceremonial and doctrine of the Mass has been constantly added to even since that date, it is very disingenuous to saddle on the Apostles all the un-apostolic and un-primitive teaching and ceremonial of Rome, by applying the name of Mass to that Sacrament which the Apostles termed Breaking of Bread, the Lord's Supper, or the Communion."[3]

While there appear to be differences in details, yet the priesthood powers and authorities (other than the Mass) claimed by the two Churches—Anglican and Roman—seem to be essentially the same.

3. Relying upon the scriptures of Matt. 18:18-19, Mark 16:15-16, and John 20:21-23, Lowndes classifies the priesthood powers claimed by the Anglican Church under seven headings:[4]

First. "The power to 'teach all nations,' or make disciples of them," which is regarded as "the first duty of the Episcopate and Priesthood."

Second. "The power or duty of planting missions among the heathen."

Third. "The power of baptizing," and Lowndes admits that as to baptism both Anglicans and Romans "have departed from the scriptural and primitive practice."[5] This is characterized as "the third official duty or power of the Apostles," and "of the Christian Priesthood."

Fourth. "The power of binding and loosing, and of remitting and retaining sins." Speaking for the Anglicans, Lowndes adds "three further divisions of the duties and powers of the Apostolate and Christian *sacerdotium*," as derived from the "power of teaching whatsoever things Christ had taught."

Fifth. "The power of administering the Holy Eucharist."

Sixth. "The power of offering sacrifice."

Seventh. "The power of teaching the moral law."

In another place Lowndes lists the "official duties of the Christian Priesthood" thus:

"(1) Doing what He had done at the Last Supper,

"(2) Evangelizing the world

"(3) Making disciples

"(4) Baptizing and

"(5) Teaching His commands till the end of the world."[6]

The Russian Church considers: "The Priestly office and yoke consists principally in four parts: i. Teaching; ii. In living holily; iii. In ministering the Sacraments; iv. In praying for the people." The Eastern Church regards the duties of its priests as covering the following: "preaching, discharging the Sacred Ministry of the Word of Truth, offering gifts and spiritual sacrifices, and renewing God's people through the laver of regeneration."[7]

With this outline of the priesthood functions

claimed by the numerically great Christian Churches having a regular priesthood system, we may go on with our examination of what the Bible Scriptures say about the matter.

We may add that we have deliberately refrained from making much use of modern revelation, even where it makes clear matters that the Bible leaves somewhat cloudy. We have done this because non-members of the Church do not accept our modern revelation, and because we believe that all matters herein discussed, may be made sufficiently clear from the Bible if the Good Book is looked to carefully and understandingly.

---

[1]See Talk No. 13. [2]Lowndes, *Vindication of Anglican Orders*, p. 150, Sentence 64. [3]*Op. cit.*, p. 386-387, and see XIII above, and authorities there cited. [4]Lowndes, p. 301-2. [5]*Op. cit.*, p. 325. [6]*Op. cit.*, p. 290. [7]*Op. cit.*, p. 301.

b. *The Savior's Authority and Works*

Jesus declared to the Disciples on the Mount in Galilee, "All power is given unto me in heaven and in earth." Preaching to the multitude after the Seventy departed Jesus said: "All things are delivered unto me of my Father."[1] John proclaimed: "In the beginning was the Word, and the Word was with God, and the Word was God. The same was in the beginning with God. All things were made by him; and without him was not any thing made that was made. In him was life; and the life was the light of men. . . . He was in the world, and the world was made by him, and the world knew him not. . . .And the Word was made flesh, and dwelt among us, (and we beheld his glory, the glory as of the only begotten of the Father,) full of grace and truth."[2] Paul declared to the Hebrews that by the Son, God "made the worlds,"[3] and that "through faith we understand that the worlds were framed by the word of God, so that things which are seen were not made of things which do appear."[4]

By modern revelation, we are told as to things of this earth: "And by the word of my power, have I created them, which is mine Only Begotten Son, who is full of grace and truth. And worlds without number have I created; and I also created them for mine own purpose; and by the Son I created them, which is mine Only Begotten."[5]

Talking to the Pharisees in the Treasury of the Temple, Jesus said: "I am not alone, but I and the

Father that sent me. . . . If ye had known me, ye should have known my Father also." A little later on the same occasion, Jesus declared to the Jews: "He that sent me is true; and I speak to the world those things which I have heard of him. . . . I do nothing of myself; but as my Father hath taught me, I speak these things. And he that sent me is with me: the Father hath not left me alone; for I do always those things that please him. . . . I speak that which I have seen with my Father: and ye do that which ye have seen with your father. . . . But now ye seek to kill me, a man that hath told you the truth, which I have heard of God: this did not Abraham. . . . For I proceeded forth and came from God; neither came I of myself, but he sent me. . . . It is my Father that honoreth me. . . . I know him. . . . Before Abraham was, I am."[4]

In the prayer of the Great High Priest on the Mount of Olives before he went into Gethsemane to pray on the night before the crucifixion, Jesus voiced the same sentiments again and again: "Father, the hour is come; glorify thy Son, that thy Son also may glorify thee: as thou hast given him power over all flesh, that he should give eternal life to as many as thou hast given him. And this is life eternal, that they might know thee the only true God, and Jesus Christ, whom thou hast sent. I have glorified thee on the earth: I have finished the work which thou gavest me to do. And now, O Father, glorify thou me with thine own self with the glory which I had with thee before the world was. I have manifested thy name unto the men which thou gavest me out of the world: thine they were, and thou gavest them me; and they have kept thy word. Now they have known that all things whatsoever thou hast given me are of thee. For I have given unto them the words which thou gavest me; and they have received them, and have known surely that I came out from thee, and they have believed that thou didst send me. ... I have given them thy word; and the world hath hated them, because they are not of the world, even as I am not of the world. ... As thou hast sent me into the world, even so have I also sent them into the world. ... And the glory which thou gavest me I have given them; that they may be one, even as we are one: I in them, and thou in me, that they may be made perfect in one; and that the world may know that thou hast sent me, and hast loved them, as thou hast loved me. Father, I will that they also, whom thou hast given me, be with me where I am; that they may behold my glory, which thou hast given me: for thou lovedst me before the foundation of the world." (John 17:1-8, 14, 18, 22-24.)

Thus Jesus, the Christ, acted for the Father, God; he had from the Father all power in heaven and in earth; he did and said nothing of himself; he spake what he had heard the Father say, and did what he had seen the Father do. The power he possessed and the authority he exercised were divine, they emanated from God himself.

What were these powers, these authorities?

At Jesus' baptism in the Jordan at the hands of John, the Father declared, as the Holy Ghost descended, "This is my beloved Son, in whom I am

well pleased."[7] At the time of the transfiguration
the Father declared: "This is my beloved Son, in
whom I am well pleased; hear ye him."[8]

From his return from the wilderness after the
temptation, until the final days in the Temple before
the crucifixion, Jesus taught to individuals (as to
Nicodemus,[9] and as to the woman of Samaria[10]),
to his disciples continuously, to groups large and
small, and to great multitudes, on the Mount and
on the plain and at the seashore, in the precincts of
the Temple, the Gospel of Jesus Christ, unfolding the
divine teachings step by step, as fast as his disciples
and listeners, steeped in the service and traditions
of the Mosaic law, could learn and understand.

But this work of teaching was but part of his
divine service. Beginning with the healing of the
nobleman's son,[11] he went about healing the sick for
the full term of his mission, sometimes one only of
a group, as the impotent man at the pool of Bethesda,[12] or one only when importuned thereto, as
Peter's wife's mother;[13] and at times, but rarely, he
healed all the sick brought to him: in Gennesaret,[14] at
Decapolis,[15] on a plain of Galilee,[16] at Capernaum
after healing Peter's wife's mother.[17]   He healed
those sick with palsy,[18] and at another time he healed
a man with dropsy.[19]   He healed lepers[20] and the
man with the withered hand in Galilee.[21]   He healed
of unspecified illness, the centurion's servant,[22] and
the woman stricken for eighteen years.[23]   He healed
the woman with the issue of blood;[24] restored the
ear of Malchus, the servant of the high priest.[25]   He
healed the deaf,[26] and the blind and dumb in Caper-

naum,[27] again in Capernaum two blind men,[28] another in Bethsaida,[29] in Judea a man born blind,[30] and Bartimæus near Jericho.[31]   He raised people from the dead: the son of the widow of Nain,[32] the daughter of Jairus,[33] and Lazarus.[34]

He showed himself master of the great forces of nature, as when he turned water into wine;[35] when he stilled the storm;[36] when he fed the five thousand with five loaves and two fishes;[37] when he walked upon the sea;[38] when he fed the four thousand with seven loaves;[39] when he miraculously provided the tribute money;[40] and when he cursed the barren fig tree.[41]

He had power over the spirits of Evil, as when he cast out unclean spirits,[42] and the evil spirits from demoniacs;[43] when he healed the dumb demoniac,[44] and cast out a devil from the daughter of the Syrophenician woman;[45] again when at Mt. Hermon he healed the demoniac whom the disciples could not heal;[46] and when he cast out a dumb devil in Judea.[47]

These were the things which Jesus did, even as he had seen and heard of his Father. These were the things he did under the power and authority his Father gave him. These are the things he did as the Great High Priest after the order of Melchizedek. These things are manifestations of the power and authority of the true Priesthood.

[1]Matt. 28:18; 11:27; see Luke 10:22. [2]John 1:1-4, 10, 14. [3]Heb. 1:2. [4]Heb. 11:3; see also 3:2-4. [5]Moses 1:32-33. [6]John 8:16, 19, 26, 28-29, 38, 40, 42, 54-55, 58. [7]Matt. 3:13-17; Mark 1:9-11; Luke 3:21-22. [8]Matt. 17:5-8; Mark 9:2-8; Luke 9:32-35. [9]John 3:1-21. [10]John 4:4-42. [11]John 4:46-54. [12]John 5:2 ff. [13]Matt. 8:14-17; Mark 1:29-34; Luke 4:38-41. [14]Matt. 14:34-36; Mark 6:53-56. [15]Matt. 15:29 ff; Mark 7:31-37. [16] Luke 6:17-19. [17]Matt. 8:16; Mark 1:29-34; Luke 4:40. [18]Matt. 9:2-8; Mark 2:1-12; Luke 5:17-20. [19]Luke

14:1-4. [20]Matt. 8:1-4; Mark 1:40-43; Luke 5:12-14. [21]Matt. 12:9-14; Mark 3:1-6; Luke 6:6-11. [22]Matt. 8:5-13; Luke 7:1-14. [23]Luke 13:10-17. [24]Matt. 9:20-23; Mark 5:25-34; Luke 8:43-48. [25]Matt. 26:50-56; Mark 14:46-52; Luke 22:49-53; John 18:10-12. [26]Mark 7:32-37. [27]Matt. 12:22-23. [28]Matt. 9:27-31. [29]Mark 8:22-26. [30]John 9:1-41. [31]Matt. 20:29-34; Mark 10:46-52; Luke 18:35-43. [32]Luke 7:11-17. [33]Matt. 9:18 ff.; Mark 5:23 ff.; Luke 8:41 ff. [34]John 11:17-46. [35]John 2:1-11. [36]Matt. 8:18-27; Mark 4:35-41; Luke 8:22-23. [37]Matt. 14:14-21; Mark 6:33-34; Luke 9:11-17; John 6:1-14. [38]Matt. 14:24-33; Mark 6:45-52; John 6:16-21. [39]Matt. 15:29 ff; Mark 8:1-9. [40]Matt. 17:24-27. [41]Matt. 21:18-19; Mark 11:12-14. [42]Mark 1:21-28; Luke 4:31-37. [43]Matt. 8:28-34; Mark 5:1-20; Luke 8:26-39. [44]Matt. 9:32-34. [45]Matt. 15:22-28; Mark 7:25-30. [46]Matt. 17:14-21; Mark 9:14-29; Luke 9:37-43. [47]Luke 11:14-36.

c. *Paul on the Old and New Covenant, the 'Changed Priesthood'*

These were the divine powers Christ possessed and exercised to the blessing of men. He possessed them because, as he declared, "All power is given unto me in heaven and in earth." "All things are delivered unto me of my Father."[1] He was as Paul declared over and over again, the "Apostle and High Priest of our profession," the high priest "after the order of Melchisedec. . . . Who is made, not after the law of a carnal commandment, but after the power of an endless life. . . . For the law made nothing perfect, but the bringing in of a better hope did; by the which we draw nigh unto God. . . . The Lord sware and will not repent, Thou art a priest for ever after the order of Melchisedec: By so much was Jesus made a surety of a better testament. . . . We have such an high priest, who is set on the right hand of the throne of the Majesty in the heavens; a minister of the sanctuary, and of the true tabernacle, which the Lord pitched, and not man. . . . For if that first covenant (Aaronic) had been faultless, then should no place have been sought for the second. . . . Behold, the days come, saith the Lord, when I will make a new covenant with the house of Israel and with the house of Judah: Not according to the covenant that I made with their fathers in the day when I took them by the hand to lead them out of the land of Egypt; because they continued not in my covenant, and I regarded them not, saith the

Lord. For this is the covenant that I will make with the house of Israel after those days, saith the Lord; I will put my laws into their mind, and write them in their hearts: and I will be to them a God, and they shall be to me a people. . . . In that he saith, A new covenant, he hath made the first old. Now that which decayeth and waxeth old is ready to vanish away. . . . Then verily the first covenant had also ordinances of divine service, and a worldly sanctuary" (the tabernacle).[2]

Then after briefly describing the tabernacle and its contents, and the entry into the holy place by the priests, and into the Holy of Holies by the high priest, and of the sacrifices they offered up, Paul continues, as to the sacrifice: "Which stood only in meats and drinks, and divers washings, and carnal ordinances, imposed on them until the time of reformation. But Christ being come an high priest of good things to come, by a greater and more perfect tabernacle, not made with hands, that is to say, not of this building; neither by the blood of goats and calves, but by his own blood he entered in *once* into the holy place, having obtained eternal redemption for us. For if the blood of bulls and of goats, and the ashes of an heifer sprinkling the unclean, sanctifieth to the purifying of the flesh: How much more shall the blood of Christ, who through the eternal Spirit offered himself without spot to God, purge your conscience from dead works to serve the living God? And for this cause he is the mediator of the new testament, that by means of death, for the redemption of the transgressions that were under the first testament, they which are called might receive the promise of eternal inheritance."³

The whole of this discussion of Paul's goes to the point of a *new* covenant that does away with the *old*, and he stresses, in explanation, and points out the difference between the Aaronic sacrifices and Christ's atonement, and shows forth the difference in the effect of each. Thus it was the *old* covenant Priesthood, the Aaronic, with its priests and high priests, in contrast with the *new* covenant Priesthood "after the order of Melchisedec," with Christ as the Great High Priest.⁴ A little earlier in his epistle than the words last quoted, Paul had said: "If therefore perfection were by the Levitical priesthood, (for under it the people received the law,) what further need was there that another priest should rise after the order of Melchisedec, and not be called after the order of Aaron? *For the priesthood being changed*, there is made of necessity a change also of the law."⁵ (Italics ours.)

And the changed law that came is the Gospel of Jesus Christ, "the power of God unto salvation,"⁶ and with the changed law came the '*changed priesthood.*'

Christ, the presiding and officiating High Priest "after the order of Melchisedec," under this law, did away with animal sacrifices, as the price of forgiveness for transgressions. Modern revelation makes clear that the sacrifices from Adam to Christ were "a similitude of the sacrifice of the Only Begotten of the Father, which is full of grace and truth."⁷

After the great sacrifice of the Son, then, instead of bulls, heifers, goats, lambs, pigeons, the first fruits, and the first sheafs, there came the sacrifice of a humble heart and a contrite spirit and true repentance, embracing a confession and a forsaking of the sinful way,[8] offered by the transgressor, and the Great High Priest, exercising the powers and authority he had from God, forgave the repentant sinner and commanded, "Go, and sin no more."

Under the 'old covenant,' the benefits of the amends made by the transgressors, resulted normally from the ministrations of the Levitical Priesthood, offered according to the Mosaic law. Under the "new covenant," 'the changed law,' 'the changed priesthood,' the blessings thereby provided were worked out through the ministrations of those holding the Priesthood after the order of Melchizedek, that is, first by Christ himself, the Great High Priest, and then by his Apostles and the Seventy called and ordained by Christ himself, these working both before and after the crucifixion. The blessings of the 'changed law' were forgiveness for the sin, the bestowal of health, of strength, the restoration from bodily ills, indeed even of life itself, relief from the afflictions of evil spirits, and the giving of the gifts of the Holy Ghost. And, with one possible exception only,[9] and this turns on another principle, there is no record of the conferring of these blessings save only by those who held the Priesthood which Christ conferred upon them, or later by those who received that Priesthood from those whom Christ had so en-

355

dowed, or still later by their successors, though for at most not more than two centuries.

A word may be said as to the name of the *new* covenant, the Priesthood which Christ brought and left, the Melchizedek Priesthood. Before the days of Melchizedek, it was called "the Holy Priesthood, after the Order of the Son of God"; the name was changed to Melchizedek Priesthood, to avoid the too frequent use of the name of the Supreme Being. The Melchizedek Priesthood embraces the Aaronic.[10] This Melchizedek Priesthood is also referred to as the "holy order of God";[11] "after the holiest order of God";[12] "the Priesthood which is after the order of Melchizedek, which is after the order of mine Only Begotten Son."[13] The Prophet Joseph referred to it as "the highest and holiest Priesthood, and is after the order of the Son of God,"[14] and again, "the Melchizedek High Priesthood was no other than the Priesthood of the Son of God."[15] Paul spoke of the Priesthood as "after the order of Melchisedec."[16]

We have, in the foregoing, and pursuant to the earlier statement of our intention, deliberately refrained from making much use of modern revelation because we wished to establish our points by Bible Scriptures. We shall hereinafter but rarely depart from this practice. But we may here notice some of the more important references to Priesthood, its bestowal, powers, functions, and authorities, in modern revelation, and for convenience will run them in the text. There are many others to which reference will be found in any good concordance. [D.C. Secs. 13, 20, 76, 84, 86, 107, 113, 124, 127, 128, 132 (vs.

5-7, 45-47); *Documentary History of the Church,* II, p. 477; III, p. 385; IV, p. 207; VI, pp. 183, 363; Talks Nos. 21 and 22.]

[1]Matt. 28:18; 11:27; and see Luke 10:22. [2]Heb. 3:1. [3]Heb. 5:6, 10; 6:20; 7:16, 19, 21-22; 8:1-2, 7-10, 13; 9:1, 10-15. [4]Parry, *Joseph Smith's Teachings,* p. 123. [5]Heb. 7:11-12. [6]Rom. 1:16. [7]Moses 5:7. [8]D. C. 58:43. [9]Mark 9:38 ff.; Luke 9:49-50. [10]D. C. 107:3-6. [11]D. C. 77:11. [12]D. C. 84:18. [13]D. C. 124:123. [14]*Documentary History of the Church,* IV, p. 207. [15]*Op. Cit.,* II, p. 477. [16]Heb. 5:10.

d. Christ's Bestowal of the Priesthood upon the Twelve and the Seventy

1. The choosing and ordaining of the Twelve.

At the commencement of the great Galilean ministry, on a mountain in Galilee, Christ called "unto him whom he would: and they came unto him. And he ordained twelve, that they should be with him, and that he might send them forth to preach," and "he gave them power against unclean spirits, to cast them out, and to heal all manner of sickness and all manner of disease."[1]   These were the power and authority which Christ bestowed upon them at the time he ordained them and which they exercised for the rest of their lives. They already held some degree of Priesthood for they had been baptizing.[2]

2. The first mission of the Twelve.

Soon after their choosing, he sent them forth to preach as Apostles under the power (the Priesthood) that he had conferred upon them at their ordination as apostles, with a charge that forbade them to go to the Gentiles, or to the Samaritans, but "rather to the lost sheep of the house of Israel." The Apostles were to declare that the kingdom of heaven was at hand; they were to heal the sick, cleanse the lepers, raise the dead, cast out devils. Christ declared: "freely ye have received, freely give." He was seemingly referring to the powers and authority given at the time of their ordination. They were to take neither purse nor script, for they were traveling amongst Israel. They were given power to bestow peace upon the worthy house, and to withdraw that peace if the house proved unworthy. Power was also given to mark for judgment those who would not receive them, by shaking the dust from their feet, and the judgment was to be less tolerable than that visited upon Sodom and Gomorrha.[3]

He admonished them that he sent them "forth as sheep in the midst of wolves." Peering into the future, he warned them that they would be brought before councils, governors, and kings, that they would be scourged, that when brought to trial they should take no thought of their defense, "for it shall be given you in that same hour what ye shall speak. For it is not ye that speak, but the Spirit of your Father which speaketh in you,"[4]— the power and authority which Christ himself had, for he declared to the Pharisees: "I speak to the world those things which I have heard of him . . . as my Father hath taught me, I speak these things."[5]

He pointed out how their work would bring dispute and hatred among closest kin, how they would be persecuted and what they should then do; instructed them to preach fully the truths he had told them, to fear not bodily harm, but to fear him who could destroy body and soul, in hell; and as showing God's care about them, he voiced that inexpressibly beautiful thought,—"Are not two sparrows sold for a farthing? and one of them shall not fall on the ground without your Father. But the very hairs of your head are all numbered. Fear ye not therefore, ye are of more value than many sparrows."

He declared the reward of loyalty and the

punishment of disloyalty, saying, "Think not that I am come to send peace on earth: I came not to send peace, but a sword,"—a sword to be waged against unrighteousness and sin, that would tear apart families till "a man's foes shall be they of his own household." He commanded that allegiance to him should be paramount over all else, that whoso would not take up his cross and follow him was not worthy of him, and whoso "findeth his life shall lose it: and he that loseth his life for my sake shall find it." He concluded his charge by declaring the blessings coming to them who received the Apostles, for they received the Christ.[6]

While this charge does not specifically mention authority to baptize, they were already performing this rite, for even in the early Judean ministry, months before this time, Jesus and his disciples tarried in Judea and baptized even more than John, "though Jesus himself baptized not, but his disciples."[7] (The Inspired Version reads: "though he himself baptized not so many as his disciples.") So that before their choice and ordination as apostles, Christ had bestowed upon them authority to baptize.

Having so charged his Apostles, he despatched them to their work, while "he departed thence to teach and to preach in their cities."[8]

The Apostles "went out, and preached that men should repent. And they cast out many devils, and anointed with oil many that were sick, and healed them."[9] Luke records: "And they departed, and went through the towns, preaching the gospel, and healing every where."[10]

It is thought that the Apostles went out during the winter and that in April they returned and reported. Mark says: "And the apostles gathered themselves together unto Jesus, and told him all things, both what they had done, and what they had taught;" while Luke's record reads: "And the apostles, when they were returned, told him all that they had done," Luke's record having previously declared that "they departed, and went through the towns, preaching the gospel, and healing every where." Mark records they preached repentance, "cast out many devils, and anointed with oil many that were sick, and healed them."[11]

Thus the Apostles went out with the authority of the Priesthood which Jesus had bestowed upon them by ordination. They did the same works that Jesus did, taught the same Gospel principles that he taught, performed the same sort of miracles he performed. The record puts this beyond reasonable question. Thus they were measurably in the same relationship to the Son that he was to the Father, having in mind that they were human and the Son was divine. They were exercising the Priesthood powers Jesus had bestowed upon them at the time of their ordination and specified in the charge he gave them, Priesthood powers which Jesus held.

3. The Seventy sent out.

A few months after the Twelve returned, "the Lord appointed other seventy also, and sent them two and two before his face into every city and place, whither he himself would come."[12]

The charge he gave to the Seventy paralleled

in outline the charge given to the Twelve. Declaring the harvest was great and the laborers few, and exhorting them to pray, he sent them on their way and warned them he sent them forth as lambs among wolves. They, like the Twelve, were to travel without purse or scrip. They, also, were to leave their peace, which if "the son of peace be there," would remain, otherwise it would return to them. They were to heal the sick and say unto the people the kingdom of God "is come nigh unto you." They, too, were to shake from their shoes the dust of those cities which received them not, and upon these cities would come judgments more terrible than upon Sodom, while Chorazin, Bethsaida, and Capernaum were warned of dire judgment. He repeated to them the promise made to the Twelve: "He that heareth you heareth me; and he that despiseth you despiseth me; and he that despiseth me despiseth him that sent me."[18]

Luke then records: "And the seventy returned again with joy, saying, Lord, even the devils are subject unto us through thy name. And he said unto them, I beheld Satan as lightning fall from heaven. Behold, I give unto you power to tread on serpents and scorpions, and over all the power of the enemy: and nothing shall by any means hurt you. Notwithstanding in this rejoice not, that the spirits are subject unto you; but rather rejoice, because your names are written in heaven."[14]

Thus to the Seventy the Lord gave Priesthood powers that he had given to the Twelve; the Seventy, too, did the works Jesus did; they went before Jesus, preparing the way.

It will be well here, by way of summary, to have in mind two main essentials bearing on Priesthood powers and their exercise, which were common to the Twelve and to the Seventy.

The powers given were a present bestowal; they were not promises of a future bestowal. After the bestowal both groups actually had the powers and exercised them. Matthew records: "And when he had called unto him his twelve disciples, *he gave them power. . . .*" Mark says: "And he called unto him the twelve, and began to send them forth by two and two; *and gave them power. . . .*" Luke states: "Then he called his twelve disciples together, *and gave them power and authority. . . .*" The powers given to the Seventy were a like present bestowal. It was not a promise to bestow in the future.[15]

That the powers were presently bestowed and possessed is evidenced by the fact that they were exercised as shown by their report back to Jesus.[16]

Next, as to the powers that were given: We have already summarized the missionary service of Jesus, and that the Apostles and Seventy carried on the same missionary service as did he, exercised the same powers, performed the same sort of miracles.

As to baptism, while the authority to baptize is not specifically given in the endowment at the time of the charge to the Apostles covering their first mission, yet John tells us, as already pointed out, that Jesus was baptizing more disciples than John, that "Jesus himself baptized not, but his dis-

ciples,"[17] though the Inspired Version says that both
Jesus and the disciples baptized. Thus they were
baptizing long before their call to the apostleship and
their first missionary expedition. The necessity of
baptism for salvation had been part of the teachings of Christ from the time of his great discourse
with Nicodemus,[18] indeed from the time of Christ's
own baptism.[19]

Next, as to the geographical area and people to
whom the Apostles were sent, a point to be noted
later: They were commanded: "Go not into the
way of the Gentiles, and into any city of the Samaritans enter ye not: But go rather to the lost sheep of
the house of Israel."[20] Jesus himself had already
preached to the Samaritans, many of whom believed
on him.[21] The charge to the Seventy was different
on this point; they were sent "two and two before
his face into every city and place, whither he
himself would come."[22] We are not told the places
to which they went.

Next, the Apostles were to preach:
>(a) The kingdom of heaven is at hand;[23]
>(b) That men should repent;[24]
>(c) The kingdom of God, and they "went
through the towns, preaching the gospel. . . ."[25]

The Seventy were to preach "The kingdom of
God is come nigh unto you."[26]

Again, both Apostles and Seventy were to travel
without purse or scrip, they were to be the beneficiaries of their racial hospitality.[27]

As to those to whom the message should be
taken, also a point to be later considered: The

Apostles were to travel among their own race,—the "lost sheep of the house of Israel."

The power to remit or retain sins, is to be considered later, but we may here note that in the authority and commandment given to "shake off the dust of your feet," of the house or city that received them not, is seen the essential element of the power either to remit or to retain sin. If the house was worthy, they left their peace; if the house was unworthy, their peace returned to them. If they 'shook the dust off their feet,' as to any house or city, it was to be more tolerable for Sodom and Gomorrah, than for such place.[28]

As to the work they were to do, also to be considered later: Having said to them, "freely ye have received, freely give," having declared "all things are delivered unto me of my Father,"[29] and having given them power[30] and authority,[31] he commanded them:

(a) To exercise power over all unclean spirits, to cast them out;[32]

(b) To heal all manner of sickness and all manner of disease, to cure diseases and to heal the sick;[33]

(c) To cleanse lepers, to raise the dead.[34]

While the charge to the Seventy does not, as recorded, contain a like grant of power and authority, yet the works they reported on their return show they possessed both power and authority, for they declared, with a seeming ecstasy of joy: "Lord, even the devils are subject unto us through thy name." Then the Lord declared: "I give unto you power to tread on serpents and scorpions, and over all the power of the enemy: and nothing shall by any means hurt you."[35]

All these matters are thus urgently stressed here, because, as we shall see, the sectarian view seems clearly to be that, notwithstanding these various powers and authorities had been bestowed upon and exercised by the Apostles and Seventy upon their first mission and thereafter, yet the sectarian contention is that they were never bestowed upon the Apostles until Caesarea Philippi and Capernaum, during the Last Supper and at the subsequent meetings between the Lord and the Apostles prior to his ascension. The sectarian view is obviously erroneous.

Again we say, it must be constantly in mind, particularly in the discussions which follow, that here is an absolute, specific conferring of power and authority, it is not a prayer that such power and authority will be bestowed. Christ had the power and authority and he bestowed it upon them; then the Apostles having this power and authority, and Christ commanding them to carry on, transmitted, rebestowed, upon those called to the Master's service, after his ascension, that same power and authority, as shown by the records as hereinafter treated of. If such power and authority were not retransferred, then it was not passed down. The conversion of Paul shows that even after a call divinely made, yet must follow the regular order of ordination by those having authority.

4. The promise made at Caesarea Philippi.

The next recorded step in relation to the bestowal of Priesthood authority had its beginning in the famous conference in the coasts of Caesarea Philippi, between the Lord and his disciples. The conference is of the last importance, because of claims that are based upon it. So we will quote it in full:

"When Jesus came into the coasts of Caesarea Philippi, he asked his disciples, saying, Whom do men say that I the Son of man am? And they said, Some say that thou art John the Baptist: some, Elias; and others, Jeremias, or one of the prophets. He saith unto them, But whom say ye that I am? And Simon Peter answered and said, Thou art the Christ, the Son of the living God. And Jesus answered and said unto him, Blessed art thou, Simon Barjona: for flesh and blood hath not revealed it unto thee, but my Father which is in heaven. And I say also unto thee, That thou art Peter, and upon this rock I will build my church; and the gates of hell shall not prevail against it. And I will give unto thee the keys of the kingdom of heaven: and whatsoever thou shalt bind on earth shall be bound in heaven: and whatsoever thou shalt loose on earth shall be loosed in heaven."[36]

It may, in the first place, be noted that, as to the keys of the kingdom and the power to bind or loose, this is not a present grant or bestowal of keys, but a promise to bestow. We shall consider the actual bestowal shortly.

In the next place, the words, "thou art Peter, and upon this rock I will build my church; and the gates of hell shall not prevail against it," are relied upon as establishing a claimed primacy for Peter, out of which has been built the claimed primacy of the Roman Church. The Latter-day Saints avow the primacy of Peter in the Presidency of Peter, James, and John, but deny the primacy of Peter as contended for by the Roman Church. (See Talk 9, where this point is discussed.)

The Latter-day Saints declare that the Church of Christ is to be built upon Christ as the foundation, and not upon any mortal man. If it is built upon a mortal man, then it is his Church and not Christ's Church. Christ here spoke of "my church," not Peter's church.

Furthermore, the Latter-day Saints declare that the *rock* upon which Christ would build his Church is the rock of revelation: "Blessed art thou, Simon Barjona: for flesh and blood hath not revealed it unto thee, but my Father which is in heaven. . . . and upon this rock I will build my church," etc.

On this whole point we may repeat here the quotation we made[87] from the learned Catholic scholar, Dollinger (excommunicated in later life for refusal to adhere to the dogma of the infallibility of the Pope):

"Of all the Fathers who interpret these passages in the Gospels (Mt. xvi.18, Jn. xxi.17), not a single one applies them to the Roman Bishops . . . not one of them whose commentaries we possess — Origen, Chrysostom, Hilary, Augustine, Cyril, Theodoret, and those whose interpretations are collected in catenas — has dropped the faintest hint that the primacy of Rome is the consequence of the commission and promise to Peter! Not one of them has explained the rock or foundation on which Christ would build His Church of the office given to Peter to be transmitted to his successors, but they understood by it either Christ Himself, or Peter's confession of faith in Christ; often both together. Or else they thought Peter was the foundation equally with all the other Apostles, the Twelve being together the foundation-stones of the Church."[38]

We may note again that here was a promise to confer power,—"I will give," not a present bestowal.[39]

In passing, it may be observed that Douay's note, to the words "loose on earth" (of verse 19 of the text) is that *"loose on earth"* means loosing the bands of temporal punishments due to sins, which is known as an indulgence and that the power to grant indulgences is here bestowed.[40]

There was in this incident no further development of Priesthood powers beyond the promise "I will give," which was to be fulfilled a little later. We should keep in mind that "the *keys* of the kingdom of heaven" were to be given later.

5. The Transfiguration, the Special Witness to Peter, James, and John of the divinity of Jesus the Christ.

Some six days after Caesarea Philippi Jesus took Peter, James, and John to a high mountain to pray,—"St. Peter who loved Him so much (John xxi.17), St. John whom He loved so much (John xxi.20), and St. James who should first attest that death could as little as life separate from His love (Acts xii.2)."[41]

As Jesus prayed, his countenance changed, "his raiment was white and glistering," "exceeding white as snow; so as no fuller on earth can white them," and he "was transfigured before them: and his face did shine as the sun."[42]

Two men, Moses and Elias, appearing "in glory," came and talked with Jesus "of his decease which he should accomplish at Jerusalem," including his resurrection. "But Peter and they that were with him were heavy with sleep: and when they were awake, they saw his glory, and the two men that stood with him."[43]

When the two men departed, Peter said to Jesus, "Master, it is good for us to be here: and let us make three tabernacles; one for thee, and one for Moses, and one for Elias. For he wist not what to say; for they were sore afraid." "While he yet spake, behold, a bright cloud overshadowed them: and behold a voice out of the cloud, which said, This is my beloved Son, in whom I am well pleased; hear ye him. And when the disciples heard it, they fell on their face, and were sore afraid. And Jesus came and touched them, and said, Arise, and be not afraid. And when they had lifted up their eyes, they saw no man, save Jesus only."[44]

As the vision closed and Jesus and the Apostles descended from the mountain, "Jesus charged them, saying, Tell the vision to no man, until the Son of man be risen again from the dead." "And they kept it close, and told no man in those days any of those things which they had seen," but as they went down the mountain they questioned "one with another what the rising from the dead should mean."[45] Under some confusion as to the coming of Elias first, Jesus told them Elias had already come, and the disciples "understood that he spake unto them of John the Baptist."[46]

But the Prophet Joseph has told us, speaking under inspiration, regarding the keys of the Priesthood, that "the Priesthood is everlasting. The Savior, Moses, and Elias, gave the keys to Peter, James, and John, on the mount, when they were transfigured before him."[47] In the revelation given the Prophet in April, 1829, (concerning the New Testament account of the incident of the resurrected Jesus on the seashore in the early morning with the Apostles, when Jesus told John that he might "tarry" till Jesus came) it is revealed that the Lord said to Peter: "Yea, he (John) has undertaken a greater work; therefore I will make him as flaming fire and a ministering angel; he shall minister for those who shall be heirs of salvation who dwell on the earth. And I will make thee (John) to minister for him (Peter) and for thy brother James; and unto you three I will give this power and the keys of this ministry until I come."[48]

Thus to the three Apostles, Peter, James, and John, the presiding Priesthood quorum, were given the keys of the ministry, to have and to hold "until I come." This was the Priesthood element of the transfiguration.

Peter was not alone; James and John were

equally with him; but Peter stood at the head of this presidency; and this is Peter's place, the head of three.

Thus the divinity of Christ had shown forth; as he prayed, he appeared in glory, his face shining as the sun, his raiment whiter than any fuller's earth could make it, and glistering; two heavenly beings, Moses and Elias, came in their "glory" and conversed with him about his decease, "which he should accomplish at Jerusalem," and of his resurrection; when these left, a bright cloud overshadowed them, and out of it came the voice of the Father himself testifying: "This is my beloved. Son, in whom I am well pleased; hear ye him."

So was witnessed the divinity of Jesus the Christ by his own physical appearance, by his converse with heavenly beings about his decease—his death and resurrection—by the voice of the Father himself declaring the Sonship of Jesus, a witness given to none other of the Apostles (so far as the record goes), so showing the primacy of the three over all the rest. They knew from the testimony of the senses, given by God himself, that Jesus was the Christ. They were special witnesses.

6. The bestowal of the binding and loosing power, probably at Capernaum.

Shortly after the transfiguration on the Mount, Jesus and his Apostles were at Capernaum. In the course of a great discourse, Jesus fulfilled the promise made at Caesarea Philippi when he had said: "And *I will give* unto thee the keys of the kingdom of heaven: and whatsoever thou shalt bind on earth shall be bound in heaven: and whatsoever thou shalt loose on earth shall be loosed in heaven."[49]

For Jesus now declared to the Disciples before him, not to Peter alone, but to all: "Verily I say unto you, Whatsoever ye shall bind on earth shall be bound in heaven: and whatsoever ye shall loose on earth shall be loosed in heaven."[50]

Thus all the Apostles, not Peter alone, possessed the power of binding and loosing, these keys of the kingdom of heaven.

It is not without significance that while Douay annotates and explains the passage (Matt. 16:19) in which Jesus *promises* to bestow this power—this passage of promise immediately follows Peter's confession and Christ's affirmation that Peter's knowledge was a revelation from the Father—yet Douay leaves, without any comment at all, this passage (Matt. 18:18) which actually bestows the power. It is obvious that this last passage (Matt. 18:18) destroys utterly the claim of primacy, based on Matt. 16:19, which the Roman Church claims for Peter. This question was considered and disposed of in our Talk 9. Peter was one only of the Apostles who held this authority, the other Apostles being equal with him therein. Peter was the presiding head of the presidency of the Priesthood composed of Peter, James, and John.

From the point of view of the Roman and Anglican churches, we come now to the most important incidents of Christ's life as affecting the bestowal of Priesthood upon the Apostles.

Before considering them we may once more

briefly review the Priesthood situation up to this time, for our minds should be clear on this matter:

Early in his ministry the Savior had given the Apostles the authority to baptize—they held that much Priesthood authority. Later he ordained them Apostles, and bestowed upon them additional Priesthood power and authority.

Thereafter, Jesus sent the Apostles on a missionary journey among "the lost sheep of the house of Israel," and gave them power and authority against unclean spirits to cast them out, and to heal sickness and all manner of disease, to raise the dead, declaring "freely ye have received, freely give," and instructing them to preach "the kingdom of heaven is at hand." He gave them also power to determine whether sins should be forgiven, or retained, by their shaking the dust off their feet.

Next he sent forth the Seventy "into every city and place, whither he himself would come"; they were to preach "the kingdom of God is come nigh unto you," to heal the sick, to leave peace in the house or place to which they came, or shake the dust off their feet and leave them under the condemnation of Sodom, and other cities named. Returning, the Seventy declared: "Lord, even the devils are subject unto us through thy name,"—so exercising certain powers of the Priesthood possessed and exercised by the Apostles, all after the pattern of the work of Jesus himself.

Then came the conference at Caesarea Philippi, the confession of Peter, the declaration from Jesus that Peter's knowledge came from the Father, that upon this principle Jesus the Christ would establish his Church, and that he would give to them the binding and loosing power.

Then the Transfiguration, with the bestowal upon them of the keys, with the special witness to Peter, James, and John of the divinity of Jesus, culminating in the declaration of the Father himself that Jesus was the Father's Beloved Son.

Lastly, the bestowal by Jesus of the binding and loosing power (some of the *keys* of the kingdom) upon all the Apostles, not upon Peter alone.

We again repeat, we must remember at this point of time the Apostles held all this Priesthood power and authority,—a fact that is fatal to the claim that the Priesthood was bestowed after this time, though it may be some *keys* were bestowed to a greater extent than they had been previously enjoyed.

Since Anglicans and Romans seem to regard the order of events as important during the latter days of the ministry of Jesus, we shall, in what follows, take as the order thereof, that given by the great scholar, Edward Robinson, in his *English Harmony of the Gospels*, the Revised Edition, with additional notes by M. B. Riddle.

7. The administration of the sacrament at the Last Supper. (Robinson, Sec. 136)[51]

We shall take first, Christ's administration of the sacrament to his Apostles (except Judas, who had already left the Chamber, with the parting message, "That thou doest, do quickly"[52]) at the Last Supper, the Lord's Supper.

Since both Anglicans and Romans seem to regard the administration of the eucharist, the Mass for the Romans, as the most important of their priesthood functions, we may well quote the full account in the three gospels, and add thereto the one from I Corinthians, that we may miss nothing.

Matthew's account reads thus:

"And as they were eating, Jesus took bread, and blessed it, and brake it, and gave it to the disciples, and said, Take, eat; this is my body. And he took the cup, and gave thanks, and gave it to them, saying, Drink ye all of it; for this is my blood of the new testament, which is shed for many for the remission of sins. But I say unto you, I will not drink henceforth of this fruit of the vine, until that day when I drink it new with you in my Father's kingdom."[53]

Mark's account is in this language:

"And as they did eat, Jesus took bread, and blessed it, and brake it, and gave to them, and said, Take, eat: this is my body. And he took the cup, and when he had given thanks, he gave it to them: and they all drank of it. And he said unto them, This is my blood of the new testament, which is shed for many. Verily I say unto you, I will drink no more of the fruit of the vine, until that day that I drink it new in the kingdom of God."[54]

Luke's record is in these words:

"And he took bread, and gave thanks, and brake it, and gave unto them, saying, This is my body which is given for you: this do in remembrance of me. Likewise also the cup after supper, saying, This cup is the new testament in my blood, which is shed for you."[55]

Paul, writing to the Corinthians, says:

"For I have received of the Lord that which also I delivered unto you, That the Lord Jesus the same night in which he was betrayed took bread: And when he had given thanks, he brake it, and said, Take, eat: this is my body, which is broken for you: this do in remembrance of me. After the same manner also he took the cup, when he had supped, saying, This cup is the new testament in my blood: this do ye, as oft as ye drink it, in remembrance of me."[56]

For our purposes, the essential words are:
As to the bread,—

> Matthew, Mark, and Paul: "Take, eat: this is my body."
>
> Luke: "This is my body which is given for you."
>
> Luke and Paul: "This do in remembrance of me."

As to the wine,—

> Matthew and Mark: "He took the cup, and gave thanks, and gave it to them."
>
> Luke: "Likewise also the cup after supper."
>
> Mark: "They all drank of it."
>
> Matthew and Mark: "This is my blood of the new testament, which is shed for many."
>
> Matthew: "For the remission of sins."
>
> Luke: "This cup is the new testament in my blood, which is shed for you."
>
> Paul: "This cup is the new testament in my

blood: this do ye, as oft as ye drink it, in remembrance of me."

The following points may be noted:

There is here no bestowal, nor any suggestion thereof, of any new power or authority. The ceremony bears no resemblance at all to the ceremony incident to the ordination of the Twelve, to the conferring of the powers and authority incident to the sending out of the Twelve and the Seventy, or to the conferring of the power to bind and loose, on which occasions power and authority were given. This is a direction, a command to the Apostles thereafter to perform this ceremony "in remembrance of me." Their authority so to do is recognized as already possessed.

The ceremony is to be performed in remembrance of him, and of the shedding of his blood for the remission of sins, that is, in remembrance of his atonement and of its effect upon the sins of men. Paul's words are: "this do ye, *as oft as ye drink it*, in remembrance of me."

There is no word here of a grant of power to sacrifice; it is a remembrance in bread and cup of his sacrifice, his atonement made *once* and for all time.

There is not even a hint here of the doctrine of transubstantiation, under which Christ is re-sacrificed thousands of times a day—each time a Roman priest performs Mass.[57] This phase of the question was briefly discussed in Talk 13.

Nevertheless, the Romans appear to claim that the Apostles were ordained at the Last Supper and that the words "this do" were the ordaining words by which he conferred the Priesthood upon the Apostles. Lowndes comments: "They have done this because they have been forced more and more to justify their teaching by appealing to Scripture, just as they magnified the power of St. Peter, not out of reverence to the Scriptures, or from a humble desire to be obedient in all things to the revealed Word of God, but because, having for purposes of dominion and overlordship extended the powers and prerogatives of the See of Rome, they afterwards sought, when pressed to defend their claims, to justify themselves by a solitary text of Scripture. A text which, however, they cannot twist into a conveyance of authority, but only into a promise of authority. Likewise, having magnified a certain aspect of the Holy Eucharist, they seek for confirmation of that view in predating the commission of the Christian Priesthood to the Eleven. They maintain that the Apostles were ordained or consecrated on the night before the betrayal."[58]

Lowndes further says: "There is not a single allusion in the Scriptures to any reference to the Lord's Supper in connection with ordination. . . . When notwithstanding the clever plan of starting an Index Expurgatorius, by which all learning might be kept 'cribbed, cabined and confined,' she found that she had to offer some apology for these additions, she brought forward this view of a preordination so as to justify her words and ceremonies. It needs only to be added that if her view of this pre-ordination be a valid one, then certainly there has been no Christian ministry in Christendom at any time. For certainly there is no trace of any ordination to the Priesthood or to the Episcopate by any form or ceremony looking back to the Last Supper as the *fons et origo* of the Christian ministry."[59]

We repeat our own finding that there was no bestowal of any priesthood at the Last Supper, as an incident of the partaking of the sacrament.

8. The promise of the Holy Ghost made at the Last Supper. (Robinson, Sec. 138)

We shall consider next, Christ's promise of the Holy Ghost made in the chamber on the evening of the Lord's Supper. Speaking to the Apostles of his going away, the Lord said:

"And I will pray the Father, and he shall give you another Comforter, that he may abide with you for ever; even the Spirit of truth; whom the world cannot receive, because it seeth him not, neither knoweth him: but ye know him; for he dwelleth with you, and shall be in you. I will not leave you comfortless: I will come to you. . . . But the Comforter, which is the Holy Ghost, whom the Father will send in my name, he shall teach you all things, and bring all things to your remembrance, whatsoever I have said unto you." A little later in the evening, the Lord said: "Nevertheless I tell you the truth; it is expedient for you that I go away: for if I go not away, the Comforter will not come unto you; but if I depart, I will send him unto you. And when he is come, he will reprove the world of sin, and of righteousness, and of judgment: of sin, because they believe not on me; of righteousness, because I go to my Father, and ye see me no more; of judgment, because the prince of this world is judged."[60]

Here was no bestowal of the Holy Ghost, no endowment with any power and authority. Here was only a promise.

But we may properly here note some further events, out of their due order.

The Apostles being gathered together after his resurrection and before the ascension, Jesus commanded them that they should not depart from Jerusalem, but wait for the promise of the Father,[61] "which, saith he, ye have heard of me. . . . But ye shall receive power, after that the Holy Ghost is come upon you: and ye shall be witnesses unto me both in Jerusalem, and in all Judæa, and in Samaria, and unto the uttermost part of the earth."[62]

There is still no bestowal of the Holy Ghost; only a promise.

Jesus ascended, the Apostles tarried in Jerusalem till Pentecost, then "there appeared unto them cloven tongues like as of fire, and it sat upon each of them. And they were all filled with the Holy Ghost."[63]

This would seem to be a fulfillment of the promise Jesus made. The Holy Ghost came after the ascension of Jesus, because it could not come until he had left. Pentecost is the first recorded visit of the Holy Ghost upon the Apostles after the promise of Jesus to send him, made on the night of the Lord's Supper.

9. The instructions to the Ten in the Upper

Chamber in the evening following the morning of the resurrection. (Robinson Sec. 167)

The next incident having to do with power and authority, in the post-crucifixion mission of Christ, is that occurring in the evening following the morning of the resurrection. The Apostles, all but Thomas, sat at meat discussing the happenings of the day, the appearances of the resurrected Christ, and listening, with disbelief, to the story of the two who had seen him on their way to Emmaus. Suddenly, the doors being shut, Christ appeared amongst them. (Douay cites this entry of Christ into a room that was closed, as supporting the doctrine of transubstantiation: if Christ could make his whole body present in a closed room, he could make the same body present in the sacrament.) The Apostles were "terrified and affrighted, and supposed that they had seen a spirit." Christ "upbraided them with their unbelief and hardness of heart, because they believed not them which had seen him after he was risen." He said to them: "Behold my hands and my feet, that it is I myself: handle me, and see; for a spirit hath not flesh and bones, as ye see me have."[64]

He ate broiled fish and honeycomb with them. Calling their attention to certain scriptures, "then opened he their understanding, that they might understand the scriptures, and said unto them, Thus it is written, and thus it behoved Christ to suffer, and to rise from the dead the third day: and that repentance and remission of sins should be preached in his name among all nations, beginning at Jerusalem. And ye are witnesses of these things."[65]

Then follow in the gospels Mark, Luke, and John, the passages upon which both the Anglican and Roman Churches seem to rely to support their contention that the Priesthood was conferred upon the Apostles at this time.

Before proceeding with this account, we again call attention to the fact that the Priesthood had been bestowed upon the Apostles many months before this time; they had been ordained; and they had exercised these powers in their work. This is abundantly clear from what has preceded.

These basic passages read:

Mark's account is as follows:

"And he said unto them, Go ye into all the world, and preach the gospel to every creature. He that believeth and is baptized shall be saved; but he that believeth not shall be damned. And these signs shall follow them that believe; In my name shall they cast out devils; they shall speak with new tongues; they shall take up serpents; and if they drink any deadly thing, it shall not hurt them; they shall lay hands on the sick, and they shall recover."[66]

Even a casual reading of these words shows that there is here no statement of bestowal of power and authority. When Christ chose and ordained the Twelve, he "gave them power" to heal all manner of sickness and disease and to have power over unclean spirits. When he sent them forth on their first mission, they were given authority to preach, though the area of their missionary work was restricted, and they were to preach the kingdom of heaven was at hand. Baptism was not specifically mentioned on those occasions, but they had been baptizing almost from the beginning,[67] and the necessity of baptism for salvation had been part of the Lord's teachings and practice since the great sermon of Christ to Nicodemus,[68] indeed from the time of the baptism of Jesus by John, that all righteousness might be fulfilled.[69] The signs that should follow the believer had been richly experienced, after, at any rate, the mission of the Twelve and the Seventy, upon the latter of whom was specifically conferred, after their return from their first mission, the "power to tread on serpents and scorpions, and over all the power of the enemy: and nothing shall by any means hurt you."[70] There is not one line or intimation or suggestion that these powers and authority were ever taken from the Twelve and Seventy, and obviously these passages just quoted assume the possession of these powers and authorities by the Apostles, and declare who else may enjoy certain of them.

We repeat: There is no direct statement or suggestion here in Mark's record that Christ is on this occasion bestowing any power and authority. The Apostles already had the Priesthood. We have already called attention to this situation, and noted that we would refer to it again, as we have now done.

As to the jurisdiction of the area of their labors, —as stated above, the Apostles, on their first mission, were to confine their work to "the lost sheep of the house of Israel";[71] now they are to go into all the world. The authority to preach they had long held, certainly after their ordination as Apostles. This merely extends their field of operations; it is not a bestowal of Priesthood; this, we again say, they already held.

Luke's account runs thus:

"And, behold, I send the promise of my Father upon you: but tarry ye in the city of Jerusalem, until ye be endued with power from on high."[72]

This was obviously a renewed promise to bestow upon them the Holy Ghost, already promised to them in the Supper Chamber, and they are told to tarry in Jerusalem until it comes, as it did later at Pentecost.

There is here no bestowal of any power or authority, nor is the need thereof even suggested.

John adds to the account of Mark and Luke, the following:

"And when he had said this, he breathed on them, and saith unto them, Receive ye the Holy Ghost: Whose soever sins ye remit, they are remitted unto them; and whose soever sins ye retain, they are retained."[73]

It will be noted that there are two parts to this passage,—one relating to the Holy Ghost and the other to the remission of sins. We will consider them in their order.

As to the Holy Ghost:

We must remember that in Luke's record of this very occasion, Jesus told the Apostles they should "tarry ... in the city of Jerusalem, until ye be endued with power from on high." This saying is not consistent with a bestowal of the Holy Ghost as of this particular occasion when they were assembled to eat. In Acts is an account of a meeting of Jesus and the

Twelve, a meeting which Robinson places *some time after* the resurrection, while the occasion we are discussing happened in the evening of the morning of the resurrection. In Acts, Jesus is recorded as commanding "they should not depart from Jerusalem, but wait for the promise of the Father, which, saith he, ye have heard of me. . . . But ye shall receive power, after that the Holy Ghost is come upon you."[74] It would appear that the coming of the Holy Ghost was at this time (just before the ascension) still in the future.

In the Supper Chamber, it will be recalled, Jesus said he would pray the Father "and he shall give you another Comforter, that he may abide with you for ever . . . But the Comforter, which is the Holy Ghost, whom the Father will send in my name, he shall teach you all things, and bring all things to your remembrance, whatsoever I have said unto you."[75] This last passage tells some of the things that the Holy Ghost was to bestow upon the Apostles when they received it. But this was not to be a bestowal of the Priesthood; for, as we have seen, they already possessed the Priesthood, which is the power and authority to act for and in the name of the Lord.

A little later in the same evening Jesus said: "It is expedient for you that I go away: for if I go not away, the Comforter will not come unto you; but if I depart, I will send him unto you."[75a]

It does seem clear from the record that this insufflation with the words "Receive ye the Holy Ghost," was not a present bestowal thereof, because they had to tarry and did tarry in Jerusalem (as the

Lord commanded them) for days thereafter, before the Holy Ghost came at Pentecost, and during which time of waiting, the Apostles "all continued with one accord in prayer and supplication,"[76] doing nothing other than filling the vacancy in the Twelve, caused by the death of Judas.[77]

What meaning then is to be given to the words: "Receive ye the Holy Ghost." This question has given the commentators some trouble.

There seems to be an agreement that *receive* should be more properly rendered *take*, as of a gift, with the idea that the recipient may accept or reject the gift. Furthermore, it is said the absence of the definite article in the Greek text before the words "Holy Ghost," seems to imply that the gift bestowed is not made in all its fulness. This latter concept seems to find considerable favor with the commentators.[78]

Plummer in the Cambridge Bible notes, dismisses with little ceremony the idea that *take ye* should be considered as a promise to give; so to do, he says, would be an "unnatural wresting of plain language."

Yet having in mind the matters already considered, and especially the command, given some time before this occasion, to tarry in Jerusalem till the Holy Ghost should come, and that some time later the Holy Ghost came at Pentecost, and his statement during the Last Supper, "If I go not away, the Comforter will not come unto you; but if I depart, I will send him unto you," having these things in mind there is surely ground for the view that *take ye* was a direction (in one sense a promise) to accept the Holy Ghost when it came as it did at Pentecost. This latter, it is submitted, could, on the whole record, be the true view, notwithstanding its summary rejection by Plummer.—We come back here, as elsewhere, to the possible tampering with gospel texts by translators and others, both by "ignorant translators, careless transcribers, or designing and corrupt priests."

The suggestion that the bestowal on this occasion was to cover the ordinary mission of the Apostles and that the Pentecostal bestowal was for their extraordinary mission as being the first propagators of the Gospel,[79] seems neither a sound nor adequate explanation. But in any event, this is not a bestowal of the Priesthood. The Holy Ghost is not the Priesthood; the Holy Ghost is the third member of the Godhead, who has special functions and duties. The Holy Ghost is not the power and authority bestowed upon the Apostles by Jesus, for this was bestowed and exercised long before the meeting on this evening of the day of the resurrection when the Christ uttered these words.

Now, with reference to the remission of sins:

The form used here by the Savior is the same form he used in conferring the binding and loosing powers,[80] which is a bestowal of power. However, both Anglicans and Romans appear to make identical the power to bind and loose and the power to retain or remit sins. If these were identical, then Anglicans and Romans are in this dilemma: either the binding and loosing power given the Apostles at Capernaum had been abrogated or withdrawn, and there is no word in the Scriptures that even suggests that Christ ever withdrew from them a power that he once granted; or it was a re-bestowal of a power the Apostles already possessed, which would be a vain gesture about a sacred power of which the Christ would not be capable.

The answer to this seeming dilemma is that the binding and loosing power is a different power from the retaining and remitting power, and this difference modern revelation makes abundantly clear.

Furthermore, as to the power of retaining and remitting of sin, we must remember the power given to the Apostles and Seventy as they went on their first missions,—that they leave peace or shake the dust from off their feet and leave a judgment.

But assuming this to be a completely new bestowal of power, yet it still is not a bestowal of the Priesthood, for, again we may note, they had held the Priesthood from very early in their ministry (witness their baptizing).[81] This, if a new bestowal, is merely the bestowal of a new power, another key, in the Priesthood, or perhaps better, a bestowal of the full power of that of which they had before only a part; but it is not a bestowal of the Priesthood itself. We should here recall Caesarea Philippi and the assurance given to Peter that *keys* of the kingdom would be given. At this point we should recall the discussion on *Keys and Powers of the Priesthood* which is given above in Talk 22.

10. Jesus on the seashore with Peter and the rest who had gone fishing. (Robinson Sec. 169)

This is the oft cited and narrated incident when
Jesus thrice asked Peter, "Lovest thou me?" and
Peter thrice answered, "Yea, Lord; thou knowest
that I love thee," and Christ thrice repeated his in-
junction, "Feed my sheep." But this is not a bestowal
of any power or authority, but a command to Peter
to go forward in an authority and power which were
already his.[82]

11. Jesus and the Apostles on the Mount in
Galilee with five hundred brethren. (Robinson Sec.
170)

Jesus came to the Apostles and the five hundred
in the mountain, all apparently worshipping, but
some doubting. "And Jesus came and spake unto
them, saying, All power is given unto me in heaven
and in earth. Go ye therefore, and teach all nations,
baptizing them in the name of the Father, and of the
Son, and of the Holy Ghost: teaching them to observe
all things whatsoever I have commanded you: and,
lo, I am with you alway, even unto the end of the
world."[83]

As to verse 18 above, "All power is given unto
me in heaven and in earth,"—long before this the
Lord had said, "All things are delivered unto me of
my Father."[84] This is a declaration of the authority
Christ held. This is no new announcement and so
can have no such special significance as Romans and
Anglicans attach to it. It is in fact merely a renewed
assurance of this power which he held, a part of
which total power he had given them. For long before
he had given the Twelve *power*, when they first went
out,[85] he then saying unto them, "freely ye have re-

ceived, freely give."[86] He had given unto the Seventy *powers*, some of them identical with the powers that Jesus recited to the Twelve in the room where they sat at meat with doors closed and Christ suddenly appeared amongst them.[87] If the Seventy had these powers (as they did) then the Apostles had them for the apostolic calling includes the rights, authorities, and powers which the Seventy possess.

Thus, again, these words are merely a reassurance of his power and authority that he had in the past bestowed upon them, and of his right to command them.

As to verse 19 (teaching all nations and baptizing), this is a mere reiteration of the command he had given them in the room where they sat at meat, in the evening following the morning of the resurrection,[88] with the additional instruction that they should baptize in the name of the Father, Son, and Holy Ghost. The power for all this, the authority of the Priesthood, they had possessed since their ordination and first mission, and as to baptism, a power they held even before their ordination as the Twelve.[89] The command to teach "all nations" was, as already pointed out, merely a command to enlarge, geographically, their field of labor, not a bestowal of Priesthood.

And verse 20 merely repeats the charge to preach that was given to both Apostles and Seventies when Jesus sent them on their first missions.

There is here no bestowal of the Priesthood, but only a repetition for emphasis of instructions already given.

12. The Lord appears to all the Apostles at Jerusalem. (Robinson Sec. 171)

Jesus had now been "seen of them forty days, and speaking of the things pertaining to the kingdom of God: and, being assembled together with them, commanded them that they should not depart from Jerusalem, but wait for the promise of the Father, which, saith he, ye have heard of me. For John truly baptized with water; but ye shall be baptized with the Holy Ghost not many days hence. . . . But ye shall receive power, after that the Holy Ghost is come upon you: and ye shall be witnesses unto me both in Jerusalem, and in all Judæa, and in Samaria, and unto the uttermost part of the earth."[90]

Following this discourse Christ "lifted up his hands, and blessed them,"[91] and he ascended into heaven, a cloud receiving him out of their sight.[92]

There is in this incident no indication of any bestowal of the Priesthood; there is a reiteration of the extent of their missionary field; there is also a promise of power following their baptism with the Holy Ghost. But this was not in its nature or effect a bestowal of the Priesthood. It was the promise of power that was to come from the Holy Ghost.

Thus there is no record of the bestowal of the Priesthood upon the Twelve by Jesus at any time during the last week — the Passion Week — of the Savior's mortal life, though certain keys were either bestowed or amplified. As the record clearly shows, the Priesthood had been bestowed upon the Twelve early in the ministry of Christ, and they had exercised its powers in their work under his direction.

Furthermore, there is no mention in these incidents of the Passion Week, of some of the Priesthood powers previously conferred on the Twelve. Those great powers manifested in the miracles he performed to alleviate human suffering are not mentioned. The Savior seems, during these last days, to be mainly concerned with emphasizing certain broad phases and principles of the future work of the Twelve: that they were to carry the Gospel to everybody throughout the world (this command was necessary to overcome their Israelitish narrowness and bigotry so inconsistent with the new covenant); that they were to baptize for the remission of sins and he instructed them in the ritual of baptism; that (as the later labors of the Twelve show) they were to confer the Holy Ghost; that they were to be witnesses of the Christ to whomsoever they should come; that they should partake of the sacrament of bread and wine, typifying his flesh and blood, in remembrance of him.

The Priesthood authority for all this had been given long before the Passion Week, though as stated, certain keys were added upon or bestowed, during this period.

The doctrine that the Priesthood powers came during this week thus falls of its own weight. The doctrine was framed to give substance to the dogma attaching to the celebration of the eucharist, the Mass, which has come to be the chief function of the Roman priesthood.

We have repeatedly pointed out and emphasized in the foregoing pages that Christ bestowed his

Priesthood by positive, declaratory words of bestowal and endowment. While in the great intercessory prayer in the Garden,[93] he besought the Father to bless the Apostles, that prayer was for the help of the Father towards the Apostles and the world; it was not in terms nor in sense and purport for an endowment or bestowal of powers and authority. Thus the record stands that the Chirst always bestowed his power and authority by a declaratory endowment.

Moreover, as will later appear, the Apostles conferred the Priesthood by the bestowal thereof accompanied by the laying on of hands. Paul said to Timothy: "Wherefore I put thee in remembrance that thou stir up the gift of God, which is in thee by the putting on of my hands"; and again: "Neglect not the gift that is in thee, which was given thee by prophecy, with the laying on of the hands of the presbytery."[94]

While a consideration of the ordinals of the great Anglican and Roman churches might be more fully appreciated a little later, after a better background has been built, yet it seems desirable to note certain characteristics of the Roman ordinal at this point. We shall use the text of the English translation of the ordinal as given by Lowndes, who states that it is the translation made by the Very Rev. J. S. M. Lynch, D.D., Ll.D., and "approved of by the Roman Catholic Archbishop Corrigan, May 4, 1892."[95]

It should be said that the Roman ordinal ceremony is of so complicated a nature that one quite unacquainted therewith (as is the writer) may not be sure one thoroughly understands its details, but the essential parts seem reasonably clear. It appears that the ordination is part of or is made in connection with the saying of the Mass.

It may be said to begin with that the Roman ordinal contains no declaratory bestowal of the priesthood such as was made by the Savior, save only as to remitting and retaining sins, which is a *key* of the Priesthood, not the Priesthood itself. As to the Priesthood portions of the ordinal, there are only prayers for the bestowal of its powers and authority, not an actual bestowal.

The whole ceremony of the ordination is made up mostly of prayers for the bestowal upon the candidate of powers covering his ability to live righteously and to perform certain services for others.

We shall confine our attention chiefly to the declaratory parts of the ceremony.

As the text runs, in the forepart of the ceremony, the officiator places both his hands on the head of the candidate, but "saying nothing," nor is any silent prayer indicated. All the "Presbyters" present, or at least three of them, also silently impose their hands.

Then, by the text, the officiator, "as well as the Priests" present, extend their hands over the candidate, while the officiator prays:

"Let us, dearly beloved brethren, beseech God the Father Almighty to multiply His heavenly gifts on this His servant, whom He has chosen for the office of the Presbyterate and enable him to fulfil by

His help, what he undertakes through His favor. Through Christ our Lord."

Obviously, here is no bestowal, only a prayer that the Father will multiply heavenly gifts. Furthermore here and for some time further in the ceremony (as the text goes), the candidate is spoken of as "the one who is to be ordained" (*ordinandus*), so clearly this imposition of hands and the prayer accompanying it is not considered as bestowing the Priesthood, otherwise he would have been spoken of as "one ordained" (*ordinatus*) as he is spoken of later on in the text.

The ordination text then proceeds with prayers only and explanations and accompanying ceremonials, till a point is reached where the officiator, in connection with a rearrangement of the vestments which the candidate wears, makes this declaratory statement:

"Receive the yoke of the Lord; for His yoke is easy and His burden light."

Then, after a further adjustment of vestments, the officiator says:

"Receive the Priestly vestment by which charity is signified; for God is powerful to make you grow in charity."

This is a bestowal of vestments but not of the Priesthood. Further prayers follow in the text; at the conclusion of the first one, are the words: "May he, through the homage of Thy people, transform bread and wine into the Body and Blood of Thy Son by stainless benediction."

Here again is a prayer for power, not a bestowal of power even as to the Mass.

Then, under the text, and following a chant or reading by the officiator, the candidate is anointed with oil, with a prayer, and next the officiator presents to the candidate (still *ordinandus*, one to be ordained) a chalice (cup) containing wine and water, and a paten containing a "Host." Meanwhile, so runs the text, the officiator says:

"Receive power to offer sacrifice to God and to celebrate Mass, as well for the living as for the dead. In the name of the Lord."

We have already noted[96] that in the sacrament of the Last Supper, the Lord said nothing about the Apostles offering sacrifice. He administered the sacrament with the command they should do this in remembrance of him. Nothing he then said could be justifiably interpreted as bestowing upon them the power to offer sacrifice. He spoke of his own sacrifice for the sins of the world, but he did not direct them to sacrifice him again throughout all time, thousands of times a day, the world over.

But under the ordinal text itself this is not a bestowal of the Priesthood, but only a power to perform one of its functions, as the ordinal seems to recognize, for after this sacrifice clause is recited, the candidate is still described in the text as *ordinandus*, one to be ordained. The ordinal thus considers him still unordained.

Then follows in the text of the ordination, directions for certain ceremonials on the part of the officiator with reference to his ring, the washing of his hands "with a small piece of bread," his going to "his seat or faldstool if the Mass is chanted, otherwise to the Epistle side, where, having placed his mitre, he proceeds with the Mass as far as the Offertory."

The ordinal proceeds: "In the meanwhile the *ordained Priest (ordinatus sacerdos)* stands and washes his hands," etc. Thus somewhere between the time coming after the imperative "Receive power to offer sacrifice" etc., and the accompanying ceremonial of the officiator, and the proceeding with the Mass to the Offertory, the priesthood is evidently presumed to have been bestowed. There have been no declaratory words of bestowal; there has been no imposition of hands; there has been no prayer. None of these simple requirements for bestowing the priesthood have been performed at the time when the Priesthood is presumed to have been bestowed.

Following prayers and more ceremonials by the officiator, as provided in the text, and as the Mass evidently goes forward, a time comes when the officiator "places both hands on the head of the man kneeling (the candidate) before him, saying to him:

"Receive the Holy Ghost; whose sins thou shalt remit they are remitted to them; and whose thou shalt retain they are retained."

This is apparently the first and only place in the ordinal where a priesthood power is declared, and here it can not be a claimed bestowal of the priesthood, but at most a *key* thereof, for the candidate is already *ordinatus*—ordained. We have al-

ready pointed out that the reception of the Holy
Ghost is not a reception of the Priesthood. It did not
come to the Apostles till long after they had received
the Priesthood. Moreover under modern revelation
we know that the Holy Ghost comes after baptism
and at confirmation.

Thus the modern Roman ordinal does not confer
the Priesthood, nor is there any place where clearly
it is pretended so to do. Furthermore, it is interesting to observe that while the ordinal purports to give
authority to remit or retain sins, the authority to
carry on the ceremonial of transubstantiation is only
prayed for.[97]

The foregoing is the Roman ordinal for priests.
The Roman ordinal for bishops apparently is not
dissimilar, except that he has the commandments:
"Receive the staff of Pastoral Office . . . Receive this
ring, the signet of faith. . . . Receive the Gospel."

Perhaps a few of the words of the oath of the
Bishop might be of interest:

"I will strive to preserve, to defend, to increase,
and to promote the rights, honours, privileges, and
authority of the Holy Roman Church, of our Lord
Pope, and of his aforesaid successors. . . . I will attack, and, as far as I am able, follow up heretics,
schismatics, and rebels to our said Lord, or his aforesaid successors."[98]

[1]Mark 3:13-14; Matt. 10:1; Luke 6:12-16. [2]John 4:2. [3]Matt.
10:5-15; Mark 6:9-11; Luke 9:1-6. [4]Matt. 10:16-20. [5]John 8:26,
28. [6]Matt. 10:21-42. [7]John 4:1-2. [8]Matt. 11:1. [9]Mark 6:12-13.
[10]Luke 9:6. [11]Mark 6:12-13, 30; Luke 9:6, 10. [12]Luke 10:1. [13]Luke
10:2-16. [14]Luke 10:17-20. [15]Matt. 10:1; Mark 6:7; Luke 9:1; 10:1.
[16]Mark 6:30; Luke 9:10; 10:17 ff. [17]John 4:2. [18]John 3. [19]Matt.
3:13-17; Mark 1:9-11; Luke 3:21-23. [20]Matt. 10:5-6. [21] John 4:41.
[22]Luke 10:1. [23]Matt. 10:7. [24]Mark 6:12. [25]Luke 9:2, 6.

[26]Luke 10:9. [27]As to the Apostles,—Matt. 10:9-10; Mark 6:8-9; Luke 9:3-4; as to the Seventy,—Luke 10:3-4. [28]As to the Apostles,—Matt. 10:12-15; Mark 6:11; Luke 9:4-6; as to the Seventy,—Luke 10:10-16. [29]Matt. 10:8; 11:27; see also Luke 10:22. [30]Matt. 10:1; Mark 6:7. [31]Luke 9:1. [32]Matt. 10:1, 8; Mark 6:7. [33]Matt. 10:1, 8. [34]Matt. 10:8. [35]Luke 10:17, 19. [36]Matt. 16:13-19; Mark 8:27-29; Luke 9:18-21. [37]See Talk No. 9. [38]Quoted, Hastings, *Encyclopaedia of Religion and Ethics*, sub voce *Infallibility*, pp. 270b, 271a; see for fuller discussion of the claims of the Roman Church, with accompanying references, Talk No. 9. [39]Lowndes, *Vindication of Anglican Orders*, p. 289. [40]See Douay's Version for the Catholic explanation of the passages telling of the incident of Caesarea Philippi. [41]Maclear's note, *The Cambridge Bible*, St. Mark. [42]Luke 9:29; Mark 9:2-3; Matt. 17:2. [43]Luke 9:30-32, Mark 9:10. [44]Mark 9:5-8; Matt. 17:5-8; Luke 9:32-35; see notes under each citation in *The Cambridge Bible*. [45]Matt. 17:9; Luke 9:36; Mark 9:10. [46]Matt. 17:13; Mark 9:10-13. [47]*Documentary History of the Church*, III, p. 387. [48]D. C. 7. [49]Matt. 16:19. [50]Matt. 18:18. [51]*Robinson's English Harmony of the Gospels*, Revised Edition, Notes by M. B. Riddle. [52]John 13:27. [53]Matt. 26:26-29. [54]Mark 14:22-25. [55]Luke 22:19-20. [56]I Cor. 11:23-25. [57]See Talk No. 13 for a discussion of this point, and of the figurative use of the words, "Take, eat: this is my body." [58]Lowndes, p. 291. [59]*Op. cit.*, p. 295; see also pp. 402 ff. [60]John 14:16-18, 26; 16:7-11; see as to the two Comforters, *Documentary History of the Church*, III, pp. 380-381; McConkie, *The Holy Ghost*, p. 64 ff. [61]John 14:16, 26; Luke 24:49. [62]Acts 1:4, 8. [63]Acts 2:3-4. [64]Luke 24:37, 39; Mark 16:14. [65]Luke 24:45-48. [66]Mark 16:15-18. [67]John 4:2. [68]John 3. [69]Matt. 3:13-17; Mark 1:9-11; Luke 3:21-23. [70]Luke 10:19. [71]Matt. 10:5-6. [72]Luke 24:49. [73]John 20:22-23. [74]Acts 1:4, 8. [75]John 14:16, 26. [75a]John 16:7. [76]Acts 1:14. [77]Acts 1:15 ff. [78]See notes under John's chapter and verse, in Matthew Henry, *An Exposition of the Old and New Testament; Clarke's Commentary and Critical Notes;* Schaff's edition of Lange, *A Commentary on the Holy Scriptures, Critical, Doctrinal, and Homiletical;* Cook's edition of *The Bible Commentary* by Bishops and Other Clergy of the Anglican Church; Plummer's notes, *The Cambridge Bible*. [79]Lowndes, p. 291. [80]Matt. 18:18. [81]John 4:2. [82]John 21:15-17. [83]Matt. 28:18-20. [84]Matt. 11:27. [85]Matt. 10:1 ff.; Mark 6:9 ff.; Luke 9:1 ff. [86]Matt. 10:8. [87]Mark 16:17-18. [88]Mark 16:15-16. [89]John 4:2, and supra. [90]Acts 1:3-8. [91]Luke 24:50. [92]Acts 1:9. [93]John 17. [94]II Tim. 1:6; I Tim. 4:14. [95]Lowndes, p. xxxiii. [96]Talk No. 13. [97]Lowndes, pp. 179 ff.; xxxiii ff. [98]*Id.*, pp. xlvi, xlix, ff.

e. Ordinations

Having in the preceding pages considered the functions — the powers and authorities — of the Priesthood as conferred by Jesus and as understood and practiced by the Apostles, we may now turn our attention to the manner of conferring the Priesthood.

We shall first briefly consider the form of ordination, that is, the manner of ordaining, during the ministry of Jesus and thereafter in the Apostolic Church, as shown by the New Testament accounts. Thereafter, we shall give some attention to the departures from the original form.

It may be fairly said that sectarian scholars and commentators are guilty of wrenching the Scriptures from their plain statement and meaning in order to give support to their ecclesiastical perversions. This seems particularly true of those belonging to sects that have no priesthood system and who, in effect, profess the belief that all who are righteous have equal authority in representing God and Christ and in conducting His and the Son's work. It is enough to say on this particular point, that such a doctrine runs contrary to the whole recorded history of God's dealing with man from Adam down through the Apostolic Church. That God must have, to represent him, special agents who are divinely called and led, is so fundamental a concept that even pagans, including those of the highest intellectual development, have recognized and implemented it

even in their idolatry. Since God is God and has a
plan of life and salvation, any other system than
that of an ordered direction and government would
bring chaos and so defeat the plan. Indeed, we now
have chaos in religious teachings because the great
body of men have departed from the commandments
of God and have repudiated and lost his Priesthood.
Humanity is too numerous and too diverse to be
run on a town meeting plan in matters affecting
the eternal welfare of all of God's children under
his divine plan.

At this point we may recall the words of Burgon
and Miller, already quoted.[1]

"Another cause why, in very early times, the
Text of the Gospels underwent serious depravation,
was mistaken solicitude on the part of the ancient
orthodox for the purity of the Catholic faith. These
persons, like certain of the moderns, Beza for example, evidently did not think it at all wrong to
tamper with the inspired Text. If any expression
seemed to them to have a dangerous tendency, they
altered it, or transplanted it, or removed it bodily
from the sacred page. About the uncritical nature
of what they did, they entertained no suspicion:
about the immorality of the proceeding, they evidently did not trouble themselves at all. On the
contrary, the piety of the motive seems to have been
held to constitute a sufficient excuse for any amount
of licence."[2]

As an illustration of the kind of tampering to
which Burgon and Miller refer, we may note an
instance that Lowndes records:[3] In a Catholic edition

of the Bible of 1686, a phrase in the text of Acts
13:2, which reads: "As they ministered to the Lord,"
was changed to read: "As they offered to the Lord
the Sacrifice of the Mass." This particular corruption has been eliminated from the present official
text.[4]

Before proceeding to a piecing together of the
scattered accounts of ordination (that is, endowment
or bestowal of the Priesthood) as appearing in the
New Testament, in order to get some idea of the
actual Priesthood investing ceremony, we should
have in mind the following facts:

First: Every translator, whatever his ability
and whatever his integrity, of necessity translates
every sentence, phrase, or word, in accordance with
his knowledge and understanding of the subject matter. If he has no knowledge of the subject matter the
foreign expression is meaningless to him, and he
translates giving the rendering that expresses what
he thinks the text should say or mean. This factor
is of particular force where men's faith or convictions as to certain subjects are involved. The translation must fit into their own thinking. This is true,
it must again be said, where there is the utmost
integrity and intellectual honesty. This factor finds
its maximum opportunity where texts date back for
many hundreds of years and so have been subject to
the many vicissitudes that have accompanied the
copying and recopying of manuscripts in different
languages, by scribes of various and sometimes seemingly indifferent aptitudes, learning, and skill, to
which confusing circumstances must be added the

translation of the texts into one language and then the translation of that translation into other languages. As one contemplates the possibilities, under such conditions, of a complete loss of the truths embodied in the original texts, the man of faith can clearly see that the Lord has performed not one, but many miracles, in preserving so faithful a text as we now have. The man of faith can see, too, the wisdom, indeed the inspiration of the Prophet Joseph when he said: "I believe the Bible as it read when it came from the pen of the original writers. Ignorant translators, careless transcribers, or designing and corrupt priests have committed many errors."[5]

Second: In considering the question of ordination in the New Testament, we note that in several places where the A.V. (King James translation) uses the word *ordain* or *ordained*, the R. V. (Revised Version) and D. V. (Douay Version) use *appoint*. While in one sense, the matter is merely one of the meaning to be attached to words, yet, as some priesthoodless sects put great store in the use of the word *appoint*, as showing, they contend, the lack of necessity for any priesthood, we should remember these facts:

Holy Writ, from the beginning, has recorded the existence and functioning of priesthood in the service and worship of God: Cain and Abel offered sacrifice, Cain unacceptably, Abel acceptably; whenever there has been a true Priesthood, there has been a false one (Moses and Pharaoh's magicians, Elijah and the priests of Baal, and the corrupting native priesthood that afflicted Israel during her whole history); God has vindicated his Priesthood (the Korah, Dathan incident; and Moses as against Aaron and Miriam); God has demanded that his Priesthood shall function according to his directions (the Nadab and Abihu incident); and the transgressions of men have been forgiven through the operations of his Priesthood (Aaronic Priesthood and Order).

So in what follows regarding *ordination*, we shall assume, as we have already pointed out, that Christ did set up a Priesthood organization in his Church;[6] that, as history conclusively proves, his Church was built up, directed, and governed by his Priesthood; and that he specially endowed and gave direct and specific powers to his Apostles and the Seventy in order that they might perform the service and do the works he did and which he commanded them to carry on, and which his Apostles after his death did carry on. It is entirely clear from the Scriptures that not every believer in or follower of Christ was given the power and authority to perform his service and to do his work, but only those specifically called thereto. The incident of Simon seeking power to bestow the Holy Ghost is completely in point.[7] So it has been in all times—and no Scripture can be found contrariwise—that all those who rightfully undertake to carry on his work as his servants, must be specially and specifically authorized thereto. As our own Articles of Faith declare: "We believe that a man must be called of God, by prophecy, and by the laying on of hands, by those who are in authority to preach the Gospel and administer in the ordinances thereof."

We shall now see what the New Testament record shows on the matter. And in this examination we must keep in mind that one positive statement of a practice is worth more than countless numbers of mere absences of statements. We cannot accept the principle invoked by that mythical judge who tried a man for murder and acquitted him because, while the prosecution produced two men who testified they saw the accused murder his victim, the defense produced eight men who did not see him. This is not a true preponderance of evidence.

In our search, we shall use the A. V. (King James translation) in preference to either the R.V. (Revised Version) or the D.V. (Douay Version, Catholic)—though noting differences—because the A.V. accounts are consistent with what modern revelations tell us is the true order. We feel that the Lord may have inspired the A.V. translators to translate the texts they used as they did, in order to leave some record of the true order.

A few further preliminary points should be made.

As already indicated, there is in the New Testament no single account that carries all the procedure incident to a full ordination. It will appear as we proceed that the accounts piece together into a very simple ceremony, indeed, so simple and, it would seem, so well understood, that none of the Apostles or writers of Holy Writ deemed it necessary to set it out in detail. A statement that there was an ordination, or a setting apart, or a laying on of hands to endow with authority, was quite enough to carry to those to whom the epistles were addressed and to whom the gospels first came, the full fact of the ordinance.

If there had been any such elaborate ritual and ceremony, with all the accompanying pomp and circumstance that now constitute the bestowal of orders in certain of the great Churches, there would surely have been some account thereof in the New Testament Scriptures, just as there are accounts in Old Testament Scriptures of the Levitical consecration of priests, which these modern rituals ape. That there is no such mention or even allusion thereto in the New Testament is strong presumptive evidence that no such ceremonies existed, for surely Paul in his epistle to the Hebrews, would have mentioned something about the new ordinance if an elaborate one existed, or would have told of the applicable portions of the old, instead of confining himself to distinguishing the *old* covenant from the *new*, to noting the Priesthood change, and to saying practically nothing about endowing with the changed Priesthood. The facts of history conclusively show that the elaborate ceremonies now used in the Catholic Churches (Roman, Anglican, Eastern, Russian) were of slow growth over the early centuries. They were not the ceremonials of the Apostolic Church, nor of the centuries immediately following.

As to the *fact* of ordination:

Mark records that Christ "ordained twelve, that they should be with him, and that he might send them forth to preach, and to have power to heal sicknesses, and to cast out devils."[8]

Peter declared, after the ascension, when they prepared to choose one to take the place of Judas: "Beginning from the baptism of John, unto that same day that he was taken up from us, must one be ordained to be a witness with us of his resurrection."[9]

This set the order for those who were to possess the powers with which Christ endowed the Twelve. This was an endowment of the higher Priesthood, and an addition to the power the Twelve already possessed to baptize.

The record is that Paul and Barnabas, journeying through Iconium, Lystra, and Antioch, "had ordained them elders in every church."[10]

Paul told Titus he was to "ordain elders in every city" in Crete.[11]

Paul told Timothy: "I am ordained a preacher, and an apostle."[12]

We may here appropriately note the following proper additional uses of the term *ordain*:

Paul, speaking on Mars Hill to the Athenians, and pointing out their idolatry and their ignorance, which theretofore God had winked at, and of which they should now repent, declared: "Because he hath appointed a day, in the which he will judge the world in righteousness by that man whom he hath ordained."[13]

Writing to the Hebrews of the Levitical Priesthood, Paul declared: "For every high priest taken from among men is ordained for men in things per-

taining to God, that he may offer both gifts and
sacrifices for sins."[14]

Again Paul said to the Hebrews: "For every
high priest is ordained to offer gifts and sacrifices."[15]

We call attention next to the fact that Paul,
writing to Timothy, said first: "Whereunto I am
ordained a preacher, and an apostle . . . a teacher
of the Gentiles in faith and verity." But in his
second epistle to Timothy he said: "Whereunto I
am *appointed* a preacher, and an apostle, and a
teacher of the Gentiles."[16]

On the face of the English text, the following
observations may be made on these two passages:
Either Paul regarded *ordain* and *appoint* (or the
equivalent word or phrase in the Greek or Latin
texts) as equivalent, in which event *ordain* must
be considered the dominant term, for (according to
Mark) Christ *ordained* the Twelve; or, on the other
hand, the use of *appoint* in II Timothy must be considered as meaning an appointment or a designation
to preach to the Gentiles, he already being *ordained*
to the apostleship. In I Timothy, preacher, apostle,
and teacher of the Gentiles are terms indicating
the extent of his authority. On this premise, the two
passages are wholly consistent, one declaring his
Priesthood and calling, the other his assignment to
a specified service.

However, arguments of this sort, based on the
English translation are not fully persuasive. And
it may be stated here, as well as anywhere, that
probably there is no existing record (at least none
has been found) of any of Christ's words or teach-

ings in the original language in which he spoke. The oldest and best texts we have are only translations of his words and teachings. What we use are translations of those translations, and this translation of ours, the English text, has been subject to all the vicissitudes and irregularities noted and suggested in Talk 25. We may not, therefore, safely rely upon critical analyses of the grammar or verbiage of the English texts. By the same token, we may observe that critics may not confidently rely upon the texts of which the English text is a translation, for the parent text of the English text was in its turn a translation.[17]

Thus mere verbiage may not be too strongly relied upon, either *pro* or *con*, in any discussion, and yet critics—"higher critics"—are prone to attach the greatest value to verbiage (usually the verbiage of Latin or Greek texts which have been subject to all the vicissitudes Burgon and Miller recite) when it suits their purpose so to do, and to cast it aside with little ceremony when against them.

In a number of important passages the R.V. and the D.V. use the word *appoint* where the A.V. uses the word *ordain*. The following table will show some of these differences, and also the agreement or otherwise of the Inspired Version (Joseph Smith's version) and the German and French texts, which latter have been furnished to me by Elder Max Zimmer.

	A.V.	R.V.	Douay	I.V.	German
1. Mark 3:14	ordained	appointed	And he made that twelve should be with him	ordained	ordained
2. Acts 1:22	ordained	must become a witness	must be made a witness	ordained	same as R.V.
3. Acts 14:23	ordained	appointed	ordained	ordained	ordained
4. Acts 17:31	ordained	ordained	appointed	ordained	decreed
5. I Tim. 2:7 (cf. II Tim. 1:11)	ordained	appointed	appointed	ordained	appointed
6. Titus 1:5	ordain	appoint	ordain	ordain	provide
7. Hebrews 5:1	ordained	appointed	ordained	ordained	appointed
8. Hebrews 8:3	ordained	appointed	appointed	ordained	set apart
9. Jude 4	ordained	written of beforehand	written of long ago	ordained	same as R.V.

The French version uses *ordain* in 1 and 8 above; the phrase "a witness of his resurrection" in 2; *set apart* in 3, 5, 6, and 7; *appoint* in 4; and "written beforehand" in 9.[18]

From what modern revelation has made known to us regarding the Priesthood, it would seem that *appoint* as used in the passages cited below should have been translated *ordain*: Luke 22:29; Hebrews 1:2 (the commissioning of the Son for his work); Hebrews 3:2 (same as Hebrews 1:2); I Chronicles 6:49 (commissioning of Aaron and his sons).

From the knowledge we Latter-day Saints have of the meaning, purpose, and function of the Priesthood, the word *ordain* as used in the A.V. in the passages quoted above, fits exactly what we know must have taken place on the occasions concerning which the word is used, — the ordaining of the Twelve, the words of Peter regarding the practice followed by Jesus, the ordaining by Paul and Barnabas, the ordaining of Paul. We shall therefore go forward accepting the A.V. text in these matters, for there is no apparent difference in circumstance or purpose between Jesus *ordaining* the Twelve, Paul and Barnabas *ordaining* elders (where all texts but the R.V. use *ordain*) and the other occasions where some translators use the word *appoint* or a phrase in place of the word *ordain*. We have support in this view because in the I.V. the word used is *ordain* as in the A.V. and the Prophet would surely have caught, even in his preliminary work, such a gross inaccuracy if it had existed. We may with reason feel that King James' translators had inspiration when they set forth the true order, by using the word *ordain*.

Modern revelation makes clear that men must be endowed with the Priesthood by proper *ordination* before they carry on the functions incident to that Priesthood.

A further word may be said about the word *appoint*. The priesthoodless sectarians wish to give to the word *appoint* as used in the New Testament, the meaning of *designate* or *name*, indeed, their system requires them so to contend. But the word *appoint* may connote other elements besides a mere naming. For example—a man *appoints* an agent, but he must, in important matters, go beyond the mere naming in order to make the appointment legal,—he must draw up and sign a written document giving to the agent the powers he wishes to be exercised. Under the Constitution of the United States, the President, with the approval of the Senate, *appoints* ambassadors, ministers, consuls, judges, and various other domestic officers, but this mere naming is not sufficient,—an oath of office must be taken, a commission must be issued, and he must be inducted into office.

So much for the *fact* of *ordination.*

We shall now go to the method or manner of ordination.

It seems clear that men were *ordained,* or *endowed,* had their Priesthood powers *bestowed* upon them, by the laying on of hands, or, in the equivalent phrase, by the imposition of hands.

The Scriptures show that this was the manner in which men were ordained. It is not recorded as to every ordination, but, as already pointed out, the ceremony of ordination was so simple in the Apostolic Church, in contradistinction to the elaborate ritual of the ordination of priests under the Mosaic law, that there was no need for recording the details each time, for the details were few and easily remembered.

There are certain accounts of the laying on of hands, which scholars affirm were incident to the bestowal of ecclesiastical powers. They are as follows:

When the Greeks complained that the Hebrew widows were better cared for than the Greek widows, the Twelve called the disciples together and explaining that the other duties of the Twelve were so great they could not "serve tables," asked for nominations of men whom the Twelve (not the body of disciples) might "*appoint* over this business." (Note what is said above about *ordain* and *appoint*.) The disciples did as requested and named Stephen and six others "whom they set before the apostles: and when they had prayed, *they laid their hands on them*."[19] It seems certain from the narrative that this occurrence took place in the early days of the Apostolic ministry after the ascension. This seems clearly an *ordination,*[20] and while the sectarian view appears to be that these men were ordained deacons, it is clear that their functions were those appertaining to a bishop under modern revelation, and as we indicated in our Talk 8.

Again, Paul writing to Timothy admonishes: "Wherefore I put thee in remembrance that thou stir up the gift of God, *which is in thee by the putting on of my hands*."[21] In his first epistle, Paul indicates that not only did Paul place his hands upon the head of Timothy in this ordination, but that elders joined with Paul in the ordination. Paul said: "Neglect not the gift that is in thee, which was given thee by prophecy, with the laying on of the hands of the presbytery."[22]

This incident is generally accepted by scholars as the occasion upon which the Priesthood, or some grade of it, was conferred upon Timothy by Paul, others joining in. Some affirm Timothy was thus ordained a bishop.[23]

An instance may be taken from the Old Testament. The occasion is of such importance that the whole text may be quoted: "And the Lord said unto Moses, Take thee Joshua the son of Nun, a man in whom is the spirit, and lay thine hand upon him; and set him before Eleazer the priest, and before all the congregation; and give him a charge in their sight. And thou shalt put some of thine honor upon him, that all the congregation of the children of Israel may be obedient. And he shall stand before Eleazar the priest, who shall ask counsel for him after the judgment of Urim before the Lord: at his word shall they go out, and at his word they shall come in, both he, and all the children of Israel with him, even all the congregation. And Moses did as the Lord commanded him: and he took Joshua, and set him before Eleazar the priest, and before all the congregation: and he laid his hands upon him, and gave him a charge, as the Lord commanded by the hand of Moses."[24]

The consummation of this ordination is recorded in Deuteronomy: "And Joshua the son of Nun was full of the spirit of wisdom; for Moses had laid his hands upon him: and the children of Israel hearkened unto him, and did as the Lord commanded Moses."[25]

Quite obviously this was not an ordination to the Aaronic Priesthood, for Joshua was of Ephraim, not of Levi; yet Joshua took Moses' place as leader of Israel and it would seem exercised direction over the priests of Aaron and the Levites.[26]

From modern revelation we know that Moses received the Melchizedek Priesthood from Jethro, his father-in-law; that the Lord would have established that Priesthood in fleeing, wandering Israel, but that they rejected it; and that God took it away from Israel, though "the lesser priesthood continued, which priesthood holdeth the key of the ministering of angels and the preparatory gospel."[27]   After Moses, other individual prophets held the Melchizedek Priesthood, down to Elijah, who was the last.[28]   The facts recorded are consistent with the bestowal of the Melchizedek Priesthood upon Joshua by the authority and hands of Moses.

Thus the ceremony of laying on hands, or the imposition of hands, was undoubtedly an essential part of the ordination ceremony in the Apostolic Church, and, as already stated, the ceremony was so simple that it was not considered necessary to write it out in detail in recording every occasion.   Maclean, writing on Christian ordination in Hastings, says, "In the whole of the early period ordinations to every grade were simple, consisting of prayer (usually a single prayer) and laying on of hands . . . St. Luke does not mention all the details on every occasion. . . . After the Apostolic Age we have no descriptions of ordinations till the 4th cent., but then they become plentiful."[29]

The laying on of hands has always been an important element of religious ceremony and ritual with Israel and with the early Christians.

It was part of the ritual incident to the sacrifice of the scapegoat under the Aaronic ceremonies;[30] of the bullocks offered as sin and burnt offerings;[31] of the goats offered as a sin offering;[32] of private burnt offerings.[33]

Jesus laid hands on the sick in his ministrations

of healings;[34] so also the Apostles[35] and others duly authorized by them.[36] The imposition of hands was part of the ceremonial of bestowing the Holy Ghost following baptism.[37] Hands were also laid, it would seem, on repentant sinners.[38] Paul and Barnabas had hands laid upon them prior to their departure to Seleucia, thence to Cyprus on a mission.[39]

Thus it is clear, under the Priesthood order of the New Testament,—first, that men must possess the Priesthood of God in order to perform *Priesthood* functions; next, that men must be ordained, that is, have bestowed upon them that Priesthood in order that they may possess it—if a man is to be an agent he must be properly constituted an agent; last, the constitution of any agency for the Lord, is accomplished by a positive bestowal of power—such as Christ gave to the Seventy and the Apostles—accompanied by the laying on of hands, the imposition of hands.

---

[1]Talk No. 25. [2]Burgon and Miller, *The Causes of the Corruption of the Traditional Text*, p. 211; and see also Paton, in *A New Standard Bible Dictionary*, sub voce *Old Testament Text*. [3]Lowndes, *Vindication of Anglican Orders*, p. 430. [4]See Douay Bible, Acts 13:2. [5]See Talk No. 25. Note also that we have three principal translations of the Bible into English: 1. King James Translation, called the *Authorized Version* (A.V.), which we use. This Bible is "Translated out of the original tongues: and with the former translations diligently compared and revised, by His Majesty's special command." 2. The Revised Translation, called the *Revised Version* (R.V.), "Translated out of the original tongues, being the version set forth A.D. 1611, compared with the most ancient authorities and revised, A.D. 1881-1885, newly edited by the American Revision Committee, A.D. 1901, Standard Edition." (The British have also prepared a similar revised translation, which differs somewhat from the American Revised Version.) 3. A Catholic Bible, an official text known as the *Douay Version* (D.V.), which differs in some important particulars (e.g. substituting *penance* for *repentance*) and is "Translated from the Latin Vulgate; and with the other translations diligently compared." 4. We have also "The Holy Scriptures, Translated and corrected by the Spirit of Revelation by Joseph Smith, Jr." However, as the Prophet never

completed the work on this revision, it is not quoted by us as authoritative, but it is consulated as of interest. However, that portion of it which is found in the Pearl of Great Price, there printed as the Book of Moses, and the Olivet Discourse, beginning with the last verse of Matthew 23, and continuing through Matthew 24, are authoritative. See *Three in One* edition of the Book of Mormon, Doctrine and Covenants, and Pearl of Great Price. For exact status of this *Inspired Version*, see *Documentary History of the Church*, I, pp. 215, 324, 341. [6]Talk No. 8. [7]Acts 8:9 ff. [8]Mark 3:14-15. [9]Acts 1:22. [10]Acts 14:23. [11]Titus 1:5. [12]I Tim. 2:7. [13]Acts 17:31. [14]Heb. 5:1. [15]Heb. 8:3. [16]I Tim. 2:7; II Tim. 1:11. [17]See Hastings, *A Dictionary of the Bible*, one volume, sub voce *Language of New Testament, Language of Christ*. [18]Elder Max Zimmer. [19]Acts 6:1-6. [20]Maclean in Hastings, *Encyclopaedia of Religion and Ethics*, sub voce *Ordination*, p. 540b. [21]II Tim. 1:6. [22]I Tim. 4:14. [23]Lowndes, p. 228. [24]Num. 27:18-23. [25]Deut. 34:9. [26]Num. 13:8; 34:-17; Deut. 3:28. [27]D.C. 84:26. [28]D.H.C., IV, p. 207ff. [29]Hastings, *Encyc.*, sub voce *Ordination*, p. 541a. [30]Lev. 16:21. [31]Num. 8:12; Lev. 8:14 ff. [32]II Chron. 29:23. [33]Edersheim, *The Temple*, p. 87 ff. [34]Mark 1:41; 6:5; 8:23; Luke 4:40; 5:13; 13:11 ff.; Matt. 8:15. [35]Acts 28:8. [36]Acts 9:12, 17. [37]Acts. 8:17-19; 19:5-6. [38]I Tim. 5:22. [39]Acts 13:3 ff.

f. Simony

Before coming to the final phase of our consideration of the "falling away" in Priesthood, there is one matter we may briefly consider because, even on the assumption that the Church possessed the Priesthood at one time, it throws doubt on the transmission thereof from one to another in the Church, centuries before the Reformation.   We refer to *simony*.

The temptation to traffic for gold in the Priesthood and its powers, found early example in the Primitive Church, when Simon, the Sorcerer, to whom we have already referred, offered money to Peter and John for the bestowal upon him of the power that on whomsoever he should lay his hands, they would receive the Holy Ghost.   Peter rebuked him saying: "Thy money perish with thee, because thou hast thought that the gift of God may be purchased with money.   Thou hast neither part nor lot in this matter: for thy heart is not right in the sight of God."[1]

The purchase and selling of clerical offices, termed simony, afflicted the Church in the early centuries following the disappearance of the Primitive Church.

Beginning with Paul of Samosata (A.D. 260-270), the evil showed its head in widely separated parts of the Christian world.   The Council of Elvira in Spain (A.D. 305) forbade fees for baptism.   This practice obtained also in the East.   The *Apostolic*

Constitutions (A.D. 375) speak against simony, and the *Apostolic Canons* (A.D. 400) forbid giving or receiving the episcopate, presbyterate, or diaconate for money. The Council of Sardica, A.D. 347, (Sofia, Bulgaria) denounced bribery in the election of bishops or the transfer of bishops from one see to another. The Council of Antioch (A.D. 341) forbade a bishop, on his deathbed, to appoint his successor, and the *Apostolic Canons* forbid nepotism in the choosing of clerics. The ecumenical Council of Chalcedon (A.D. 451) forbade simony and the giving of bribes for appointments. The Emperor Justinian in his *Novellae* (A.D. 534-565) provided that an oath be taken against simony by the elected bishop and by the doctors.

So, also during the whole remaining early period of the Church, council and synod condemned simony, but the sin thrived.

In the medieval period in the West and the East, the practice continued, with continued efforts to control it on the part of councils and synods, and in modern times the evil and the fight against it have continued.

In England the evil seems to have been dealt with by an act of Parliament as late as 1898.[2]

Under the rule of Peter as against Simon, the succession of any Priesthood tainted with simony, and its legitimacy, must be seriously questioned.

As might be expected, great confusion came into the Church because of simony and apparently the evil cast doubt on the legitimacy of ordination of many of the clergy. Uncertainty increased because of the annulment of ordinations performed by certain Popes in the early and middle medieval centuries (Constantine II, A.D. 769; Formosus, end of ninth century), and of decisions for and against such ordinations. Later, in the eleventh century, because ordinations were then also annulled on account of simony, the ruling was made that "a simoniacal Bishop can give nothing in ordination, because he has nothing."[3] These measures inevitably threw general doubt on the descent of the Priesthood.

In A.D. 1075, Gregory VII, (Hildebrand) who took vigorous measures against simony, wrote to his friend Hugo of Cluny: "In the West, South, or North, scarcely any bishops who have obtained their office regularly, or whose life and conduct correspond to their calling, and who are actuated by the love of Christ instead of worldly ambition."[4] Leo IX, an "Hildebrandian pope," had before this taken vigorous measures against simony, prohibiting it "on pain of excommunication, including the guilty bishops and the priests ordained by them."[5]

Thus the line of descent of their priesthood in the Western Church inevitably took on an uncertainty, not only as to descent, but, under the rule that he who had no Priesthood gave none, uncertainty as to their actual possession of their Priesthood. This situation was further complicated by the fact that there were, at times, rival popes, and also popes who, it was charged, obtained their own papal throne by simoniacal practices, which by the rule announced by the Church as noted above, would seem to rob all their acts of legality.[6]

All this presents serious question as to the descent of the Priesthood authority which they claim to possess, for both popes and bishops were simoniacal, so possessing nothing they gave nothing.

[1]Acts 8:13 ff. [2]See on whole subject, Hastings, *Encyclopaedia of Religion and Ethics*, sub voce *Simony*. [3]Actions of Popes Leo IX, 1049-1054; Gregory VII, 1073-1085; Urban II, 1088-1099,—Lowndes, *Vindication of Anglican Orders*, I, p. 96 ff., quoting Janus; *id.* p. 539 ff. [4]Quoted, Schaff, *History of the Christian Church*, V, pt. I, p. 26. [5]Schaff, *op. cit.*, p. 13. [6]Alexander VI (Borgia), A.D. 1492; Julius II, 1503, — Hastings, *Encyc.*, sub voce *Simony*, p. 526b-527a; and see Benton, *The Church Cyclopaedia*, sub voce, *Simony*.

g. The Priesthood Disappeared Because of Failure to Transmit It

We may again call attention to the character-istic feature of the bestowal of Priesthood authority by Jesus,—it was an actual bestowal, not a prayer to the Father to bestow.

When he *ordained* the Twelve, "he gave them power," and authority. When he sent them out, he said, "freely ye have received, freely give."

To the Seventy he said, "Behold, I give unto you power."

At the time of Peter's great confession at Caesarea Philippi, the Lord said he would give there-after the *keys* of the kingdom and the power to bind and loose on earth, to be ratified in heaven.[1] Later, probably at Capernaum, he bestowed the keys thus promised as to binding and loosing in these definite, precise words: "Whatsoever ye shall bind on earth shall be bound in heaven: and whatsoever ye shall loose on earth shall be loosed in heaven."[2] (See for a discussion of *keys*, Talk 22.)

We might note in passing that there was no such power in the Priesthood of Aaron.

Again, when the Apostles were assembled in the room to which they had gone in fear of the Jews, in the evening of the day of the resurrection, the Lord appeared unto them and confirmed or bestowed certain keys in definite, precise terms: "Whose soever sins ye remit, they are remitted unto them; and whose soever sins ye retain, they are retained."[3]

A partial bestowal, at least, of these keys for remitting or retaining sin had been given to the Twelve and Seventy as he sent them on their first missions,—the power to shake the dust off their feet and so pronounce judgment.

There is no such authority as this in the Aaronic Priesthood.

Still later in Galilee, after declaring to his Apostles, "All power is given unto me,"—he had long before declared to the multitude, "All things are delivered unto me of my Father"[4]—the Lord reaffirmed the commission to his Apostles given at the time of their first mission, but making world-wide the field of their operations, with this command: "Go ye therefore, and teach all nations, baptizing them in the name of the Father, and of the Son, and of the Holy Ghost."[5]

This authority was no part of the Priesthood given to Aaron.

We should again note that these words are none of them a petition to the Father to give power; they are not a promise to bestow the power at a later time. They are a present, definite command to exercise an existing power and authority.

For the sake of brevity, we shall hereafter speak of this whole group of gifts, powers, and authorities, so conferred by the Christ upon his Apostles, as the Apostolic powers, although as we know from modern revelation, some (the power to baptize for instance, which was conferred in the early days of the Savior's ministry)[5a] were incident to the Aaronic Priesthood as now bestowed, and some to the Melchizedek, though of course the Apostles, possessing powers and authorities of both Priesthoods, could administer in the Priesthood functions appertaining to both.

We should again note further the utter simplicity of this ordinance of bestowing power and authority by the Lord. There was no elaborate ceremony, no pageantry, no pomp.

So it was when, in this Last Dispensation, John the Baptist, standing on the banks of the Susquehanna River, and placing his hands upon the heads of Joseph Smith and Oliver Cowdery, conferred upon them, and so restored to the earth, the Aaronic Priesthood in these words:

"Upon you my fellow servants, in the name of Messiah I confer the Priesthood of Aaron, which holds the keys of the ministering of angels, and of the gospel of repentance, and of baptism by immersion for the remission of sins; and this shall never be taken again from the earth, until the sons of Levi do offer again an offering unto the Lord in righteousness."[6]

Note well that here is an actual, present bestowal of the Priesthood, accompanied by the imposition of hands. It is not a prayer for the bestowal of the Priesthood or the Priesthood powers.

And with like simplicity and definiteness the Melchizedek Priesthood and Apostolic authority were conferred on the same men by Peter, James, and John.[7]

This bestowal by the Baptist of the Aaronic Priesthood, and by Peter, James, and John of the

Melchizedek Priesthood, was in strict accord with the procedure of the Apostolic Church, as the early Church records show. For convenience, we again quote Maclean: "In the whole of the early period ordinations to every grade were simple, consisting of prayer (usually a single prayer) and laying on of hands. . . . St. Luke does not mention all the details on every occasion. . . . After the Apostolic Age we have no descriptions of ordinations till the 4th cent., but then they become plentiful."[8]

Before we pass on to the consideration of certain early forms of ordination to see how far these meet the forms of the Apostolic Church, we will note a few principles which the Roman Church lays down governing the bestowal and passing on of the priesthood.

On the "Ides of September" (a Roman heathen date designation), in 1896, the Pope of Rome issued an *Apostolicae Curae*—Bull—declaring ordinations under the "Anglican rite" to be "absolutely null and utterly void." (*Apostolicae Curae*, Sentence 97.) In the course of his consideration of the validity of the Anglican Orders, the Pope laid down certain fundamental principles that we should have in mind. The quotations herein made are from Lowndes' *Vindication of Anglican Orders*, and from an English translation (which Lowndes uses) of the Latin text, the translation being made by the Catholic scholar, A. S. Barnes.

In speaking of the Anglican Ordinal and of certain additions made thereto over the years, the *Apostolicae Curae* (hereafter indicated as A.C.) says:

"But even if this addition could give to the form its due signification, it was introduced too late, as a century had already elapsed since the adoption of the Edwardine Ordinal, for, as the Hierarchy had become extinct, there remained no power of ordaining." (A.C. Sentence 66.)

That is to say, if the form of ordination fails to bestow the priesthood, then additions to the form cannot operate to make it a sufficient form so that priests ordained after the form is amended shall be properly ordained, because under the first form the Hierarchy (apparently bishops, priests, and ministers) "had become extinct" and "there remained no power of ordaining." This is a most important principle.

Again the Bull says:

"Hence, if vitiated in its origin, it was wholly insufficient to confer Orders, it was impossible that, in the course of time, it would become sufficient, since no change had taken place." (A.C. Sentence 81.)

That is, mere lapse of time will not make a good and sufficient ordinal out of a bad one. The sentence immediately succeeding (Sentence 82) points out how *"vain"* are additions.

Lowndes concedes these principles. He says:

"We boldly affirm that if the Edwardine or Elizabethan Ordinal, as administered by the then living Bishops, did not make Priests, then no subsequent change in the Ordinal could ever operate so as to make laymen into Priests at the hands of a man who was not a Bishop, because he himself was con-

secrated under a defective Ordinal. We unshrinkingly affirm that the Consecrator is greater than the
words. That for making a man a Bishop or a Priest
there is necessarily before all things a Bishop. Hence,
if the Elizabethan Bishops were laymen no subsequent change in the wording of the Ordinal could
ever make Priests of laymen, and that no 'course of
time,' no matter how prolonged, could be of avail."⁹

Two other matters should be mentioned here:

In connection with ordinations in the post-
Primitive Church, it became the custom to hand to
the one being ordained, the chalice (the cup from
which is drunk the wine) and the paten (the plate
on which is the bread). It is said this custom may
have come from the Levitical law, where Moses
placed unleavened bread in th ehands of Aaron,¹⁰
but with an added influence from pagan Rome where
the Pontifex Maximus handed the emblems of his
office to the newly-made priest.¹¹ Pope Eugenius
IV (1431-1447) held that the giving of the chalice
and paten, the *traditio instrumentorum*, was the
"matter" (the essential part of the ceremony of ordination) of the ceremonial; and that the "form"
was "Take (or receive) the power of offering sacrifice."¹²

However, this view of Eugenius was later given
up by the scholars, though apparently the idea is
still clung to by many Roman ecclesiasts.¹³ Nor is
this reluctance to abandon this dogma as to "form"
difficult to understand, when we recall the expression
of Leo XIII that the *"grace and power" of the Priesthood "is chiefly the power 'of consecrating and of*

offering the true body and blood of the Lord,'"
(A.C. Sentence 64) which seems obviously to refer
to the dogma and cult of transubstantiation.

But the official view expressed in the Bull of Leo
XIII (from which we are quoting) is that imposition of hands is the "matter" (A.C. Sentence 63),
and apparently that "Receive the Holy Ghost" is the
"form." (A.C. Sentences 64 and 69.)[14] This "receive" was not brought into the ordinal until the
darkest part of the Middle Ages.[15]

It might be added that Lowndes affirms that the
traditio instrumentorum is "neither ancient nor
scriptural," nor is "the form 'to offer sacrifice' or
to say Mass."[16]

Lowndes points out that in earlier times, the
imposition of hands, instead of being considered by
the Romans as *the* essential "matter" in ordination
as it is now, was then "not considered as an essential
in confirmation by the Romans, and was not given
in countless cases."[17]

With the technical meanings of "matter" and
"form," and the distinctions between them, we are
not here concerned. The whole subject is abstruse
and confusing to the uninitiated. The only points
to be noted here are that it was at one time held there
must be a *traditio instrumentorum* as the *matter*,
and that now imposition of hands is the *matter*, and
that, apparently, the imposition of hands is now considered necessary to a valid ordination but that this
was not so in earlier times. Futhermore, at one time,
"Take the power of offering sacrifice" was regarded
as the *form*, but now the words, "Receive the Holy

Ghost" is to be taken as the *form*. For our purposes we have no concern as to which is the official dogma. We are interested only in the dogma that one of the "matters" and one of the "forms," whichever one they may be, must be present in the ceremonial to constitute a valid ordination under the Roman rule.

We shall now pass to certain of the early ordinals—the texts used in ordaining men to the priesthood or one of its grades. Lowndes affirms he has collected and placed side by side all the forms of ordinations he has been able to gather together.[18]

Before proceeding to examine these forms we should again make sure to have clearly in mind that Jesus actually *bestowed* powers, he did not pray that they would be bestowed, and likewise the Apostles after him,—as Paul and Timothy; and that the Apostles ordained by an ordinance of bestowal by the laying on of hands. We should also carry in mind the Roman dogma regarding "matter" and "form."

Apparently the earliest ordinal that has been found is that taken from the Canons of Hippolytus (A.D. 236). The text we have is a translation from the Arabic (made by Achelis) into Latin. Probably the original was in Greek, of which no remnant has been found. Therefore the whole text must be viewed, rather than a particular word or phrase. But the scholars seem agreed that the text may be relied upon for the general sense and purport of the prayer. The text as given by Lowndes reads as follows:

"O God, the Father of our Lord Jesus Christ, the Father of mercy, and God of all consolation,

Who dwellest on high, and beholdest the lowly; Who
knowest all things before they are made; Who hast
appointed the bounds of the Church, by Whose command it cometh to pass that a righteous race en-
dureth from Adam, by reason of that Bishop, which
is the great Abraham; Who hast ordained governments and principalities; look down upon Thy servant N., giving him Thy power and the effectual
Spirit, which by Thine only Son, Jesus Christ our
Lord, Thou gavest to the holy Apostles, who laid
the foundations of the Church in every place, to the
honor and glory of Thy Holy Name. Forasmuch as
Thou knowest the hearts of all men, grant unto him
that he may without sin watch over Thy people, and
worthily feed Thy great and holy flock.

"Bring it also to pass that his conversation may
be higher than that of all the people, without any
falling away.

"Bring it also to pass that he may be envied of
all men for his excellence, and accept his prayers and
oblations which he will offer to Thee day and night,
and may they be a sweet savour unto Thee. Give also
unto him, O Lord, the Bishoprick (or Presbyterate),
the spirit of clemency and power for the remission of
sins; give him authority to loose all the chains of the
iniquity of evil spirits, and to heal all diseases, and
tread down Satan quickly under his feet, through
Jesus Christ our Lord, by Whom be all glory to Thee
with Himself and the Holy Ghost, world without end.
Amen."[19]

Maclean, after stating that following a prayer
by the officiator that the Spirit might be given to

the candidate, and that he might live worthily, gives
the concluding words of the Hippolytan prayer as
follows: "Receive his prayers and offerings which
he shall offer to thee day and night, and may they
be to thee a sweet savour. Give also to him, O Lord,
the episcopate and a mild spirit, and power to forgive sins; and give him ability to loose all bonds of
iniquity of demons and power to heal all diseases,
and bruise Satan under his feet shortly, through our
Lord Jesus Christ, by whom be glory to thee, with
him and the Holy Ghost, for ever and ever. Amen."[20]

It will be noted, as already indicated, that this
is a *prayer for power*, not a *bestowal* thereof. This
is a prayer that priesthood powers will be given,
not the *power* to preach that the kingdom of heaven
was at hand, to bestow peace and to mark for judgment, not the gift of the power to heal the sick
and to cast out devils and unclean spirits, the powers
(among others) that Christ gave the Apostles, and
which they exercised; but a prayer that God will
give power. This is not the like powers given to the
Seventy, and by them also exercised, but a prayer
for such powers. This is not the bestowal of the
keys "whatsoever thou shalt bind on earth shall be
bound in heaven: and whatsoever thou shalt loose on
earth shall be loosed in heaven," given to the Apostles,
nor the other keys bestowed, "whose soever sins ye
remit, they are remitted unto them; and whose soever
sins ye retain, they are retained," with which the
Apostles were endowed. This is not the command
and commission to go into all the world preaching
the Gospel, "he that believeth and is baptized shall

be saved; but he that believeth not shall be damned," which the Apostles received. All this is missing, and in place of it is a prayer that God will give certain powers.

There being no pretense of passing a power, of bestowing power and authority, and there being no sign of an intention actually to pass or bestow, and there being a seeming consciousness, evidenced by the absence of words of endowment, that they had no power to bestow and authorize, it follows that no such power or authority did pass nor was it bestowed; and thus the Priesthood was lost by the middle of the third century, and the great Churches make no claim of a restoration since that time.

The conclusion is inescapable that the sectarian Churches of the world do not now possess, and have not possessed, certainly since the middle of the third century, the Holy Priesthood of God and the power and authority to administer therein and thereunder. No amount of twisting and turning, of interpreting and wrenching texts from their true meaning, can change this fact, for such it is.

As to the exactness of the wording of the ordinal of Hippolytus, as already stated, this cannot be regarded as fixed, for scholars affirm that probably the prayers of the early ordinations were frequently extemporaneous. But Lowndes says this was the ordinal used by the Roman Church until the Council of Nicaea (A.D. 325).[21]

The scholars agree (as already stated) that in the early centuries the rites were extremely simple, a laying on of hands and a prayer. Maclean says:

"The extreme simplicity of the earliest rites continued for many centuries in both East and West, and it was only by slow degrees that they became more elaborate."[22]

In *The Dictionary of the Apostolic Church*, sub voce *Ordination*,[23] Maclean further says: "We are not told that our Lord gave directions to the apostles as to the method by which they were to appoint officials for the Church. Indeed, it is not a little remarkable that what Western theologians of a later day called the 'matter' and 'form' of ordination could neither of them have been taken from the incidents recorded in the gospel narratives which have come down to us. For in Jn 20:22 f. (we need not stop to inquire whether these words were addressed to the Ten or to a larger number of disciples) our Lord is said to have 'breathed' on those present, whereas *the apostles and those who came after them used, without any known exception, laying on of hands as an outward sign, and to have pronounced a declaratory and imperative formula*, whereas the disciples always (till the Middle Ages) used by way of 'form' a prayer only." (Italics ours.)

Every Church claiming its priesthood authority through the Catholic Church, Eastern or Western, Anglican or Roman, is in precisely the same situation as to the possession of the Holy Priesthood, for this Priesthood "falling away," this loss of Priesthood, transpired before there was more difficulty than quarreling and disputing among the various branches of the Church presided over by bishops, as for example Rome and Carthage, Alexandria and

Antioch, that is, before the great schism between the East and the West.

But the Roman Church is in the present position of having now laid down in the *Apostolicae Curae*, (Leo XIII) certain indispensable requirements for the passing of the priesthood, which the ordinal of Hippolytus does not meet.

Maclean, in the quotation last made, refers to the Roman "matter" and "form," in ordination. Disregarding the changes in their dogma over the centuries as to just what particular thing is "matter" and what "form," we may note that the "form" described in the *Apostolicae Curae*, that is, the declaratory phrase "Receive the Holy Ghost," does not appear in the ordinal of Hippolytus, indeed, the Holy Ghost is not even mentioned in the prayer. Maclean says, speaking of the early ordinals: "It must be noticed that in the ordination of bishops and presbyters there is no trace of an imperative formula like 'Receive the Holy Ghost,' such as we find in the mediaeval and modern books in the West."[24] Apparently the Eastern Churches have never used the imperative form.[25] As already stated, the imperative "Receive the Holy Ghost," was not brought into the "office of ordination" until the middle ages,— "the darkest days of Popery," as Lowndes quotes Churton as saying.[26]

Thus, under the Roman rule and dogma, the ordinal of Hippolytus is fatally defective as to "form" and the ordinal could not bestow the Priesthood.

Furthermore, there is nothing in the ordinal as

given that shows that there was an imposition of hands accompanying the prayer, and Pope Leo declares that the imposition of hands is the "matter" of a due ordination. Lowndes in qualifying the ordinal as sufficient to bestow the priesthood,[27] assumes that imposition of hands accompanied the prayer but indicates that without this rite the ordinal would be insufficient. But the fact is the ordinal itself makes no mention of the imposition of hands; but if it did, it would still be fatally defective for it *bestows* nothing; it merely prays for bestowal.

Thus, in "matter" also, this ordinal, from the point of view of Pope Leo XIII, is fatally defective; it could not bestow the Priesthood.

Since this ordinal would not, under the Roman dogma as announced by Leo XIII, bestow the Priesthood, it necessarily follows that those so "ordained" would not possess the Priesthood, and since, as pointed out above, one cannot bestow a Priesthood which one does not possess, 'the Hierarchy became extinct and there remained no power of ordaining.' (See A.C. Sentence 66.)

On these bases, it is a mathematical demonstration that the Roman Church and all its offspring are without the Holy Priesthood of God, and have been for at least seventeen centuries.

We may reiterate: It cannot be claimed by any of those Churches that an ordinal may be so amended as to confer the Priesthood, because while the mere wording of the ordinal could be changed to a proper form, yet it would be wholly ineffective unless implemented by one holding the proper Priesthood authority, and, as we have seen, no member of their hierarchy has possessed that power and authority, certainly since the ordinal from the Canon of Hippolytus was used as the form.

To repeat again: The Romans are especially estopped from affirming that alterations or additions can amend or make good a vitiated ordinal, for Leo XIII expressly affirmed this could not be done (A.C. Sentence 81), and furthermore, mere lapse of time will not do it. The *Apostolicae Curae* says: "Hence, if vitiated in its origin, it was wholly insufficient to confer Orders, it was impossible that, in the course of time, it would become sufficient, since no change had taken place." (A.C. Sentence 81.)

As Lowndes says in a passage already quoted, "We unshrinkingly affirm that the Consecrator is greater than the words. That for making a man a Bishop or a Priest there is necessarily before all things a Bishop. Hence, if the Elizabethan Bishops were laymen no subsequent change in the wording of the Ordinal could ever make Priests of laymen, and that no 'course of time,' no matter how prolonged could be of avail."[28]

But the existing Roman ordinal (which we have already glossed) "is really a succession of new rites,"[29] many of which came in before the Reformation and so are now common to all priesthoods claiming under the original Catholic rite. Maclean notes some of them in his brief summary at the end of his article *Ordination* (*Christian*) in Hastings. One of the earliest ceremonies that was added to the ordination was the holding of the Gospel-Book over the candidate—under the Roman ordinal since the 11th century the book is delivered to the candidate; anointing with oil in the ordination came in from the Gallican Church, appearing in Britain as early as the 6th century, whence it passed to Rome and thence to the Armenians and Maronites, who alone of the Eastern Churches have it; the clothing with vestments was an addition; so the addition of the badges of office, to the bishop a ring and staff, to the presbyter a chalice and paten with the elements prepared for the Mass—these coming into the ordinal in the 7th and 8th centuries as the result of the fusion of the Roman and Gallican rites[30]—at which time also came in a rearrangement of the prayers in the ordination ceremonies, and also a replacing of the time of the imposition of hands; before and after the Reformation, the imperative or declaratory formulae "and the delivery of the insignia of office change the centre of gravity of the office from a prayer to God to ordain to an act done by the ordainer. . . . The only doctrinal development that calls for notice is found in the Western pre-Reformation pontificals.   In these the function of offering sacrifice is greatly emphasized in the ordination of a presbyter. This is the case both in the ordination prayers and in the comparatively modern imperative formulae."[31]

For all the elaborate pomp and ceremony and regal and paganistic regalia, accompanying the present ordination ceremonies, there is not one word of New Testament Scripture authority nor any scriptural intimation. It seems clear that the vestments, at least in part, and some of the ceremonial used in the Mass, came from the Aaronic rituals of the Levitical Priesthood as prescribed in the Old Testament.[31a] These were adopted in disregard of the careful disquisition which Paul gave to the Hebrews on the *old* and *new* covenants.

One cannot read the history of this repeated corruption of the simplicity of the Apostolic ordination ceremonial, without a feeling that consciously or subconsciously, along during the centuries, there came to the heirarchy, or some member of it, a suspicion, at least, of the insufficiency of all this pageantry for bestowing the priesthood, and then came an uninspired reaching out for something that would cure their spiritual malady.

Of a truth, Leo XIII spoke more wisely than he wit, when, for some seemingly non-essential, even trifling changes made in the Anglican ordinal, he laid down the principle, fully applicable to the Roman Ordinal, that "in vain" had the Anglicans "made some additions to the Ordinal," because "vitiated in its origin" it 'was impossible that, in the course of time, it could become sufficient,' since "as the Hierarchy had become extinct, there remained no power of ordaining," even if the changes and additions made would have been sufficient had they been introduced before the death of the hierarchy. One cannot escape the recollection of Nathan and David and the one little ewe lamb, and David's condemnation of himself.[31b]

While all the foregoing has been predicated upon the ordinal from the Canon of Hippolytus, the case does not rest just there. Some might contend that somewhere some properly ordained priest might have been still functioning and so pass the Priesthood by a proper rite. This has not been alleged, so far as observed, and if alleged, the finding of that priest and the tracing of his priesthood would not be possible under the circumstances and conditions found in the post-Primitive Church, nor would it be applicable to the existing hierarchies.

But other early ordinals, used by the Church, or its branches, are known, which have the same fatal defects that vitiate the Hippolytus ordinal. The early ones collected by Lowndes (all he could find, he said)[32] bring us down from the time of Hippolytus (A.D. 236) to the time of Gregory the Great (A.D. 590-604). Those listed are: Apostolical Constitutions (fourth century);[33] Coptic and Jacobite Syrian (fifth century);[34] Missale Francorum (sixth century);[34a] Leonine Sacramentary (sixth century);[35] Nestorian (middle of sixth century);[36] Maronite (date uncertain);[37] Armenian (sixth century).[38]

But all of these are also precatory; none pretends to bestow or endow by declaratory or imperative words such as Christ used.

Since the Leonine Sacramentary (sixth century) seems to be considered by some Roman writers as "the form," and as it appears further that the prayer was "attached to the laying-on of hands," (though after the prayer was offered, and it would seem, that when hands were imposed, the candidate was still *ordinandus*, or the one to be ordained), we quote the full prayer of the ordinal as given by Lowndes:

"O Lord Holy, Father Almighty, Eternal God, Who art the Giver of honours and the Distributor of dignities, through Whom all things prosper, by Whom all things are sustained and do continually increase for the well being of men through the ordinances of Thy Providence: Wherefore also the Priestly degrees and the Levitical offices have increased by the institution of mystic Sacraments, so that, even as Thou didst appoint the Chief Pontiffs to be the principal rulers of the people, so Thou hast chosen also men of the next order and of a lower dignity, to be unto them as helpers in work and fellowship.

"Thus, in the desert, Thou didst engraft the spirit of Moses into the minds of the seventy wise men, thus didst Thou impart to Eleazar and Ithamar, the sons of Aaron, the full authority which Thou hadst given to their father, so that the ministry of Priests might suffice for the offering of saving victims, and the Sacraments might be more frequently offered. With this providence, O Lord, Thou hast added teachers of the faith, as companions to the Apostles of Thy Son, by whose ministry they have filled the whole world with their preaching. Wherefore, we beseech Thee, O Lord, bestow these aids also upon our infirmity, who feel, inasmuch as we are weaker than they, the need of multiplied helpers. Bestow, we beseech Thee, Almighty God, on this Thy servant the diginity of the Priesthood (*Presbyterii*), and renew within him the spirit of holiness, that he may obtain from Thy acceptance, O God, the office of second dignity, and by the example of his conduct provide a model of godly life. May he prudently co-operate with our order, and may all manner of virtue be in him reflected, so that when he shall have come to render a good account of the stewardship entrusted to him, he may obtain the reward of eternal happiness.

"Through the same Lord Jesus Christ, Who liveth, etc."[39]

By the time of this ordinal, the absorption of the Aaronic rites was seemingly begun. The Levitical Priesthood is stressed. The Melchizedek Priesthood is not mentioned. There is no evidence that the difference between the *old* and the *new* covenant, 'the changed priesthood,' is in their minds. They seem to have forgotten that Christ was the Great High Priest after the order of Melchizedek.

There is still no pretense of a present bestowal of a Priesthood power. The ordinal voices no authority to do the works that Jesus and the Apostles did. It is a prayer of beautiful verbiage but of barren substance.

As to the Romans, it does not meet the requirements laid down by Leo XIII, because the "form" he demands, "Receive the Holy Ghost," is not present. It is thus fatally defective for the Romans. It may be, though it does not appear in the text, that the "matter," the imposition of hands, demanded by Pope Leo is present, but if so, as stated above, the candidate was still considered unordained[40] at the conclusion of the prayer. Thus this ordinal cannot stand the test of

validity presented by the Pope himself, so for them
no priesthood passed, and it must be said of ordination under this ordinal, even as Pope Leo XIII says
of the ordinations under the Anglican Ordinal: "We
pronounce and declare that Ordinations carried out
according to the Anglican rite (The Leonine Sacramentary) have been, and are, absolutely null and
utterly void." (A.C. Sentence 97.)

Logic and the facts of history (to appeal to
which is said to be treason) demonstrate beyond a
question to the open mind that the Holy Priesthood
of God had disappeared from the earth by the middle
of the 3rd century; that devices and makeshifts
adopted by the hierarchy to restore it failed utterly
so to do, the heirarchy all the time getting further
and further away from the truth; and that a restoration of the Priesthood was an absolute essential if the
salvation and exaltation of men was to be brought
about.

Looking at what Christ did in the exercise of
his powers received from the Father, and what the
Apostles and Seventy did under Christ's ordination,
and by his direction, both during Christ's life and
after his ascension; contemplating that these servants of the Lord were specifically endowed with power and authority to heal the sick, cast out devils, and
unclean spirits, cure all manner of diseases, raise the
dead, bring the elements and forces of nature under
control, bind and loose for time and eternity, retain
or remit sins, and preach the Gospel of salvation with
the authority of Almighty God through the ministrations of the Only Begotten, having all this in mind,

one can see the abyss of error into which the hierarchy has let the people fall, when they must look for succor in their trials and tribulations, not to the ministrations of the Priesthood of Almighty God but to visits to shrines, to pictures, to images of wood and stone, to the graves of mortal men and to dead men's bones. Would the Christ say to the sectarian priests of today as he said to the Pharisees and scribes in that most scathing indictment ever spoken in mortal tongue to men: "Woe unto you, scribes and Pharisees, hypocrites! for ye are like unto whited sepulchres, which indeed appear beautiful outward, but are within full of dead men's bones, and of all uncleanness."[41]

Is not the justice clear of Christ's words to the Prophet on the occasion of the First Vision, ". . . that all their creeds were an abomination in his sight; that those professors were all corrupt; that: 'they draw near to me with their lips, but their hearts are far from me; they teach for doctrines the commandments of men, having a form of godliness, but they deny the power thereof.' "

This is not to say that there are not now nor that there have not been, millions of God-fearing men belonging to the Catholic religion (used in its broadest sense), nor that there have not been over the centuries, millions upon millions of men who were honest, true, and righteous, according to their standards, living over the centuries. To bring salvation to these, if they choose to accept the gift, we build Temples and do work for them, exercising the binding and loosing power bestowed upon the Prophet Joseph and by due authority passed to his successors.

But it is to say that their system is based in error, even as the Lord said to Joseph.

To cure all this, the Gospel was restored to the earth, and with it came the restoration of the Holy Priesthood after the Order of the Son of God,—the Higher or Melchizedek Priesthood, including the Lesser or Aaronic Priesthood.

We repeat here the ordination to the Aaronic Priesthood of Joseph and Oliver at the hands of John the Baptist:

"Upon you my fellow servants, in the name of Messiah I confer the Priesthood of Aaron, which holds the keys of the ministering of angels, and of the gospel of repentance, and of baptism by immersion for the remission of sins; and this shall never be taken again from the earth, until the sons of Levi do offer again an offering unto the Lord in righteousness."[42]

As pointed out above[43] the Melchizedek Priesthood was restored soon after the Aaronic, the ordination being of like bestowal by the Apostles Peter, James, and John; and the keys of the Priesthood followed in due course.[44]

Every ordination to the Priesthood of whatever grade in the Church of Jesus Christ of Latter-day Saints, is a present bestowal and endowment of the Priesthood—not a prayer that the Lord will bestow some of its incidents—with all the gifts, powers, authorities, and functions thereunto appertaining, with a reminder of the duties and obligations as to righteous living that run therewith; and of what these gifts, powers, authorities, and functions consist, is set out in the revelations from the Lord to his Prophet, Seer, and Revelator, and found printed in the Doctrine and Covenants.

There is no withholding, no abating, no shrinking, no deviating, no running away from the full recorded powers conferred by Christ upon his Priesthood while he moved upon the earth.

I close this book with my own testimony to these things, and I pray in the name of the Redeemer that he will give to those who may read what I have said and written, the knowledge that only by obedience to the laws and commandments of the Restored Gospel shall we certainly attain to immortality and eternal life.

---

[1]Matt. 16:19. [2]Matt. 18:19. [3]John 20:23. [4]Matt. 11:27. [5]Matt. 28:19. [5a]John 4:1-2. [6]D.C. 13. [7]D.C. 18:9; 27:12-14; 128:20. [8]Hastings, *Encyclopaedia of Religion and Ethics*, sub voce *Ordination*, p. 541a. [9]Lowndes, *Vindication of Anglican Orders*, p. 275. [10]Lev. 8:26ff. [11]Lowndes, p. 207. [12]*Id.* pp. 138, 204-205, 487, 530, *et alia.* [13]*Id.* pp. 209 ff., 487 ff. [14]*Id.*, p. 205 ff. [15]*Id.*, p. 167. [16]*Id.*, p. 298. [17]*Id.*, p. 539. [18]*Id.*, pp. 212, 447, 537. [19]*Id.*, pp. 447-48. [20]Hastings *op cit.*, p. 542a. [21]Lowndes, p. 450. [22]Hastings, *op. cit.*, p. 541a, 551b. [23]*Dictionary of the Apostolic Church*, sub voce *Ordination*, p. 115. [24]Hastings, *op. cit.*, p. 542. [25]Lowndes, p. 477. [26]*Id.*, p. 167. [27]*Id.*, p. 449. [28]*Id.*, p. 275. [29]*Id.*, p. 280. [30]Hastings, *op cit.*, p. 543b, 551b, 552a. [31]*Id.*, p. 552a; also Lowndes, pp. 280, 295. [31a]See Talk 13. [31b]IISam. 12. [32]Lowndes, pp. 212, 447, 537. [33]*Id.*, pp. 450, cxxxv. [34]*Id.*, pp. 452, cxxxvi-vii. [34a]*Id.*, pp. 453, cxxxviii. [35]*Id.*, pp. 455, cxliv. [36]*Id.*, pp. 459, cxxxix. [37]*Id.*, pp. 460, cxl. [38]*Id.*, pp. 462, cxli. [39]*Id.*, pp 455-456. [40]*Id.*, p.457. [41]Matt. 23:27. [42]D.C. 13. [43]Talk 19. [44]See Talk 22.

ACKNOWLEDGMENTS

Grateful acknowledgment is extended to the publishers of the copyrighted works listed below, who have kindly given permission to reprint the quotations used in the text:

G. BELL & SONS, LTD., London, for *The Causes of the Corruption of the Traditional Text of the Holy Gospels*, by John William Burgon, 1896.

A. & C. BLACK, LTD., London, for *Encyclopaedia Biblica*, 1899.

ENCYCLOPAEDIA BRITANNICA, Chicago, for *Encyclopaedia Britannica*, Ninth Edition.

FUNK & WAGNALLS COMPANY, New York, for *The New Schaff-Herzog Encyclopedia of Religious Knowledge*, 1908; and *A New Standard Bible Dictionary*, 1925.

THE JUDSON PRESS, Philadelphia, for *A Manual of Church History*, by Albert Henry Newman, 1899.

LONGMANS, GREEN & CO., INC., New York and London, for *The Doctrine of the Church of England on the Holy Communion*, by Frederick Meyrick, 1908.

THE MACMILLAN COMPANY AND THE CAMBRIDGE UNIVERSITY PRESS, New York, for *The Cambridge Bible for Schools and Colleges*, 1881-1893.

CHARLES SCRIBNER'S SONS, New York, for *The Ante-Nicene Fathers*, edited by Alexander Roberts and James Donaldson, 1899; *Dictionary of the Apostolic Church*, edited by James Hastings, 1916; *A Dictionary of the Bible*, edited by James Hastings, 1902; and *Encyclopaedia of Religion and Ethics*, edited by James Hastings, 1928.

ROBERT C. TERRY, Chestnut Hill, Mass., for *Terry's Guide to Mexico*, 1928.

BIBLIOGRAPHY

Ante-Nicene Fathers, The, edited by Alexander Roberts and James Donaldson, notes by A. Cleveland Coxe, Charles Scribner's Sons, New York, 1899.

Bible Commentary, The, edited by F. C. Cook, Charles Scribner's Sons, New York.

Book of Mormon, The.

BURGON, JOHN WILLIAM, *The Causes of the Corruption of the Traditional Text of the Holy Gospels*, arranged, completed, and edited by Edward Miller, George Bell and Sons, London, 1896.

BURNS, ISLAY, *The First Three Christian Centuries*, T. Nelson and Sons, London, 1884.

Cambridge Bible for Schools and Colleges, The, J. J. S. Perowne, general editor, The University Press, Cambridge, 1881-1893.
    St. Matthew, notes by A. Carr.
    St. Mark, notes by G. F. Maclear.
    St. Luke, notes by F. W. Farrar.
    St. John, notes by A. Plummer.
    The Acts of the Apostles, notes by J. Rawson Lumby.

Church Cyclopaedia, The, edited by A. A. Benton, L. R. Hamersly & Co., Philadelphia, 1884.
    "Cardinal," by A. A. Benton.
    "Councils, Aecumenical," by W. J. Gold.
    "Pope," by H. H. Loring.
    "Simony," by A. A. Benton.

CLARKE, ADAM, *Commentary on the Bible*, The Methodist Book Concern, New York.

Dictionary of the Apostolic Church, edited by James Hastings and others, Charles Scribner's Sons, New York, 1916.
    "Ordination," by Arthur John Maclean.

Dictionary of the Bible, A, edited by James Hastings, 1908.

Dictionary of the Bible, A, edited by James Hastings, and others, Charles Scribner's Sons, New York, 1902.
    "Bible," by Alexander Stewart.
    "Bishop," by Henry Melville Gwatkin.
    "Canon," by Vincent Henry Stanton.
    "Peter," by Frederic Henry Chase.

Doctrine and Covenants, The.

EDERSHEIM, ALFRED, *The Temple, Its Ministry and Services as They Were at the Time of Jesus Christ*, Fleming H. Revell Company, London, 1874.

Encyclopaedia Biblica, edited by T. K. Cheyne and J. Sutherland Black, Adam and Charles Black, London, 1899.
    "Gnosis," by Gustav Adolf Julicher.
    "Idolatry and Primitive Religion," by George F. Moore.
    "Simon Peter," by P. W. Schmiedel.

Encyclopaedia Britannica, The, Ninth Edition, A. and C. Black, London, 1889.
    "Constantine," by W. Browning Smith.
    "Crusades," by Geo. W. Cox.

Encyclopaedia of Religion and Ethics, edited by James Hastings, Charles Scribner's Sons, New York, 1928.
    "Agapetae," by Hans Achelis.
    "Arianism," by Frederick John Foakes-Jackson.
    "Assumption and Ascension," by John Henry Bernard.
    "Baptism, Early Christian," by Kirsopp Lake.
    "Bible," by William Sanday.
    "Celibacy (Christian)," by George Cross.
    "Concubinage (Christian)," by David Schley Schaff.
    "Coptic Church," by Philip David Scott-Moncrieff.
    "Councils (Early Christian)," by Darwell Stone.
    "Councils (Mediaeval Christian)," by David Schley Schaff.
    "Councils (Modern Christian)," by Herbert Thurston.
    "Crusades," by Herbert B. Workman.
    "Eucharist (to End of Middle Ages)," by James Herbert Srawley.
    "Gnosticism," by Ernest Findlay Scott.
    "Greek Orthodox Church," by Sergei Victorovich Troitsky.
    "Images and Idols (General and Primitive)," by Count Gohlet D'Alviella.
    "Indulgences," by Auguste Boudinhon.
    "Infallibility," by William Alexander Curtis.
    "Mary," by James Cooper.
    "Ordination (Christian)," by Arthur John Maclean.
    "Papacy," by Alfred Fawkes.
    "Propitiation (Roman)," by A. C. Pearson.
    "Relics (Primitive and Western)," by John Arnott MacCulloch.
    "Saints and Martyrs (Christian)," by Herbert Thurston.
    "Simony," by Arthur John Maclean.

GIBBON, EDWARD, *The Decline and Fall of the Roman Empire,* notes by H. H. Milman, International Book Company, New York, 1845.

HEFELE, CHARLES JOSEPH, *A History of the Christian Councils,* translated and edited by William R. Clark, T. & T. Clark, Edinburgh, 1871.

HENRY, MATTHEW, *An Exposition of the Old and New Testament,* James Nisbet and Co., London, 1875.

History of the Church of Jesus Christ of Latter-day Saints, The Deseret News, Salt Lake City, 1902.

Holy Bible, The (Authorized Version).

Holy Bible, The (Douay Version).

Holy Bible, The (Revised Version), 1901.

Holy Scriptures, The (Inspired Version).

LANGE, JOHN PETER, *A Commentary on the Holy Scriptures, Critical, Doctrinal, and Homiletical,* translated and edited by Philip Schaff, Charles Scribner & Co., New York, 1870.

LOWNDES, ARTHUR, *Vindication of Anglican Orders*, James Pott & Co., New York, 1897.

MCCONKIE, OSCAR W., *The Holy Ghost*, Deseret Book Company, Salt Lake City, 1944.

MEYRICK, FREDERICK, *The Doctrine of The Church of England on the Holy Communion*, Longman's, Green and Co., London, 1908.

Millennial Star, The Latter-day Saints', Volume XVI, Liverpool, 1854.

New Schaff-Herzog Encyclopedia of Religious Knowledge, The, Funk & Wagnalls Company, New York, 1908.
>   "Assumption, Feast of the," by John Thomas Creagh.
>   "Canon of Scripture," by Theodor Zahn.
>   "Immaculate Conception," by Philip Schaff-David Schley Schaff.
>   "Mary, Mother of Jesus Christ," by Otto Zoeckler.
>   "Mass (The Doctrine)," by Ferdinand Friedrich Wilhelm Kattenbusch.
>   "Mass (The Liturgy)," by Paul Gottfried Drews.
>   "Pope," by Emil Sehling.
>   "Saints, Veneration of," by Gottlieb Nathanael Bonwetsch.
>   "Soul and Spirit, Biblical Conceptions of," by Clarence Augustine Beckwith.

New Standard Bible Dictionary, A, Funk & Wagnalls Company, New York, 1925.
>   "New Testament, Canon of," by Kirsopp Lake.
>   "Old Testament, Canon of," by W. G. Jordan.
>   "Old Testament Text," by Lewis Bayles Paton.

NEWMAN, ALBERT HENRY, *A Manual of Church History*, The American Baptist Publication Society, Philadelphia, 1899.

PARRY, EDWIN F., *Joseph Smith's Teachings*, The Deseret News, Salt Lake City, 1931.

Pearl of Great Price, The.

RANKE, LEOPOLD, *The History of the Popes*, translated by E. Foster, George Bell and Sons, London, 1874.

ROBERTS, B. H., *A Comprehensive History of The Church of Jesus Christ of Latter-day Saints*, published by the Church, Deseret News Press, Salt Lake City, 1930.

ROBERTSON, JAMES C., *History of the Christian Church, From the Apostolic Age to the Reformation*, Pott, Young and Co., New York, 1874.

ROBINSON, EDWARD, *A Harmony of the Four Gospels in English*, revised edition by M. B. Riddle, Houghton, Mifflin and Company, Boston, 1889.

SCHAFF, PHILIP, *The Creeds of Christendom*, Harper & Brothers, New York, 1899.

.... *History of the Christian Church*, Charles Scribner's Sons, New York, 1889.

TALMAGE, JAMES E., *A Study of the Articles of Faith*, Church of Jesus Christ of Latter-day Saints, Salt Lake City, 1924.

TERRY, T. PHILIP, *Terry's Guide to Mexico*, Houghton Mifflin Company, Boston, 1928.

BIOGRAPHICAL NOTES ON AUTHORITIES CITED

ACHELIS, HANS, D. THEOL., D. PHIL., Professor of Church History, University of Halle; has published, among others, *Das Symbol des Fisches* (Marburg, 1888); *Acta sanctorum Nerei et Achillei* (Leipsic, 1890); and an edition of the works of Hippolytus, in collaboration with G. L. Bonwetsch (Leipsic, 1897).

BECKWICK, CLARENCE AUGUSTINE, A.B., A.M., D.D., S.T.D., Professor of Systematic Theology, Chicago Theological Seminary; author of *Realities of Christian Theology* (New York, 1906); departmental editor, *New Schaff-Herzog Encyclopedia of Religious Knowledge*.

BENTON, REV. ANGELO AMES, M.A., Professor of Mathematics and Chair of Greek and Latin, Delaware College, Professor of Dogmatic Theology, University of the South; editor, *Church Cyclopedia* (Philadelphia, 1884).

BERNARD, JOHN HENRY, D.D., D.C.L., Archbishop of Dublin, Provost of Trinity College, Dublin; author or editor, among others, of Kant's *Criticism of Judgment* (1892); *The Works of Bishop Butler* (London, 1900); *The Pilgrimage of St. Silvia* (1896); and publications of The Palestine Pilgrim's Text Society.

BLACK, J. SUTHERLAND, M.A., LL.D., assistant editor, *Encyclopaedia Britannica*, editor, *Encyclopaedia Biblica*, (1899).

BONWETSCH, GOTTLIEB NATHANAEL, Th.D., Professor of Church History, University of Göttingen; author, among others, of *Die Schriften Tertullians untersucht* (Bonn, 1878); and *Die Apokalypse Abrahams, das Testament der vierzig Märtyrer* (1898).

BOUDINHON, AUGUSTE, Docteur en Theologie et en Droit canonique; professeur de droit canon a l'Institut catholique de Paris; Chanoine honoraire de Parie et de Nice.

BURGON, JOHN WILLIAM, B.D., Dean of Chichester; author, among others, of *A Plain Commentary on the Four Holy Gospels* (8 vols., 1855); *The Last Twelve Verses of the Gospel according to St. Mark Vindicated and Established* (1871); *The Revision Revised*, articles against the *Revised Version of the New Testament* (London, 1883); and *The Causes of the Corruption of the Traditional Text of the Holy Gospels* (London, 1896).

BURNS, ISLAY, D.D., Professor of Church History, Free Church College, Glasgow; author of *The First Three Christian Centuries* (London, 1884).

CARR, REV. A., M.A., Fellow of Oriel College, Oxford, Assistant Master at Wellington College; editor of St. Matthew in *The Cambridge Bible* (Cambridge, 1893).

CHASE, REV. FREDERIC HENRY, M.A., D.D., Christ's College, Principal of the Clergy Training School, Cambridge, Examining Chaplain to the Archbishop of York; Bishop of Ely; author, among others, of *Chrysostom* (London, 1887); *The Old Syriac Element in the Text of Codex Bezae* (1893); and *The Gospels in the Light of Historical Criticism* (1905).

CHEYNE, REV. THOMAS KELLY, M.A., D.D., Oriel Professor of the Interpretation of Holy Scripture at Oxford, Fellow of Balliol College, Canon of Rochester; among his independent works, in addition to numerous contributions to standard works of reference, are, *Notes and Criticisms on the Hebrew Text of Isaiah* (London, 1868); *Founders of Old Testament Criticism* (1893); editor, *Encyclopaedia Biblica* (London, 1899); and *Traditions and Beliefs of Ancient Israel* (1907).

CLARKE, ADAM, LL.D., F.S.A., etc., Wesleyan preacher, commentator, and theologian; published besides his *Commentary on the Bible* (8 vols., Liverpool, 1810-26), among others, a *Biographical Dictionary* (6 vols., London, 1802) and its supplement, *The Biographical Miscellany* (2 vols., 1806).

COOK, FREDERIC CHARLES, M.A., Canon of Exeter, Preacher at Lincoln's Inn, Chaplain in Ordinary to the Queen; most important work was done for *The Speaker's (Bible) Commentary* (10 vols., London, 1871-72); and in addition thereto, among others, *The Origins of Religion and Language* (1884); and *Letters Addressed to the Rev. H. Mace and the Rev. J. Earle* (1885), in which he argued for the unity of language and a primitive divine revelation to man.

COOPER, JAMES, D.D., HON. D. LITT., D.C.L., Professor of Ecclesiastical History in the University of Glasgow; edited, among others, transactions of Aberdeen and Scottish Ecclesiological Society (1886-1903); *Cartularium Ecclesiae Sancti Nicolai Aberdonensis* (2 vols., Aberdeen, 1888-92); and made English translation of the Syriac *Testament of Our Lord* (London, 1902, in collaboration with A. J. Maclean).

COX, REV. SIR GEO. WM., English miscellaneous and historical writer; wrote, among others, *Aryan Mythology* (1870), and *Introduction to the Science of Comparative Mythology* (1881).

COXE, ARTHUR CLEVELAND, D.D., Second Bishop of Western New York; works upon theological topics include *Absolution and Confession* (New Haven, 1850); *The Criterion*, defining his position concerning the Oxford movement (New York and Oxford, 1866); and notes on *The Ante-Nicene Fathers* (1899).

CREAGH, JOHN THOMAS, D.D., Professor of Canon Law, Catholic University of America, Washington, D. C., lecturer on Religion at Trinity College, Washington, D. C.; author of *Remarriage After Divorce* (New York, 1905); and Department Editor, Liturgics and Religious Orders, in *The New Schaff-Herzog Encyclopedia of Religious Knowledge* (New York, 1908).

CROSS, GEORGE, M.A., PH.D., D.D., Professor of Systematic Theology

in the Rochester Theological Seminary, Rochester, N.Y.; author
of *The Theology of Schleiermacher*, (1911).

CURTIS, WILLIAM ALEXANDER, D.D., D.LITT., Professor of Biblical
Criticism in the University of Edinburgh; author of *Religion,
Yesterday, To-day, To-morrow* (Edinburgh, 1903), and *A History of Creeds and Confessions of Faith in Christendom and
Beyond* (1911).

D'ALVIELLA, COUNT GOBLET, PH.D., LL.D., Belgian Minister of State,
Member and Vice-President of the Belgian Senate, Professor
of History of Religions in the University of Brussels, Hibbert
Lecturer, 1891, Commander of the Order of Leopold; author of,
among others, *Migration of Symbols* (1891), and *The Contemporary Evolution of Religious Thought in England, America and
India* (1885).

DONALDSON, SIR JAMES, LL.D., Principal and Vice-Chancellor of St.
Andrews University, Principal of the United College of St.
Salvator and St. Leonard; books include: *A Critical History of
Christian Literature and Doctrine from the Death of the Apostles
to the Nicene Council* (3 vols., London, 1864-66); *The Westminster Confession of Faith and the Thirty-nine Articles of
the Church of England: the Legal, Moral, and Religious Aspects
of Subscription to Them* (1905); and editor of *The Ante-Nicene
Fathers* (Edinburgh, 1867-72).

DREWS, PAUL GOTTFRIED, TH.D., Professor of Theology, University
of Berlin, Professor of Practical Theology, University of Halle;
author of, among others, *Humanismus und Reformation* (1887);
Der evangelische Geistliche in der deutschen Vergangenheit
(Jena, 1905); and joint editor of the *Monatsschrift für die
kirchliche Praxis*.

EDERSHEIM, ALFRED, Biblical scholar, Vicar of Loders, Dorsetshire,
Warburtonian Lecturer, Preacher to the University of Oxford
and Grinfield Lecturer on the Septuagint; works include, *History of the Jewish Nation after the Destruction of Jerusalem by
Titus* (Edinburgh, 1856); *The Temple, Its Ministry and Services as They Were at the Time of Jesus Christ* (London, 1874);
and *Sketches of Jewish Social Life in the Days of Christ* (1876).

FARRAR, THE VEN. FREDERIC WILLIAM, D.D., Archdeacon of Westminister, Dean of Canterbury; among his numerous publications
are, *Life of Christ* (2 vols., 1874); *The Early Days of Christianity* (2 vols., London, 1882); and St. Luke in *The Cambridge
Bible* (1894).

FAWKES, ALFRED, M.A., Vicar of Ashby St. Ledgers.

FOAKES-JACKSON, FREDERICK JOHN, D.D., F.R., HIST. S., F.R.L.S.,
Fellow of Jesus College, Cambridge, and Hon. Canon of Peterborough Cathedral, Briggs Graduate Professor of Christian
Institutions at Union Theological Seminary, New York; author
of, among others, *The History of the Christian Church* to A.D.
337 (London, 1891); *A Biblical History of the Hebrews* (Cambridge, 1903), and *Christ in the Church* (London, 1905).

GIBBON, EDWARD, the historian of the Roman Empire; author of *The Decline and Fall of the Roman Empire* (1776-88).

GOLD, REV. PROF. WILLIAM JASON, Warden, Western Theological Seminary, Chicago, instructor exegesis and liturgics; author of, among others, *Method of Liturgical Revision*, (1886); *Report on the Standard Bible*, *Gen. Con. Jour.*, (1898); and editorial contributor to *Living Church*, Chicago, (1888-98).

GWATKIN, REV. HENRY MELVILL, M.A., D.D., Fellow of Emmanuel College, and Dixie Professor of Ecclesiastical History in the University of Cambridge, author of, among others, *Studies of Arianism* (Cambridge, 1882); *Selections from Early Christian Writers* (1893); and editor of *The Cambridge Medieval History*.

HASTINGS, JAMES, M.A., D.D., Fellow of the Royal Anthropological Institute, Member of the Council of the Palestine Exploration Fund; editor of *A Dictionary of the Bible* (5 vols., Edinburgh and New York, 1898-1904); *Dictionary of Christ and the Gospels* (2 vols., 1906-07); *Dictionary of the Bible* (1 vol., 1908); *Dictionary of the Apostolic Church* (1916); *Encyclopaedia of Religion and Ethics* (1928); and *The Expository Times*.

HEFELE, CHARLES JOSEPH, D.D., German Roman Catholic prelate and ecclesiastical historian, Bishop of Rottenburg, Professor of Theology in the University of Tubingen; author of, among others, *History of Introduction of Christianity in Southwestern Germany* (Tubingen, 1837); *The Apostolic Fathers* (1839); and *Conciliengeschichte* (Freiburg, 1855-74).

HENRY, MATTHEW, non-conformist minister and commentator; in addition to celebrated commentary, *An Exposition of the Old and New Testaments* (5 vols., London, 1708-10), wrote, among others, *A Scripture Catechism* (1702); and *The Communicant's Companion* (1704).

JORDAN, W. G., D.D., Professor of Hebrew and Old Testament Exegesis, Queen's University, Kingston, Canada.

JULICHER, GUSTAV ADOLF, D.D., PH.D., Professor of Church History and New Testament Exegesis, Marburg; author of, among others, *Die Gleichnisreden Jesu* (2 vols., Freiburg, 1888-99); *Introduction to the New Testament* (1894); and *Paulus und Jesus* (Tubingen, 1907).

KATTENBUSCH, FERDINAND FRIEDRICH WILHELM, PH.D., THD., Professor of Dogmatics, University of Halle; author of, among others, *Lehrbuch der vergleichenden Confessionskunde*, i. (Freiburg, 1892); and *Das sittliche Recht des Krieges* (Giesen, 1906).

LAKE, KIRSOPP, M.A., D.D., TH.D., LITT.D., PH.D., Winn Professor of Ecclesiastical History, and Professor of History, Harvard University, Honorary Fellow of Lincoln College, Oxford; author of, among others, *Text of the New Testament* (1898); *The Codex Sinaiticus* (1921); *The Beginnings of Christianity* (1920-1933); and also translator of many works, including *The Apostolic Fathers* (1912).

LANGE, JOHANN PETER, D.D., German theologican and exegete of the Evangelical school, Professor of Theology at the University of Bonn; author of, in addition to his well-known *Commentary*, among others, *Biblische Dichtungen* (2 vols., Elberfeld, 1832-34); *Grundriss der theologischen Encyklopadie* (Heidelberg, 1877); and *Grundriss der Bibelkunde* (1881).

LORING, REV. H. H., contributor to *The Church Cyclopaedia.*

LOWNDES, ARTHUR, D.D., Bishop, Doane Memorial Church, S. Amboy, N.J., St. Mark the Evangelist, Philmont, N.Y., Chaplain, Peekskill, N.Y., in St. Gabriel's School; Rector Ch. of the Transfiguration, Freeport, N.Y.; editor of *Church Eclectic,* (1900-1908); author, *Vindication of Anglican Orders,* (1899); *Christ, the Life of the World* (1914); and collaborator with Rev. Dr. Dix in, *History of Trinity Parish* (1898-1906).

LUMBY, J. RAWSON, D.D., Norrisian Professor of Divinity; editor of The Acts of the Apostles in *The Cambridge Bible* (1891), and contributed to *The Speaker's (Bible) Commentary,*

MACCULLOCH, JOHN ARNOTT, HON. D.D., Rector of St. Saviour's, Bridge of Allan; Hon. Canon of the Cathedral of the Holy Spirit, Cumbrae; Examiner in Comparative Religion and Philosophy of Religion, Victoria University, Manchester; Examining Chaplain to the Bishop of St. Andrews; author of *The Religion of the Ancient Celts.*

MACLEAN, ARTHUR JOHN, D.D., Bishop of Moray, Ross, and Caithness; author of, among others, *Dictionary and Grammar of Vernacular Syriac* (Cambridge and Oxford, 1895-1901); *Ancient Church Orders; Recent Discoveries Illustrating Early Christian Life and Worship* (London, 1904); and editor of *East Syrian Liturgies* (1890-92).

MACLEAR, THE REV. GEO. FREDERICK, D.D., Warden of St. Augustine's, Canterbury, and Head Master of King's College School, London; works include, *A Class-Book of the New Testament History* (1862); *Apostles of Mediaeval Europe* (London, 1868); and St. Mark in *The Cambridge Bible* (1881).

MCCONKIE, OSCAR W., Judge in Third Judicial District of Utah, member of Salt Lake City Commission, and President of the California Mission of the Church of Jesus Christ of Latter-day Saints; author of *The Holy Ghost,* and *Dialogue at Golgotha.*

MEYRICK, THE REV. FREDERICK, M.A., Rector of Blickling, Norfolk, and Non-Residentiary Canon of Lincoln Cathedral; works include, *Scriptural and Catholic Truth and Worship* (1901); *Is Dogma a Necessity?* (1883); and contributed to *The Speaker's (Bible) Commentary* (1876-1895).

MILLER, EDWARD, M.A., Wykehamical Prebendary of Chichester, arranged, compiled and edited *The Causes of the Corruption of the Traditional Text of the Holy Gospels,* by John William Burgon (1896).

MILMAN, REV. HENRY HART, English ecclesiastical historian and poet, Dean of St. Paul's, London, Professor of poetry at Oxford, and Bampton lecturer; besides editing Gibbon's *History of the Decline and Fall of the Roman Empire* (1838), he edited many other works, and wrote, among others, *The Character and Conduct of the Apostles Considered as an Evidence of Christianity* (Oxford, 1827); and *The History of the Jews* (London, 1830).

MOORE, REV, GEORGE FOOTE, D.D., President and Professor of Hebrew in Andover Theological Seminary, Andover, Mass.; besides articles in the *Encyclopaedia Biblica*, he has written, among others, *Commentary on Judges* (New York, 1895); and edited Judges for the *Polychrome Bible* (2 vols., 1898-1900).

NEWMAN, ALBERT HENRY, D.D., LL.D., LITT.D., Professor of Church History at Southwestern Baptist Theological Seminary and Baylor University, Department Editor of Church History of the *New Schaff-Herzog Encyclopedia of Religious Knowledge*, and author of, among others, *A History of the Baptist Churches in the United States* (New York, 1894); *A History of Anti-Pedobaptism* (Philadelphia, 1897), and *A Manual of Church History* (1900-03).

PATON, LEWIS BAYLES, PH.D., D.D., Nettleton Professor of Old Testament Exegesis and Criticism, Instructor in Assyrian and Cognate Languages, Hartford Theological Seminary, Hartford, Conn., Director of the American School of Archaeology in Jerusalem; author of, among others, *The Early History of Syria and Palestine* (New York, 1902), and *Jerusalem in Bible Times* (Chicago, 1908).

PEARSON, A. C., M.A., LITT.D., Regius Professor of Greek in the University of Cambridge; editor of, among others, *Fragments of Sophocles;* Euripides' *Helena, Heraclidae,* and *Phoenissae;* and *Zeno and Cleanthes: Fragments.*

PEROWNE, JOHN JAMES STEWART, D.D., Bishop of Worcester, Hulsean lecturer, member of Old Testament company of Bible revisers; author of, among others, *Immortality* (Hulsean lectures, 1868-1869); *The Doctrine of the Lord's Supper* (1887, 1899); and general editor of *The Cambridge Bible for Schools* (Cambridge, 1877, sqq).

PLUMMER, THE REV. ALFRED, M.A., D.D., Master of University College, Durham, Fellow and Tutor of Trinity College, Oxford; editor, St. John in *The Cambridge Bible* (1892); and author of, among others, *The Gospel according to St. Luke,* in *The International Critical Commentary.*

RANKE, LEOPOLD VON, German historian (1795-1886), fifty years with University of Berlin; among works translated into English are, *Civil Wars and Monarchy in France; History of England; State of Germany after the Reformation;* and *The History of the Popes.*

RIDDLE, MATTHEW BROWN, D.D., Professor of New Testament Exegesis in Hartford Theological Seminary and at Western Theological Seminary; editor of the American standard edition of the *Revised Version of the Bible;* author of *Story of the Revised*

New Testament, American Standard Edition (Philadelphia, 1908); and revised portions of the American edition of *The Ante-Nicene Fathers* (New York, 1886-1888); edited Robinson's *A Harmony of the Four Gospels in English*, (Boston, 1889).

ROBERTS, REV. ALEXANDER, D.D., editor, *The Ante-Nicene Fathers* (Edinburgh, 1867-72).

ROBERTS, BRIGHAM HENRY, one of Seven Presidents of Seventies, Church of Jesus Christ of Latter-day Saints, editor and writer; author of, among others, *The Gospel* (1888); *Outlines of Ecclesiastical History* (1893); *Defense of the Faith and the Saints; A Comprehensive History of the Church of Jesus Christ of Latter-day Saints.*

ROBERTSON, JAMES CRAIGIE, M.A., Canon of Canterbury, and Professor of Ecclesiastical History in King's College, London; author of, among others, *How Shall We Conform to the Liturgy of the Church of England?* (London, 1843); *Plain Lectures on the Growth of the Papal Power* (1876); and *History of the Christian Church to the Reformation* (1874).

ROBINSON, EDWARD, D.D., LL.D., Professor of Biblical Literature in the Union Theological Seminary, New York; author of, among others, *Biblical Researches in Palestine, Mount Sinai, and Arabia Petraea* (1841); *A Harmony of the Four Gospels in English* (1846); and *A Greek and English Lexicon of the New Testament* (1850).

SANDAY, WILLIAM, D.D., HON. D.D., HON. LL.D., HON. LITT.D., Lady Margaret Professor and Canon of Christ Church, Oxford; Chaplain in Ordinary to H. M. the King; Fellow of the British Academy; author of, among others, *The Authorship and Historical Character of the Fourth Gospel* (London, 1872); *Criticism of the New Testament* (1902); and *The Life of Christ in Recent Research* (1907).

SCHAFF, DAVID SCHLEY, D.D., Professor of Church History, Lane Theological Seminary and Western Theological Seminary; contributed to *Bible Dictionary* of his father, Philip Schaff; wrote *The Life of Philip Schaff* (1897); and continued the *History of the Christian Church*, by his father (vol. v., parts 1 and 2, 1907-10).

SCHAFF, PHILIP, D.D., LL.D., Professor of Church History, and of Biblical Literature, Union Theological Seminary, New York; editor of the original *Schaff-Herzog Encyclopaedia;* wrote and edited numerous works, among the most important of which were *History of the Christian Church* (New York, 1853); the American edition of Lange's *Bibelwerk* (25 vols., New York, 1870); *The Creeds of Christendom* (3 vols., 1877); *Through Bible Lands* (1878); and *A Companion to the Greek Testament and the English Version* (1883).

SCHMIEDEL, PAUL WILHELM, D.D., Professor of New Testament Exegesis at the University of Zurich; author of, among others, *Quae intercedat ratio inter doctrinam epistolae ad Hebraeos missae et Pauli apostoli doctrinam* (Jena, 1878); *Jesus in*

Modern Criticism (London, 1907); and edited R. Seydel's *Religionsphilosophie* (1893).

SCOTT, ERNEST FINDLAY, B.A., D.D., Professor of New Testament Criticism in Union Theological Seminary, New York; Professor of New Testament Literature in Queen's University, Kingston, Canada; author of, among others, *The Fourth Gospel: Its Purpose and Theology* (1906); *The Apologetic of the New Testament* (1907); *The Nature of the Early Church* (1941).

SCOTT-MONCRIEFF, PHILIP DAVID, M.A., Assistant in the Department of Egyptian and Assyrian Antiquities in the British Museum.

SEHLING, EMIL, DR. JUR., Professor of Ecclesiastical and Commercial Law, University of Erlangen.

SMITH, W. BROWNING, Sub-editor of the Encyclopaedia Britannica (9th Edition).

SRAWLEY, JAMES HERBERT, D.D., Canon and Chancellor of Lincoln Cathedral; Examining Chaplain to the Bishop of Lichfield; author of, among others, *The Epistles of St. Ignatius, Translated with Introduction and Notes* (2 vols., London, 1900); and *The Catechetical Oration of St. Gregory of Nyssa* (Cambridge, 1903).

STANTON, REV. VINCENT HENRY, M.A., D.D., Fellow of Trinity College, and Ely Professor of Divinity in the University of Cambridge; author of, among others, *The Jewish and the Christian Messiah* (London, 1887); and *The Place of Authority in Matters of Religious Belief* (1891).

STEWART, REV. ALEXANDER, M.A., D.D., Principal and Primarius Professor of Divinity, St. Mary's College, University of St. Andrews; author of *Handbook of Christian Evidences* (Edinburgh, 1892), and *Life of Christ* (London, 1905).

STONE, DARWELL, M.A., D.D., Principal of Pusey House, Oxford; author of, among others, *Christ and Human Life* (1901); *The Invocation of Saints* (1903); and *A History of the Doctrine of the Holy Eucharist* (2 vols., 1909).

TALMAGE, JAMES EDWARD, member of Council of Twelve Apostles, Church of Jesus Christ of Latter-day Saints, and geologist; President of University of Utah; author of, among others, *The Book of Mormon, an Account of its Origin* (1899); *The Articles of Faith* (1899); *The Great Apostasy* (1909); and *Jesus the Christ* (1915).

TERRY, T. PHILIP, author, lecturer, Fellow Royal Geog. Soc.; author of, among others, *Terry's Pocket Interpreter* (Spanish) (1890); and *Terry's Guide to Mexico* (1909).

THURSTON, HERBERT, BA., S.J., Joint-editor of the *Westminster Library for Priests and Students*; author of *Life of St. Hugh of Lincoln, The Holy Year of Jubilee,* and *The Stations of the Cross.*

TROITSKY, SERGEI VICTOROVICH, Master of Theology; Instructor in the Alexander-Nevskij Theological College at Petrograd; Member

of the Imperial Archaeological Institute of Petrograd; attached
to the Chancery of the Over-Procurator of the Most Holy Synod.

WORKMAN, HERBERT B., M.A., D.LITT., D.D., Principal of Westminster
Training College; Member of the Board of Studies in the
Faculty of Theology, London University; author of *The Dawn
of the Reformation, The Letters of John Hus, Persecution in the
Early Church, Christian Thought to the Reformation.*

ZAHN, THEODOR, TH.D., LITT.D., Professor of New Testament
Exegesis and Introduction, University of Erlangen.

ZOECKLER, OTTO, PH.D., TH.D., Professor of Church History and
Apologetics, University of Greifswald, author of *Kritische
Geschichte der Askese.*

INDEX